Published by Scrivenings Press LLC
15 Lucky Lane
Morrilton, Arkansas 72110
https://ScriveningsPress.com

Printed in the United States of Americ

Paperback ISBN 978-1-64917-216-7

eBook ISBN 978-1-64917-217-4

Editors: Erin R. Howard and Shannon Taylor Vannatter

Cover by Linda Fulkerson, www.bookmarketinggraphics.com.

SHARKTOOTH *Island*

A Collection of Novellas

Susan Page Davis
Linda Fulkerson
Elena Hill
Deborah Sprinkle

OUT OF THE *Storm*

Susan Page Davis

Chapter One

August 1830

Laura Bryant whirled around the floor, letting the music propel her. The naval officer she danced with gazed at her attentively, his face flushed as he took only quick glances away to make sure they didn't crash into another couple. Laura wasn't sure she liked his fascination with her and kept her head turned to the side to avoid his searing gaze.

At least sixty people were crowded into the ballroom of the hotel, and the side doors were open wide to let in a sea breeze. Kingston, on the island of Jamaica, was beautiful, and a lovely place to hold a party, but in summer its heat hardly eased at sunset. With this many people in one room and the constant motion and excitement, Laura was roasting. The men must be stifling in their uniforms and formal jackets.

Her gown was the only one she'd brought along on the voyage, and it was two years old, but what did that matter? No one in Kingston had ever seen her wear it before. She'd thought it was modest, but now she wished the neckline was higher.

Her partner couldn't seem to stop making downward glances toward her bodice.

She spotted her father near the refreshment table, talking to their host, Captain Edwards. Both men owned merchant vessels. Edwards's ship was significantly larger than Bryant's schooner, but he held her father in high regard. She was glad they'd met up so far from home. Papa needed friends around him to ease the melancholy he'd carried since her mother died.

The music ended, and she stepped back from her partner and applauded, wishing they'd stopped closer to her father. She hoped she could escape the lieutenant.

"May I get you a glass of punch?" he asked.

"Oh, I—" She looked around desperately and was thankful to spot someone she knew passing by. "Mr. Dryden, I believe you owe me a dance." Her cheeks heated even more as she spoke, and she felt very forward, waylaying Edwards's second mate like that.

But he stepped up like the gentleman she knew he was.

"Miss Bryant. This is the perfect time for me, if it is for you."

"Delighted." She looked back at the lieutenant. "You'll excuse me, please."

He nodded but didn't look pleased.

"Thank you," she whispered, gazing up at Alexander Dryden as the music resumed and they glided away. "You've no idea how grateful I am."

His devastating smile put the finishing touches to his conquest of her heart, though she would never admit so much to a gentleman. Especially when she'd only met him twice before, as both the captains and their crews went about their business in port. He'd caught her interest on their first encounter.

"It's my pleasure to assist you," he said. "I take it the company you were in wasn't enjoyable."

"Not in the least. He made me shudder every time he looked at me. I felt like a shark's next meal."

"Then let us think of more pleasant things. Has your father finished loading his cargo?"

"He hopes to get more coffee tomorrow. And your captain?"

"We sail with the morning tide. We're full up with sugar and coffee."

So she wouldn't see him again. What a pity. Her father would offload his cargo in Portland, Maine, but Captain Edwards sailed out of Boston. The old friends only met occasionally, and more often than not in a foreign port.

"So this is a farewell party."

"In a sense," Dryden said. "The captain wanted to gather his friends from the ships in port, and also some of the Kingston officials. It doesn't hurt to court the government men in a port where you frequently do business."

"Indeed." Captain Edwards must be doing very well for himself in his Caribbean trade to throw an event like this, Laura thought. Her father could never afford such an extravagant party. In fact, their comfort next winter depended heavily on their getting home safely with their load of finest coffee.

She observed the other women dancing as they flitted about. Her first impression of her dress was bolstered as she surveyed their fashions. Her neckline was indeed more modest than most.

"Are you looking for someone?" Dryden asked.

"Oh, no. Sorry. I was just taking note of the other dresses and wondering if mine was out of fashion."

"Your gown is lovely."

Her face was already warm from the warmth and exercise, but she felt her cheeks heat even more. "Thank you."

Their number together ended, and Dryden offered her refreshment, but she shook her head.

"I'd like to get back to Papa, Mr. Dryden, if you can see him."

Dryden, who was a good eight inches taller than her, glanced around and smiled. "He's yonder, talking to the governor's man and Captain Edwards."

He guided Laura swiftly through clusters of other guests to her father's side.

"Ah, there you are, Laura." Captain Bryant eyed her and Alex with satisfaction. "I wondered where you'd got to."

"She's been in good hands, if Dryden's been with her," Captain Edwards said.

"Yes, he rescued me after the last dance but one, from a rather boring partner," she said. Her father would worry if he knew one of her dance partners had shown wolfish tendencies.

"Laura, this is Mr. James. Sir, my daughter."

The government official bowed. "It is an honor, Miss Bryant."

She smiled and gave a little curtsey.

"I'm surprised you're pulling anchor tomorrow," her father said, turning back to Edwards and his interrupted conversation. "I heard there are pirates lurking about outside the harbor."

"Can't dawdle about in port for long," Edwards replied. "We'll be fine. We're well armed."

Laura glanced at Alex, but his expression remained impassive. He must not be worried either. Perhaps her father was overly cautious, since he had his only daughter aboard the *Arundel*. This was her first voyage with him.

"It's the storms you should worry about," said James. "I

think we're due for a big one in a few days. They hit hard this time of year."

"We'll get ahead of it," Captain Edwards said. His confidence reassured Laura. With his swift ship, he probably would outrun the tropical storms, and likely any pirates in the vicinity as well.

Alex leaned down close to her ear. "Would you care to dance again?"

She gave him a wide smile. "I'd love to." The concerns of the journey left her as he led her back onto the floor. She faced him and placed her hand on the shoulder of his broadcloth jacket, no doubt his Sunday best. In Alex Dryden's arms, a sailor's problems were the farthest things from her mind. If only his ship wasn't leaving for Boston tomorrow.

ALEX LEFT the hotel whistling the tune he'd danced to last with Laura. By the end of it, they'd established that they should use first names with each other. That was also when Alex had decided he was at least five fathoms deep in love.

Overhead, the stars glittered. The fresh sea breeze cooled him down a bit, but he'd have endured the overheated ballroom longer if he'd been able to stay with her. Meeting Laura was easily the highlight of this voyage.

He loved his job on the ship under Captain Edwards, but now could imagine a future life on land with ... a woman like her. He smiled as the fragrant breeze from the harbor rippled his hair. A few more voyages with Captain Edwards, and he'd have enough to start his own business. Then he'd stay on dry land.

He turned toward the dock. The captain and his first mate had stayed behind at the party, but Alex had to relieve the man on watch. Their vessel was anchored between Bryant's schooner and a brigantine, and the crews were sociable, mingling in their off hours when they weren't loading and unloading cargo. Maybe he'd catch another glimpse of Laura in the morning before they weighed anchor.

Two men sprang out of the shadows in front of him. Alex stopped short, his heart racing. He ought to have been more aware of his surroundings. The crew had all been warned that the harbor held some evil men and they should be wary.

One of the roughnecks was bigger than him, and both looked bound for mischief. The shorter man was easily twice Alex's age, but he had the air of a hardened seadog. The large man smiled at him. Alex flinched when he saw the man's upraised knife. His companion held a revolver, aimed straight at Alex's chest.

"What do you want?" he managed to choke out, though he thought he knew.

"Just come along easy with us, lad," said the older man. "We've need of you on the *Herring*."

Alex wondered if he had any chance of fighting them off. Not a very large chance, he decided, but it was worth a try. If only he could distract them somehow.

"I'm already employed," he said hastily. "I'm signed with Captain Edwards."

"Aye, we've heard of him," said the big fellow. "And of you. You're handy with a hammer, they say. We've a few bits need fixin' on the *Herring*."

"Look, Captain Edwards needs me. I don't have much, but I've got a couple of Spanish dollars in my pocket." Alex reached slowly toward his side. "If you—"

Something hit Alex on the back of the head. He sucked in a breath, but the stars and the thugs' faces grew hazy.

Chapter Two

Several days later, Laura stood in the bow of her father's schooner, *Arundel*, facing forward. They were headed home, and she could hardly wait to see the rocky shores of New England again.

Her first trip to the Caribbean with Papa had been exciting. Often, her thoughts drifted back to the interesting young man she'd met at Captain Edwards's party. She would likely never see him again. Best to forget about Alexander Dryden.

That seemed impossible, though. She'd learned during their conversation that he was not only Edwards's second mate in the crew of fifteen, but also served as the ship's carpenter. He'd told her he planned to make a few more voyages to build up his savings and then stay ashore and build furniture. Somehow, Laura's dreams of her future had come to include a carpenter's workshop, somewhere near Boston.

"We're in for some weather," Captain Bryant yelled, snapping her out of her daydreams.

He was right. The sky had darkened, with ominous black clouds rolling in from the west, completely blocking the sun that had shone so merrily this morning. The wind had picked up, too, tugging at Laura's shawl and whipping loose tendrils of hair against her face. Though they hadn't endured a large storm before leaving Jamaica, Mr. James's prediction appeared to be coming true now.

Papa's crew scurried about the deck, tying off sheets and securing anything that could move when the deck rolled. Laura walked astern as quickly as she could, but the deck pitched beneath her feet. At last she joined her father in the stern and clung to the taffrail, near where he stood at the wheel. She could tell it was fighting him, pulling against his strong arms as he strove to keep them on course.

"Take in the mainsail," he yelled.

"How can I help, Papa?" She raised her voice against the wind's howl.

"Get below. And take that crate!" He nodded toward a loose wooden box that skidded across the deck toward the sail locker. She'd brought it up earlier to sit on when the sun was bright.

Laura hurried to corral the crate and hefted it toward the open hatch. The men sprang to take in canvas, so the schooner wouldn't fight the wind so badly. She hesitated, wondering if she should offer to help them. Her father had taught her the rudiments of sailing during calmer weather. She enjoyed being more than just another piece of cargo for them to haul about.

"Sail ho!"

She turned toward Old Philip's shout and saw him pointing off the bow, two points to larboard. A trim vessel ran before the storm in a path that would intercept theirs.

"Pirates." Eli turned to the captain. "They'll board us."

"Not in this storm," Captain Bryant said.

Old Philip shook his head. "They're coming on fast. Should we raise sail again? Can we outrun 'em?"

"Have to try." The captain set his mouth in a grim line and pulled hard on the wheel to turn it, altering their course eastward into the Atlantic, away from the mainland and the pirate ship.

"Raise the main topsail!" Captain Bryant had ordered his three sailors to reef those sails just minutes ago.

"What about the storm, Papa?" Laura gazed with dread at the darker clouds that melded with the sea astern. Usually in a storm, her father had the men take in the sails and let the schooner ride the waves wherever the wind took them. When the gale blew itself out, they could make sail again and get on with their voyage.

He gritted his teeth, and his bushy eyebrows lowered. "We can try to keep out of the worst of that, or we can try to lose that shipload of hellions. Me, I prefer to take my chances with the storm and God Almighty. Now get below, girl."

Already, huge drops of rain splattered on the deck. The sails snapped and the hull creaked. Laura worked her way to the hatch and took one last glance toward the pirate ship. It did, indeed, seem a little closer.

She climbed backward down the ladder, shifting the box down step by step. If she took the narrow stairs facing forward, she was sure she'd pitch off at the first lurch of the buffeted schooner.

She had two steps to go when one of the men slammed the hatch shut. The roar of the wind was muffled, and the darkness of the hold enfolded her. Laura froze for a moment, clutching the crate with one hand and the railing with the other. Her heart felt as though it would pound right out of her chest. She hauled in deep, shaky breaths until she was calm.

Cautiously, she felt her way down with her toes until she stood on the lower deck, solid though rolling beneath her. She walked slowly along the narrow companionway, her elbow keeping contact with the bulkhead, until she reached the door to her tiny cabin.

Inside, she placed the crate where it wouldn't be thrown about. She didn't dare try to light a candle, knowing the heaving waves could throw her off her feet at any moment. Fire of any type, even a candle, was forbidden on board when they faced bad weather, so there was no chance of losing control of a blaze.

She lay on her bunk for a long time, feeling the ship's struggles and clinging to a rope handle fixed to the head of the bed. Now and then she heard a faint shout, but the noise of waves crashing against the hull and the shrieking wind covered all other sounds.

At last the waves grew less violent and the wind diminished. When the youngest sailor, Daniel, shouted, "Give us a hand!" to his friend Eli, she heard his words clearly.

Laura rose and threw her shawl on the berth then felt her way to the hooks on the wall. She lifted down a canvas cape and tugged it on over her dress. A matching hood covered her hair and shadowed her face. The foul-weather gear wasn't flattering, but now she felt ready to go on deck and see if she could help Papa and his men.

When she emerged from the hatch, rain pounded her head, the deck, everything. At least the wind was less violent and the waves not quite so huge. Daniel and Eli were perched up on the mast, furling the mainsail. Old Philip stood below, tugging on a line.

Laura turned to the wheel, which her father struggled to hold steady.

"Go below, girl!"

"I want to help."

"Then put your weight on the larboard side of this wheel. When we get the sails in, I'll let her drift."

"Oh, Papa."

"I know, I know, but you can't outwork a gale. 'Tis still black to the west, and I don't think we're through with it yet. We'll let the storm take us where it will, and when it's over, we'll take our bearings and set a new course."

At last the sails were tucked in below the spars, and Daniel and Eli climbed down to the tilting deck. Laura wished she could make some hot coffee for them, but they'd have no fire in the galley until the sea was calm again.

Her father persuaded her to go below deck. Once down the ladder, she heard their muffled shouts and yearned to go up again, but she knew she would only distract her father. He could handle the ship better if she stayed safely out of sight and out of the way.

After an hour of cowering in her dark cabin feeling useless, Laura felt the schooner roll heavily once more, and the wind sheared around the hull, louder than a banshee. The ship gave a sudden shudder, and a loud *thud* shivered through the vessel. She clung to the edge of her berth, a lump of terror rising in her throat. Had the mast fallen? Or maybe the pirate ship had caught up and rammed them.

She gripped the bedrail and whispered a prayer of desperation. "Lord, don't let us sink! Protect us, Heavenly Father!"

Finally the wind stopped shrieking around the hull, and the rain abated to a gentle pattering on the deck. Instead of plunging up and down, *Arundel* rocked over the waves with an almost regular rhythm.

Laura found she could stand up without danger of sprawling. She pulled on the damp foul-weather gear once more and felt her way to the ladder.

When she pushed up the hatch cover, Daniel was at the

wheel. She craned her head around and spotted her father, Eli, and Philip standing at the rail on the starboard side.

"We'll wreck for certain if we can't claw our way off," Old Philip said, waving at the sea.

Laura squinted through the mist in the direction he gestured and caught her breath.

Not the sea. Philip was pointing at a not-too-distant island.

Chapter Three

"What is that place?" Laura grasped her father's elbow and stared at the spectral land that rose, dark and dreadful, before them.

"It's an inhospitable isle." Captain Bryant frowned as he studied the high, craggy ridge and the shore that seemed all large, menacing rocks. "Some call it Sharktooth Island, for the stone rising out of the sea near the tip of the land."

He pointed along the shore toward the port side of their vessel. A half mile away, Laura could just make out a solitary stone jutting up from the waves, half as high as their mainmast, she judged. It did indeed resemble a shark's tooth in shape, but instead of gleaming white, the rock was foreboding black.

She shivered. "Can we land on this island?"

"Not likely." Her father turned toward the stern. "Hold her as steady as you can, Daniel. We'll throw out a sea anchor."

The sea anchor was extra canvas, tied to sturdy ropes. When they threw it off the taffrail, it would drag behind them and slow the schooner down. But it would be hard to recover it later with the small crew. Her father must be desperate to keep them off that island.

"Some call it Ghost Island," Old Philip said softly.

Laura whirled on him. "Why?"

"They say no ship that's ever struck her has returned. Some old tars even say the island pulls vessels to her rocky shores."

A tingle crept down Laura's spine.

"I've heard a coastal trader call it Doom Island," Eli said. "And some name it Island of Secrets."

"Those are just stories," her father said firmly. "Come on, boys. Let's get at it or we'll be too far in to tack against the wind."

For the first time, Laura noticed that the foremast was broken off about a yard above the deck. That must be the *thud* she'd heard.

"Papa—"

He arched his eyebrows at her.

"Nothing," she said. "What can I do?"

"Help us get the sea anchor ready."

When they'd prepared it the rain was falling again, drumming on the planks of the deck.

"Ready?" Eli asked.

Her father sighed and eyed the shore. "I hoped we could get past the island, but with the foremast down and the rudder damaged ... No, we'll just have to try to keep off the rocks."

"If we can get out to sea, away from the land—"

"Aye, that's right, Eli. But the wind is picking up again. I fear it will drive us right onto that horrid shore."

Laura helped them drag the canvas to the stern and heave it over the rail. They all stood there panting as the ship drifted, taking the slack out of the line. After a minute, she felt the schooner pull against the weight it dragged and swing slowly around, so that the bow was pointed southward. They were closer to the jagged black shoreline than before, and she didn't see how they could avoid being thrown onto the rocks. Not with the wind so strong.

"What else can we do?"

"You should go below," Eli said.

"No." Her father laid a heavy hand on her shoulder. "I'll not have you trapped down there if we smash on those rocks or go aground in the shoals. Stay near the seaward side, and if we hit, you jump clear and swim. You hear me?" He was shouting now, above the howling wind.

"Aye, Papa." She clenched her teeth. For the men, it might be feasible to swim ashore. Her sodden wool skirts would drag her down. Would she have time to shed her outer skirt before she jumped?

"That goes for all of you." Captain Bryant scowled fiercely at Eli and Philip, then walked as steadily as he could on the rolling deck to the wheel. "You too, Daniel. If we wreck, jump off on the seaward side, away from the rocks. I think swimmers have a better chance of surviving a smash-up than those who wait for the ship to splinter beneath them and heave them onto the rocks."

"Aye, sir," Daniel said.

The jagged rocks at the base of the island drew nearer. Laura and the men huddled together in the stern.

"Can't help it," her father said, shaking his head.

Laura gazed at the nearing land. Now she could see brush beyond the rocky shore. When the clouds shifted, she thought she glimpsed jungle. Was it possible? The land definitely rose into hills or a mountain, its top still obscured by the low clouds and the driving rain.

"If we hit hard, you don't want your daughter thrown into the sea," Old Philip yelled to the captain. "Mayhap you should tie her—"

The crash came before he could finish, and Laura sprawled on the deck, which seemed to leap skyward then lodge at an angle.

"Papa," she screamed. She lifted her head to look for him, but everything whirled.

Laura awoke to darkness. The rain still came down, but it was now only a gentle patter. Once fully alert, she realized she was lying under a canvas roof, and a small fire burned nearby. Shadowy figures crouched by the fire.

"Where are we?" she asked.

"Bless me, she's awake," Old Philip said. "Cap'n, Miss Laura's with us." He turned and grinned at her. "We've fetched up on the ghost island."

"Is everyone all right?" she asked, pushing herself to a sitting position. A searing pain caught her, and she put cautious fingers to her forehead.

"More or less," Philip replied.

Her father ducked under the edge of their awning, followed by Eli.

"Well," said the captain. "All right then, girl?"

"I think so, Papa. My head aches, but I don't seem to have broken anything."

"Good," he said. "It's bad enough we broke the schooner."

Eli nodded gravely. "Lucky we weren't all smashed to bits."

She sat up straighter. "Where's Daniel?"

"Bringing one last load he salvaged from *Arundel*. I told him we'll wait till morning after that batch, to see what's left."

She hoped they wouldn't be left with nothing—no supplies and no boat to carry them away from the island. Slowly, she crawled to the edge of the shelter and looked out. Beyond the campfire, a large heap of stores sat at the base of a rocky slope. They'd piled things as far away from the surf as they could.

"We brought that stuff ashore in case the ship goes to pieces in the night and we can't save anything more tomorrow," Eli said at her shoulder. His left arm was bound close to his chest in a rudimentary sling.

"You're hurt."

"A bit. I couldn't help much in the salvaging, I fear."

"Just be glad you got ashore," Philip told him.

A few yards offshore, she could make out the hulk of the schooner, listing to starboard, caught among the rocks.

"Will she drift away?" she asked.

"We've secured her with lines, as well as we could," Philip said. "If the wind gets bad again, who knows."

Daniel climbed down *Arundel's* boarding ladder with his arms full and dropped into their tiny dinghy. As he rowed in, dodging rocks that stuck up from the water, her father walked into the waves and waded out to meet him. They hauled the dinghy, which was barely large enough to hold two men, up above the reach of the surf. The sailor and her father stood in the swash to remove the last few articles he'd managed to rescue and plodded toward the camp.

Over his shoulder, the captain carried a coil of rope and some burlap sacking, and in his hands were a hammer and a hatchet. Daniel came behind him carrying their teakettle and a lumpy sack. When they got to the pile, they added most of their supplies to it. Daniel brought the sack under the canvas.

"This is food from the galley. I'm afraid at least a third of our cargo went into the drink, where the rocks stove in the hull."

"The ship is ruined?" Laura asked, looking fearfully to her father.

"I think we can mend her," he said. "It's true there's a big hole in the hull, but it's doable. We've salvaged most of the tools, and we're resourceful. We may limp into port, but I think we'll make it. If we can't make her seaworthy, well, we can keep a fire going and hope a ship spots us here."

"Not those filthy pirates," Philip muttered.

"There now," the captain said. "Which is worse, pirates or this island? I'll take the island, thank you."

"It's only stories, right? Ghost Island, I mean. Those sailors who never return from here." Laura gave them a tentative smile, but Philip turned away with a sour expression.

Laura tried to put thoughts of spirits away from her. Better concentrate on other threats. Ghosts or not, she knew the pirates were real.

Chapter Four

Alex Dryden stood on deck in the sprinkling rain, glad the ship was somewhat stable now. The crew had dropped anchor just off the eastern shore of a craggy island, one called Sharktooth. He'd heard of the place before, and the many wrecks that had happened here. No landing place lay on the shore. Men who insisted on going there had to approach in a small boat at high tide and steer carefully to make land without damage. Even then it was chancy.

During the storm the previous day, they'd managed to stay offshore and get around the small land mass to the side that was temporarily sheltered. The high ridge that was the isle's backbone broke the raging wind out of the west. Now the sea was comparatively calm, with only a light wind and persistent drizzle—nothing like yesterday's terrifying gale. In the east, the sun struggled to break through the clouds and burn off the mist.

He hauled in a deep breath and gazed over the endless gray waves. How far were they from Europe? Were they closer to Africa than to his home? He'd only been with the pirates a few days, but already his best shirt and trousers were full of tears and stains. He had no extra clothing to change into. He probably wouldn't get any until they stole some from the crew of another vessel. He hated the thought, but he had to face the possibility.

Though he'd watched for it, he'd seen no further signs of the schooner they'd briefly pursued the day before. It had driven straight into the storm, and the pirates, wise for once, had held back. They'd let their quarry escape but managed to keep their own ship from destruction.

Alex hoped Captain Bryant hadn't wrecked on this or some other island. Because he was pretty sure the schooner they'd seen was Bryant's, and the last thing he'd want to happen to that man—and his lovely daughter—was to be overtaken and boarded by the cutthroats he sailed with now. He sent a prayer for their safety winging skyward.

A tall, gaunt crewman called Slate approached him and said in a gravelly voice, "The cap'n says you're to stay aboard while we go ashore, Dryden."

"Oh?" Alex was pleased with this verdict, but he tried not to let Slate see that. "Doesn't trust me, does he?"

"You might say that."

The crew of the *Herring* had a load of treasure they wanted to stash somewhere before they attacked another ship. That would give them room in the hold for more loot while avoiding the risk of losing what they already had.

Alex's mind started to spin possibilities of making an escape while the pirates gained land to bury their loot.

"Dudgeon will stay here with you, just to make sure you don't get any ideas, hey?"

Slate's pronouncement made Alex frown, dashing his hopes. Dudgeon was the nickname of a burly pirate given to outbursts of foul temper. Alex had no idea what the man's real name was, but if he could have picked a man from the

Herring's crew for a guardian, Dudgeon would be the very last man he'd name.

The captain of the motley crew went by Red Jensen. His hair still held hints of red in the back, but most of it was gone on top. Around the sides, it was a spiky gray. Red was well known along the lower Atlantic coast of the United States and into the Caribbean. He and his men attacked passenger ships or, more to their liking, loaded cargo vessels.

Alex had yet to be in on a sea battle with them or a capture, and he wasn't looking forward to it. The men of the *Herring* were known to be ruthless in their treatment of the crews and passengers they captured.

Dudgeon came up through the hatch from the forecastle and swung his gaze over the deck. Alex cringed but knew he couldn't avoid the man. As Captain Red and the rest of the crew loaded their longboat and dinghy with crates of spoils and chests of treasure, Dudgeon walked deliberately toward him.

"They're not leaving the whole cargo here, are they?" Alexander asked before Dudgeon could speak.

The pirate frowned. "Nay, we'll take most of the goods to Savannah and sell them. They be leaving a few things here for another day."

Just as Alex had reckoned. They wanted to sell off the valuable cargo fast, but be sure of what they wanted for themselves. If the law caught up with them, or if one of their attacks at sea went wrong, they didn't want to lose their treasure, their rum, or whatever else they'd earmarked for themselves.

"You stay where I can see you whilst they're about it," Dudgeon said.

"Aye, aye." Alex leaned on the rail, watching the rest of his captors strike out for shore. So much for dreams of escaping.

He was still angry at himself for the way he'd arrived here.

He'd been minding his own business in Kingston when those men jumped him after he left Captain Edwards's party. To be honest, he should have been more alert. His mind was too much on a certain young lady whose company he'd enjoyed that evening and too little on the dark streets he walked.

When he'd awoken in the forecastle of the *Herring*, Alex had tried to work it out in his mind. The two men had accosted him, perhaps expecting a brief struggle, and a third man had come up behind him and cracked him over the head. He couldn't remember much of the encounter, but it seemed to him that they knew who he was and had targeted him.

The first thing he'd learned after regaining consciousness was that he was now a pirate and at sea, like it or not. Kidnapped and forced to help Red Jensen and his band of robbers. And he was sure Dudgeon was one of those who'd confronted him. Three against one. It wasn't fair. But even though he knew better than to expect pirates to be fair, his situation was his own fault.

The two small boats heading for the island rode low in the water with their burdens. Landing would be tricky here at the best of times and with a lighter load. Jensen had chosen with care the time when they'd attempt making shore.

As they approached the outlying rocks, Alex held his breath. He was sure the longboat would smash, but at the last moment, a large wave came under them and swept the boat over the worst shoals. The men yelled in triumph and waved their oars skyward.

They hit the rocky land, which he couldn't call a beach, with some force, and two of the inebriated pirates flipped over the gunwales into the water. They rose dripping and waded to shore as their companions had a hearty laugh.

The dinghy was smaller and lighter, and its crew landed without mishap. All hands set to work to unload the two boats.

"Here now, fetch us some'at to eat, ya think?" Dudgeon said.

Alex eyed him in surprise. "You want me to go to the galley?"

"Where else d'ya think you'll find vittles?"

"Oh, aye." Alex headed across the deck, visualizing all the potential weapons in the galley. He glanced back and once more had to give up a promising thought. Dudgeon was only two steps behind him, his hand on the hilt of his cutlass.

"I DON'T THINK we lost much," Daniel said. "Of the rigging, I mean—other than the foretopsail and a bit of tackle. We can fix the mast and the rudder, yes?"

Captain Bryant grunted. Laura took that to mean he agreed, but he wasn't happy.

"Might be we can haul in the sea anchor and salvage enough canvas for a makeshift topsail," Old Philip said, gazing forlornly toward the waves.

Laura turned away from the crippled ship. The foresail, from the broken mast, now served as their shelter on shore. She gazed at the dripping island. How long would they have to stay here?

The storm was past, the sun's heat had begun to dry the rocks on shore, and its beams danced on the water. Beyond the shore, a tangle of inhospitable undergrowth hugged the cliffs and the side of a rocky ridge, eventually giving way to stunted trees. Higher up, thick jungle thrived. Did those trees hold fruit, or had the weather ruined it all? It was worth a look.

She turned and smiled at her father. They'd survived, and they'd make the best of the situation. If not for the crippled schooner, she might have felt carefree.

"Can you fix it, Papa?"

Her father stood amid the jagged stones that were the only beach, staring moodily at his ship.

"Aye, in good time. Philip and the boys and I can do it, but it won't be quick."

"How long?"

"Several days, maybe a week. We'll have to see if we can prop up what's left of the foremast. If not, we'll need to find a good, sturdy tree." He gazed doubtfully at the steaming jungle. "Most of the trees on this rock look misformed. Have to find a good, sturdy hardwood."

Laura gulped. "Maybe there are some on the other side of the island."

That thought didn't seem to cheer him, unlike his daughter, who always loved to explore. They walked back toward their shelter.

"It's days like this I wonder if I shouldn't have left you home with your aunts," her father said.

"We're safe now, Papa."

"Perhaps." The lines at the corners of his eyes seemed deeper than usual. "I've put my daughter in danger."

She couldn't deny that, but even so, she was glad to be here sharing the danger with him, rather than off in Maine, knitting and wondering what had happened to him and whether he would ever return home.

"Mother sailed with you once," she said.

"Yes. But we were young—"

"I'm young."

He smiled. "You are."

"And nothing bad happened on that voyage together, did it?"

"No, nothing terrible." He gave her an apologetic glance.

"We'd not been married long, and I couldn't bear to leave her behind."

Laura smiled. "I think that's lovely. Why didn't she sail with you again?"

"Well, we found that—" He cleared his throat, and his cheeks above his graying beard reddened. "Before my next voyage, we found that you were on the way."

"Oh, I see. It's my fault Mother was banned from the ship."

"In a sense." He put an arm about her shoulders. "But what a joyful time we had at the end of the journey, when I docked in Portland and you were there to meet me."

She laughed. "I expect I wasn't big enough to shake your hand."

"Oh, but you did. You held onto my finger. You were only a mite, but very determined, even then. But after that, we felt it was best that your mother stay ashore."

Laura looked out over the ocean, glad that she'd also had a chance to make a voyage with her father. She gazed up at him. "Do you regret taking her along that one time?"

"No, child. Those were sweet times."

If he would let her, she knew in that moment, she'd sail with him again. Not so much for her love of the sea, but to have every minute with him that she was allowed. But now he needed to make the *Arundel* seaworthy, or there would be no more sailing adventures together.

"Perhaps I should gather driftwood for a fire," she said. "I could make you some tea and heat up something to eat."

"That would be good. Something hot."

After a breakfast of hotcakes seasoned with ash and sand, the men set to work. Laura couldn't find a basket, so she emptied the stewpot Daniel had salvaged and carried it with her in case she found some fruit. The men were at the schooner, trying to make it more stable so they could begin the repairs.

"Papa," she called, "I'm going to have a look up there." She pointed toward the least steep part of the ridge.

Her father waved to acknowledge that he'd heard her and turned back to help the men sort through the broken planks they'd salvaged.

She climbed a couple of boulders then worked her way above the worst of the rocks, to where weeds and small bushes had found a foothold. She was able to walk upward slowly if she was careful not to trip on vines and undergrowth. Many of the plants she had no name for, and none at this point grew above her waist. But if she could get higher up, toward the ridge, she would find good-sized shrubs and even a few trees.

No path appeared, so she climbed precariously from spot to spot, wherever the route seemed least steep. After a while she came to an almost horizontal ridge along a cliff, where she could look down and see the captain and his men working on the schooner, trying their hardest to patch the hole in the hull so the vessel could at least float. Apparently they would worry about the rudder for steering it later.

A cleft rose gradually in a fold of the mountain—Laura thought of it as a mountain, even though by mainland standards it was probably not more than an abrupt, steep hill. She met a small stream and bent to cup water in her hand. To her surprise, it was fresh and sweet. *Thank you, Lord!*

She followed the cleft's curve upward, plucking a few brilliant blossoms as she went and dropping them into her pot. She spotted a gull, perched on a rock surrounded by thick bushes. Wouldn't it be nice to bring in some fresh meat for the stewpot?

She picked up a small rock and slowly drew her arm back,

eyes glued to the bird. She let fly, and the rock actually hit the gull, but it spread its wings and flew off with an affronted squawk.

Oh, well, she thought. Maybe next time. If she'd had the slingshot she'd learned to use as a child, it would have hurled the rock harder, and she'd have had the bird. At least she hadn't lost her good aim.

About a third of the way to the summit, she paused for breath and looked around. She could no longer see the men because she'd traveled too far to the side, and her view was now shielded by the cleft. But distant, sporadic hammering confirmed they were still hard at work.

To her left was a black area among the foliage, and she frowned at it. Surely that couldn't be an opening in the cliffside? Her pulse tripped. What had she discovered?

Slowly, she worked her way toward it. Vines twined around her ankles, and she wished she'd brought a knife of some sort. At last she stood before the black area, and it was indeed a hole in the rock wall.

Laura smiled in delight. She'd found a cave! What would Old Philip say when she told him? Probably he'd insist that ghosts would issue out of it at midnight, or some such rubbish.

She set down the kettle and peered inside, wondering if she dared enter. Not without a candle, she decided. Snakes and insects could be hovering inside, waiting for a hapless human to trespass. She straightened and considered whether she wanted to climb up here again today. The men would want another hot meal. She'd better wait and return tomorrow. Mildly disappointed, she picked up the kettle and set off for camp.

"There you are," her father cried as she approached the campfire. "Thought we'd lost you."

"No, I'm fine. Didn't find anything edible, though."

The captain came to stand beside her. "Philip thinks we can patch 'er up with a few days' hard work. We've lost a good deal of merchandise—"

"I'm sorry, Papa."

He shrugged. "We'll get by. I'll sell what's left and pay off the men. We won't live as high this winter as we'd hoped, is all."

Laura was used to living a spare life. They almost never had money to splurge with. When her father returned from a voyage, all was well for a while, but when the money ran out, provisions were scant and the captain had to go off on another voyage. They'd lived that way for years. Her mother had been philosophical about it, cherishing the times when her husband was at home and working hard to make their supplies last when he was away.

"Eli rescued your portmanteau."

"He did?" Laura said. "How wonderful." At least she would have her extra clothing.

"And this was floating in the hold." He stooped to pick up her small gathering basket.

"Wonderful." On her next foraging hike, that would be easier to carry than the kettle.

Eli came up with an armful of driftwood and dropped it near the fire ring as they spoke. "You might not think it's so wonderful when you see your baggage," he declared with an apologetic smile. Everything's soaked. You'll want to take out your clothes and dry them by the fire."

"Or just lay them out on the rocks," her father said. "The wind and sun will dry them."

"What about your clothes, Papa?"

"Mine are all right, but poor Eli and Daniel are only left with what's on their backs until we get to some port."

She set about her preparations for the next meal, then excavated the waterlogged portmanteau. Eli was right. Her clothing was bedraggled and smelled of seawater. She spread out each item, hoping the men wouldn't venture too close while her undergarments were exposed.

A few bolts of cotton material had been among the cargo in the hold, she recalled. If they hadn't been lost, perhaps she could get hold of them and stitch them each an extra shirt. Her sewing kit had survived, inside her portmanteau. She set it open on a rock, so that the spools of thread would dry.

Of course, Daniel and Eli might not like to wear the bright calicos they'd purchased in the islands. The thought made her smile as she poked about their meager foodstuffs to plan what they could eat for supper.

ALEX SAW his chance as he scraped up the coals in the stove. Dudgeon stood in the galley doorway, gazing toward shore. No telling how long he would keep his back turned. Alex stooped over the coal scuttle as though he would build up the fire and grasped the short poker tightly.

While he didn't really want to hurt the man seriously, he knew he must strike hard enough to put the big man out of commission for at least several minutes. Dudgeon was one of the most disagreeable men among the pirate crew. Alex could imagine clearly some of the nefarious deeds he had committed.

He's a thief, and probably a murderer. If I don't do this, I'll be with them for a long time, and they'll make me into a thief and a murderer too. If the law catches them while I'm aboard, then I'll hang alongside them.

Loathsome as his task was, he had no choice. Alex swallowed hard and took a stealthy step toward his guard.

Dudgeon turned just as he swung the poker. The big pirate gave a roar, but it was too late to stop. Alex put more strength behind his swing as Dudgeon yanked his huge knife from his belt. The poker came down on the side of his brow.

The pirate stared at Alex, and Alex stared back. Blood ran down Dudgeon's face, over his eye and into his beard. For a long moment, Alex thought he would recover his strength and stab him, despite the staggering blow. Then, ever so slowly, the big man sank to his knees and toppled forward.

Alex jumped back, next to the stove. Dudgeon lay motionless on the floor. Carefully, Alex bent and laid down the poker then retrieved the knife. He stuck it in his belt. What else would he need? He'd have to hide out on this desolate island until they gave up looking for him and left. Alex questioned whether he could elude them long enough for them to reach that point, but what else could he do?

Maybe he'd need some money. If he was lucky enough to evade Jensen's crew and then meet up with another ship's captain, he could pay the man to take him aboard. It might be months or years before another ship came that close, but when it did ...

Quickly he rifled Dudgeon's pockets. The senseless man didn't stir except to haul in one big, shaky breath and then let it out. At least he wasn't dead.

Alex's fingers closed on a couple of coins. He drew them out and slid them into his own pocket. There. He really was a thief now. He climbed over the big man's torso and legs and reached the door.

Scanning the shore, he saw only one of the pirates, lounging near the beached boats. The rest must have gone off to bury their chests of loot. This side of the island seemed a bit more hospitable than the other side. Perhaps they could find some ground that wasn't too rocky and dig a deep hole.

Alex considered how to leave the *Herring*. He couldn't sail the ship by himself, that was certain. If he made it to shore, they would hunt him down, but what else could he do? They'd taken the only small boats.

He decided the best plan was to drop over the side of the ship farthest from shore and swim for it. If he could get around the nearest point, near the looming shark's tooth rock, the men on shore wouldn't be able to see him. He'd have to scramble ashore among the rocks, but he thought he could do it. Maybe he could hide until they gave up looking for him. Being marooned here would be better than staying with the pirates.

Cautiously he swung a leg over the far rail then lowered himself until he was hanging from the side. With a quick prayer, he let go and held his breath. The shock of the cold water hit him harder than he'd expected. He surfaced swiftly and struck out along the side of the ship. When he left its shelter, he moved as silently as he could, swimming underwater then surfacing just long enough to gulp in a new breath.

After several underwater stints, His lungs burned. He let his head break the surface and looked back. He'd done it. He could no longer see the boats on shore or the man guarding them. He struck out with quick overhand strokes, toward the towering fang of a rock.

Twenty minutes later, he struggled ashore, panting. He stopped in the shelter of a reddish boulder to catch his breath. So far, so good. A sound caught his attention, and he raised his chin, standing perfectly still to listen.

Was that hammering? He didn't know what the pirates were up to, but he'd better steer clear of the place from which that sound issued. He hurried toward the line where the brush met the rocks. The quicker he hid himself, the better.

Chapter Five

After they'd eaten, Laura cleaned up. It took a long time to heat water for their dishes with soggy driftwood for fuel. The day had turned off balmy and bright, with a light breeze ruffling her hair. If she hadn't known what a close call they'd had on arrival, she'd have thought this island a pleasant spot for a picnic.

By some miracle, her father had brought her leatherbound journal ashore safely when they left the *Arundel*. She should record this adventure in it while the light was good.

No, she had a better plan. She would walk up to the cave and do it there. Hastily, she rinsed out the last of the dishes and made sure their precious foodstuffs were put away where seabirds and waves couldn't reach them. Then she set out carrying the journal, a pencil, and a candle lantern. She took the faint path that led her above the shore, up the hillside then along the side of the incline until she came to the nearly obscured cave entrance.

She settled on a rock in the sun outside the gaping hole in the hillside and opened to the first blank page. In her previous entry, she'd described the party she'd attended with her father at the hotel in Kingston. She'd mentioned meeting the handsome Alexander Dryden. Would she ever see him again? Certainly not, if they couldn't get off this island.

After thinking for a moment, she entered the date and *Sharktooth Island*. Painstakingly, she described the storm they'd endured, the fearsome sighting of the pirate ship, and the violent landing on the island.

Papa and the men think they can repair the schooner in a few days. I hope we won't have to stay here longer than that, although the island has a rugged beauty. I'm told it's not likely that another ship would stop here and give us aid, since it is so very difficult to land here safely.

She wrote another half page, describing the rocky terrain, the high ridge above her, the stunted flora that gave way to dense jungle away from the shore, and the cave's mouth she had discovered by accident while exploring. Opposite this, she added a rough sketch of their camp on the shore, with the jagged ridge towering over them and the island's namesake jutting out of the water in the distance. On the next page, she added a sketch of the cave's opening.

After sitting still for several minutes looking down on the troubled sea, she added, *I can't seem to stop thinking about Alexander. Is it possible we could meet again one day? Perhaps Papa will stop in Boston, or Captain Edwards will run up to Maine.* She hadn't yet decided whether she would make another voyage with her father. But that might be her only hope of seeing Alexander again, and then it would only be a hope and a chance.

And a prayer, she thought. *Lord, You know best. If You want Alex and me to meet again, it's up to You to arrange it.*

She stooped to check the lantern. It was the type of metal frame in which she could light a candle and then open or close the side panels. She'd lit a new candle at the campfire and then placed it inside. It had burned down a third of its length while she walked and sat writing.

"Guess I'd better hurry if I want to see inside the cave." She rose, brushed off her skirt, and crept toward the gaping entrance. Her pulse raced. Was anything living inside? Certainly no animals large enough to attack her, but there might be snakes, spiders, or poisonous insects.

She pushed the vines aside and stepped into the opening, holding the uncovered lantern high. A space the size of a small room stood before her, about four yards wide but becoming narrower toward the back. She stepped inside and looked all around. Apart from a few rocks on the floor, the cave appeared to be empty. The wall to her left was uneven. She walked toward it and found that a fault in the stone made a ledge about four feet off the cave floor and extending about six feet at the height of her waist.

"A lovely shelf," she whispered. If anyone wanted to live in the cave, that would be a boon. They could keep their food and dishes there, if they had any. She laid her journal on it, the gilt words *Day to Day* shimmering in the candlelight.

She set her pencil beside it and smiled. Perfect. She would come back each day and add to her journal. Turning toward the back of the cave, she held the lantern high and stepped carefully into the narrower part. The dark ceiling made her wary. She examined its contours carefully. No bats had better swoop down on her.

To her surprise, the back wall didn't close completely, but became a passageway between the rocks. Laura shivered but took a few steps inside. She lowered the lantern and squinted into the distance. She couldn't see any beams of light penetrating from outside. If the cave had another opening, it wasn't very close.

The rock walls nearly touched her on either side, and the ceiling was so low she had to stoop. Again she thought of bats, or perhaps even worse, spiders, lurking up there, waiting to drop into her hair. Her heart pounding, she backed up into the main room of the cave.

"I think I'll save that for another day," she said aloud. Maybe if there was time, she'd bring Daniel up here and see what he thought. Daniel was about her age and the adventurous type. She didn't think she could coax her father, Old Philip, or Eli up here. But if Daniel came along and they each carried a lantern, they could scout along the cavern and see how far it went. Who knew? There might even be some interesting minerals in there.

The light from the entrance beckoned her. As she stepped out into the brilliant sunlight, her eyes pinched shut against the glare of its rays on water. For a moment, she hesitated, squinting, until she could open her eyes fully without pain.

She looked behind her at the dark opening. Should she put the vines back in place? No. Nobody else would venture here to find the cave.

Perhaps she should go back and retrieve her diary. No, even if Daniel didn't want to come, she'd return tomorrow. The journal would be safe and dry in there, more so than down on the shore. She blew out the candle and hurried along the path. She needed to prepare supper for the men. Would she find anything besides rice and beans? Maybe one of them would have time to do a little fishing.

She glanced up toward the ridge above her. She'd toyed with the idea of climbing up there so she could see what was on the far side of the island. Maybe she could follow the freshwater stream upward to its source. The sun had moved noticeably. She'd spent more time at the cave than she'd realized, but there was still a little time she could call her own.

Carrying the lantern, she hurried down to the shore. The four men were all out at the schooner, working on the repairs. There was a little time before she had to return to the campfire.

She grabbed the water bucket, emptied its meager contents into the kettle left hanging over the remains of their fire, and added a good measure of dry beans to soak and simmer. With the empty bucket, she hurried toward the stream. They'd all given thanks for its presence. It meant they would have fresh drinking water as long as they were forced to remain here, and they could fill their casks before leaving the island.

After filling the bucket, Laura left it in the path where they usually accessed the stream. She walked beside the water until the bushes and rocks became too difficult to maneuver. Peering down into the rivulet, she considered wading upward, but that wouldn't do. If she kept her shoes on, she'd ruin her only pair. If she took them off, the rocky bottom would shred her feet.

Moving a little to one side, she set out to make her own path toward the summit. The going was rough, but she was making progress. Almost at the top of the ridge, she was surprised to find the water gushing from a crevice in the rock face. She laughed. "So this is the where the spring comes out. There must be an underground stream."

She stood for several minutes beside the top of the stream. When she looked down, she realized how high up she was. Hiking up here was quite an accomplishment. She glanced up once more, tempted to complete the climb and see what was on the other side of the ridge. But the ascent had eaten up her free hour. She'd better not take time now. It would take her a while to prepare the meal. Satisfied with her jaunt, she set out for camp.

The bushes before her parted, and she stopped short with a gasp. A man stepped out onto the narrow patch and stared at her. Laura's heart pounded, and stark terror rippled through her. Then she gazed into his bearded face and exhaled. It couldn't be.

"Mr. Dryden?"

"Miss Bryant. I—this is most unexpected."

She eyed his damp clothing and several days' growth of whiskers. "What—I don't understand."

"I—I was on another ship."

"Oh. And you've landed here, on Sharktooth Island? I thought that was nearly impossible."

He smiled. "And yet, here you are."

Her face warmed. "Yes, we—my father's vessel wrecked in the storm."

"No!" Concern flooded his features, and he took a step toward her. "Is your father all right?"

"He is. One of the men was injured, but we all got safely to shore, praise God."

"Indeed."

"What about your friends?" she asked.

Alex's face darkened. "They are not my friends. In fact, I am on this side of the island in an effort to escape them."

"Escape?" She eyed him closely.

"I am no longer with Captain Edwards. I was captured after the party where we last met. Against my will, I was taken aboard another ship."

"But—Captain Edwards set sail the day after the party. Weren't you with him?"

"Would to God I were. Unfortunately, a ship full of marauders was haunting the harbor. They sent a few men ashore to bring back a few more hands. I was attacked and taken prisoner. I never made it back to Captain Edwards's ship. I was forced for the last several days to serve a cutthroat known as Red Jensen."

Laura's chest tightened. "I'm so sorry to hear this. Papa will be distressed too. He and Captain Edwards are good friends."

"Believe me, I would never have left his employ if I had a choice."

"I'm sure of it. He spoke well of you."

"Well, Jensen learned of my carpentry skills. He put me to work doing some needed repairs to the *Herring*. Next, he wanted me to make him some fancy cabinetry for his cabin."

"I suppose that's better than looting other ships," Laura said hesitantly.

"Oh aye, but it was only a matter of time. When they found a victim, I'm sure they expected me to take part in the slaughter and thievery." Alex hung his head. "It pains me to admit to you that I've been pressed into service on a pirate vessel."

"And where was the navy while this was going on?"

"I fear they battened down in Kingston to wait out the storm. They won't chase after a ruthless pirate to get one man back. I do hope they'll hunt him down eventually, though, and give him his just desserts. Though I doubt they'd believe me if I told them I was there on the *Herring* against my will."

"The ship we saw in the storm." The bitter truth came to her suddenly, and she looked into his face, hoping he would deny it.

"I fear it's true. We'd set a course toward Bermuda before the gale blew up. Jensen thought maybe he could make port there, but the wind was too fierce and we were blown eastward. I spotted a small schooner as we tried to evade the worst of the gale—your father's."

Her breath whooshed out of her. "But—are you saying those pirates are ashore here right now?"

Alex nodded toward the crest above them. "On the other side."

"But how did you get over here on this side of the island? Are they a danger to us?"

"They might be. Most of them went ashore to hide the loot they'd stolen recently. I managed to get away, but when they find I'm missing, they will no doubt come looking for me."

"Oh." She swallowed hard.

"I heard hammering."

"That's my father and his crew, trying to repair our vessel."

"Then we must tell them to stop, lest they give away their presence with the noise."

Glad she hadn't thrown more wood on her cook fire, she looked up at the hilltop. "If they climb to the ridge, they might see the *Arundel* and our camp."

Alex gazed thoughtfully up the slope. "We're not far from the top. Perhaps I should take a quick look before we go down to your camp."

Before she could speak, he was dashing up the slope. Laura scrambled after him, holding on to protruding rocks and the branch of a small tree when the way was steepest. Panting, she reached his side as he peered between bushes.

"Keep low," he whispered.

Laura edged forward and carefully separated a couple of branches. She drew in a quick breath. The pirate ship rode at anchor on the waters that were almost calm now. It looked nearly twice the length of the *Arundel*. Small waves rocked it up and down peacefully. Movement on shore snagged her attention.

"I see them," she whispered. Several men moved about them below, carrying boxes and tools.

"Look." He pointed down the ridge, closer to its base.

"Oh, no." Two men were climbing the slope.

A distant gunshot reached them through the clear air.

"What is it? Do they see us?"

"No. I fear that Dudgeon, the man they left aboard with me, has awakened. He doesn't have a boat, but he'll warn them."

Even as he spoke, two of the pirates dropped their burdens and ran toward their dinghy.

"Come on," Alex muttered. "We can't stay here. We need to warn your father."

He jumped dexterously from perch to perch down the incline, with Laura half running, half sliding behind him. They reached the path proper, near the stream, and she wondered what or who had made this path. Someone must have spent time on the island. She'd seen no sign of goats or wild creatures that would make a path.

They neared the spot where she'd drawn water, and Laura tugged at his sleeve.

"Wait. If I leave the bucket, they might find it."

She pointed to where she'd left it, and Alex dashed the few yards to the spot and grabbed the bucket.

"This way," she cried turning toward the encampment.

"Hurry!" He seized her hand and pulled her along to another steep pitch, water sloshing over the bucket's rim. "I'll go first and steady you."

Chapter Six

The men in the camp had spotted them during the last bit of their precarious descent and waited for them at the bottom.

"Who's this?" her father roared as Laura dashed toward him with Alex behind her. Eli and Philip stood back a few paces with pistols pointed at the newcomer. At least they'd stopped hammering.

"It's Alex Dryden, Papa! I met him up the path. We met him at Captain Edwards's party, remember? There are pirates on the other side of the island. We must prepare in case they find us."

Laura skidded to a halt beside her father and hauled in short breaths that didn't give her enough air.

"Where is Edwards's ship?" her father asked.

"Alas, sir, it's gone away toward Boston. I came here, sadly on the *Herring*."

Captain Bryant glared at him. "Are you a pirate, then?"

"No, sir. I assure you I'm not. I was captured by them and carried aboard their ship as a slave. They were going to force me to help attack other ships and shore villages, but they don't trust me yet, so they left me on the ship with one man for a guard while they went ashore. I've escaped them, but my guard has alerted them now, and I fear they'll come looking for me."

"Papa, if they hear sounds of your repair work or smell the campfire's smoke, they'll find us quickly." Laura ran to the fire pit and poked the remaining coals apart with stick. She set the kettle aside in a crevice.

Her father turned to his three men. "Put your weapons away and hide the tools. Then we must make ourselves small, so that we can't be seen from up above."

"We can't hide our ship," Eli said.

"No, but mayhap they'll think it was wrecked and abandoned here," the captain replied.

Alex looked up the slope to the ridge. "You must hurry. We saw two men climbing the slope on the far side. If they go all the way to the top ..."

"Look lively!" Captain Bryant gathered up a piece of canvas on which they'd laid out foodstuffs. "Laura, hide the bucket behind a rock, then get out of sight."

Alex sprang to help them conceal their things as best they could.

"Our arms are limited," the captain told him. "Do you have any weapons?"

"Only this knife." He patted it at his waist. "I couldn't carry a gun when I swam for it."

"We've a shotgun, a rifle, and two pistols. Eli is our best shot, but he's broken his arm so I gave Daniel one of the pistols, and I have the other. Philip will take the shotgun." He distributed ammunition while speaking. "How are you with a long gun?"

"I'm a passable shot, sir," Alex said.

The captain nodded and handed over the rifle, a powder

horn, and a pouch of lead balls. "It shoots true if your hand is steady."

Laura went to Alex's side. "Come. I thought I'd hide between those rocks near the dinghy."

Alex frowned. "They'll see the boat and know someone came ashore after the wreck."

The youngest sailor, Daniel, heard him and walked over to them. "I can row it out and tie it to the *Arundel's* stern. It won't be as visible then."

"Ask your captain," Alex said, not wanting to overstep Bryant's authority.

Laura touched his sleeve. "We need to hurry. They could arrive any second."

Her father walked unsteadily toward them over the rocky ground. "Hunker down, Laura. Not near the ship. They'll check around it and steal anything they think useful."

"Should we hide in the jungle?" She looked toward the thick bushes that grew up near the cave. Maybe there was time for them all to climb up there, and they'd have the advantage of an elevated position. She turned to ask her father if he thought it was a good plan.

Eli gave a shout, and they all looked toward him. He pointed up the shore. A longboat manned by several pirates glided around the point near the tooth-shaped rock.

ALEX SEIZED Laura's hand and yanked her down behind a large rock. Old Philip pulled the captain toward another jumble of boulders that might conceal them. The other two, Daniel and Eli, melted into the bushes beyond the high-water mark.

Silence fell, except for the breaking waves. Alex couldn't

help peering about and wondering if they should move to another spot farther from the disabled schooner. If he'd known who did the hammering, he certainly would have warned them sooner.

He fished a lead ball from the pouch Bryant had given him and set the powder horn on a nearby rock. He didn't want to waste time when he needed to reload the rifle.

Laura stirred, and he touched her forearm, fearing she was about to stick her head around the edge of the rock for a look.

"Let me. You stay low." He shuddered to think what Captain Red's crew would do if they discovered that a maiden as lovely as Miss Bryant was hiding from them. They'd kill her father and the rest of them in a flash to take possession of her.

She nodded, and he leaned to his left, only far enough that he could see along the shore. He drew back quickly.

"The boat is much nearer. If they disembark near the schooner, I'll have to fire on them. Surprise may favor us. There are four in the boat, and we are five."

"But only four guns," she whispered, ignoring the fact that he didn't count her, only the men who presumably could engage in battle. "If they come that close, though, Papa should be able to take one with his pistol."

A blast shattered the air, and Alex whirled around. Old Philip was standing behind his rock, resting the shotgun on its crest. Captain Bryant pulled him down.

"Well, that's torn it," Alex said. "Now or never." He eased up between two boulders. The men in the boat were frantically trying to turn it away from the shore. He took careful aim and pulled the trigger. Without waiting to see the result, he ducked behind the rocks and began to reload. Another shot fired at a distance.

"Was that them shooting at us, or was it Daniel firing at them?" Laura asked.

"Don't know. Keep your head down!" Alex took another quick look, and no one fired a weapon while he peeked over the rock. "I only see two of their men rowing now," he reported.

"Weren't there four?"

"Yes. I'm pretty sure I hit one, and either Philip or the captain may have hit another. Or Daniel."

She nodded.

"You all right?" came Captain's Bryant's voice.

"Yes, we're fine," Alex called back.

They waited half a minute, then Alex bobbed up again. The longboat was coming in toward shore just yards beyond the schooner. He ducked down.

"They're very close, but they can't land now. The tide's too low. They might be able to nudge up against the stern or your schooner and climb onto it."

"Why would they?" Laura asked.

"To see if anyone's aboard. And from there, they can walk the length of your deck and step onto rock and make their way ashore, the way your lot did."

"We used the dinghy too. I think." She frowned. "I bumped my head, and they brought me ashore."

"Are you all right now?"

She put a hand up to the back of her head. "It only hurts a little, when I touch it."

He grinned. "Well, don't touch it." He still had a knot on the back of his own skull, from the night he was captured. He hoped it would shrink soon and stop hurting.

A shot sounded from close by, and he realized either the captain or Philip had fired.

"Stay down!" He rose and aimed his gun in the schooner's direction, but before he could focus on the pirates, a bullet nicked the rock in front of him, and chips flew into the air.

He sank quickly beside Laura. "They've spotted us."

"Is Papa all right?"

"I'm not sure." A wave of guilt washed over him, like the surf bathing the rocky shore. He had led the cutthroats to Laura and Captain Bryant. If they survived, could Bryant forgive him?

A hoarse shout nearby was cut off, and metal clashed against metal. Alex sprang up just as a gun roared. Old Philip sprawled on the rocks, with bright red pouring from his chest. One pirate stepped back to reload his pistol while his companion dashed toward Captain Bryant, his cutlass raised high.

Laura stifled a scream and scrambled to the edge of her refuge, poking her head around the side of the biggest rock. Alex's back was to her, but she could see beyond him to a swarthy pirate menacing her father with a gleaming cutlass.

A rifle fired, so close it hurt her ears, and she knew Alex had pulled the trigger. The man holding the cutlass crumpled into a pool of water between the boulders.

The second pirate, fumbling with a long-barreled pistol, cast it aside and pulled a long dagger from his belt.

"Papa!" She sprang forward, unable to help herself.

Her father had evidently been reloading, and she sprang to his side.

"Get back." He glared at her.

Laura was aware of Alex and the pirate with the dagger squaring off. She cowered back in her sheltered place as before, but now the pirate knew where she was. If he overcame Alex and her father, she was doomed.

She looked about for something to use as a weapon. Alex's shot pouch and powder horn were close by, but they wouldn't help. A quick glance told her Alex had laid down the rifle and was now crouched, his knife extended, waiting for the other man to make a move. Even if she could reach the rifle, which she couldn't without exposing herself, she couldn't reload it fast enough to save him or her father.

The incoming tide had nearly reached her hiding place. She glanced down as a precocious wave lapped her shoes. She peeked around the rock again while feeling the wet stones with one hand. One fit into her palm and she hefted it, then she transferred it to her right hand.

The stone was heavier than the one she'd hurled at the herring gull the previous day. Maybe she could throw it hard enough to do some good. If nothing else, it would distract the pirate and possibly give her father time to finish reloading his pistol.

She poised herself and counted under her breath. *One, two, three.*

Jumping out from her cover, she drew back her arm and focused on the cutthroat, trying to block out the sight of Alex with blood flowing from his upper arm and her father crouching behind his own stone shelter. She had to wait for Alex to move to one side, and then she threw the rock as hard as she could.

It struck the pirate on his jaw, and his head jerked back. He faltered and shook his head then glared in her direction. Laura gasped and dove down out of sight.

She held her breath, listening to sounds of a struggle set against the pounding surf. A wave surged up and washed over her feet ankle-high, soaking her from the knees down where she crouched.

"Laura!"

At her father's cry, she rose. He was leaning heavily on one of the boulders, still holding his pistol. A few yards beyond,

Alex bent over the prone form of the pirate she'd targeted with her rock. The waves sloshed over the body, and Alex dragged the man farther ashore then walked toward them.

"You're hurt," Laura said, eyeing his reddened sleeve.

"It's nothing." He looked anxiously at Captain Bryant. "Maybe we should leave them to the sea."

Another body lay between them and the longboat, where he'd fallen.

"No," her father said. "Either we'll take them out a way for a sea burial or ..."

"Where are Eli and Daniel?" Laura asked.

Alex frowned. "Still in the jungle, I think."

"I heard gunfire from that direction," her father said, gazing toward the thick foliage. "They may have encountered more of the cutthroats."

"I'll go and see." Alex said grimly to Laura, "Tend to your father and stay close. Be alert. The others will have heard the gunfire."

"How many are there?" her father asked.

"There were a dozen on the ship besides me. Here." He held out the rifle. "You can reload this. Let me take the pistol."

The long gun wouldn't be as useful in the jungle as the pistol. Laura took the rifle. "I'll do it. Unless—" She looked over to where Old Philip lay, his limbs splayed out on the rocks and the blood soaking the whole front of his shirt.

"I fear there's nothing to be done for our friend," her father said gently. "Get Alex's bullet pouch."

She hurried back to their hiding place, and when she returned with the pouch and powder horn, Alex was halfway to the thick bushes where Daniel and Eli had disappeared. Had it only been a few minutes ago? It seemed like hours since the pirates' longboat had appeared at the end of the island.

As she watched Alex approach the dense foliage, a shot rang out a little distance inland. She caught her breath.

"Steady," her father said. "Get the shotgun. We must needs reload that too. I taught you to use one."

"Yes, Papa." He'd taken her out to shoot birds a couple of times at home in Maine. Her hands shook as she pulled it from beneath Philip's lifeless arm and set about reloading it.

Two more shots sounded. She stopped her task and looked to her father.

"Easy now," he said. "Shotgun ready?"

"Yes." Her voice shook. Had they lost Alex, so soon after finding him? And what of Eli and Daniel, their dear friends?

"And I've the rifle," her father said steadily. "If any of those cutthroats burst from the jungle, I'll shoot first. You hold fire until they're closer. We have to reload as fast as possible."

"Yes, Papa."

When she was satisfied that the shotgun was ready, she stood and leaned it on the rock her father and Philip had sheltered behind. The waves were again encroaching on them.

"The tide's rising, Papa. Should we move higher up the beach?"

He snorted. "I wouldn't call this a beach, but you're probably right." She took hold of his arm in an effort to guide him over the rock, but he shook free. "Pick out your own way. The ground is too rough here to try to keep together." He pointed to a rock ten yards away. "That one. It's not as big as those others, but the tide shouldn't reach there. If it does, it will just give us a wetting but not pull us out."

As usual, his reasoning made sense, and she let him go ahead. He was limping, and he moved very slowly, placing each foot with care.

When they'd nearly reached the boulder, she remembered

poor Old Philip and looked back. "We should have brought Old Philip up here. We can bury him later."

"He'd rather rest at sea," her father said. "If we survive this day, we'll get him and stitch him up in a sailcloth sack. If not, what will it matter?"

She shuddered. Movement along the line of vegetation caught her eye.

"Look, Papa. There's Alex and Daniel."

Her father rested his weapon's barrel on the top of the rock and waved to the two men. "Don't forget to keep watch behind as well."

Laura whirled and gazed at the empty shore behind her. The rocky beach was nearly under water now, but no one moved against the backdrop—only the surf and the bushes fluttering their leaves in the sea breeze.

"Was the tide this high before?" she asked.

"It's barely reached our fire ring. But you're right, it does seem a bit higher than yesterday.

"Is another storm coming?"

The captain cast an eye skyward. "I think not."

She could see now that Alex was supporting Daniel, who walked awkwardly, stumbling as they wove among the rocks.

"Daniel's hurt," she said.

"Do you think so?" Her father squinted and watched their slow progress. Soon they could make out dark blood staining his left pant leg.

"No one seems to be following them." She hauled in a ragged breath.

When the two reached them, Daniel flung himself down on a smaller rock and pulled in deep, raspy gulps of air.

"Eli's dead," Alex said.

Captain Bryant's chin sank. "I feared it when I saw you."

"They were attacked by two pirates in the jungle. Daniel shot one, and the other got to Eli."

"He only had a knife," Daniel choked out. Tears ran down his cheeks. "He came at me after he'd done for Eli. I couldn't reload. I held him off for a little bit, but he got at me just as Alex came crashing through the brush." He looked up at Dryden. "I'm in your debt."

"Don't be silly. We're all in this together."

"That be two more," Captain Bryant said. "We killed four here. You said there were twelve?"

"Aye." Alex cast a worried glance toward the ridge.

"We've lost two." The captain said no more.

Laura's heart ached at the thought of Eli and Philip never making it home. Old Philip considered the Bryants his family, but Eli had a wife and a little son back in Maine.

"What now?" Daniel asked.

"They'll want that longboat," Alex said, glancing uneasily toward the shore. The pirates' boat had been run up on the rocks, but the rising tide was rocking it. Soon it would float away.

"Should we secure it?" Laura asked.

Her father frowned. "Perhaps, but that would draw them to us."

"Can we use their boat to get home?" She looked into his face, seeking wisdom.

But the captain shook his head. "Not to get all the way to the mainland. It's too risky in an open boat."

"Riskier than facing the rest of the pirates?"

Alex cleared his throat. "Perhaps I should climb up to the ridge and see if I can tell what they're doing."

"Perhaps, but don't put yourself in danger if you can help it."

"How long will it take to finish the repairs on the schooner?" Alex asked.

The captain looked very helpless at that moment. "With only me and Daniel, and with him being hurt ..."

"You have me," Laura said.

"And me." Alex squared his shoulders. "I'll go take a look from the top. We need to know if they're coming for us."

"Be your pistol loaded?" Captain Bryant asked.

"Aye."

The older man nodded. "We'll make ready every weapon we have and await your return. If you hear a shot, make haste."

Alex nodded. "I will at any rate, but if I hear such sounds, I'll turn back immediately." He stuck the pistol through his belt.

"Take this too." Daniel held up a long dirk with a horn handle.

"The pirate's knife." Alex took it.

Laura was sure he'd had a knife when she first met up with him. Where was it now? She peered along the shore, but the pirates' bodies were hidden by rocks, and she couldn't tell if Alex's knife was now wedged in one of them.

"I'll be back soon, brother," Alex said to Daniel. He nodded to the captain, and his eyes lingered a moment on Laura's face.

"God speed," she said.

Alex turned away. His long strides had him at the edge of the jungle in seconds.

"I should have sent my spyglass with him," Captain Bryant said.

"I could follow after him with it," Daniel said.

"Nay, you're hurt."

"Let me take it." Laura ran to the biggest hidden cache of supplies. She knew the pack where her father had stowed his small telescope. Her hand closed around it. She lifted her skirts and ran for the path they'd followed to the stream.

The wind brought her a faint shout, and she turned around. Her father was waving frantically. She turned an ear toward him. All she could make out was "No," but she decided he was demanding that she come back and not run off alone.

"I'll be with Alex," she called, but the wind blew her words back at her. She hovered only an instant thinking she might not be doing the right thing. Was she being utterly foolish to run off and leave the camp? Surely if she ran her fastest, she'd catch up with Alex before he reached the stream. She'd be safe with him.

Their trips to get fresh water had begun to define a path. She pushed herself up it. Alex was no longer in sight, and her breath came in short gasps. She slowed to a walk, clutching the spyglass with one hand, trudging upward one step at a time.

Wind lifted the leaves and fronds all around her. She cast uneasy glances sideways into the lush, inhospitable greenness. Somewhere, a bird croaked. Stepping with more care, she tried to survey the ground before she placed each step. There might be snakes here, too, though she'd seen none in the past two days.

She was recovering her wind when a bush to the right of the path rustled and swayed. Laura stifled a scream. Where was Alex? She ran forward, away from the camp and, she hoped, toward Alex.

Chapter Seven

Alex pushed through the brush, trying not to make too big a disturbance. Beyond the spring, there was no path, and he didn't want to alert his enemies of his presence.

Despite his precautions, the route he and Laura had taken when they tore down the slope was as clearly visible as if they'd marked it with arrows pointing the way. Bent stems and broken fallen leaflets were as obvious as signposts. He clenched his jaw and pressed on.

Panting, he gained the summit. By crawling over some rocks and peering through the bushes, he was able to see the *Herring,* still riding at anchor where he'd left it a few short hours ago. Several men were in the jollyboat, rowing toward the ship.

Had they really killed half the *Herring's* crew?

Thanks be for that.

If only he had a spyglass. He couldn't tell who was in the jollyboat. Was one of the rowers Captain Red? Dudgeon still stood on the deck, he could tell that much. He squinted at the small boat. Three men there. Where were the other two?

Maybe they'd already gone to the ship, when Dudgeon first sounded the alarm. Or were they on foot, seeking a way around the island to discover the fate of the longboat's crew?

Alexander drew back, lest the men were even now climbing the other side of the ridge toward him. Though he couldn't see movement below him, he didn't dare stand up or make any other move that would give him a better view. Best go back to camp and see about mending the *Arundel* as quickly as possible.

Turning, he froze in his tracks. Red Jensen stood between two large shrubs, a bandanna shielding his bald head from the sun and a crafty smile on his face. One arm was clamped around Laura Bryant's waist, and in his other hand was a pistol, pointed at her temple.

Alex's stomach clenched and he had to grind his teeth to keep from groaning. His gun was still thrust through his belt, as he'd needed both hands to complete the rugged climb.

The pirate captain nodded pleasantly. "So there ye be, Dryden. Best be getting back to the ship."

Alex's heart raced. If he tried to draw his own pistol, the pirate captain would shoot him point blank and make off with Laura. He had not the slightest doubt of that.

What was she doing up here? He'd left her below, with her father and Daniel. Had they been attacked again? He'd heard nothing to alarm him. Laura stared at him, her eyes wide with terror, her face blanched and her arms limp at her sides.

He swallowed hard. "I see you know there's another ship landed on this island."

"Aye, we heard a few gunshots back along." Red smiled craftily. "This lovely creature brought me a spyglass."

Red turned around slowly, hauling Laura with him. When his back was turned to Alex, he could see a collapsed spyglass protruding from the pirate's belt at the back of his waist. He tensed. If he jumped now, would Red discharge the pistol and kill Laura? Was it worth a try? He put one foot forward.

Too late. Red completed his circle, so that he and Laura again faced Alex.

Laura shook all over. She tried to say something, but Red tightened his hold about her waist and she flinched, her face strained in an awful grimace.

"I reckon she thought to spy on us," he said with a chuckle. He sobered suddenly. "Or she was bringing the spyglass to you."

So he hadn't been down to the camp. Unless he was close by during the earlier clash in the jungle and hung back to save his own skin. He most likely didn't know what had happened earlier.

"The strangers have killed all your longboat crew."

Jensen's face darkened. "You lie."

"No," Alex said. "They've killed six in all. I saw Carle go down myself, not long ago. I'm surprised to see you up here on your own."

"Looking for stragglers. We're ready to sail." The pistol moved slightly. "Looking for you too. Dudgeon says you done him a bad turn."

"I made my escape."

"And now you're taken again."

Alex considered his options. Was there even a sliver of a chance he could rescue Laura and return her to Captain Bryant? Red Jensen needed him badly. The *Herring* had needed him before. Now, with half his crew gone, Jensen needed him even more. How likely was he to shoot the deserter? He would see an able-bodied seaman as a highly desirable commodity. But would he see Laura as more valuable?

They stood eyeing each other keenly. Alex hated to think what Laura's fate might be with Jensen. Abuse her? Sell her?

On the other hand, the pirates would be hard-pressed to sail the *Herring* as it was. Every man lost now would make it even harder. And this was one place they did *not* want to be marooned. Perhaps he could get Captain Red to start moving to rejoin his crew and catch him unawares along the way.

"We'd best go back to the *Herring* now, before the crew of that schooner finds you here," Alex said.

Red smiled. "You first, lad. Over the top and down the other side. My men will bring the jollyboat in for us and Rourke."

So, he was right. Another man was still roaming the island. Alex raised his chin. "They'll do well to land it again in those rocks."

"The tide is high now."

Alex didn't move.

"Go on now! We'll come along behind you. Won't we lass?" Red gave Laura a squeeze, moving his hand a little higher along her bodice. If possible, Laura's face went even whiter. Her eyes pleaded with Alex. In that instant, he made his decision. He wouldn't let her be taken to the *Herring*. If he couldn't stop Jensen, he would die trying.

He stared into the pirate's eyes. "I'm staying. I'll take my chances with the schooner."

"I'll drop you where you stand." Red moved his right hand, turning the pistol away from Laura's head, toward Alex.

They stood unmoving for a second. If only Laura were free and had a rock to throw!

Jensen sneered at him. "If you won't come, I'm leaving you here. Dead. The lady and I will get along fine without you. Now, drop the pistol."

Hesitantly, Alex removed his gun from his belt. He crouched and laid it on a nearby rock.

A call came from a distance, faint on the wind. "Cap'n Red!" It had to be Rourke, the sixth remaining pirate.

Jensen's eyes flickered.

Now or never. Alex dove toward him from his crouching position, shoving Jensen back and down the slope, driving most of his weight onto the pirate's gun hand, forcing it to the side. The pistol discharged.

No impact. Alex had a real chance now. As he and Captain Red fell, Laura tumbled away from the pirate, rolling down the rocky path. Alex and Red both fell backward, into a clump of inhospitable bushes. Branches scratched his cheek and his arms, but Alex paid them no mind. The pirate had dropped his pistol. Alex drove his fist into Red's stomach then pushed away. He leaped to his feet and labored the few steps upward to where he'd left his own pistol.

Whirling toward his foe, he aimed the gun at Jensen, who was pulling himself up, using a bush to stabilize himself. Twenty feet beyond him, Laura pushed herself shakily to her feet. She was farther down the slope than either of them. "Run," he shouted.

Captain Red jerked around to see where she was, but Laura was already scrambling along the path toward her father's camp.

"Hold it, Jensen," Alex said. "I can kill you now, or you can go join Rourke and go back to your ship. Take what men you have left and leave this island."

He wanted to look behind him. Surely Rourke had heard the gun's discharge. Not daring to take his eyes off Jensen, Alex walked toward him instead, one downward step at a time. The man was so surprised that he didn't react in time to thwart Alex.

Grabbing the pirate captain, Alex whipped behind him and faced the crest of the ridge. He held his pistol's muzzle to Jensen's temple and his other arm circling the man's throat from behind. "Don't move. I won't hesitate to pull the trigger."

Above them, a man peered over the top of the rocky slope.

"Cap'n?"

"Stop right there," Alex yelled. "I've got Captain Red. There's another ship anchored below me, and they've killed six of your men and disabled your longboat. Take your captain and go back to the *Herring*. Leave this place at once."

Rourke stared round-eyed at him and Jensen. "Is he lyin', Cap'n?"

"I'm not lying," Alex roared. "You want to know who's dead? I'll tell you." He named off four of the pirates. "They were in the longboat. And Smiley and Carle were afoot. They were killed down below in the jungle."

Rourke's eyes widened.

"I've got Carle's knife in my belt right now," Alex shouted. "One of their men took it off him when he killed him. Then he gave it to me."

"Why didn't they kill you?" Rourke croaked out.

"Because they knew I was an honest man."

As he held Jensen, Alex felt the man give a laborious swallow.

"I fear he speaks truth." Jensen's hoarse statement seemed to convince Rourke, whose chin sank a good inch.

Alex shoved the captain away from him, toward the ridge, still holding the pistol aimed at him. With his left hand, he pulled out the horn-handled dirk. "You see Carle's knife. I do not lie. Now go, the both of you. Leave this island while you can, or the men of the other ship will hunt you down."

Red stumbled to his feet and looked back with narrow, calculating eyes.

I should have killed him. Alex ground his teeth together. *Forgive me, Lord.*

"Go," he called again.

Rourke's hand went to his waist, but Alex could see he had only a dagger, not a gun.

"Don't even think it, Rourke."

With a curse, Rourke grasped his captain's arm and helped him up to the summit.

Captain Bryant's spyglass! Alex considered asking for it, but it was too late. Bryant would consider it a good trade for his daughter's life.

Pistol poised, he waited until both pirates disappeared over the top. He dashed to the spot where Jensen's empty pistol had fallen, scooped it up, and scrambled down the slope, choosing his footing with care. A sprained ankle now would doom them all.

Glancing backward once, he saw no sign of the two pirates. As he turned toward the camp, his thoughts returned to the innocent people down there.

Laura!

How amazing that he'd met up with her and Captain Bryant again, and how terrible that his escape had brought the cutthroats down upon them. He set his jaw, determined to see them and Daniel safely out of this fix. He sent up another quick prayer as he ran. *Father, give me wisdom. Show me how to keep Laura safe.*

He saw her running down the lowest slope. He yelled her name, and she swiveled her head then stopped. When he reached her, he pulled her to him, holding her against his chest.

"Laura, Laura! I'm so sorry."

Her little laugh sounded a bit hysterical. "It's I who am sorry. I did a very foolish thing, coming after you like that."

"But you're safe now." He looked down into her precious face.

She returned his gaze, her lips trembling. Before he could reason with himself, Alex dipped his head and kissed her lightly. Her hands slid around him, but she pulled back when she touched the extra pistol. She looked up at him, then glanced quickly away, her face reddening.

"I'm sorry," he said quickly.

"Stop saying that. You have nothing to apologize for."

He swallowed hard. Did she mean ...?

"Come." He reached for her hand. "We must get to your father."

When they came within sight of their camp, Captain Bryant stood in the pirates' longboat, hacking at it with a hatchet. Alex was amazed, as his words to Jensen were now fulfilled. The schooner's crew had disabled the pirates' longboat.

Daniel sat on a large boulder, cradling the rifle and constantly turning his head in vigil. His left leg bore a bloody rag bandage that Alex suspected came from one of Laura's petticoats. The watchman spotted Alex and started to aim the gun at him. Alex waved, and Daniel lowered the barrel and returned his signal with a grin.

Alex hurried down the rest of the way and out through the surf to the longboat, with Laura close on his heels.

"What are you doing, sir?"

Captain Bryant lifted his head and turned toward Alex, the hatchet in his hands. "I feared Daniel and I would be left alone, and I thought we could get the *Arundel* fixed much faster with a few boards from this boat. We heard a gunshot."

"All is well, sir."

The captain nodded and turned to survey his work. "If we can get what is useful and sink this boat, it will slow the pirates down and deprive them of one reason to attack us." The captain blinked at him in the searing sun. "What happened, Dryden?"

"Alex saved me from a pirate, Papa," Laura said.

Alex said evenly, "It was Red Jensen."

"That cur."

"The shot you heard went wild. All is well, for the moment."

"Praise God."

Alex nodded and looked back toward the stream path. "When I first got to the top, some were rowing their jollyboat out to the ship. At least one was on deck. I couldn't account for two of their men, but then Laura and I met up with them."

The captain's mouth skewed. "I told her not to go, but she didn't hear me."

"I'm sorry, Papa." Laura's whole face drooped.

Bryant said curtly, "You both survived."

"After I disarmed Jensen, I sent them both back to their ship," Alex said. "I could have killed the captain, but I feared if we killed any more, they'd not have enough crew to man the sails."

The captain stared at him. "Probably so."

"What if they return?" Laura asked.

"Then they return." Her father cast a troubled glance toward the stream path.

"Good reason for us to get under way as fast as we can." Alex looked at the damaged boat. "Now, show me what wood you want, sir, and I'll take over. You can join Daniel on watch."

Bryant looked doubtful.

"Go, Papa," Laura said. "Those pirates might come back. They're angry with us now."

The captain handed the hatchet and an iron prybar to Alex with a sigh. He pointed out the planks he wanted most.

"Get my daughter ashore before you sink the boat. I'll not lose her through any foolishness."

"Aye, sir."

Bryant plodded toward shore. Laura took the hatchet and waded into the three inches of water in the bottom of the longboat. Her hair streamed out in the wind, and her face was wind-chapped and rosy. Alex tried to distract himself from her beauty.

"You should have a hat," he said.

"Lost when we wrecked."

He nodded and eyed the stern of the boat, which already held more water than he liked. "Your father said to get this thwart and a couple of the side boards."

"Yes. They don't need much more to patch the hull. When we've got those, we should push her out if we can and let her sink."

Alex hadn't seen the damage to the schooner up close, so he couldn't disagree. He went to work with the tools, removing the pieces the captain asked for from the longboat, and a couple more for good measure. He hated destroying a perfectly good boat, but he could see the sense of it, since they couldn't take it with them.

As he freed each piece, Laura took it and tossed it inland. The water in the boat deepened. When it was up to his ankles, he stopped.

"Come, or we won't get out without a soaking." Her father had enough reasons to dislike him as it was. No sense adding more.

They both clambered over the bow. Laura stood in water to her knees, and Alex was tempted to swoop her up and carry her. But he had the tools, and there were a couple of boards that would float away if he didn't grab them out of the surf, now that it was just beyond its highest and beginning to ebb.

When he was nearly out of the surf, he heaved the tools as far as he could onto the shore and flung the boards after them. Then he turned back and grasped Laura's hand just as a large wave caught them, sloshing as high as her waist. She clung to his arm as she lost her footing and let him pull her to his side.

"There she goes." Alex nodded toward the longboat.

Laura looked back in time to see the receding wave catch the longboat's hulk. It floated awkwardly out from the rocks and slipped beneath the water.

Chapter Eight

There was no shore left below the bottom of the craggy slopes. Laura sat on a rock above the surf, watching, ever watching. Salt water pummeled her with every wave, teasing, threatening, but it never swept over her this high up.

At last it stopped reaching her hem, then touched not even her shoes. It only left crusty lines like rime across the woolen skirt. She could only hope that it wouldn't fall apart from the beating the cloth had taken, but would hold together until they reached civilization once more and she could replace it. Even so, she was thankful for what she had. Poor Daniel's extra clothes had all washed away from the crippled schooner.

Alex had carried Old Philip's body up out of the surf and laid it at the edge of the jungle, alongside Eli's. Then he'd worked with her father and Daniel, determined not to give up until full darkness stopped them. Laura sat on the high rocks until the water receded, straining her eyes to be sure the pirates did not return.

As the sun sank lower, the schooner floated free of the

rocks, only held close by ropes they'd tied around boulders at low tide.

Alex stood knee-deep in water in the stern, painstakingly patching the holes in the hull. Twice she saw him go over the side and dive below the surface so he could do something on the underside. She held her breath until he resurfaced each time, then breathed a prayer of thanks as her father and Daniel helped him back on board.

She checked behind her. Surely if the pirates were going to attack again, they'd have done it by now. Water, birds, and leaves moved, but no humans. She turned northward again and studied the shoreline, the bushes, the boulders.

The captain furthered the repairs mostly by handing Alex tools, nails, and pieces of wood. Daniel couldn't do much with his leg wound. He sat on the deck watching Laura and the jungle, or he stood leaning on a long stick that Alex had fashioned into a crude crutch for him, watching their progress.

The sun sank into the sea to the west, slashing fiery streaks through the clouds. Laura saw a dark form move out from the land toward the open sea, beyond the pointed Sharktooth Rock and the end of the island.

"Ahoy," she yelled.

Her father and Alex didn't hear, but Daniel was at the *Arundel's* bow. He heard and looked her way. Laura waved and pointed at the ship departing to the northwest. Daniel saw it and gave a shout. He turned to her father, clapped him on the shoulder, and pointed out the receding vessel.

The three men waded ashore in the dark with Daniel carrying a lantern and the others carrying tools they didn't dare leave aboard the partially repaired schooner.

"I think we can finish it tomorrow," Alex said, helping her down from her perch.

"Really? I thought it would take longer."

"The worst holes are patched. There's still some caulking needed, and the foremast and a few other small things. The captain will be the final judge of her seaworthiness, but I think that if we bail out the hold tomorrow, we'll be able to tell if we dare leave here."

"Some of the cargo is ruined. Most of it, in fact," the captain said. "At least a dozen barrels are somewhere in the drink, and much of the rest is waterlogged. But alas, if we escape with our lives, 'tis a blessing."

"Aye," Laura whispered, thinking of Old Philip and Eli, who would never return home.

"It seems our foes have left for good," Daniel said.

"They had to run while they had enough able bodies to do it," Alex replied. "I feared they might try to steal our smaller vessel."

"Praise God they did not." The captain looked around. "Well, if we're to have a hot supper, we'll need a fire. Get up above the high water line, boys, and fetch some dry wood, if you find it."

"If not, we'll eat cold bean soup," Laura said. "There's no more bread."

Her father grunted and set the lantern on a rock. "Now that the cutthroats have gone, perhaps you can fish tomorrow while we set the *Arundel* to rights."

"Gladly, Papa." She stepped to his side and kissed his cheek. She started to turn away but stopped. "Oh, Papa, I fear I lost your spyglass to the pirate."

"I'm aware," her father said grimly. "The Lord has given me three pair of younger eyes to help sail us home."

Laura opened her mouth and closed it.

The next morning, Laura rose at dawn and looked through the sad little cache of provisions they had left. She would fish indeed today.

Overhead, a gull gave its harsh cry, and she looked up. Maybe if she climbed the ridge, she could find some birds' nests and glean a few eggs. She was sure her father would forbid her from doing that. Now that they'd overcome the threat of the pirates, he wouldn't want her to take any more risks. More likely she could catch a bird. These sea fowl would be tough, but if she got one early, she could stew it all day while the men worked.

Her father stirred and sat up with a moan. She tiptoed past Alex and Daniel's sleeping forms and approached him.

"Are you all right, Papa?"

"Just stiff."

She knew he was in pain, but it wouldn't do to contradict him.

"Here, let me help you up." She held out a hand. When he grasped it, she noticed how wrinkled his skin was, and how frail he looked.

A few minutes later, they walked slowly among the rocks together. He paused by a tide pool and pointed. "There. Get those mussels, child. If you can find enough, we'll make a meal of them."

Laura found only three in the tiny pool between the rocks. There was too little soil for the bivalves to burrow into on this stony island. She put them in her basket and straightened.

"Papa, if we get home safe, we'll have very little to get by on this winter. You said most of the cargo is ruined or washed overboard." She sought his somber eyes. "How will we live this winter?"

"There's a wee bit in the bank." He sighed. "Not much. It won't be enough to pay Daniel. And I'd like to give Eli's widow some money. At least as much as I'd have paid him for this voyage."

"Of course." Old Philip was all alone and had no family, at least none that he knew.

He'd told the tale of how he'd been apprenticed to a sea captain at the age of nine and lived most of his life on ocean-going vessels. He claimed he didn't remember his parents, or whether he'd been in an orphan home, only that he'd belonged to Captain Miles for seven years and then whatever sailing master he served under.

He loved the sea, or perhaps more accurately, he hated land, distrusted it, especially cities. He'd lived a hard life and known several harsh masters. When he landed on Captain Bryant's ship, Philip considered it good fortune. He'd found a home and a friend. Gladly, he'd stayed with Bryant for the past twenty-five years and grown into 'Old Philip.' To Laura, he'd been like a doting uncle. She would miss him terribly.

While the men worked on the schooner, she rambled among the rocks. She found only a few more mussels, enough for them each to eat two. That wouldn't be enough to feed hard-working men.

She spotted a bird a bit smaller than a gull as it landed a few yards away. Stooping, she chose three rocks. They would have a stew for supper, or she'd know the reason why. Sneaking forward, she tried to keep an eye on the scavenging bird, but she had to watch her footing as well. To her chagrin, the bird flew off just as she came within throwing range.

A shout reached her on the wind, and she turned back toward camp. Alex was climbing over the boulders holding a long rod—a fishing pole. She hurried toward him.

"We found this floating in the hold." Alex extended it to her.

"It's Philip's."

He nodded. "Your father said to bring it to you and maybe you could catch something."

"Thank you. I'll try, since the birds are not cooperating with me."

Alex laughed. "A nice, tasty sea bass would go down better than a stringy old gull."

"You're probably right." She quickly examined the line wrapped around a short stick. A hook was attached. All she needed was some bait. Maybe she should give up one of her hard-earned mussels for the risk of a real catch.

She spent two hours fishing, sitting on a big rock as the tide ebbed around her. Finally she was able to remove to one farther out. Its sides were slippery, and she banged her knees painfully climbing to the top. At last her efforts were rewarded, and she hauled in a codfish that was nearly strong enough to pull her into the water.

As she left the rock planning to take her catch ashore, Alex hopped toward her from stone to stone.

"Look at you," he cried. "That's a monster!"

"It's by far the biggest fish I've ever caught," she admitted.

"We saw you fighting it, and your father told me to come help you. But I see you've got the best of him."

"I hope the best of him will be how he tastes when we eat supper."

Alex laughed. "Come on. I'll clean it for you."

"Don't they need you on the *Arundel*?"

"She's all patched. They're just scooping out the last of the bilge."

"We'll leave soon, then?"

"We thought tonight, on the next high tide. That will give us time to load everything and make sure she's sound enough to carry us to the mainland."

"My bones are getting old," Captain Bryant declared, setting a coil of rope and a bag of cooking gear down on the deck of the *Arundel.*

"You're not old, Papa," Laura cried.

He frowned and looked over the water. The sun was sinking into the waves westward, in a blaze of vermillion and puce.

The captain shook his head. "I don't know if we can handle her without more men."

"You've got Alex and me, Papa. Last month you said I was as good as a seaman. And you and Daniel will be able to help some."

"I expect you're right. But it's a long haul." He let out a sigh. "I do hope Daniel will be all right. When I dressed his leg, it looked angry and red, probably from working in the ship's hold. That bilge water couldn't be good for it."

"It's infected?" Laura caught her breath. They could lose Daniel after all.

"We need to get him to a surgeon as soon as we can, poor lad."

"Did you douse it with whiskey?" she asked.

"Aye, but still ... Let us hurry."

All their gear was now aboard except for the heavy mainsail they'd used as a tent.

"You stay here and put away what things you can," Laura said. "I'll go help Alex with that last bit of canvas." She minimized the work of folding and transporting the sail. She knew the two of them would strain every muscle to carry it over the jagged rocks, but they couldn't sail without it.

Both of them puffed, wheezed, and scraped their knees, but at last the big canvas was aboard. They set about attaching it to lines and hoisting it into place on the yardarm. It took all three working together to prepare the rigging, but at last Captain Bryant gave the order.

"Weigh anchor."

Laura sprang to the capstan with Alex and helped him pull up the anchor chain while her father stood at the ship's wheel. Daniel's work that day had pulled his wound open, and he now lay below in his hammock. Laura knew he suffered pain and fever, but they'd done all they could for him at present. Captain Bryant had even dosed him with a bit of rum from a bottle he'd kept in his cabin for medicinal purposes.

"I hope Daniel can sleep while we get under way," she told Alex.

"I do too. The best we can do for him now is set sail toward home."

As they'd hoped, when the anchor left the bottom, the ship began to move. The moment it rested on deck was a relief for all of them. Laura gladly joined Alex near the mast, to haul up the mainsail. She would have to do a man's work for the next few weeks, but she was glad to serve as a sailor if it meant the four of them would reach home alive.

"Daughter! Come here," the captain called.

Laura went to him, and he guided her hands to spokes of the big wheel. "Hold her as steady as you can. We're done with danger of wrecking again on that cursed island. I'll help Alex with the rest of the sails if you can hold us on course for a few minutes."

He'd shown her the basics earlier in their journey, and she knew what to do. It was harder than it looked at first glance, but she leaned her weight into the task when the wheel tried to defy her. Above her, pinpricks of stars gleamed here and there in the vast sky. She shivered as the wind increased. When her father returned, he looked up at the stars and then nodded.

"Near enough, girl. Near enough. Go and rest."

She walked toward the hatch but paused to have one last look back at the island. At its northern tip, Sharktooth Rock pointed skyward while waves swirled around its base.

"Goodbye, island," she whispered.

Alex came up beside her. "Any regrets?"

"Plenty." She thought of Eli and Old Philip, lying below, stitched up in canvas and awaiting their burial tomorrow, when they were out of sight of land and running before the wind. "I won't miss the island, though."

"Same here." He reached out and brushed back an unruly lock of her hair. "I thought I'd never see you again when we left Kingston."

"And I—oh!" She whirled back toward the rail. The island was a distant shadow on the water, and she could no longer make out Sharktooth Rock, but she'd sketched it in her journal. "Oh, no."

"What is it?" Alex asked just behind her.

She jumped and turned to face him. "My journal. I left it in the cave."

"What cave?"

"I found it the second day we were there. I wrote in my journal and left it inside, on a rock shelf. I meant to go back each day and write more in it. But with the pirates and everything ..."

"You forgot it."

"I don't know as I'd have been able to go fetch it anyway."

His dark eyes regarded her steadily in the moonlight. "I'd have gone for you."

"Thank you." She felt her cheeks flush and hoped he couldn't see it. Having Alex retrieve her diary was the last thing she wanted. What if he glanced inside and saw what she'd written about him after that ill-fated party in Jamaica?

"Don't worry," he said. "I wouldn't open it."

Her face felt like it had burst into flames. Could the man read her thoughts, then?

"I appreciate that."

Alex smiled. "I'll get you a new one when we touch land."

"Thank you." She probably wouldn't remember all the details she'd written on the first leg of their voyage, but there was much to tell since she'd last opened the journal. She would write in the new one all about the pirates and how she and Alex were reunited on the island, and how he'd helped save them and fix their schooner.

"We wouldn't have made it without you," she said softly.

He gazed at her and leaned slowly toward her. Laura closed her eyes and felt his wind-chapped lips brush hers. Her heart raced. What was she supposed to do now? Nothing, she supposed. It wouldn't be proper. She certainly couldn't fling herself at him, though she wanted to. Besides, her father could probably see them, silhouetted against the sky. Would he give Alex a tongue-lashing after she'd left the deck?

"Go and rest," Alex said. "The captain and I will see us through the night."

"I know Papa can't do it alone," she said, "but we need to spell each other so that we all get to sleep. Wake me at the end of this watch."

"No need."

"I'm ready to assist." Even to herself, she sounded a bit stubborn, much like her father.

He gazed into her eyes for a long moment, and Laura stared back.

"I'll wake you when it seems best," he said. "You'll need your strength tomorrow, I'm sure. It will be a difficult task, taking this schooner home with only three of us able-bodied."

Laura nodded soberly. Only two able-bodied, if one were

honest. Her father had been slammed about more than he admitted in their wreck, but he did his best to hide it. "We can do it."

SHE AWOKE to a knock on the door of her tiny cabin. She sat up and swung her legs over the edge of the berth. "I'm awake."

"Take your time," her father replied. "All is calm."

Even so, she hurried. When she opened the door, he was waiting near the ladder.

"Do you sleep well?" he asked.

"Much better than on the island."

"Good." His eyes crinkled. "Alex and I had a long chat in the midnight watch."

"I told him to wake me sooner."

"No, we put our time to good use."

Was he smiling?

"I believe Alex Dryden is a good man," the captain said.

Laura swallowed hard. "I think so too, Papa."

"He asked if I would allow him to court you."

Speechless, she stared at him in the light spilling down from the hatch.

"I told him that was your decision," her father went on. "But if you are in favor, I have no objection."

She took three breaths and then was able to meet his gaze. "I have no objection."

"So. This doesn't mean you're promised to him. It just gives him the opportunity to explore the possibility."

"I understand, Papa."

"Good. I let him know how I expect my daughter to be treated."

She wanted to laugh, but he was so serious she couldn't. "Yes, Papa."

"You treat him well too. Don't tease the man. Don't keep him hanging. But don't allow it to go on if you have doubts."

She thought about that for a moment and nodded.

"That young man has the skills to provide for a family," her father said, "and he's old enough to know what he wants in a wife. He thinks he sees that in you. Have you thought about what you want in a husband?"

She wanted to scream, "For years now," but instead, she said, "Some. I want a hard worker. A man who is honest and loyal." After a silence, she added, "A man who will love me." She'd written those things in her journal. Would someone else find it one day? They would think her a silly young girl. But she'd meant every word.

"I want no less for you," her father said. "Don't let yourself be talked into less."

"I won't, Papa."

His smile broke out, and he looked ten years younger, the way he had before Mother died.

"Go on," he said. "I intend to sleep through the watch."

She hurried up the ladder and through the hatch into blazing sun. When her eyes adjusted, she turned toward the stern and found Alex watching her with a placid smile on his lips. She made her way to the wheel.

"What shall I do first?"

"Find a place to sit. We have a good breeze, and we're making steady for Charleston."

"Charleston? We're putting in there?"

"It's the closest port without fighting the wind, and your father and I agree that Daniel should see a physician as soon as possible. If we can hold this course, we'll be there by tomorrow morning."

"So soon?" She'd thought Sharktooth Island was much farther from the mainland, more isolated.

"With God's grace and a fair wind."

Laura drew a deep breath and faced forward—west, toward home. Recalling her father's words about his midnight chat with Alex, she tried to ignore the heat in her cheeks. She glanced toward Alex. He was smiling as he held the wheel steady. Was he thinking about it too?

"So, Charleston tomorrow."

"Have you been there?" he asked.

"No. Have you?"

"Twice. Perhaps I can show you around, if the captain can spare us for an hour or two. It's a lovely city."

She couldn't quite meet his gaze, but she said, "I'll look forward to it."

And to the rest of the future before her, with the promise it held.

About Susan Page Davis

Susan Page Davis is the author of more than one hundred books. Her books include Christian novels and novellas in the historical romance, mystery, and romantic suspense genres. Her work has won several awards, including the Carol Award, two Will Rogers Medallions, and two Faith, Hope, & Love Reader's Choice Awards. She has also been a finalist in the WILLA Literary Awards and a multi-time finalist in the Carol Awards. A Maine native, Susan has lived in Oregon and now resides in western Kentucky with her husband Jim, a retired news editor. They are the parents of six and grandparents of eleven. Visit her website at: https://susanpagedavis.com.

A PASSAGE OF *Chance*

Linda Fulkerson

Chapter One

March 1893
Charleston, South Carolina

Raucous laughter echoed through the grand hallway. Melody Lampert sighed. She closed the cover of Mark Twain's latest novel and rose from her comfortable cushion in the petit salon. "Boys," she muttered with a slight head shake. Padding across the carpeted floor, she grasped the doorknob and gave it a slow twist to prevent waking those in the upper-floor bedchambers who might have managed to remain asleep despite the disturbance.

Another wave of guffawing boomed through the house, quickly followed by the incessant ringing of a bell. Melody gasped and hurried her steps, stopping for a brief moment to catch her breath near the smoking room's intricately carved double doors. Her deep intake of air brought with it the suffocating stench of cigars. She stifled a cough and tugged one of the doors until it flung open. Smoke billowed from the chamber.

She rushed across the room and grabbed the bell from her cousin's hand. "Reginald Emerson, you'll wake the entire household."

"'Twas my intent. How else shall a man fend off starvation?" Brandy laced his breath.

"Well, I certainly don't wish for you to wake Grandmother." A slight shudder rumbled through her. She met her cousin's eyes. Had he noticed? "Why didn't you use the bell pull?"

Andrew Newsome, their nearest neighbor and a close friend of Reginald, laughed. "He tried." The young man spat the words between guffaws. "But he yanked so hard, it broke, so he found that handbell and used it instead."

Reginald looked past Melody's shoulder. A bewildered look crossed his face. "Where is Enid?"

"In bed, I suppose. She retired two hours ago. It's nearly half-past ten." The grandfather clock opposite the room's hearth gonged, as if to confirm her statement.

She surveyed the room. A pile of plates topped with discarded bread crusts sat precariously beside a near-empty decanter. At least someone had attempted to tidy up. Returning her gaze to the table strewn with cards and coins, she noticed a new person in the quartet of gamblers.

A smattering of freckles dotted the newcomer's face. Melody noticed that the young man's ill-fitted jacket strained against thick biceps and exposed at least two inches of skin at the wrist.

Her scrutiny obviously unnerved him because he tugged at his too-tight collar.

"Where is Peter?" Although directed at no one in particular, she kept her focus on the new man, his green eyes having captured her attention.

"He fell ill," Andrew answered. "So, I brought Padric

Murphy as a last-minute replacement. He's the mechanic of my new yacht."

Mechanic? Her gaze fell to Padric's hands. Strong. Tanned. Not manicured. She couldn't recall ever seeing a workingman's hands. Not this close, anyway. Suddenly remembering her manners, she gave a quick curtsy and spoke. "Melody Lampert." She extended her hand, palm down. "Pleased to make your acquaintance, Mr. Murphy."

Padric stood, grasped her hand, and gave it a hearty shake. "Same to you, Miss."

The remaining three men laughed at his faux pas.

"Mr. Murphy is an *Irishman*," said Reginald, contempt oozing off his last word.

A deep blush reddened Padric's face. "Excuse me," he muttered and crossed to the coat rack in two swift strides. "It's time for me to bid you all goodnight." He reached for his hat.

"But we need a fourth for the game," whined Edward Randolph, another neighbor of Melody and Reginald.

Andrew stood. "Yes, Padric. Please stay. The night's still young. I'm most certain Mr. Emerson meant nothing from his comment."

Padric's eyes cut toward Reginald then flickered back to Melody. "And I'm most certain he did." He bowed slightly, his focus never wavering from her face. "Goodnight, sirs, Miss."

She grasped the sleeve of his coat. "Mr. Murphy, please, do stay. I apologize for the lack of manners displayed by my cousin. I shall prepare more refreshments." She reached for the stack of dishes.

"Allow me." He shrugged out of his overcoat, flung it back on the hook, and scooped up the plates. "Where to?"

As his long strides followed her short, scurried steps, Melody felt the warmth of his breath on her neck. "Just this way, Mr. Murphy. The kitchen is through there." She held open the door and gave a nod toward the sink. "You may set the dishes in there, please."

She tiptoed to reach the cupboard containing the breadbox.

"Need some help?" Padric leaned past her, barely brushing his hand against hers as he easily retrieved a fresh loaf. "Is it normal for the mistress of the house to know her way around the kitchen?"

Melody sucked in a breath. How much should she tell this stranger? That there was nothing *normal* about this household? That she not only wasn't the mistress, but barely ranked above the servants? That she was trapped in this house? In this life? With no hope of escape? She exhaled slowly. "My grandmother rented the house for the winter. We shall soon return to the Hamptons." She busied herself with slicing the bread.

"Ah. That explains the accent. I didn't think you were from this area." He looked around the room and pointed toward the icebox. "Do you need something to go with the bread?"

She nodded. "Looks like I'm not the only one familiar with a kitchen." A small giggle emerged from her throat. The sound startled her.

"No offense intended, but I didn't grow up with the luxury of servants. Or even a mother. Father and I learned to fend for ourselves when it came to food." He returned to the workspace with an array of meats and cheeses.

"No offense taken. I also didn't grow up with servants." She sighed. "Which is why I'm here now."

He turned to face her and lifted an eyebrow.

"I ... um ..." Melody chided herself for bringing up a topic she couldn't broach.

Padric held up a hand and shook his head. "I'm sure there's a story there that I'd love to hear, but perhaps we'd best feed your cousin and his guests before they mutiny." He grinned as he piled a generous portion of meat onto a slice of bread.

"I agree." Relief washed over her. She savored the genuineness of his smile. How long had it been since she'd been in the company of someone who treated her without contempt?

As they finished the meal preparation, Melody's lips remained silent, but not her mind. Questions swarmed through her brain. What had possessed her to loosen her tongue in the presence of this easygoing Irishman? And why had her body betrayed her with near swoons and shivers at his proximity?

She attempted to shush such silly thoughts. It wasn't like he would or could provide her a means of escape. He was simply a man coerced to fill the fourth space at a poker table. Nothing more. Besides, her grandmother would never allow a man of his lowly standing to court Melody. In fact, her grandmother would never allow anyone to court her.

Ever.

Chapter Two

Padric positioned the platter of sandwiches and sliced fruit in one hand while he used the other to open the door for Melody. A brief but sweet smile rewarded him. The few young women of her position he'd encountered would have roused one of the servants rather than venture into a kitchen and risk callousing one of their dainty hands. But then she'd hinted that her status wasn't one of wealth.

"Thank you," she murmured as she moved past him.

Her voice held a song-like quality. *Melody.* The name suited her perfectly. He'd barely crossed the threshold when a chorus of chaos assaulted his ears, drowning out his thoughts of a certain blue-eyed beauty. It was just as well. He had no business entertaining thoughts of a lady of her class.

"But it's boring."

Padric recognized the sniveling voice. Edward. He'd done nothing but complain all evening.

"What's boring?" Melody asked as she placed a sandwich on a plate and handed it to Reginald. She repeated the process until each of the men had been served, then she arranged some fruit on a plate for herself.

"Money." Andrew accepted the food, nodding his thanks. "Edward wants us to buy into the next game using something besides money."

Despite the gnawing emptiness in his gut, Padric forced himself to take normal-sized bites, wondering what his father had scrounged for supper.

"Some of us only have our allowance and don't have the freedom to bet away family treasures," Reginald explained.

And some of us have neither an allowance nor *family treasures.* Padric risked a glance at Melody. She looked bemused. Was she thinking the same thing? The lady had her secrets. That was for certain. But didn't everybody? He prayed she would never discover his.

Andrew stood and brushed the crumbs from his trousers. "All right, gents. Surely we can come up with something of value to pacify Edward's whim." He moved over to the game table, which had been cleared of its clutter, and motioned to the empty chairs. "Shall we?"

"I'll put up one of our finest fillies. She's never been beaten," Edward announced.

Reginald took his place at the table. "Has she ever been raced?"

Edward's face reddened, and Padric stifled a grin.

"A horse? Something the winner must feed and water and keep alive?" Andrew slung his chair around and straddled it backwards.

"Don't scoff. She comes with a top-notch pedigree," Edward said. "You have something better?

Andrew paused for a moment. "Of course. My yacht. It's docked in Savannah. We plan to sail it up the coast this summer instead of taking the train home."

"And it's yours to wager?"

"Yes, Reggie. An early gift for my upcoming university graduation." Andrew reached for the decanter and emptied its contents into his glass. "What about you?"

Reginald cleared his throat. "I'll wager an island."

"An island?" Andrew sounded intrigued. "What island? Where is it?"

"Not too far from here—a short distance from Savannah. It's called Sharktooth Island."

"Sharktooth Island?" Padric spoke without thinking, and when all heads turned toward him, he wished he'd kept his mouth shut.

"You've heard of it?"

"Heard of it? Oh, yes. My grandfather's been there."

"Really?" Reginald sounded doubtful. "Well, here's your chance to win it. If, that is, you have something to wager."

"Oh, I have something."

"What?" the others asked in unison.

Padric leaned in close, his voice barely above a whisper, and said, "I'll wager a story."

REGINALD WAS the first to protest. "A story? Seriously? First you say your grandfather has visited Sharktooth Island. Now you want to buy into a poker game where each of us is risking something of great value. How do we know you're not a liar? What proof do you have that your so-called story is worthy of betting?"

Melody held her breath while Padric listened to her cousin's rant. In truth, Reggie had a valid point. How could a story possibly be equal to the price of an island or a yacht or a top-pedigree racehorse?

The Irishman scooted away from the table and strode to the coatrack. He reached inside the pocket of his overcoat and pulled out a small pouch. Returning to the table, he gave the bag a gentle shake. A leather-bound book and two gold doubloons fell out.

Padric opened the book.

Melody gasped. "It's a journal."

He nodded. Intricate script filled the first half of the book's pages. He flipped to the volume's middle and stopped at a drawing of an island. Set in rough water, a jagged section of the landmass jutted into a steep, tooth-shaped crag. "Sharktooth Island." He placed his finger on the signature. *Fergus O' Murchadha, 1847*. "My grandfather. Murchadha means 'Sea Warrior.' When he and my grandmother arrived in this country, their name was changed to Murphy, but he preferred his Irish name."

Padric turned another page. The next sketch showed a map of the island. A rough mark encircled part of the drawing.

"What is that?" Melody asked.

He nodded. "The cave where the journal and doubloons were found."

"And where there were two doubloons, there are likely to be more." Reginald's eyes glowed with greed.

"Perhaps." Padric snapped the book shut and tucked it into the bag.

"Are those Brasher doubloons?" Edward reached for one of the coins.

Padric quickly grabbed it and placed the two gold pieces back in the pouch alongside the journal. He shook his finger in mock scolding manner. "Not so fast. First, the game. Then, I share the story with the winner."

"And what if *you* win?"

Padric leaned back in his chair and let loose a hearty laugh. "Then I'll have a nice yacht to live on and a horse to sell."

Chapter Three

Reginald splayed his cards on the table. "Queens over nines."

Mutterings and head shakes followed as the other players folded their hands.

"All right, gents. Looks like I'm the proud owner of a new yacht, a young filly, and a pair of Brasher doubloons." He held an open palm toward Padric. "Hand 'em over."

"I never bet the coins."

Melody stifled a giggle.

"Wha—"

"'Tis true, cousin," Melody confirmed. "He never promised the gold or the journal—only the story."

Andrew nodded. "Just be glad the game was cards and not knife throwing. No one can beat Padric Murphy when it comes to tossing a blade."

Reginald raised an eyebrow as he looked toward Padric. "Interesting." He stacked the cards and scooted them to the edge of the table. "Let's hope the story I won is also interesting, Mr. Murphy."

"Yeah. And like you said, there's bound to be more gold where that came from." Edward gave Reginald a friendly pat on the back.

"Plus, don't forget the island," added Andrew. "You could build an ocean resort on it."

"That's not a bad idea," Reginald said. "I was wondering what good it would do for me to own an island."

"Half an island."

All heads turned to face Melody.

"What nonsense is this?" Reginald demanded.

"When Grandmother stripped my mother's and my names from the family's holdings, she overlooked one obscure piece of property—Sharktooth Island. Check the deed, if you wish. My name is on it. And since it's the one piece of my mother's inheritance that wasn't stolen from me, I claim half the island and its contents, be it gold or other treasure."

"How do you know this?"

"Last year when Grandmother fell ill, her lawyer came calling to go over her accounts and make sure all was in order, just in case ..." She paused for a moment and met her cousin's eyes. "You were away at school."

"So, you saw fit to meddle through an old woman's business?"

"I-I ... well ..."

"Stop the family squabbling," Edward interrupted. "It's not like we don't all know the situation." He continued in a mocking singsong voice, "Melody's mother was disinherited for marrying a commoner, and now poor, sweet Melody must marry into money to regain her share of the inheritance."

Andrew cut in. "Too bad we didn't realize how lovely you'd become when Edward, Peter, and I swore a pact with Reggie that none of us would seek to court you, so he'd be the sole heir." He gave her a wink. "But half an island, Reg. Today's your lucky day!"

"Enough!" Reginald held up his hand.

Edward and Andrew shrank back as Reginald turned to face Padric. "Since I suppose the horse is at Edward's farm back in Rhode Island and my yacht is docked in Savannah, I'll lay claim to my story now, if you please, Mr. Murphy."

"Edward asked if the coins were Brasher doubloons. Aye, they are." Padric settled back in his chair.

Melody held her breath and soaked in the words of his smooth brogue.

"Over one hundred years ago, Mr. Brasher's mint struck only a few of these coins." He pulled one out of his pouch and held it up between his thumb and forefinger. "And, according to me da, they must be returned to the island to break the curse."

Melody gasped. "Do you believe that?"

He looked at her, green eyes hooded with an emotion she couldn't identify, and shrugged. "It matters not what I believe. Da believed it. And he made me swear an oath as he lay dying." His eyes misted, and he cleared his throat. "And now, here's your story, Mr. Reginald. Many years ago, when my great-grandfather was a young lad, he sailed on a merchant vessel. That same ship was captained by the father of the young lady whose journal I showed you. They ran aground on Sharktooth Island, and she discovered the cave."

"Is that where the pirate treasure was hidden?" Edward asked.

An annoyed look crossed Padric's face as he continued, ignoring the question. "The ship's crew had to leave hurriedly, as some unsavory men were in pursuit."

"Pirates," Reginald whispered, which drew another glare from Padric.

"Sir, you've won a story, but to receive your prize, you'll need to let me tell the tale."

"Yes, of course. Please continue."

The clock struck twelve. Padric waited, more patiently than his audience, Melody observed, until the final gong sounded.

"In her rush to escape, Miss Laura left her journal. She was distraught about it, and it touched the heart of my young great-grandfather. He made a silent vow to return to the island, recover the journal, and get the book back to her. It became his life's quest. And when he was older, he returned to the island and found her book."

Padric stretched and covered a yawn. "My granda was a young man when he and his father, now the first mate, set out on that journey. Great-granddad sent out a half-dozen crew members in pairs to help him find the cave. The two fellas who located the journal's cave also discovered a small chest. It was too heavy for them to haul down the ridge unaided, but they were loath to tell the others of their find.

"The story goes that one of them joggled the lock and popped it open. Another pair of scouts arrived just as the two were bickering. The stouter of the first two hoisted the chest, but he was acting the maggot and angered the second man, who pushed the first man backward. With the weight of the chest, the bigger man lost his balance and slipped into a black hole."

"With the chest? The treasure fell into the hole too?" Reginald's voice cracked.

Padric nodded. "Aye, according to the witnesses. But unbeknownst to them, the first man had already pocketed two doubloons." Padric lowered his voice again. "They found 'em on him after the death bringer came for him."

"He died?" Melody dared to ask.

"Aye, Miss. Back in those days, death was never very far

from a ship's crewman." He met her eyes for a moment. "He'd been telling his mates how he was going to live in luxury once they made land, but no one paid him attention since he was one of those braggarts where all of his geese were swans."

"How did he die?"

Padric paused for a moment, and Melody wondered if he would answer her question. "The passage was fraught with bad luck. A high wind had fouled the lines, and the man with the doubloons was a rigging monkey. He scrambled up the mast, but something went awry, and he fell. The halyard caught 'im by the throat. Hung just as sure as a noose." Padric looked downward and whispered, "My granda witnessed it."

Melody squirmed in her seat.

"Sorry, Miss."

She shook her head. "No, it's all right. I did ask."

Padric nodded. "Granda said the captain locked away the coins, but he was found murdered in his cabin the next morn. Before they reached land, much of the crew died from the fever. The survivors figured it was because someone had stolen from the island. Because rumors of a curse had swirled around Sharktooth Island for generations, the crew pronounced the rumors as truth.

He paused to catch his breath. "What was once greed transformed to terror. No one wanted responsibility for the coins. My great-grandfather was tasked with keeping them safe, since he was the one who'd sent the men to search for the diary. Not long after he took them home, his wife died."

"But nothing has happened to you since you took possession of the doubloons," said Reginald.

"You have known me for five hours, and yet you know of my life?" A burdened look covered Padric's face. "I have witnessed things ... done things ... that no man should have seen or done. And *that* is why the doubloons must be returned. As well as the young woman's journal. My da said the island is calling them back."

"You truly believe the island is cursed?"

Reginald waved off Melody's question and stood. "Andrew, how far along is the yacht?"

"We hadn't yet hired a compliment of servants or crew for the journey homeward, but the ship itself is ready to sail."

"Hmm." Her cousin paced back and forth for a moment before stopping in front of Padric Murphy. "You want to return the items. I want to see my island. My yacht is apparently in need of a crew, and you're an experienced mechanic who comes from a long line of sea warriors." Reginald slapped Padric on the back. "Perhaps we can come to an accord, Mr. Murphy."

"Surely you don't intend to leave those valuable gold pieces on that spit of rock, Reggie."

Reginald silenced Edward with a glare. "What I do or don't intend to do is of no concern to you. And besides," –his face contorted into a sneer—"Mr. Murphy has already made it clear that the doubloons are not mine."

Chapter Four

Savannah, Georgia

Melody tapped her hand on her lap, waiting for the footman to hop down from his station and open the carriage door. Although the ride on the Charleston & Savannah Railway had been a pleasant one, she was anxious to see the one piece of her parents that her grandmother hadn't swindled from her.

"'Tis a bad idea, Miss." Enid glanced out the window toward the marina. "He'll never allow you aboard. He already said as much when he told you to take the train home. He'll be furious when he discovers you bought tickets to Savannah."

"You worry too much." Melody dismissed her maid's concern with a wave of her hand.

Enid opened her mouth to protest, but the door swung open, interrupting any objections the girl may have uttered.

Melody held her gloved hand toward the footman and eased her skirts out of the carriage. "Thank you." She offered him a smile and paused as Enid exited the vehicle behind her. Within a few minutes, their trunks were loaded onto a pushcart, and a young worker rushed toward them to maneuver the cart to the dock.

"Where to, Miss?" A smattering of dirt dusted the boy's once-white shirt, and his broad smile revealed a set of dingy teeth that matched his clothing.

Melody scanned the array of white yachts, each tucked into a slip of blue water, awaiting some grand adventure. She noted one near the shore, gangplank extended, with a flurry of activity as servants hustled to load the boat with supplies. Squinting against the morning sun, Melody spotted Reginald on the deck of the yacht moored next to the one being loaded. He looked splendid in his new ship's captain attire. "That one." She pointed toward the magnificent vessel.

"The *Destiny*? Ah, she's a fine one, Miss."

Destiny. She hadn't heard the ship's name the night her cousin won it from their neighbor. It had seemed like theft to her, to claim such an expensive piece of property from another during a game of chance.

Andrew had appeared aghast at his loss, but when he returned the following day with the papers signing the yacht over to Reggie, he announced he'd just commissioned a prominent shipbuilder to begin construction on a larger, more extravagant one. As she approached the craft rising out of the water, it was difficult to imagine a ship more luxurious than this one.

"A quick trip to and from the island, Enid. That's what Reginald told Mr. Murphy. Then they will return here to collect the crew for the journey home."

"Will they load the vessel with supplies for the longer voyage then?"

"Yes, I suppose. Although I haven't been privy to the details. Are you ready, Enid?"

The maid shook her head and laughed. "No, but does that matter?"

Melody stepped cautiously onto the gangplank. "Permission to come aboard, Captain." She curtsied as she stated the practiced words in a firm tone.

Shock registered on Reginald's face, but he glanced about him and quickly recovered. He reached for her hand and planted a light kiss. She knew the gesture was meant for show, not as a display of affection. "Have you come to see me off, cousin, before you head north?"

Glancing toward the luggage cart behind her, she shook her head. "No. I've come to join you."

He dropped her hand so quickly it nearly slapped her side before she righted it. "I'm afraid that won't possible. This is a man's cruise."

"Yet I'm certain I saw Edward's sisters board just moments ago. And you will surely have servants, some of which will be female. Correct?"

"We're taking this little jaunt without taking the help. But I see you've brought Enid. Even though this will be a short trip, it'll be good to have someone along who can feed us." He gave a slight bow toward their maid. "Besides, dear cousin, *you* are not a servant."

"Am I not? You've never treated me as an equal, even though we are co-owners of this island."

"That has not yet been confirmed."

Melody pulled a document from her travel case and unfurled it.

"You brought the deed?" His face blanched.

"It's my sole possession, so yes, since Grandmother's

attorney informed me about it, I have kept it with me. If you explore and possibly find something valuable, then I intend to be there to claim my fair share." With a harumph, she tucked the page back into her bag.

"Do you not trust me?" Reginald smirked.

"Not in the slightest."

"Nor do I trust you and your phony document."

"Please step aside, Captain. Unless you wish to escort me to my quarters."

"Speaking of quarters, there are none available. I've assigned all the suites to our passengers."

"Who all is coming?"

"Andrew and Edward. Also, as you noted, Edward's sisters." He smiled through clenched teeth, nodding to those bustling about him. "But you and Enid may help yourselves to the accommodations in the steerage. I believe Mr. Murphy will be staying there as well. Bon voyage, cousin!" He gave a mock salute, spun on his heel, and walked away.

"This idea has been even worse than your plan to march onto the deck this morning. Don't know why I bother with trying to keep you in line, Miss Melody." Enid quickly stuck her head through the doorway and peered up and down the passageway. Ducking back into the lavatory, she said, "It's clear."

"Thank you, Enid." Melody grinned. "But admit it, we'll have a bit of fun during the voyage, right?"

"If you call hanging my head over the ship's rail fun."

Melody pouted. "I'm sorry you haven't taken well to the sea in the past. Perhaps this short trip will be better."

"Don't mind me. You'd better get on out there, Miss, 'fore that man of yours comes out of his quarters."

"That man of—"

"Don't deny he hasn't caught your eye. Besides, he's the only reason you're sneaking around, right? Your cousin knows where you are, so you ain't hiding from him." Enid harrumphed and pushed Melody toward the exit. "Go!"

The heavy door creaked as Melody tugged it open far enough to squeeze through. She glanced down the passageway toward the quarters she'd been sharing with Enid. Twenty steps. But the doorway to Padric Murphy's room was situated between her current position and her goal. She paused, listening for any sign of movement in the mechanic's living space. The constant rumble of the ship's engines drowned out any sounds she may have heard. She sucked in a breath and stepped over the threshold.

Before her foot hit the deck for the fifth step, Padric's door opened and slammed against the bulkhead. Melody stood face to face with the handsome Irishman.

A slight gasp escaped from his mouth. "Miss Lampert? What are ye doing here? This is the servants' area."

"I-I ..." Melody faltered.

"You're a lady, Miss. A woman of your standing shouldn't be wandering around the belly of a ship."

"You obviously know nothing of my *standing*, Mr. Murphy." She almost laughed at the word.

"Let me help you to the upper deck, where you belong." He reached for her hand. "Does your cousin know you're on board? I'm sure he'll want you staying in one of those nice suites above."

She jerked her hand away. "*He* is the one who sent me down here!"

"Why would he—"

The ship lurched, sending Melody off balance. Padric reached to steady her in his strong arms. As he grasped her shoulders, a loud crash sounded, and the entire vessel thudded to a halt.

"Wh-what just happened?" she managed.

"I believe we just ran aground."

Chapter Five

Padric pulled Melody against him, holding tight as the ship swayed. "Are you all right, Miss?"

"Y-yes. Did you say we crashed?" She made no attempt to move away from him.

"I think so. I need to go see what happened. Please go back to your cabin."

"Where is Enid? She was right behind me." Melody pointed to the lavatory. She opened the door. "Enid?"

The maid stepped forward. "Is it safe to—Oh, my. Hello, Mr. Murphy."

Padric reached out a hand. "Pleased to meet your acquaintance, Miss Enid."

She extended her hand and shook his.

The ship suddenly listed, throwing Melody forward. Her head struck the bulkhead.

He caught her before she hit the deck, but blood oozed down the side of her face. Seawater trickled at their feet. "We're taking on water. Is there anyone else down here?"

Enid shook her head. "Not that I know of."

Padric lifted Melody into his arms and stepped on ladder's first rung. "Let's get out of here. Are you able to climb?"

"Yes. Go!"

He carried Melody upward, careful to maintain his balance in the unstable vessel. When they reached the upper deck, voices carried over the ship's groans.

"I told you to pay attention," Andrew screamed. "Now look what you've done to my ship!"

"*My* ship. Remember? I won it fair and square," snarled Reginald.

"Well, *your* ship is sinking, Captain." Andrew spat the words.

Padric sidestepped debris cluttering the deck. He turned around and saw a jagged tooth-shaped mound jutting upward from the ocean. "Sharktooth Island," he murmured. "We've already angered her."

Reginald spun around at the sound of Padric's voice. "You can't anger an island." When his gaze caught sight of his cousin, he gasped. "What happened? Is she—"

"She fell and hit her head. She's a bit groggy, but I think she'll be fine. I need to get her off this boat before it sinks to the depths. Is there a medical bag in the galley?"

"Sink? Do you think it's going to sink? As in all the way down?"

"There's already water in the steerage area."

"What shall I do? Andrew, is there a bilge pump?" Reginald yelled.

Padric pushed past the two men and flung the Jacob's Ladder over the starboard side. He had no time for such nonsense. "Hang on, Miss Melody. We're going ashore. Watch your step, Miss Enid."

The maid nodded and followed Padric as he clutched

Melody close against his chest with one arm and maneuvered down the rope rungs.

Melody moaned and her eyes flickered. "Wh-what happened?"

"Stay still. The ship hit a rock and is sinking. I'm carrying you to the island." He reached the water and sloshed through the shallows until they reached a small stretch of sand. He laid her on the ground and examined the gash on her head.

Enid rushed over and knelt beside Melody. "Will she be all right?" Worry creased her brow.

He nodded. "I think so. The cut is small and in her hairline. Head wounds tend to bleed a lot, so it looks worse than it is." He ripped a piece of cloth from his shirt and dabbed at the gash.

Enid touched her hand lightly to Melody's forehead. "The bump is rising outward, which is a good sign."

Padric noticed the others scrambling from the yacht. The rear end of the vessel protruded from the water, as if mimicking the island's jagged mountain.

Andrew and Reginald were still arguing about the ruined ship. Edward hurried down the ladder, leaving his sisters to fend for themselves.

Ominous clouds swirled overhead. "A storm is brewing." Padric pointed to the darkening sky. "We'll need to find shelter or build a lean-to of some sort. Is anyone else hurt?" He helped Melody sit, resting her head against his chest and keeping a steady arm around her.

"My dress is ruined!" squealed Edward's eldest sister. Padric remembered the younger one calling her Florence. She looked back at the creaking hunk of wood and metal, slowly slipping downward. She pointed toward Padric. "My brother says you're a mechanic. Go fix the ship! There's a ball this evening in Savannah, and I intend to be there." She turned to her sister. "Daphne, I heard Mr. Peter Hartley will be in attendance. Perhaps he'll ask me to dance. Do you remember him?"

Her younger sister nodded, a swoony look forming on her face. "How could I forget?" She batted her eyelashes and clutched her hands to her chest.

"Ladies, the ship is beyond repair. Unfortunately, your Mr. Hartley will have to wait for his dance," Padric said. "Right now, we must focus on finding a safe shelter to ride out the approaching storm. We'll also need to find a source of fresh water and gather wood to build a fire."

"What about food? We haven't lunched yet," Edward whined.

"Food can wait." Padric glanced around the group from person to person. All eyes focused on him, searching for answers. He couldn't take charge of this rabble. He couldn't be responsible for the lives of others. Not again. Not ever. Yet, he knew in his heart that none of them had the skills or knowledge necessary to survive this ordeal. If he didn't help them, they would die.

Just like the others had.

Chapter Six

Padric sighed. Why had he attempted to take charge of the situation? Edward was right, though. They would need food eventually.

Melody straightened a bit, easing away from him. Padric instantly missed the warmth where she had leaned against his chest. "My deed to the island. It's in my cabin."

"I'll go back and retrieve it from the ship."

"No. It's too dangerous."

"But without proof, your cousin may not grant you ownership," Enid said.

"It doesn't matter."

"No," he said quietly. "You've already lost your parents and your mother's inheritance. I won't let you lose this property too. And perhaps I can find a medical bag and some food while I'm on board."

Edward glanced toward the half-submerged yacht then upward at the jagged, tooth-like formation. "We've already angered the island. It's as if it knows the gold stolen from it is close."

"Not you too, Ed!" Reginald shook his head. "Curse, smurse. That's the most ridiculous thing I've ever heard." He glanced over his shoulder at the sinking vessel.

"Go. I'll tend to Miss Melody," Enid whispered.

"I'll be quick." Padric hesitated and glanced at the darkening sky. Reaching inside his vest, he pulled out the small pouch and handed it to Melody. "Keep this hidden, and keep it safe."

She nodded and winced, lifting her hand to the small lump on her forehead. "But you don't have to—"

He touched a finger to her lips and walked away. "Reginald, I'm returning to the ship. I'm going to see what supplies are available. Can you set up a shelter? And search for fresh water and firewood?"

"Yes, yes." Reginald waved a dismissive hand. "I can build a shelter. We built forts when we were boys, right Edward? Andrew?"

Andrew nodded. "From kits our fathers bought for us."

"But you don't need to go back to the ship. I'd hate to have to rescue you." A loud creak from the yacht punctuated Reginald's remark. "On second thought, if you're dumb enough to go back, I'd probably let you go down with the ship."

"Isn't that the Captain's responsibility?" asked Andrew.

Reginald silenced him with a scowl.

"Something of vital importance was left behind," continued Padric. "I'm going to retrieve it."

"The map? You forgot the map?" Reginald sounded frantic. "How could you have forgotten it? That map is our only hope of finding the cave and the gol—." He waved the Irishman toward the sinking ship. "Go! And hurry up about it!"

Padric left him to believe the assumption. He turned toward Melody and knelt beside her.

She gave him a tentative smile. Enid had wiped most of the

blood from her face, and her color had improved. "Be careful," she whispered. "Come back to me."

Without thinking, he bent over and planted a light kiss on her cheek. "Aye. I will, Miss." He gave her a quick wink and hurried toward the ship's ladder.

THE UNSTEADY VESSEL complained against his weight as he mounted the rope rungs. Now hanging at an awkward angle, Padric struggled to hoist his body upward. Once he reached the upper deck, he grasped whatever he could to maneuver without sliding into the submerged portion. He managed to reach the hatch leading to the galley. Melody's berth lay beneath it.

Holding a handle with one hand, he stretched until he could touch the lever of the lower deck's hatch. Padric's arm muscles protested as he pulled himself toward the opening that accessed the steerage area. He had to get her document. Even though it was only an obscure island, that property was all she had. If Melody's deed was lost to the depths, her cousin would never consent to split the property, leaving her penniless. Of course, according to Edward, she could marry a society man and restore her inheritance. He pushed the thought from his mind.

Padric used what he could for handholds, pulling himself along the galley's bulkhead. He found the cabinet marked with a medical symbol and jerked it open. The ship shuddered. He felt his way inside the deep hold until his fingers touched a bag. He slung it over his shoulder and searched the galley for other supplies.

Due to the newness of the ship and the shortness of their planned excursion, little food was available. A few jars of vegetables and meats had crashed to the deck, so he carefully avoided slipping on their contents so he wouldn't fall on the broken glass.

He bagged some smoked meat and a few potatoes that survived the crash, then eased his way toward the lower deck, whispering a prayer along the way.

Melody watched Padric's retreating figure as long strides carried him toward the once-magnificent *Destiny*. Was he her destiny? She shook her head and immediately regretted the slight movement.

"Are you all right, Miss?" Enid placed a gentle hand on Melody's arm.

"Yes. Thank you. I may need your help to get up, though."

"Are you sure that's wise?"

"I'm fine. Just a bump and a scratch." She offered a smile that she hoped reassured the young woman.

Reginald walked over and reached a hand toward her. "Need some assistance, cousin?"

She took the offered hand, and between his help and Enid's, Melody stood. "Thanks."

He gripped her upper arm tighter than necessary and leaned close to her ear. "Pity the deed with your name on it is buried beneath the sea. When I have Mr. Arnold redraw the document, I'll make sure he corrects Grandmother's oversight."

Melody shrugged loose from his grasp. "Excuse me while I check on the other passengers."

She noticed the Randolph sisters holding each other and sobbing. As she approached, Melody realized their tears flowed because they would likely miss the evening ball in Savannah.

Melody chanced a glance backward at the yacht. No sign of Padric, but she reminded herself he'd only left moments earlier.

Was it true, what his father thought about the island being cursed? Had they angered it? She'd never put much stock in superstitions or religion.

Enid scurried up beside her. "What now, Miss?"

She pointed toward Andrew and Edward, who were making their best attempt at constructing a lean-to. "It looks like the men are busy building a shelter. I suppose you and I can gather wood for a fire and search for something palatable to eat."

"I've already collected a fine batch of berries." Reginald held out a cloth remnant that formed a makeshift basket, filled with dark-colored fruit.

Melody startled at his voice. "I-I didn't hear you approaching."

"You must keep your wits about you at all times in the wild, cousin. This island is likely fraught with all sorts of dangers. Even without the curse."

She shivered, despite the mild temperature.

"Would you like some berries? There are plenty."

Melody shook her head. "Let the others eat first. I'm not hungry at the moment." Concern for Padric outweighed any hunger pangs. She turned to Enid. "If you're hungry, go ahead and eat."

The maid eagerly grabbed a handful of the dark fruit. "Thank you, Mr. Emerson."

He smiled broadly and nodded, popping a few berries into his mouth. "I'll be off to share these with the others now." He made a mock gesture of a hat-tip, his cover likely lost at sea.

"Look, Miss. There's some driftwood. I'll go fetch an armful." Enid skipped down the small slip of sand toward a small pile of wood.

A large water droplet splatted against Melody's face. She hurried to help Enid gather the wood. If it became rain drenched, the hope of lighting a fire would be lost. Heavy footsteps sounded behind her, and she spun around to face Padric. His torn shirt and trousers were soaked, but he appeared to be well, and if the broad smile indicated anything, in good spirits.

"Padric." Her words came out in a breathless whisper, and she forced herself to remain still rather than rush into his arms, which she longed to do. "You're back." She returned his smile.

He reached out and brushed a tendril from her face. "I promised a lady I'd come back to her."

She felt a blush warming her cheeks. "You're wet. We must get the fire going before you catch your death of cold!"

Padric lifted the small load of driftwood from her arms. "Aye. I'll get busy with it, then." He nodded toward Edward and Andrew, who were struggling to place branches atop their make-shift shelter. "I see the lads are still working on the lean-to."

She opened her mouth to respond, but a gagging scream halted her. "Enid?"

Melody ran toward her handmaid, who was bent over, retching near the water's edge. Her skin was a ghastly gray, and her legs crumpled beneath her just as Padric reached to catch her.

"Enid, what happened?" Melody fought to catch her breath.

Padric eased her onto the beach. "Did you eat anything from the island?"

The young woman nodded. "So dizzy."

Padric rushed to the water and tore a strip of cloth from his shirttail. He dipped it in the cool liquid and wrung out the excess moisture as he hurried back. Melody sank to the ground and laid Enid's head on her lap. She wiped the maid's face with the damp cloth and looked up at Padric. "Berries. Reginald picked berries for us."

"And you?" Worry creased his brow. "Did you eat as well?"

Melody shook her head. "No. I was ... I was too concerned about your welfare to eat."

He smiled. "As you can see, I am fine, Miss Melody." He knelt beside Enid. "How many berries did you eat? Five? Ten? More?"

"A handful," she managed. "Perhaps ten or more."

"Certain berries can cause devastating effects, but most, when eaten in small amounts, can make one quite ill, but the illness will pass quickly." He patted her on the shoulder and stood. "Oh, I almost forgot. I found some potatoes, smoked meat, and pickled herring in the galley. I'll start a fire and prepare a meal for those who are able to eat." He gazed into Melody's eyes. "And I collected your treasure as well, Miss Melody." With a wink, he hurried back toward the others.

Chapter Seven

Padric found his fellow passengers in various stages of misery, but none appeared to have life-threatening repercussions from the berries. Andrew and Edward had abandoned their attempts to build a shelter, both muttering curses about the cursed island. Within a short time, Padric had the lot tucked beneath a craggy rock overhang with a fire blazing nearby.

Putting the few supplies he retrieved from the ship to good use, he set out a bucket to catch rainwater. Melody had the herring and potatoes sizzling in a small skillet for those who felt like eating, while Padric worked to extend the shelter by weaving large branches he and Melody had gathered.

Thunder rumbled overhead, and lightning flashed between the clouds. Satisfied he could do nothing further to ease the discomfort of the group, he settled in for what he figured would be a long, miserable night. He patted the small pouch tucked beneath his shirt. *Tomorrow.* His thoughts of returning the island's property were so clear, he wondered if he'd spoken the word out loud.

Edward and his sisters huddled in the back corner of the crevice. Padric could hear the girls' whimpers mingled in between Edward's moans. Reginald lay sprawled near the fire with Andrew curled in a fetal position not far from him. Melody sat beside Enid, who had somehow managed to doze despite the situation.

He caught Melody looking his way and offered her what he hoped was a reassuring smile. "Best get some rest, Miss Melody. I'll keep watch."

"But you need your rest too," she protested.

Padric nodded. "Perhaps I can catch a nap tomorrow when everyone feels better, but someone needs to keep the fire going tonight." He didn't elaborate on the reasons why a fire was necessary. No need to frighten her. Beyond the obvious uses such as warmth and light, a fire would ward off creatures of the night. Smoke would keep the insects at bay. Most nocturnal creatures avoided a fire's brightness.

But no matter how long or how fiercely the fire burned, it couldn't protect him from the memories.

He stared into the flickering flames, watching sparks ease upward, lifted by the light breeze. His thoughts drifted as easily as the glowing cinders. Even if this island were cursed, it had nothing on the hauntings within his mind.

Tomorrow. He would find the cave. Return the gold. Seek a solution to get off the island. Reginald was the ship's captain. Let him command the party. Padric would follow the leader. Do as he was told. And keep a watchful eye. But he wouldn't take charge.

He couldn't be responsible for the death of one more person.

MELODY JERKED AWAKE. What was that noise? A scream? She blinked her eyes against the morning sun rays and eased Enid's head off her shoulder so she could move. She glanced at the group lying in various positions. Someone was gone. Daphne. And Padric. He was no longer by the fire, which had diminished to a small pile of ash and coals.

She eased upward and tiptoed to the edge of the shelter. The scream ripped through the silence. Melody stilled, determining the direction of the cry. Padric rushed over, carrying an armload of sticks and driftwood. Some pieces were obviously debris from the wrecked yacht. He set it next to the dying flames.

"What was that?"

Melody shook her head. "I don't know, but Daphne is gone." Others in the group stirred.

Edward jumped up, striking his head against the low-hanging rock formation. He fell to his knees, muttering a curse. "Where is my sister?" he yelled.

"The noise I heard came from over there." Melody pointed.

Edward scrambled on all fours until he'd cleared the rocky slab. Unsure what to do, Melody followed as he hurried in the direction she had indicated.

Padric's voice sounded behind her. "Tend to the fire!"

She glanced over her shoulder to see her cousin moving toward the pile of driftwood. A moment later, Padric was beside her.

Edward called out to Daphne.

"I'm over here!" she shouted. "I can't move."

Fears of all sorts rushed through Melody's mind. What had happened to the poor girl to prevent her from moving? Was she injured? But her voice sounded strong, so perhaps she would survive whatever ordeal had befallen her.

The trio scrambled between the boulders and stopped.

Daphne stood, pressing her back against the rocky cliff, and near her feet lay the carcass of a half-eaten sea turtle.

"*That* is why you screamed?" Padric pointed at the dead creature. "And why you said you couldn't move?" Exasperation laced his voice.

"I'll not have you speak to my sister in that tone, Mr. Murphy." Edward assumed a rigid stance.

Padric gave a half bow toward the frightened young woman. "My apologies for my gruffness, Miss, but if we're to survive this ... this situation, we mustn't panic over harmless things."

"And who put you in charge, Mr. Murphy?" Edward demanded.

Padric stepped back. "No one." He turned toward the camp. "No one at all." His voice was barely audible.

Melody remained quiet as she matched his gait. She heard Edward quizzing Daphne, a few paces behind them.

"Don't you realize it's dangerous to go off gallivanting alone on this cursed strip of land?"

"Do you think the island is cursed, Edward?" Daphne asked. "Is ... is that what happened to that poor animal? The curse got it?"

"It was killed because something more powerful than it was hungry. There is no curse. But the island is still dangerous. Why did you leave the camp?"

"I-I needed a moment of privacy, brother. In case you haven't noticed, there isn't a necessary on this island."

A smirk crossed Padric's face. But the girl was right. The narrow beach was barely wide enough to walk along. As long as they remained stranded here, privacy would be nonexistent.

Her last thought triggered a frightening realization. How long would they remain stranded here? She'd read of sailors, marooned for heinous crimes, who'd been left abandoned with nothing more than a day's supply of rations. Some were granted a one-shot pistol. Criminals or not, she shuddered at their fates.

"Cold?" Padric asked.

She shook her head. "No. Just wondering what will become of us. What if something ... more powerful than us gets hungry?" She met his gaze. "Are we going to die here?"

Padric stiffened at her question, then answered in a soft voice, "Not if I can help it."

Chapter Eight

The party breakfasted on the remaining supplies Padric had found in the yacht's galley. Melody was grateful her shipmates had recovered quickly from their bout with the berries.

"It's time for me to locate the cave. I shouldn't be gone long," Padric said and strode away from the shelter.

Melody hurried to catch up with him. "I want to go with you."

"You're not going without me." Reginald blocked his path. "Don't think I can't see through your scheme."

"What scheme?"

"And now you're playing innocent."

"What are you talking about, Reggie?" Melody asked.

He placed an arm across her shoulders. "Pity you're too naïve to see through his façade. Can't you tell he's been pretending to be sweet on you so he can take control of the island? The treasure?"

"What?" Padric stepped toward them.

Melody backed away slightly. Was Reginald right? Had

Padric been playing on her emotions? Her hopes of finding a loving home someday? Even though she doubted it was possible, she still dreamed of one day becoming part of a real family instead of the sham life she currently lived.

"Do you believe him?" Padric gazed into her eyes and gave a nod toward her cousin.

She looked downward, unable to face him.

"Melody?"

Tears misted her eyes. How could she have been so foolish to have fallen for his charms?

He tipped her chin upward with one finger. "Surely you don't believe him."

"You risked your life to retrieve the deed with my name on it. Without that, you knew Reggie could lay claim to the entire island, and I'd be penniless. Did you do that for me? Or in hopes of future gain for yourself?" A tear trickled down her cheek.

"So you got the deed back?" Reggie's lips twisted.

"You've perpetuated the rumors about the island being cursed, although I doubt you believe it," she went on, gazing at Padric. "And even though you claim to not want to lead the group, you offer advice. Leadership. Everyone looks to you. We trusted you. Hoped in you." She jerked her head away from his touch. "To be honest, I'm not sure what to believe. About you. The island. Anything."

Reginald pulled her closer to him, glaring over his shoulder at Padric.

Padric sighed. "Fine. You've obviously made up your mind about me and my motives." He shook his head. "Let's get on with it, then. The sooner we finish what we came to do, the sooner you'll be rid of me."

"That is, if we can find a way off this cursed island," muttered Reginald.

PADRIC OPENED the journal and thumbed through it until he found the map. He scanned the terrain, attempting to line up his grandfather's sketch with his surroundings.

"What's wrong?" asked Reginald.

"Things have changed since this map was drawn."

"You're stalling. Give me that!" He reached for the journal.

Padric spun away from Reginald. "Be careful. That book is decades old." He looked toward Melody. "You think I returned to get the deed so I could swindle the island from you. But I could have found it at any time. I have the map. If I were trying to trick you, I wouldn't have shown it to you."

Before she could answer, Reginald cut in. "Nonsense. You had to show the map to prove you had a story worth buying into our hand with. And now, instead of heading toward the cave that supposedly holds all the answers, you're delaying. That book is likely a phony, just like you." He took Melody's hand. "Come along, cousin. We don't need him. We'll just search until we find the cave. The island isn't that big."

She pulled away. "I think it's best if we stay together. Too many things have happened since we arrived here."

"Now you're on his side?"

"I'm not on anyone's side. But think about it, Reginald. You've never showed me a moment's affection in all the years I've lived at Mapleleaf Manor. Yet now you're acting as if we're close. And don't forget who crashed the yacht. And fed poisonous berries to the group." She wiped her eyes on her sleeve. "I don't know who to believe."

Reginald paled at her statement. He opened his mouth but shut it without speaking.

Padric glanced back at the map and studied the landscape. Squabbling would get them nowhere. "There." He pointed to a rock shelf up and to the left. "Is that the place circled on the map?"

Melody shielded her eyes with her hand and looked upward before returning her gaze to the journal. "It's definitely similar." She turned toward Reginald. "Ready to climb?"

He stared at the jagged hill before them. "That's ridiculous. No one can reach that ledge. Are you sure you're not just trying to get us killed so you can have the gold?"

Padric felt his patience slipping. He gritted his teeth and spoke through them. "If you don't want to go, then stay here. No one is forcing you to go." He turned to Melody. "Miss Lampert, it won't be an easy hike. Especially in what you're wearing."

She glanced down at her ruined dress and turned toward her cousin. "I see you changed to fresh clothes this morning. Do you still have your other trousers in your knapsack?" Melody pointed to the bag strapped to his shoulders.

"What are you thinking?" Reginald's voice squawked.

"Give me your other pair of pants." She reached for the bag. "Besides, if I'm wearing your clothes, that'll leave more room to stuff gold in your bag. Correct?"

He reached in his sack and tossed her the dirty and damp trousers. "You're daft, cousin. I thought it before, but now I'm certain. When Grandmother hears of your shenanigans on this trip ..." He paused. "Does she even know you're here? That you've left the house?"

Melody waved away his questions. "Now, if you two will be gentlemen and turn your backs while I step behind this tree, I'd be most grateful."

Chapter Nine

Melody swatted another gnat, forcing herself not to complain like her cousin, who had muttered nonstop for the past hour. She looked upward. The ledge hovering above them appeared no closer than it had when they began the ascent. What she would give for a drink, but Padric had been strict about rationing the scant amount of rainwater they'd collected before the clouds cleared.

A sound to her left caught her attention. Running water? She'd read of unfortunate souls, stranded for long stretches without proper nourishment, who imagined things even to the point of insanity. The noise grew louder. She veered off the path Padric was clearing, intent on investigating the sound. Pushing back thick vegetation, she spotted a short waterfall pooling in a cluster of rocks. "Padric!" she called.

He immediately ceased his thrashing ahead of her. "What is it? Are you all right?"

"Over here. I've found fresh water!"

The two men broke through the undergrowth, and Melody pointed to the cascading flow.

Reginald wiped his brow and eagerly pushed past her, kneeling down. He alternated gulping handfuls of the rippling stream and splashing the liquid on his face.

"Good job!" Padric grinned at her. "This can be the difference between our survival and ..."

"Our demise?" she finished his sentence.

"Yes." He knelt beside her as they both drank. "I've read the scripture about deer panting for water, but even though I've been through many scrapes in my life, I never knew true thirst until this ... adventure."

It seemed Padric Murphy was full of surprises. "It's been a long time since I heard someone quote from the Bible."

"Well, I didn't exactly quote it." He smiled.

"Enough chatter," Reginald snapped. "Don't you think this find is worth sharing with the others? They've barely wet their tongues due to the rationing." He glared toward Padric.

"Of course they should be told." Padric glanced toward the suspected cave entrance and back toward the area they'd traversed. "They are likely on the verge of dehydration following the ... the berry incident."

"Right. Then I volunteer to go back and tell them," said Reginald.

"You trust us to continue to the cave?" Melody eyed him doubtfully.

"If that even is the cave entrance, cousin, then yes. Continue onward. I'll head to the camp, and we'll fill the bucket for all to drink." He about-faced before waiting for a response.

"We'll resume our climb once you've quenched your thirst," Padric said, his voice soft.

Melody's conscience clenched. How could she have doubted him when all he'd done was good for the group? Was it Padric she doubted? Or was it her inability to trust anyone after experiencing so much betrayal in her life? She offered him a smile. "I'm ready."

He reached for her hand and pulled her back to their original path. "I hope your cousin can easily find his way back to the stream." He cut away some of the thicket to expose the waterfall's location.

Another hour of maneuvering over the rough terrain left Melody longing for the stream below them. She looked out toward the ocean. Gentle whitecaps topped the sea. She could barely make out the yacht's stern poking above the waves. As she leaned for a better angle, she lost her footing and slipped. A loose rock tumbled downward, clinking along the rocky terrain as it fell.

A scream caught in her throat as a strong arm caught her, preventing her from plunging downhill.

"Th-thank you." Melody caught her breath.

"Let's take a rest." He patted a small boulder.

She sat on the rock and scooted over to make room for him next to her.

Glancing upward, he said, "It's not much farther. We'll need to work our way to the left in order to climb onto the ledge. Miss Melody, if you're the praying sort, lift up a petition that this is the cave's entrance."

"I'm afraid I'm not the praying sort. Are you?" She was unsure how much to pry.

His eyes met hers with a steady gaze. "Aye, I do believe there's a God in heaven who hears our cries. But most of my prayers are selfish pleas for forgiveness. Ever since ..." He sucked in a deep breath.

"What is it?" she asked.

He gazed into her eyes for a long moment. "About ten years ago, I was aboard a merchant vessel with my father. A storm blew in, and the ship broke apart. Before the sea sucked him to its depths, he told me to save the crew." Padric paused. "I caught a piece of plank and pulled myself onto it. I tried to reach the others, but the waves ... the waves swept them away from me." Tears misted his eyes.

"You must have been just a boy."

"I was twelve." He faced downward. "I woke up on a spit of land not much larger than the one we camped on last night. Only this stretch was strewn with the bodies of my shipmates." His green eyes shimmered behind unshed tears. "And that's why I should never be in charge."

Melody placed her hand on his forearm. "You must know that wasn't your fault."

"Aye. But there's still an ache in my gut. When the wind rushed in, my da said it was the sea searching for its lost gold. That it must be returned to the cursed Sharktooh Island. I'd never heard of the place until then. But when I got old enough, I vowed to do just that."

She placed her hand on his arm, not sure what she could say to comfort him.

He blinked. "So, when your cousin offered me the position of mechanic on the yacht, I determined to make this trip the one to fulfill my vow. Curse or no curse, I made a promise to my father. That is why I'm here."

"Did someone rescue you?"

"Aye. By God's grace. A pirate ship had been closing in on us. They veered away from the storm, and when it passed, found land." He swallowed hard. "They put me on board while they searched for valuables. We hadn't picked up a load yet, so there wasn't much."

He paused, and Melody could almost see the memories reflecting in his eyes. "I was certain my shipmates had all perished, but—"

A shout rang out through the jungle, interrupting Padric's tale.

"Murphy! You hornswoggler! Did ye think I wouldn't find you?"

A bowstring twanged, and an arrow landed at Melody's feet.

Padric pushed her behind the rock, tumbling on top of her. He reached into his shirt and thrust the pouch into her hand. "Take the journal and the gold to the cave. Stay low and keep covered in the overgrowth. I'll be right behind you, but first I've got a crow to pluck."

"Wh-what's happening? Who shot at us?"

"At me, technically. His name's Greyson Watters, and he's come to right a wrong. Now go, and don't look back."

Chapter Ten

Melody inched her way upward, careful to remain hidden behind rocks and trees. Padric's last words echoed in her ears. *Don't look back.* She recalled a story her mother had told her about Lot's wife, a woman who looked back. Had God Himself cursed Lot's wife? Did He still curse people today? Could the island truly be cursed?

Although Melody doubted she'd be transformed into a pillar of salt, an overwhelming sense of dread enveloped her as her mind ran amuck with swirling questions. Who was this man, Greyson Watters? Why had he shot at Padric? What wrong needed to be righted?

She pushed the thoughts aside and grasped a sapling, hoisting her body onto the flat rock jutting out from the mountain, the goal she and Padric had focused on for the past two hours. Clutching crevices with her fingertips, Melody eased leftward along the ledge toward the gaping opening.

The shelf jutted out from the mountain about four feet. Wide enough to walk along, but not enough to make her feel safe about it. Forcing herself not to look down, she steadied her weight on the overhang.

As she approached the yawning darkness, Melody recalled the story of the greedy man who'd fallen into the cave's depths and realized she had no light source. Would she be doomed to the same fate? She clutched Padric's pouch close to her chest and crossed the threshold.

Keeping her hand along the rough, damp cave wall, she moved slowly, testing each step before placing her full weight downward. Within ten paces of the opening, darkness shrouded her. She spun around and could barely make out the glow from the entrance. Another horrifying idea enveloped her. She could easily get lost in the cavern. Her gasp at the thought rebounded off the rough corridor, an eerie echo that halted her progress.

Silence followed. The noiselessness was as thick as the darkness, and Melody wasn't sure which was the most unnerving. Did it matter where she left the items? Perhaps she should leave the doubloons and journal and return to the camp. Where was Padric? He'd said he'd join her soon.

Melody took another step and slipped, barely catching herself in time to prevent a fall onto the slick cave floor. Footsteps behind her shattered the silence. A shadow appeared before her. Her own shadow. It took her a moment to realize that creating a shadow required light. Melody turned toward around and saw a glimmer. "Padric?"

She found herself face to face with a stranger bearing a flickering torch. The man she presumed was Greyson Watters stood close enough for her to breathe in his foul breath. Stepping backward, Melody felt behind her for the cavern wall. At that moment, one thought pushed itself through to the forefront of all the thoughts swirling through her mind. *Escape.* The importance of that concept was not foreign to her. In fact, it had been her goal since she was taken to her grandmother's home after her parents died.

Watters tipped his hat. A mocking smirk crossed his mouth as he gave a half bow. "I'm sorry, Missy, but Mr. Murphy won't be joining us. Looks like it's just me and you." He moved closer to her, brushing aside the hair that had fallen across her face with filthy and gnarled fingers.

Heat from the torch he held grew strong enough to cause discomfort. She tried to take another backward step, but the rugged wall halted her. Cold, jagged stones pressed into her shoulder blades.

"You best be giving me the goods your Padric sent along with you. I couldn't find them on his body, and I know bringing them to the cave was his intent." He thrust his hand toward her, palm up, wiggling his fingers in a gimme gesture. "You do have it, don't you?"

His body? Tears stung her eyes. Padric wouldn't be coming to save her from this man. And she was certain Reginald and the others had no desire to exert themselves enough to climb the cliff face. If she gave this man the gold, would he be merciful to her?

Greyson grabbed a handful of her hair and jerked Melody against him. "What's the matter, Missy? Cat got your tongue? Don't you know it's rude to ignore a man when he's asked you a question? Has no one taught you how to treat a man?" He released her hair and brushed her cheek with the back of his hand. "Maybe it's time you learned." His mocking caress trickled down to her throat. "I can teach you."

Melody pushed the satchel into the man's face. "Here. The gold's in this sack. Take it."

Greed shrouded his expression. She'd seen the look before. He used his free hand to dig in the bag. A moment later, he pulled out a coin. The gold glinted in the torch's flame and reflected in his eyes. He retrieved the second coin. "You little minx. Where's the rest of it?"

"Th-that's all. The rest was lost in the cave. Years ago."

"Did your Padric tell you that? You know he's a liar and a cheat, right? Of course he'd make you believe this was all of it. He's likely hidden away the rest for himself. That's the only person he's ever thought of."

Melody stood, frozen against the cave wall. After a moment, her voice found the words. "No. Padric is kind. He's selfless. He sacrificed to take care of us after the yacht crashed."

"Your ship crashed? You mean you're stuck on this piece of rock?" The man laughed. "Now that's poetic justice."

She turned her face to avoid the stench of his rotten breath.

"I suppose your Padric never told about another shipwreck he was in."

"He told me." She closed her eyes. "He said all were lost, save himself."

Greyson spat on the cave floor. "All were lost? He told you that?"

She barely nodded.

"Liar!"

The slap that followed startled as much as it stung. Melody's eyes misted over.

"All were not lost!" His voice reverberated off the cavern walls. His face hovered mere inches from hers, and he moved his fingers to clutch her throat. "I was there. And when the crew carried Murphy away, he stood against the ship's rail, staring at the beach strewn with bodies. I was too weak to sit or stand, but I lifted my head. He met my gaze. Did he attempt to coerce the ship's crew to return for me? No. But he saw me. And he left me there to die on that forsaken spit of land."

"He was twelve years old," Melody whispered.

He pushed his thumb against her windpipe and tightened

his grip. "It wasn't a matter of age—it was a matter of right and wrong, of leaving a wounded man to die. I vowed that day to find him. To track him down. When I heard a young man at the docks asking about a ship heading to Sharktooth Island, it piqued my interest, because Murphy's father was obsessed with the place." He stared into her eyes. "The young man seemed concerned. Said his friends should have returned, and he wanted to check their welfare."

"Peter," she whispered.

Greyson loosened his grasp slightly and shrugged. "I followed your friend and stowed away on his vessel."

"Is he here?"

"I left his corpse on the ship, along with the bodies of his small crew. The vessel is moored just off this cursed island. I'll dispose of him when I return to the schooner." His lips displayed a malicious grin. "I was in a hurry—determined to finally find Padric Murphy and leave him to the same fate he left me. Unfortunately, my anger got the best of me when I saw him a few minutes ago, spoiling my chances to abandon him."

He moved his thumb in a circular motion at the base of her throat. "But, my sweet, that will be *your* fate. I will take this gold and sail off in my schooner, watching you until I'm out of sight, while you ponder what it's like to be abandoned. Left to die. A fitting revenge against that coward Padric Murphy, don't you think?"

Chapter Eleven

Padric rolled onto his side. He attempted to rise, but pain exploded along the right side of his forehead and reverberated throughout his body. He touched the source of the searing and quickly pulled his hand back. Sticky blood oozed from a wound and covered his face. Inching his body into a sitting position, he leaned against the rock and paused to catch his breath. Sweat from the slight exertion beaded across his brow. He wiped the blood from his eyes with his shirtsleeve and blinked.

Thoughts swirled amidst the throbbing ache. What happened? How long had he lain here? A wave of dizziness flooded over him. Yellow spots flickered in his line of sight. *Stay awake.* The words were futile, so he supported his back against the boulder and let the blackness come. Another thought pressed its way into his consciousness. *Melody.*

"Melody." He barely recognized the weak, gravelly voice as her name emerged from his throat. "Melody!" He repeated her name, louder, urgently. Where was she? Had she been injured too?

He closed his eyes and took a series of slow, deep breaths, willing the dizziness to subside, forcing himself to think. To remember. Snippets of time returned to him. Melody. Gone. He'd sent her to the cave. Why? Another memory fragment found its way into his thoughts. Greyson Watters. A bow shot. He reached to touch his head again. Watters had shot him.

Padric forced his frame onto all fours. He grasped the rock and pulled himself upward until he stood. Keeping a hand on the rock to balance his dazed body, he took a step. *Melody.* The thought of her enabled him to push past the pain. Past the vertigo. He grabbed a young tree and pulled himself forward, stopping to mop the trickling blood from his eyes.

He ripped off a piece of his already ragged shirt and wrapped it around his head to prevent the blood from blinding him. He had to get to the cave. Find Melody. Stop Watters from hurting her.

Was he already too late?

"Eeee-nid," whined Daphne. "Please hurry. I think I'm dying."

Enid struggled to keep up with the demands on her assistance. *Rich kids certainly were needy.* Before she reached the younger of Edward's sisters, the eldest grasped her by the wrist.

"She's fine. But *I* need you," cried Florence. "I'm sooo thirsty. Can't you fetch us some water?"

"Now, Miss Florence, you know we divvied up the last of the water an hour ago. The men done explored the area looking for water and didn't find any. You're just gonna have to be tough."

"Are we going to die?"

Enid searched the young woman's eyes. *I can't lie to her.* "Well, we're all gonna die sometime of something. I reckon only the Good Lord knows when and from what."

"If He is truly good, then why are we stuck here?" asked Daphne.

"We're stuck here because Mr. Emerson didn't listen to what your brother and Mr. Murphy was telling him, and he crashed the boat."

Heavy footsteps tromped through the brush, and a hand swept aside a small tree to reveal a red-faced Reginald. "What's that you said? Don't forget your station, Enid."

Edward spun away from the shelter he'd been working on to face Reginald. "Ah, you're back. Mission accomplished?"

Reginald shook his head. "They're still inching their way up that cliff face." He pointed upward.

Andrew stepped over to join them and gazed upward at the steep rise. "Too much for you, eh, Reg?" He gave a slight laugh.

"I returned because I have some excellent news. About a third of the way up the mountain, there's a waterfall with a small pool at its base."

"Water? You found water?" Florence almost squealed the word.

"Yes."

"Thank you, Jesus," Enid whispered.

Reginald ignored her and continued, "It's a bit of a climb, but not too strenuous. Those who are able can come along. Otherwise, we can fill the bucket and bring it back."

"And slosh it out all the way down?"

Reginald glared at Enid. "I already warned you about your place, woman."

"My *place* is that of one who has actually carried water. And it sloshes when you're walking normal." She pointed toward the peak. "Going down that hill with a full bucket will be nigh on impossible, seeings how you'll need both hands to climb and steady yoreself. How many trips you think it'll take to get each body here one swallow after it spills all along the way?"

A long period of silence followed. "Is there a bit of flat land near the waterfall?" Enid asked. "Because if so, we can move this so-called camp uphill and settle there. It ain't like the shelter is fit to cover us anyhow."

Reginald opened his mouth but Edward held up a hand to halt him. "She's right, you know. Andrew and I have made a mess of things here. I think we should all head up to the water. Together."

"Fine, then," muttered Reginald. "Let's go."

Chapter Twelve

Melody wondered if Padric had been right about God. She whispered a prayer. At this point, it couldn't hurt.

"Are you praying?" Watters scoffed. "Prayers don't work. Don't you think I prayed when I was lying on that beach, abandoned by your Padric? Abandoned by God?"

"And yet you somehow managed to get off the island," she said softly.

The flickering torchlight revealed a pensive expression on his face. "You think God saved me?"

"Well—"

Another slap jerked her head against the wall, and Melody grasped a jagged rock to steady herself. She reached to touch the back of her head. Warm moisture met her fingers.

"Step away from her."

Padric? The voice was raspy, weak, but held the unmistakable light brogue she'd come to love listening to.

"Now!"

The tone was more insistent this time, and Melody knew

without a doubt it was the voice of *her* Padric. But how? Watters said he'd killed him.

"Padric! You're alive!" She turned toward him. The waning torchlight barely lit the space between them, a gap Padric was stumbling to narrow. As he neared, she caught a glimpse of him and gasped. Blood covered one side of his face and had soaked his tattered shirt.

"Padric!" Melody shrugged away from Greyson Watters, but in one motion, he crammed the torch into a crevice and grasped her around the waist, spinning her against him. She felt a prick against her flesh and realized he now held a knife to her throat.

"Stop right there, Murphy, or she'll die."

Padric hesitated. Melody could see the grogginess in his eyes. Whatever injury he'd incurred had likely left him concussed. He staggered forward another step. "Let her go, Watters. She has nothing to do with this. This is between you and me."

"How could you leave me to die? We were mates." Sadness and disbelief lined his words. "You saw me. You knew I was still alive, and yet you let them sail off."

"I-I'm sorry. Your face has haunted my dreams ever since that moment."

"You were *haunted* by nightmares? I lived a nightmare! It was no dream for me, Padric Murphy!" He was weeping now. "And you could have prevented it."

"He was just a boy," Melody interrupted.

"Shut up, woman!" His fingers gripped her arm, pressing into her flesh deep enough to inflict pain. "You were haunted by my face? I'll give you a memory that will really haunt you. I'm going to shred her lovely face with this knife and leave her to die on this cursed spit of land. Then, I'll take you with me and let you watch her bleeding form on the beach while we sail off and abandon her."

Padric gasped. "M-Melody." He stumbled another step forward, nearly losing his balance.

Without thinking, Melody thrust her elbow into Greyson's ribcage. He crumpled away from her, lowering the blade. She reached into the bag and thrust the two doubloons into his hands. "Here. Take your precious gold. Let the island's curse pass on to you."

The gold glinted in the flickering flame, reflecting the greed in the man's eyes as she moved across the slick floor toward Padric.

"Oh, no, Missy. You're not getting away." He rushed to grab her but lost his footing. Watters yelled an expletive as he slipped. His knife clattered to the cave floor.

Melody reached Padric's side as a loud crack echoed throughout the cavern. She turned to see Watters sprawled on the ground.

Padric reached for her and pulled her against his chest and entwined his fingers into hers. "Don't look," he whispered.

"Is he—"

"He crushed his skull on the rocky floor. I doubt he survived." Padric paused. "But this time, I will check before I leave him. Stay here." He kissed her lightly on the forehead.

She released him and held her breath as Padric painstakingly made his way to the fallen figure.

"I-I cursed him." Tears pooled in her eyes.

"Oh, no, my sweet. 'Twas greed that cursed him." Padric caressed her cheek. His touch held comfort. Promise. Hope.

Light from the torch danced off the doubloons lying near Watters's body. Melody watched as Padric slowly knelt beside the man. He checked for signs of life then turned toward her and gave a slight shake of his head. "This may come in handy." He tucked the knife into his waistband.

Melody reached inside the satchel and pulled out the journal. "Wait."

"What? Are you all right?"

"I ... do you think it would be all right if I took a few minutes to record our time here before we leave Laura's diary?"

Padric shrugged. "I had actually considered that myself." The dim light reflected his smile. "I even stuck a pencil in my pouch." He handed it to her.

Wishing she had more time to record their adventure, Melody opened the book and skipped a few pages past the last entry and using her best penmanship, entered a brief summation of their story. She hugged the journal close to her chest for a moment and then set it on a rock that protruded from the cave wall.

Padric's quest was complete.

Chapter Thirteen

Padric reached for Melody's hand and helped her ease down from the ledge at the cave's entrance. He still felt wobbly, but his strength was improving. "Now, to figure out a way to return to the mainland."

Melody gasped.

"What is it?"

"Peter! The man said he'd killed Peter and sailed here on his schooner. We must find it and ... and ..."

"He killed Peter and stole his ship?"

She nodded. "That's what he told me." Melody paused for a moment. "Is it terrible to use Peter's boat? I just want—"

He drew her close against his chest, brushing her waves of hair away from his bloody shirt. "You want to go home." He kissed the top of her head. "There's nothing wrong with that. You didn't harm Peter. He wouldn't have wanted the rest of us to suffer longer."

"I suppose you're right."

"We shall return the schooner to his family." He cupped her chin and lifted it until she met his gaze. The look in her eyes melted his heart. Trust. Hope. Something else? He bent his mouth to cover hers. As their lips melded, he pulled her closer until he could feel her heart beat against his.

She jerked away and looked up at him, breathless. "I-I don't want to go home." She paused. "Grandmother ..."

"Ah, yes. She won't be pleased about this outing."

"I can't go back there. Not to live. It's time I found somewhere else. Maybe I should seek a position as a nanny. Many of the wealthy families with young children know me. But ..."

"Do you think your grandmother would ask them not to hire you?"

She nodded. A tear trickled down her cheek. "It's not my home. I don't have a home."

"Would you like one? A real home that would be yours?"

"Of course. It's been my lifelong dream." More tears. "But that isn't possible. Grandmother has frightened off all possible suitors. She's told the neighbors I'm unfit. Unworthy. Because ... because my father was a commoner."

"What was your father like? Do you remember him?"

She smiled. A beautiful sight. "I remember his laugh. He and my mother laughed together. They may have been poor—well, poor by my grandmother's standards—but I never remember being in want. And they truly loved each other." The tears fell unheeded now.

"It sounds perfect." He pulled her against him and stroked her hair, wiped the tears from her cheeks. "My parents also had that special bond. Laughter. Love."

"And now we both have nothing." She pulled away and looked downward.

He tipped her chin upward again. "We can have that. The love. The laughter." He paused. "Not the money. I mean, like your parents, we wouldn't be in want, but we wouldn't have the opulent lifestyle your grandmother has."

"Wh-what are you saying?"

Padric knelt down on one knee. "I'm saying I would be honored if you would become my wife. I can't offer you riches, but I can offer you all my heart and the promise that I will work hard and provide for you and our children."

CHILDREN. The thought of being a mother had never crossed her mind, but the thought of holding a babe against her, of tying bows into a young girl's hair, of sewing shirts and dresses ... the idea sounded wonderful. She gazed down at him. His eyes dazzled her.

"You're serious?" She was stunned. Never had she hoped to have a home. A family. A loving husband.

"More serious than I've been about anything."

Her grandmother's face flashed through Melody's thoughts. Never would she permit such a union. She pulled away from him and wiped an errant tear from her cheek. "I-I'm so sorry, but I can't."

"It is I who should apologize, Miss Lampert. I must have misread your feelings." Padric twisted away from her and worked to clear a downward path to the camp.

Chapter Fourteen

Sun rays, low in the sky, illuminated the tooth-shaped monolith. Padric continued his descent toward the others. Soon after the midpoint, he heard what sounded like laughter. And splashing. He turned to his left, holding branches off the newly carved path to allow Melody easy passage.

"It sounds like they found the waterfall," he said.

"Yes." Her voice was quiet. She thanked him and eased toward the voices.

Padric nodded in acknowledgement of her thanks, noting her eyes glistened with tears but made no mention of it. *So, we've gone from passionate kisses to polite platitudes.* He sucked in a deep breath and slowly exhaled. *Lord, help me show her the way to freedom. To true joy. To You.*

A few more paces brought them to a clearing near the pool. Florence and Daphne were knee-deep at the water's edge, splashing each other as they fell into a fit of giggles. Enid sat nearby, shaking her head, while Andrew, Edward, and Reginald fiddled with a stack of branches.

"I see you decided to move the camp near the water," Padric shouted over the girls' laughter. "Good choice."

"Yes." Reginald gave a half nod toward Enid without turning to face him. "She suggested it, actually. 'Twas easier to move what few items we had up here than sloshing a pail of water up and down the hill. Now, if only we had some food to enjoy with it."

As if on cue, Padric's stomach growled loudly. "We may have to stick a pole in the pond."

When Reginald turned around, he gasped at the sight of Padric. "What happened to you?"

He shrugged. "It's only a flesh wound, but it knocked me dizzy for a while."

Reginald raised an eyebrow. "Well, your shirt looks like it was worn in a knife fight." He slapped Padric on the back. "Glad you're okay. Did you accomplish what you came here to do?"

Were they best friends now? "Yes. With the help of Miss Lampert."

At the sound of her name, Melody glanced over her shoulder at the two men. She knelt beside the pool and cupped her hands full of water. After taking a few sips, she moved a few feet away from the group and sat, leaning against a tree.

"What's with her?" Andrew thumbed toward Melody.

Padric cleared his throat. "I'm afraid my actions upset her."

Reginald tromped toward Padric and swung a fist at him. "Why, you cad!"

Padric blocked the blow and grasped Reginald's wrist. "Not that kind of actions."

Melody jumped to her feet. "Stop it!" She turned toward her cousin. "He has done nothing wrong or unsavory."

"Then why did you arrive in tears?"

"B-because ... because he asked me to marry him."

Daphne Randolph squealed. "How exciting!" She looked at her sister. "He is rather handsome, don't you think? I mean, if he bathed and donned fresh clothes."

"He's not our kind," Florence retorted.

"What do you mean?"

"She means I'm not wealthy. And, I'm Irish. Therefore, I'm not a suitable suitor for either of you."

"But Melody isn't rich. So, she can marry you, right?" Daphne's eyes looked hopeful. "I adore weddings!"

"I'm afraid her situation is more complicated," Reginald placed his arm around Melody's shoulders.

She wrenched free from his arm and rushed through the cleared brush toward the path leading down the hill.

"Melody!" Padric called. "Come back! It's getting dark." He glanced toward Reginald. "Get a fire started and try to catch some fish."

"B-but—"

"Just do it. I'm going after her."

Melody heard Padric's footsteps nearing. Why had she allowed herself to kiss him? To glimpse a dream world in which she could never reside? Tears blinded her as she ran, giving no thought to how dangerous traversing the rough terrain could be at this speed.

A thud sounded behind her, followed by a deep voice yelling, "Arrgh!"

Had he fallen? He must still be dizzy from his head wound. She should go back. Check to see if he was all right. But then he'd mistake her concern for ... for love. Yes. That was the feeling swirling through her. But it was all for naught. She couldn't love him. She mustn't love him. She urged her weary body forward, around the mountain, away from the path he'd just cut for them.

Brush struck her in the face as she continued onward without thought to where she headed. *Escape*. The word drove her. But what was she escaping from?

She stopped, suddenly realizing this venture was in vain. She couldn't escape. Not from her feelings for Padric Murphy. Not from her lot in life. Not from this island. She crumpled to the ground and sobbed into her hands. There was no escape for her.

A deep guttural growl boomed to her left. Melody eased upward, searching for the source of the sound. The throaty growl repeated, followed by a short series of grunts. She took a step away from the noise, pressing against the mountain.

She chastised herself for being so reckless. How could she have let her emotions literally carry her away from the safety of the group? The shadows deepened as the sun eased toward the western horizon. She had perhaps an hour of sunlight left. Maybe less.

And she was lost. Alone.

The snorts and growls grew louder, and a moment later a wild boar came barreling out of the bushes, squalling. She may be lost, but she was not alone. Melody screamed.

In the scant seconds it took for the charging animal to breach the distance between them, a thousand thoughts swirled through Melody's mind. A prayer burst from her heart and through her lips. "Help me, Lord."

She hadn't prayed since the night her parents died. God hadn't listened then. Would he listen now? If not, she would soon join her parents in death. Or would she? She knew her parents would be in heaven, but would she, one who had shunned God, be welcome there? How could someone like her be forgiven? Padric mentioned grace. There was so much she didn't understand.

The hog skidded to a stiff-legged stop within a few yards of her. Through the fading twilight she could see the boar's bristled mane. Its ears cocked forward, and it snapped its mouth open and shut. Frothy saliva drooled down its chin. After emitting a lowing roar, the creature snarled and resumed its charge.

Melody braced herself for impact, but before the hog reached her, a knife sailed between them, lodging deep into the animal's neck. It squealed and staggered, then slumped in a heap at her feet. Her knees gave way, and she wobbled, crumpling downward.

Strong arms caught her, breaking her fall. She gazed into the green eyes of Padric Murphy before her world went dark.

Chapter Fifteen

Melody blinked open her eyes. Sunlight glinted off the waves below. She looked around, confused, before remembering the events of the previous evening. "There was a hog ..."

"Um-hmm." Padric pulled a piece of meat from a hand-carved skewer and handed it to her. "He was an old cuss. It has a strong flavor, but his meat will keep us fed until we get home."

Home. There was that word again. "Where are the others?"

"I imagine they camped by the waterfall. I hope no one else wandered into the wilderness."

She hung her head. "I'm sorry. I-I ..."

"You could have been killed. If that boar would have ..." He shuddered.

"Th-thank you. You saved me. Again."

He grinned and gave her a wink. "Seems like it's becoming a habit." His expression sobered. "It's a habit I'd like to continue, but—"

She held up her hand. "Please understand. I can't entertain such thoughts."

"Can you at least give me a reason?"

"My grandmother. She would never permit it." Melody sighed.

"And you must remain under her authority because ...?"

She paused. "I'd always hoped she'd reinstate my mother to the family. Even though my mother is gone. Not for the money, but for the principle of it. That my grandmother would respect her daughter's wishes and decision. But Grandmother let her pride get in the way. She said my mother was an embarrassment."

"Oh, Melody." He touched her arm.

"I guess I always hoped if I did what she said, that she'd somehow let my obedience override her disappointment for my mother's actions. That somehow, by me doing everything Grandmother wanted, she could forgive what she called my mother's 'sin.' Does that even make sense?"

He nodded. "I understand what you're saying. But there are some people who never change. Your grandmother may be one of them." He put his hand over hers. "Other than that, is there any other reason not to become my wife?"

She shook her head. "I want to. I'm just afraid."

Padric pulled her close. "Have you ever heard the words, faith casts out fear?"

"No. I don't know much about faith."

"I'd love to share more about it with you sometime. Would that be all right?"

"Yes," she said softly. "I did pray last night."

"Really? And how did God answer?"

"He sent you." She grinned and popped another piece of meat in her mouth. "We need to take some of this food to the others. I think they must be on the other side of the mountain, but I'm not sure how to get back there."

"I know a way." He pointed to the sparkling water below. "Look."

She squinted against the morning sun and saw a boat moored a short distance from the island's coast. "Peter's schooner." Her voice softened. "So, the man in the cave told the truth. He killed Peter and stole his ship."

"I'm afraid so." He held his hand toward her. "Let's pack up this meat and work our way down there. Are you ready?"

Melody nodded.

THE SUN HAD EASED midway above the eastern horizon by the time they reached the rocky shoreline.

"I'm going to swim out. I've worked on Peter's schooner before. It has a jolly boat. I'll use that to come ashore and get you. Then I can ferry the others from the other side to the ship."

"And Peter?"

"If his body is on the schooner, I will take care of him. Put him a safe place until we return to the mainland so his family can give him a proper burial."

She nodded, her eyes wet with unshed tears.

The sight of her pain over the loss of a neighbor moved him. He pulled her into his arms and held her against his chest, gently stroking her back. "He was a good man." After a few minutes, he loosened the embrace. She gazed into his eyes. He quickly covered the distance between his mouth and hers. When he finally pulled himself out of the kiss, he lifted her chin with a finger. "It will be all right." Then he turned and walked into the sea.

Long strides carried him across the waves toward the waiting ship. As he swam, he murmured a prayer for the Lord to comfort Peter's family. His arms ached when he arrived at the schooner. He turned and saw Melody watching from the rocky coast. He gave a quick salute and then tested the anchor rode, hoping it would support him enough to mount the vessel.

Padric placed hand over hand, pulling himself up the chain. When he reached the top, he stopped to catch his breath before hoisting his leg over the rail. The boat rocked gently toward him, protesting against his weight. He steadied himself on the deck and made his way toward the jolly boat. He halted at the sound of a groan.

"Peter?" He prayed it was Peter. Otherwise, Watters may have had an accomplice.

Padric moved quickly toward the moaning. He found Peter in the galley, dried blood pooled around his head and a large skillet thrown on the floor beside him. The bodies of two other men lay next to him. Padric breathed a prayer for their families and knelt beside Peter's still form.

"Peter! It's Padric Murphy. I'm here to help you."

He lifted the young man and carried him to the waiting craft. Padric struggled to lower the boat over the schooner's edge. He took turns letting each side down a little at a time to keep the craft as even as possible. Then he eased himself downward, joining the injured man in the jolly boat. Padric rowed through the rough surf. Melody's waiting form grow nearer as he cut the distance between boat and shore with each powerful thrust of the oars.

As he pulled across the shallows, he saw movement and heard a racket coming from behind Melody. Hogs were pack animals, and he uttered a quick petition that the boar he'd killed didn't have friends nearby. A moment later, Reginald and Andrew broke through the overgrowth and emerged on the rocky point next to Melody.

Thank you, Lord.

Edward, his sisters, and Enid arrived just as Padric pulled the small craft ashore.

"Peter's alive," Padric shouted, "but just barely."

"Peter? Peter Hartley is here?" Daphne pushed her way through the gathering but gasped and recoiled at the sight of the bloody young man lying in the boat.

Enid rushed forward. "I'll tend to him, Mr. Padric." She ripped a small piece of cloth from her skirt, dipped it in the cool water, and dabbed it against the blood-matted hair behind his ear.

"What happened?" Reginald glared at Padric.

Melody stepped forward. "I'm sorry I panicked last night and ran off before Padric and I could tell you about the man in the cave. He is the one who attacked Peter."

"The cave? What man?" Edward asked.

She shook her head. "Let me start from the beginning."

While Enid tended to Peter, Padric passed out pieces of roasted pork, and Melody shared about their encounter with Greyson Watters.

"So, the gold and the journal have been returned to the island." Reginald affirmed his words with a sharp nod. "I suppose our business here is done then. We need to get Peter to a doctor. How is he?"

Enid met Reginald's gaze. "It's serious, but I think he will live."

Padric turned to face Reginald. "There is one more bit of business I'd like to take care of before we return."

"And what is that, Mr. Murphy?"

"As you're the man of Mapleleaf Manor, I'd like to request your permission to have your cousin's hand in marriage."

Reginald looked back and forth between Melody and Padric. He smiled. "And I suppose you're agreeable to this request, cousin?"

"Yes. If you think Grandmother—"

Reginald shook his head and held up his hand. "I should have realized this long before now, but Grandmother has bullied us both far too long. We are adults, and it's time we made our own decisions." He put his thumbs through the buttonholes of his ragged waistcoat in a mock chest puff. "And" —he cleared his throat—"as the man of Mapleleaf Manor, I hereby grant my blessing on this union."

Enid put her hands on her hips and glared at Reginald. "And the island? You gonna let her have her half or you gonna sneak back here and steal the treasure?"

"You sure are bossy for a maid, Enid." Reginald laughed. "When we get home, I'll meet with Mr. Arnold and go through the family holdings to ensure you get your fair share of the estate." He pulled Padric and her into a bear hug and gazed upward at the foreboding tooth-shaped pillar. "As far as this island goes, I hope I never see this stretch of rock again!" He turned to face Melody. "If you want to return here and search for more gold, I certainly won't stop you."

"Want to go treasure hunting?" Melody winked at Padric.

"I have all the treasure I need right here." Padric eased out of the embrace with his soon-to-be cousin and brought his lips downward to meet those of his betrothed.

The first kiss of their engagement was interrupted by a squeal and clapping. Daphne danced around them in a circle. "Yay! A wedding! I love weddings."

Padric and Melody laughed together before resuming their kiss. One of many more kisses to come.

THE END

About Linda Fulkerson

Linda Fulkerson began her writing career as a copyeditor and typesetter at a small-town weekly newspaper. She has since been published in several magazines and newspapers, including a two-year stint as a sports writer, and is the author of two novels and several non-fiction books. In 2020, she purchased Mantle Rock Publishing's backlist and founded Scrivenings Press LLC.

She and her husband, Don, live on a ten-acre plot in central Arkansas. They have four adult children and eight grandchildren. Linda enjoys photography, RV travel, and spoiling her two dachshunds.

ISLAND *Mayhem*

Elena Hill

June 18, 1937

Off the coast of Savannah, Georgia

"Mayday Mayday! Goin ... down!"

The crackling radio tore Wilhelmina from her evening chores.

"Willie ca— ... –ear me?"

Wilhelmina turned the dial, desperately attempting to clear the signal. "This is Willie. Over."

Nothing.

She needed to hear where Lou was. "I hear you, Lou. What are your coordinates? Over."

"—see land, turn ... back. Try to—"

"Lou?" Wilhelmina wrung her hands. This can't be happening. They were just going to do a circle. Louise promised it would be routine, and she'd be home by supper.

"Find ...Willie! Yo ... fin ... us."

Lord, where are they? She never mentioned where they were flying—just 'over the ocean.' They could be anywhere. Please Lord, protect them.

Chapter One

Three Days Earlier

Tuesday Morning, June 15

Louise Krause attempted to condense masses of fabric into the tiny carrying case yet again. Why was she even bothering with the parachute? She never used them. Throwing her hands up, she shoved the nuisance aside.

Wilhelmina had been rebuilding an engine but chose that moment to peer across their workshop, a gleam in her knowing eyes. This once-cramped airplane hangar was the perfect size for the small mechanic shop Wilhelmina now ran.

"Dorothy Lou—"

"Stop it. Y-you ... just ... don't."

"I'm sorry." She set down her wrench. "Lou ..." Wilhelmina walked toward her, reaching out as if to console her. "I should never have—"

"No. You shouldn't. It's *her* name. Not mine." Louise wiped an errant tear as she jerked her shoulder away, returning to the abandoned parachute. "Never mine," she mumbled.

The long silence was deafening.

Wilhelmina squeezed Louise's shoulder and returned to the engine parts strewn across the workbench. "So, tell me. Why are you messing with that 'chute? Good news?"

Louise inhaled, regulating her breathing. She couldn't stay angry with Wilhelmina. And she did have good news. The best news.

"Your man Stanley secured a GeeBee." Louise hesitated. Did Willie know how big this was? "They want me to fly my playboy boss and his trusty sidekick before purchase." Here was the catch. "Over the Atlantic."

"Would you be comfortable doing that? I mean, how long has it been since you've taxied anyone? And have you even flown over water?"

"Of course, I have."

Wilhelmina's eyebrows shot up as she glared at Louise. Oh no—that look again. Louise might have been hasty when answering. No one needed to know she'd only flown over lakes and rivers—never the ocean. But she could do it. How hard could it be? Amelia Earhart flew to Hawaii just last month. Now she was making a trip around the world. Louise only needed to navigate the seas for a few miles, not the whole ocean. She could do this.

"Since we lost the biplane, I've only made maintenance flights for clients. No passengers. Not since before Atlanta." Louise tilted her head back in thought. "So, more than a year."

"Uh-huh. And you want your first passengers to be your boss and longtime crush?"

Louise remained silent, hoping Wilhelmina's concentration with the engine repair would quell her questions. She wasn't sure she wanted any passengers ever again. But this was the opportunity of a lifetime for any pilot—especially a female one.

The engines weren't enough of a distraction. Willie

glanced up. "Did you say a GeeBee? Aren't those the cursed planes?"

"Don't tell me you believe in curses." Louise paused, remembering poor Florence's fatal crash at the International Air Races. But designs had improved, and that was years ago. Louise would not share the same tragedy. "So, they've had a run of bad luck, but I wouldn't say ... cursed."

"Then why are you packing a 'chute? You never use those." Wilhelmina grabbed a larger wrench and growled at the stubborn bolt.

"You said it yourself, I don't fly as often anymore. As for ferrying the boss around, I'm certain they only hired me as their bookkeeper so I could be at their beck and call." Louise threw the now neatly packed fabric on the floor. "Besides, *someone* scolds me every time I go without one."

"Scold? *Me*? Never." Wilhelmina grinned. "I merely remind you of the importance of staying safe and valuing life."

"Thank you for your vote of confidence," Louise placed the parachute in the cubby containing all her flight gear and glanced at the wall clock. Grabbing another unraveled mess, she headed back to her corner. She could repack at least one more parachute before work.

"I trust you, but maybe not the plane." Willie wiped her greasy hands on a rag after the bolt finally broke loose. "I hate that you had to stop nursing school this semester, but I'm glad you get a chance to fly again." Taking a deep breath, she attacked the next bolt. "So, just Eugene and Augustus?"

"Yeah. I wish Augustus would pester someone else. It's bad enough to have the playboy boss man, I don't need his guard dog too." Louise finished the second 'chute much faster than the first. "Every time Augustus comes in with Eugene, I struggle to concentrate. His penetrating gaze and statue-like posture make me squirm."

"I'm sure his muscular physique and dive-into-me blue eyes, have nothing to do with your distraction." Wilhelmina waggled her eyebrows as she placed her tools back in their proper cubbies. "Enjoy your close quarters." Willie let a giggle slip before asking, "When is the grand adventure?"

Heat crept up Louise's neck. "Here, put this up too." Louise tossed the tightly packed bag to Willie hoping her cheeks remained unflushed. "Oh, look at the time. I must go, or I'll be late for my real job." She grabbed her purse and ducked her head as she scurried across the hangar. "We fly Friday."

"What do we want for supper?" Willie asked.

"Your choice. I'll likely be late. The books are killing me this week." She flung open the door and hesitated. "I know I've only been there a month, but it's a wonder they stayed afloat all these years. Their records are a mess. I'm trying to reevaluate the last six months." Louise crossed the threshold calling back, "Worst case, I'll bring them home to you."

"Miss 'I can figure sums in my sleep' wants my help? I feel honored," Wilhelmina shouted after a retreating Louise.

Louise walked the four blocks to Astor Realty. Excitement about the upcoming flight bubbled inside her. She was going to fly again.

Even after ...

No. She smiled at each passerby, refusing to get her spirits down. As she approached the quaint office, she stooped to pet the neighborhood stray. Today would be a glorious day.

The doorbell chimed as she entered. Nodding to Stanley, she took her seat behind the oak desk. Good. No Augustus. Maybe she could get some work done without distraction. Even in school he was a distraction. She may have been four years his junior, but she'd still noticed him. Who didn't notice him? He was the silent star of the football team. With his arm and skills, he could have gone to any college, but he remained here, keeping his best friend out of trouble.

Shaking away the memories of yesteryears, Louise focused on the records before her. The figures awaited. She pulled out expense ledgers for April, May, and June.

After eight hours, three more ledgers, and several cups of coffee, Louise was off over seven hundred dollars rather than the sixty-two that had concerned her last night.

Where was the money?

Yesterday she'd assumed the previous clerk just made errors here and there, but today ... After digging back as far as January, nothing added up. There was almost a rhythm to the missing sums, but she couldn't put her finger on it.

Could it be Eugene? He did buy a new Ford Coupe last month, and now this GeeBee ...

No. No way. But money was missing. A pattern indicated someone was taking it. Rigid, by-the-book Stanley couldn't be the culprit, so who else but Eugene? She wasn't wrong about the skewed records. This was deliberate.

What was that annoying echo? The numbers blurred.

"Miss Lou-ise?"

Startled out of her stupor, Louise glanced up to see Stanley hovering over her desk, coat in hand.

"There now. What seems to be bothering you?"

Should she bring up her suspicions? He was partner in the company, after all. Astor Realty might hold Eugene's name and claim him as the face, but Stanley was the brains behind all business decisions. They never could have survived the Depression, much less excelled, without Stanley's brilliance.

"Oh, hello, Stanley." Louise forced what she hoped was an innocent sounding giggle. "I didn't know you were still here."

"I'm off now, ma'am. That is, unless you need something."

"No. Thank you." Louise started to gather her belongings, hoping Stanley would leave without her. Yet, knowing he was a gentleman, she didn't hold her breath. "I'm right behind you."

She needed to take the documents home to Wilhelmina. Between the two of them, they could make sense of the mess.

Stanley hesitated, holding the door. His tight facial features resembled a toad's. What did Willie see in him?

It was no use. Giving up all pretense, she sat back down. "Stanley, something is wrong."

How to put her assumptions into words? "The books ... I fear I've missed something."

Stanley returned to her desk, setting down his briefcase. "Let me see."

"Here." Louise punctuated the statement by placing her finger where the errors began.

Several minutes passed before Stanley glanced up. "This is January's ledger, silly girl. Is Friday's flight already getting to you? The month is June."

With a hard swallow, Louise replied, "Yes, sir. I know. I just ... well ... it seems ... I had to go back that far to find the start. I will soon have this figured out." Her final words spilled out like a waterfall. She needed this job. Louise didn't give up her dreams of nursing only to fail her first month as a bookkeeper.

"You've spent all day on this, have you not? Put these figures on my desk. I'll see to it later this week." Stanley reached for his case. "Goodness knows it will take far more than a glance to untangle this mess."

A truer statement could not be uttered.

"Sir, I apologize. I assure you I am good with numbers. Please. Give me some more time, and I will fix this." Once he started digging, would he, like her, assume the worst of Eugene? Would they fire her?

Stanley attempted a supportive smile but his gaunt features and crooked nose failed to convey empathy. "Don't fret, my dear. We will see that all is right." He scooped up the papers, transferring them from her desk to the top drawer of his. "You just concentrate on Friday. I wouldn't want something to happen to my partner or our newest employee."

WILHELMINA PEERED at the darkening sky. Louise should have been home already. No need to have a cold supper. She placed the savory dish back in the warming box. Lou mentioned the books before leaving this morning. Could those numbers really be bothering her? She should be stressing over how to tend to patients and learning the way of a nurse—not holed up in an office with two men all day.

Wilhelmina fiddled with the flower arrangement on the table. This bouquet was one of her favorites, with little yellow buttercups contrasting the blue-violet asters. She prayed as she waited.

Thank you, Lord, for sharing your beauty and creation with me. Help me to see Your handiwork daily. Lord, I don't want to sound like a broken record, but give us means to send Lou back to nursing school in the fall. She belongs there, Lord. Tending to the sick, pouring her passion into something with meaning, not risking life and limb soaring through the heavens.

Wilhelmina squeezed her eyes tighter, One day they would catch a break. Who knew—maybe she could attend school too.

The door slammed, and Lou materialized. Nothing like perfect timing.

Your will not mine, Lord. In Your Son's name I pray. Amen.

Finishing her prayer, she grabbed her oven mitts and placed the potato casserole on the table.

"That smells divine. Sorry I'm late," Lou flung off her heels.

Wilhelmina smiled to herself. Lou tried so hard to fit in as a society woman, but it was obvious she preferred dungarees and men's boots. "No bother, 'tis still warm. How was work?"

"Frustrating."

"So, I get to go cross-eyed reviewing numbers?" Wilhelmina laughed, trying to ease Lou's tension.

"No. Stanley took them. The longer I reviewed the books, the more errors I found. They're missing nearly seven hundred dollars. He questioned me, so I guess my confusion showed." Louise ran her hands through her short wavy locks, making the already frizzy hair stand on end. Now she matched her hero—Albert Einstein—in not only brains, but looks. "How could I miss the discrepancy my first few weeks? Have I been that distracted lately?"

Wilhelmina patted her hand. "I'm sure all is well."

"I fear it's not." Louise scooped a heaping spoonful of casserole onto her plate. "Eugene is skimming. I didn't have the heart to tell Stanley tonight, but I'm sure he will notice soon enough. No way that much money disappears innocently."

"Eugene? But why? He has plenty of money. Besides, it's his company."

"Astor may be Eugene's family, and the public recognizes his pretty-boy face, but you and I both know who built the wealth. Stanley wouldn't allow Eugene to take more than his share."

"Oh, Lou, don't be so hard on them. Both are good men." Wilhelmina took a dainty bite before finishing her thought. "Trust that all is well, and it was just a misunderstanding. Who knows, maybe they forgot to give you a receipt along the way?"

"*Trust. It will be fine.* Let me guess—now you're going to tell me to pray about it too." Louise slammed down her fork and stood. "Willie, you don't get it. The world is full of bad people.

You can't just wish them good." Louise scrapped her nearly full plate back into the dish before stomping over to the sink.

At least she saved the food this time. They couldn't afford to trash any of it.

"I do believe prayer will help." Wilhelmina sighed. *What could she say to help Lou get over her anger and distrust of everyone?* Losing Papa Krause had pushed her farther from God than ever before. It was a wonder Lou trusted her. "Pray for both men. If there is embezzlement involved, it will be a difficult road to travel for all of you."

Chapter Two

A little after midnight
Wednesday, June 16

When would these midnight rendezvous stop? Soon. Once Astor was gone. Remus didn't know how to kill anyone. He needed help—thus the meeting.

Would Doc come in person or send his henchman Little Benny? Neither was welcome, but either was necessary.

Remus's heartrate thundered and his palms became clammy. Surely there would be an easier way to get rid of Astor than with his bare hands. Well, now there were two ...

That floozy figured it out. How? No matter, it was done. Her fate was sealed the moment she pointed out the missing money. She had to go, too, but when?

Together? That would work. Friday's flight? Yes. But how?

Maybe Doc would have some ideas.

Where was he? It was well after midnight.

The alley smelled of stale wine and cat urine. Why here?

Why couldn't they meet at the bar uptown? At least enjoy a drink or two during their "talk."

Remus checked his watch again. Already a quarter to one. Should he leave? He hated being in this predicament. Waiting. Like a lap dog. The longer he waited, the worse the smell nauseated him.

He'd need a drink after this meeting, or maybe a round at the tables ...

No, he couldn't go back to the tables. That was what got him here in the first place. A simple hundred-dollar advance. Then another. And another.

Two thousand dollars. How had he let it go that far, and in less than six months? Five hundred percent interest didn't sound that daunting the first time, but after four or five advances, it added up.

Remus was drowning in debt. That was it—drowning. The sea could make those two troublemakers go away. Let it take away all his worries. But how? Doc would know.

Just when Remus was ready to give up on the meeting, Little Benny rounded the corner. "Let's walk."

Chapter Three

Thursday Evening
June 17

"Here?"

"Yes, here. Isn't that great?" Louise jumped up and down, emphasizing the statement. If only Papa could see her now. Their hangar would hold a prestigious plane. Granted, she wouldn't own it, but they were housing it for several nights.

"Where will we put a plane, Lou?" Wilhelmina spun in circles scanning the small space. "I barely have room to store my current projects, much less add a plane to the mix."

"Calm down. This space was designed to be a hangar. Besides, we had Papa's old biplane in here until last year, and you still worked out of the same space."

"Okay, I guess it can stay, but that is a lot of responsibility. What if something happens to it?"

"Don't worry about it. Eugene said nothing would be our fault. It just needs a home until our flight Friday." Louise rearranged her flight gear, trying to create a bigger place. She looked over at the strewn engine pieces and tools. Willie was right. Space would be tight here, but they needed this.

"Then it's gone by Saturday, right?" Wilhelmina crossed her arms and set her feet in a fighting stance. Better not push anymore buttons.

"Yes. Gone by Saturday."

"Fine then. Tell Eugene I agree."

"No need. His pilot just landed, and the plane is being taxied over now."

"What? You agreed without asking?"

Louise grinned and gave Willie a half hug. "I told him to give me twenty minutes to convince you." Squinting at the clock, she said, "What do you know? It only took me seven."

Louise shivered with excitement. She couldn't believe she was truly in the presence of a GeeBee, and in less than twenty-four hours, she would be flying it. She glanced at Willie. Would she remain huffy? No. As soon as the glorious red machine rolled in, Willie's taut shoulders slackened, and a squeal escaped her lips.

Good. She's as giddy as I am.

Scanning the room, Louise noted her strapping young boss had brought his sidekick along with the delivery crew. Why did Augustus have to come with Eugene? Never mind Willie was right—his good looks were likely the culprit behind Louise's distraction, but she didn't like his pompous aura. Nonetheless, she refused to let him stifle her joy.

The wheels stopped rolling, and the plane settled in the corner of the small hangar. She jogged over and climbed into the cockpit. It was more spacious than she'd guessed but would still be tight tomorrow with both men joining her.

She scrambled out of the seat, jumped down, and ran her fingers down the cool metal. A girl could dream. But, for now, the dream was coming true—it was hers.

Chapter Four

Wee Hours of the Morning
Friday, June 18

Remus stumbled in the dark toward the covered plane. He refused to kill them personally, so this had to work. Why did she have to be so meticulous?

Little Benny swore it would be easy. Remus hoped he was right.

He needed something. A jug. Yes, there along the wall. That would hold the fuel. Surely no one would look to see if there was an extra.

This *would* be easy. Seen as human error or incompetence of the fairer sex.

All Remus had to do was cut the signal wire from the float to the fuel gauge. Easy, right? Significantly easier if he could see. Could he risk turning on the overhead light?

Gripping the flashlight he'd brought along for the midnight adventure, he flicked on the beam. It would have to do. The eerie yellow tint made this spacious room creepier. He ignored the shadows dancing along the walls and lifted the tarp. He cut the sender wire.

Now, for the messy part. Fiddling with the borrowed cutters, he walked across the room, set the tool on a container, and grabbed an empty fuel jug. He placed the large vessel beneath the plane's fuel tank. How much did it hold? Tapping the metal, the dull thud indicated the tank was full—as expected. The soft, rhythmic sound of fluid cascading out soothed Remus. This wasn't that hard. He knocked on the tank a final time, smiling at the echoing ting. Empty, or nearly.

Remus scanned the room for signs he'd been here. All was good. The jug was nestled back in its place. The tarp pulled tightly over the plane's nose.

Was he missing anything?

No. Time to leave. He could finally get his beauty sleep, for tomorrow all his troubles would ... pass away.

Chapter Five

Friday, June 18

Louise tried to catch Stanley's attention when he entered the office after the noon meal.

"Mr. Stanley, sir? Did you by chance have time to check those records?" Louise wrung her hands and avoided eye contact.

"Not yet. Edgar is coming over this evening." He brushed past her to his desk. "Not to worry. We will figure it out."

Louise sank back into her chair, trying to concentrate on her task at hand. Edgar? Was that who she replaced? For now, she had a job. But would she still, once he discovered how much money was missing? Could he fire her for revealing the discrepancies, or worse, would he accuse her of theft?

"Miss Louise, dear, shouldn't you be readying yourself and your flying machine? Don't get me wrong—" He hesitated and gave a nervous sounding chuckle as he made a swooping gesture. "—You look lovely. But is that outfit suitable for flight?"

She peered down at her floral dress and two-inch pumps.

No. She would never fly in this, but Astor made it perfectly clear that she must dress like a lady while at work. She had time, although Stanley was right—she needed to go home before heading to the hangar. And she still needed to go over the pre-flight.

"No, sir. I must change first, but I still have some—"

"Go now. This will wait until Monday." He nodded at her desk. "I'd much rather have you relaxed as you take my partner up in that contraption. We can't have anything happening to you now, can we?"

His nonchalance helped put her at ease. He patted her shoulders and sent her on her way.

After rushing home, she stood before her bureau, pulling out clothes. Should she wear proper women's trousers or the more practical dungaree overalls? Staring into space, she visioned herself wearing her high-waisted khakis, complimented by a navy-blue blouse, laughing and walking toward a sunset, hand-in-hand with Augustus.

What am I doing? I don't need a man.

She donned the trusty dungarees and well-worn men's boots. Still going for practical, she pulled on a long-sleeved work shirt. Her outfit was warm for June, but necessary in the cockpit. Papa's voice echoed in her mind, "Best to be fully covered and protected, because one never knows what could happen during flight."

There, on the nightstand, sat her father's old pocketknife. She picked it up, fingering the wooden handle. Closing her eyes, she muttered to the nothingness, "Miss you, Papa." She tucked the only piece of him she had left safely into the large pocket of her dungarees and headed to the door. Refusing to cry, she locked up her and Willie's one-room cottage.

THIS WAS IT. Louise had taxied the GeeBee from their small hangar to a private runway. Her stomach twisted in knots. She had flown several different planes, but never one so splendid as this. She hurried about, making any last-minute flight preparations. She reminded herself flight checklists don't care what model was being flown, just that the aircraft was ready to go.

Oh, how she wished Papa were still here to see this day—that it would be him with her soaring over the seas, not Eugene and Augustus. If not with Papa, then she longed to fly alone. But Eugene needed to be aboard to see if an island was a worthy investment.

Too bad Eugene only wanted this beauty as a loan and was more interested in buying Sharktooth Island. Who would want a lousy island that wasn't even on the map when he could have this luxury for a third the price?

Louise continued readying the plane, referencing the checklist. Parachutes—three were tucked into the tiny cockpit. How would they all fit if there was barely room for her?

Maybe if it were just her and Eugene, but propriety called for a chaperone, so there would be three of them. If socialites thought hanky-panky could happen in a cockpit mid-flight, they were way off base. Crowding three people in a space meant for two was more unacceptable to Louise than being alone with Eugene. She removed the 'chutes. One would do them no good, and there just wasn't room for all three.

Peering across the room, she checked the time. Only three, and the flight wasn't scheduled until four o'clock. Setting down her clipboard, Louise perched on a stool near Willie's workbench, recalling last night's conversation with Eugene. He'd emphasized that he had no plans of buying the aircraft—he just needed quick and easy access to some mysterious island southeast. He quoted a rumor stating the island held treasure, yet it also possessed a curse. Thankfully, Willie was still tidying up and missed hearing the tales and legends.

After the brief discussion with Eugene and knowing Willie was already leery of the racer's curse, Louise stated that the flight was merely a luxury ride. Nothing fancy, and no need to see them off. They would fly for an hour and be home before dinner. There was no need to worry.

She marked off the last item on her list and squinted at the clock's face once again. It was time. All was set. They had refueled last night before leaving the hangar. Instruments and radios good. Propeller good. The engine purred like a kitten, ready for takeoff. Now, where were the guys?

"Mayday Mayday! Goin ... down!"

The crackling radio tore Wilhelmina from her evening chores.

"Willie ca— ... –ear me?" Wilhelmina turned the dial, desperately attempting to clear the signal. "This is Willie. Over."

Nothing.

She needed to hear where Lou was. "I hear you, Lou. What are your coordinates? Over."

"—see land, turn ... back. Try to—"

"Lou?" Wilhelmina wrung her hands. This can't be happening. They were just going to do a circle. Louise promised it would be routine, and she'd be home by supper.

"Find ...Willie! Yo ... fin ... us."

Lord, where are they? She never mentioned where they were flying just 'over the ocean.' They could be anywhere, Lord. Protect them.

Frantically, Wilhelmina's fingers moved by rote memory as

she turned the dial, scanning all channels, searching for any more clues. This wasn't happening. Still nothing. No signal, not even static. Louise was gone. What could she do? Stanley. Yes, he should have coordinates, or at least a direction, right? It was his partner's investment, after all.

Wilhelmina sprinted down to Astor Realty. Barging in, she scanned the room for Stanley. "T-the plane ... dow ... on!" She shook uncontrollably. The sobs came so fast and hard, she feared she would pass out.

Stanley rose. Striding over to her in two steps, he settled his hands on her shoulders. "Calm down. Take a breath. Now try again. What's wrong?"

Wilhelmina took a final sob and closed her eyes, "Lou. There was a mayday call from Lou." She paced toward the corner chair, only then seeing a second man peering over ledgers sprawled on the desk. Taking a deep breath, she sat and slowly repeated her dilemma, "The plane crashed. I lost signal. I can't accept that they are gone without looking. What can we do?"

Stanley gazed out the front window. "Let's go see if they left a flight log."

Leaving the stranger behind, the two headed back to Wilhelmina's workshop.

"Do you know the coordinates? Or where they were headed? Lou told me nothing." Her words flowed faster than her jogging pace. "We have to tell the Coast Guard something, so they can begin a search."

"Darkness will soon be upon us. Let me make some calls and set out in the morning. No need to involve the military unless we fail to find them tomorrow."

Willie glanced back as she entered the mechanic shop. "Stanley, can we wait that long? How can they survive?"

Longing for a reassuring hug or words with better comfort,

she scrutinized Stanley's hazel eyes. She recognized determination. He could do this. He would save her best friend.

Stepping backward, Stanley said, "I have only the legend. The Coast Guard will want more. Let me set up a search party. We will regroup tomorrow."

"Legend?"

"Didn't Lou tell you? They were flying to Sharktooth Island."

Chapter Six

Louise pulled harder on the stick, yet the plane continued to plummet. What was wrong? All gauges and readings showed clear, but the fast-approaching sea claimed otherwise. Eugene's death grip on the seat and Augustus's mutterings proved neither man was ready to meet his maker.

Why didn't she keep the parachutes onboard? It was going to be too crowded, and this was supposed to be an easy twenty-minute flight. Oh, well, nothing she could do. They were going down. Now.

"Brace yourselves. This will be rough, but I think I can land us."

"Where?" Eugene's roving eyes scanned the seas.

"Back on your mysterious island."

Augustus tucked his head between his knees.

"I wouldn't do that." Louise pulled on his shirt collar, then pointed at her control panel. "This dash won't survive the impact."

Both men blanched.

"Don't worry. We'll survive, but the plane won't. I think it's better to sit up than snap your neck by cowering." Louise calmly tried the radio one last time, but it was no use. "Ready boys? Here we go ..."

Time stood still.

The forceful landing thrust all three forward, slamming their heads into the dashboard. Louise eyed the right wing as it quivered. In slow motion, the once sturdy extension severed from the plane's body and flew past the cockpit. The now lopsided fuselage coasted aimlessly through the shoals. Finally, the wreckage settled. Did they survive?

Louise flinched as a bloodcurdling scream ripped through the silence. "Wha—"

"My leg!" Augustus's words echoed throughout the small space.

Springing into action, Louise unbuckled and popped the top off the cockpit. They had to get out of here. No telling how long the plane's body would rest on this rock. She had no idea how deep the water was, but she refused to succumb to a watery grave after managing the landing.

"Eugene, are you hurt? Can you move? Augustus needs help." She tried to keep her voice steady, but they must act fast.

"I hit my head, but I-I think I'm okay."

She considered how to free Augustus's leg. The plane's nose had crumpled like an accordion, and the mess rested on his lap. Too much pulling could cause more damage. A quick assessment proved he had no compound fractures, but blood oozed through his pant leg.

"Good. Grab his arm. This plane is going to sink."

Struggling to think despite the ringing of her ears and the spinning surroundings, Louise pulled Papa's pocketknife from her dungarees. She cut Augustus's pants, freeing his leg but revealing a large gash. One problem at a time. Get out of this mess, then they could patch up the guard dog.

Chapter Seven

Alive? They were still alive, how could this be? Did he not empty out enough fuel? Doc would be furious if he found out they survived the crash. If. If he found out. And *if* they survived.

Remus's head ached, and he longed for a drink to clear his mind and calm his nerves. But that would have to wait. For now, he needed to act the part. Be the concerned friend, find the chump, and kill him.

He would search high and low. Search not for the blubbering idiot, but for himself. Doc demanded payment. And he would get it.

Remus had to negotiate with Little Benny last week. He claimed Doc would accept Astor's death, since Remus was due to inherit. A watery grave for Astor. That was all he had to do—drown the sap, and his worries would wash away.

But no. He survived.

Chapter Eight

Cutting Augustus free took far too long. Thank goodness for long sleeves. Eugene aided in tying off the gash, but they were barely able to stanch the bleeding. The two managed to half swim, half drag the semi-conscious Augustus through the shoals.

Although the waters were shallow, the crags and seabed were unforgiving. Eugene nearly drowned when he caught his ankle on some seaweed that pulled him under. By pure luck, they found a rhythm and made it to shore.

Louise gasped for air as their trio sank onto the island's rocky shore. They made it. How long had it been? She peered at her unticking watch—no use. She gazed at the sky. There, on the horizon, not only was the sun sinking, but so was their ride home. The fuselage bobbed. Only the cockpit was visible above the waves.

How could this happen? It must be nearing eight o'clock.

Eugene's voice ripped Louise from her reverie. "What of Gus's leg? Can you fix it before we lose daylight?"

Right. *Focus, Louise. You have training. These men are depending on you.*

Shaking her head to clear her thoughts, she muttered, "Go get some of your seaweed. We'll use it as bandage. And maybe a stick, for balance."

As Eugene retreated back to the water's edge, she eased Augustus higher on the scant shore for better lighting. The setting sun reminded her they would need shelter, too, but that would have to come later.

She softened her voice, speaking as if Augustus were a child. "This will hurt." Spying a small stick, she handed it to him. "Here. Bite down. I'm going to pull away the makeshift bandage and feel if the bones are broken."

"Do what you must." His clipped words did nothing to hide his pain. He clenched the stick between his teeth.

Electricity zinged through Louise as she ran her hand along his ankle. *That was strange.* Did he feel it too? Shaking away those thoughts, she continued her inspection and carefully grazed her hands beside the raw, torn flesh of his shin.

"Let me see if your knee will bend ... slowly." Gently, she took his bare leg in her hands, easing it upward and toward his torso. Good. Based on touch, just the gash. No fractures. The real trick would be to keep infection out of the wound. The long period of seawater lapping against the wound should have helped clean out any debris.

"Does anywhere else hurt?" She gingerly brushed the back of her hand across his forehead as if to soothe him, all the while checking for heat of fever or clamminess of shock. Warm. As he should be.

Spitting out the stick, he gave her a wobbly smile. "No. Just that scratch." The scoundrel had the audacity to wink.

Eugene scurried over to them and handed her several strands of seaweed and a large limb. "Will these work?"

Not the supplies she was accustomed to, but they would do. After ensuring Augustus's "scratch" was clean, Louise secured his leg with the slimy mess.

Turning her attention from Augustus to Eugene, she said, "Now, let's have a look at you. Anything hurt?" She gave him a quick-once over.

With a rueful smile, Eugene pointed to a knot on his forehead. "Want to kiss this goose egg better?"

Two winks in less than an hour. A girl could get used to this.

"He'll live. Now let's look for shelter." Augustus made to stand, but Louise and Eugene set hands on his shoulders in unison.

"Hold your horses, cowboy. Let's not ruin Miss Louise's handiwork."

"Why don't you two stay here, and I'll gather some firewood, seeing as how I'm the only uninjured one." Louise refrained from winking but gave each man a smile, hightailing it up to the tree line before they had a chance to stop her escape.

Louise scanned her surroundings—nothing but trees and rocks. The last of the sun's light ebbed. Darkness would soon fall. How long had she been wandering? Ten minutes? Twenty? She should take her meager stack of wood back down to the men. Would they be here long enough to need this? *Did Willie hear enough of her transmission to send help? Why did she agree to fly to this cursed island?*

Eugene had spent the entire flight telling of pirates, lost treasure, and curses. He claimed that anyone who dared trespass on the island would come to an untimely end—of course that fact was what spurred this whole trip into action. From the air, she'd deemed the island uninhabited, so maybe there was truth to the tales. Louise didn't wish to find out.

Somehow, she wandered out of view of the shore. *No, I won't fall prey to the curse.* Louise backtracked, picking up her pace. With night falling and the distraction of eerie noises, she tripped on a large stone. Throwing her precious firewood skyward, she thrust out her hands to break the fall, but she instead took hold of a crude opening.

A cave? Shelter for the night, perhaps? Refusing to become the island's next victim, she left her sticks and marched back to the shore.

Squinting through the twilight, she found the duo where she'd left them. "Do you think we can move? I found a cave over by the tree line." Pointing in the direction from where she'd come, she said, "I left my kindling by the entrance. We can rest there for the night."

"Here buddy, give me your hand. We'll have you up and running in no time." Eugene's slight nod in her direction proved he perceived the risks they were taking with Augustus's injury. Maybe she'd judged the playboy wrong. He acted levelheaded.

"Do you think anything else is using your cave for shelter?" Augustus asked through gritted teeth.

"I sure hope not, but we can get a fire going at the entrance, then investigate."

Eugene chimed in, "I vote we draw straws to see who gets to explore."

"Why? Are you scared?" Louise said as they drew up to the entrance.

"Of course not, but I didn't want to steal your chance." Eugene gave her his second wink of the night.

When they reached the opening, she asked, "So, were

either of you Boy Scouts? I don't know how we are going to start our fire without supplies."

"Ease me down here." Augustus pointed to the stone Louise must have tripped on earlier. "Bring your kindling back up here. I think if we get it stacked just right, I can use friction to make a spark and start a flame."

Louise gathered some smaller twigs. She hoped Augustus understood what he was talking about. A fire would serve many purposes tonight—light, warmth, and protection.

Chapter Nine

Late Evening
Friday, June 18

Remus paced the small alleyway. How did they survive? He needed a fix. Doc didn't have to know. Just one or two bets in the back alley—to clear his head. Then he'd make a plan.

Doc had given him until the twenty-first to pay up his two thousand or kill Astor. Should he give up on the killing and work on getting the money?

Remus was still short four hundred, but with some luck he could earn it back tonight, then he wouldn't have to worry with Astor or the doll.

Well, he still needed to deal with the girl. One way or another—she was onto him. No one could know he'd been skimming off the Astors.

Just one or two bets. To clear his head.

Remus walked to a lesser-known craps game. He couldn't afford to let Doc see him at his usual hangout.

Remus threw the dice at an angle, banging them against the back wall. Seven or eleven. Seven or eleven. Seven or ...

Snake eyes. Again. How could this be?

Three hours later Remus was down nearly two hundred. Should he attempt a double or nothing? No, that's what got him in this mess. He started the night hot with a seven, then met his point on the next two rolls. He rolled an eleven but got cocky with a double or nothing bet and started rolling snake eyes, over and over. Now, he needed to stop and figure out how he could come up with six hundred dollars in forty-eight hours.

Was that Little Benny? A bulky man pushed through the crowd with ease. The streetlight provided just enough glow to show Benny's pearly whites in a smile of recognition.

Drat. They found him. And with just a few questions, they'd learn he just lost two hundred.

Remus stooped to pick up his latest bet before the dice were thrown. No use waiting for the inevitable. He had to leave. Now.

Tonight's losing sealed the deal. He scrambled to blend into the crowd before Little Benny caught up with him. Remus ducked down a side street and ran for home. No need sobering up, he didn't want to be lucid for what happened next.

He would have to find Astor. And kill him.

Chapter Ten

Saturday Morning, June 19

Louise woke to smoke wafting in from the remaining embers and soft light entering the cave. They survived the night. If she were on speaking terms with the Lord, she'd thank Him.

Easing around the still snoring men, she left the comfort of shelter to seek food. Her rumbling stomach reminded her she hadn't eaten since breakfast yesterday. What sort of sustenance could this island offer?

Louise began her exploration by heading to the coastline. She wanted to get a good look at the crash site now that there was light and no panic. About two hundred yards offshore, she could see a wing and part of the fuselage sticking out the of the water. She remembered the water being fairly shallow. While it took them much longer last night, she should be able to make the swim in a half-hour today. Maybe the radio managed to stay dry. If so, she could try again to reach Willie.

Pacing along the beach, she refused to spend more effort on

what-ifs. They needed food. Then she could trudge back to the wreckage to call for help. Where were the cattails? Didn't Willie say those were edible? Or did she say those were only freshwater? Why did Louise ignore her friend's never-ending knowledge and survival skills?

As she wandered back toward their camp, she remembered seaweed clinging to her legs last night on the swim to shore. That was for sure edible, but she'd save it as a last resort. She wanted real food. But what? Berries, maybe? Melodic hymns of songbirds hung in the morning breeze. Paydirt. Where there were birds, there were berries.

Moving farther inland, she hit the jackpot. Using the overalls' flap, she created a pouch in her dungarees and filled it with the various berries. Louise's mouth began to water. They needed fresh water too. For now, the berries alone would have to do the trick.

Did Eugene mention a waterfall in all his tales? That would be bliss.

She peered skyward. Maybe the overcast skies would turn into a light summer shower. She dreaded the possibility of those beautiful clouds turning into a terrible thunderstorm instead. Either way, they should make some sort of system to catch the water—just in case.

Murmurs filtered out of the cave's entrance as Louise rounded the last corner. Then a frantic Eugene emerged.

"There you are!"

"What's wrong? Has Augustus's leg worsened?" Louise jogged the last few steps, making sure to sidestep the still smoldering fire.

"No. We just woke to you missing. Why would you leave without telling us?"

So, they do care if I'm gone. "Sorry to bring alarm, but I figured after a fitful night you needed your beauty sleep."

Trying to lighten the mood, Louise pointed to Eugene's typically pristine hair, now mussed. "Clearly it didn't work, though."

"Very funny." Eugene self-consciously finger combed his hair as the two entered the cave.

"Good. You found her." Augustus was still pale but had energy enough to rise.

"She was never *lost*, and therefore couldn't be *found*," Louise said as she pulled berries out of her pockets. "Both of you sit. Let's eat and discuss how we plan to escape this cursed island."

"Don't be ridiculous." The edge in Eugene's voice proved Louise would not sway him to her side of the argument. How did he not see the logic in her plan?

"Both of you calm down." Of course, Augustus would call for order. Back to good old guard dog instead of helpless invalid.

Louise took a deep breath, "I am calm. Give me one good reason why we can't at least *try* my plan. As long as the radio isn't underwater, I can get it to work."

"How do you plan to get to that mess to even see if the radio's busted or not?"

"I swam here, didn't I? I can swim back."

Maintaining an even, logical tone, Augustus's baritone chimed back in, "Eugene, are you clear headed this morning? Can you manage to go with—"

"Wait! Are you serious? You think this plan has merit?"

Louise nearly squealed with joy. Never in a million years did she think Augustus would agree, let alone back her.

"No, I don't think it will work at all." At Augustus's reply,

Louise's heart sank. "But I think we can use the canvas from the wings to make a raft. And if you both go, you can bring back twice the supplies in a single trip."

Louise's face flushed as she tried not to scream at the men. "So, I'm supposed to risk my life hauling back supplies and you aren't even going to let me try to call for help first?"

"By all means, try to radio out while you are at the wreckage, but I don't think it will work." Augustus nestled himself back down into a seated position, wincing as he said, "No extra risk of life and limb if you plan to go anyway, but I do want you to bring back some fabric. Oh, and if any wood from the fuselage is usable, try to bring it back too."

"Fine." Louise turned toward the sea. "We'd better go now, or we'll waste another day."

As she stormed off, she could hear both Augustus and Eugene muttering back and forth. "Maybe she is right. A radio call will be easier than trying to construct and control a raft out of here."

"You think that thing will work after a dunk? It didn't work when we were in the air!"

"At least humor her, but don't be all day about it."

"You don't have to tell me to hurry. I don't want to tempt the curse."

"There isn't a curse. It ..."

Louise finally walked beyond earshot. The shoreline was much closer this morning where the tide crept up. She slid off her boots and waded into the water. No need making them any soggier—they were almost dry from last night's venture.

The stones near the water were as soft as carpet beneath her toes. Years of rough treatment beneath the waves had smoothed their surfaces. But she remembered from last night's venture that the rocks protruding above the surface were jagged and dangerous. Several times during their swim to safety, the wind had nearly thrashed their bodies against the towering crags.

A curse. Could they really be in for trouble? If half of the stories Eugene recounted as they flew were true, then the three of them were going to need some luck. Or Wilhelmina's God.

Chapter Eleven

Wilhelmina needed to work. She'd left the confines of their small cottage and flower garden, choosing instead to be productive. But what to do? Her focus waned, and her heart was not in it today. Down the street, Stanley was gathering men and organizing the search party. He claimed it would be best for her to sit close to the radio. In case ...

She assumed he refused to deal with a blubbering female, should they discover the worst. Wilhelmina could not lose Louise. She was more than a friend, after all. They were raised as sisters. The girls met in grade school after each had lost her mother. Father was at a loss as to how to raise a child, crippled by grief, so he sought refuge in the bottle. Prohibition became his downfall, and Wilhelmina was orphaned before she reached double digits.

Thankfully, Louise's father had more sense. Nearly a dozen years ago, Papa Krause took Wilhelmina in as a second daughter. He had taught both little girls everything—from engines and flying to flowers and cooking. But he, too, was taken before his time. Everyone she loved died young. Wilhelmina shook her head. No. She could not worry before there was cause. Louise was alive. She had to be. She was a fighter.

Gathering the necessary tools, she headed to the workbench. She turned at a faint crackle. Was that—? She sprinted over to the radio. Her hands took to the dials, seeking any hint of noise.

" ... southeast ... f— miles..."

Louise? Oh, you survived the night! Thank You, Lord! But where are you? Tell me more.

"Repeat coordinates. Over."

Could she risk going over to Astor Realty to tell Stanley?

"—crashed ... on island ... sou—"

Wilhelmina remained silent willing Lou to give more information.

"Willie—"

There. She was calling her name. Definitely Louise. "Hang in there Lou. We'll find you."

After a full half-hour of silence, Willie released her pent-up breath. It was over, but ... she had something. She could assume they flew southeast a distance. Was it forty or fifty miles? Regardless, they now had a starting point.

She glanced at the clock. A quarter to ten. Would Stanley still be here? She ran to see.

The door slammed, and she lingered in the small office entrance. Stanley and Edgar hovered over a large map, surrounded by several men, standing at attention. Good—the search parties hadn't left. She could give them a direction.

"Stanley?" For all her bravado earlier, her voice barely escaped in a whisper.

"Miss Wilhelmina. May we help?"

"The radio. Another broken transmission, but I managed

to get a direction." She finally fully stepped inside, wringing her hands together as her message sailed from her mouth, "They flew southeast. Forty or fifty miles. They're on an island."

LOUISE THREW ASIDE the crackling radio. While she fiddled with the knobs, willing Wilhelmina's voice to tune in, Eugene was hacking away at the wings and tail fins. Who could have guessed a propeller blade was sharp enough to saw wood?

She was wrong—the radio was useless.

Now to throw all efforts into Augustus's raft theory. They must escape this island, and soon. She could not spend another night here. The night's chill and dampened clothes left them snuggling for warmth. Somehow there was comfort in Augustus's soft snores and the light touch of his arm around her waist. No. She needed no man. Men were trouble. That was Dorothy's problem—she'd trusted in men.

Louise methodically spent the next hour cutting and preserving the wing's fabric. Augustus was right—the water-resistant material would make a fine sail. That was, if they managed to construct a raft.

"Do you think we can do it?" The words left Louise's mouth before she could take them back.

"Gus thinks so, and if anyone can work magic with sub-par tools, he can."

"So, if we manage to guide ourselves out of this mess—" Louise stretched out her arms, "—how do we expect to make it the fifty or more miles back to Savannah?"

"We'll know soon enough." Eugene flashed his pearly white teeth. "Adventure begins tomorrow morning. Or it will if we can get these supplies back to Gus soon. Tonight."

"I hope he found a magic wand while we've been slaving away out here," Louise muttered under her breath.

After another three hours of work, Louise and Eugene slowly made their way back to the shore. Augustus had sketched a blueprint for the raft in the sand. Louise unloaded the neatly folded material while Eugene scooted the scrap wood up. Augustus instructed Louise to strip some cloth for ties since they had no nails. The trio worked to interlace strips between the logs, forming the base. Louise hated to admit it, but this crazy scheme just might work.

Eugene fastened a single pole upward with the largest piece of fabric as a makeshift sail. "Pray for wind."

Louise shook her head, doubting God had time to get them out of this mess.

They slid the newly formed raft to the water's edge.

"Moment of truth ..." Augustus sucked in a deep breath.

The structure wobbled, but managed to stay afloat. Could leaving really be this easy?

"It works!" Eugene jumped for joy, pumping his fists in the air.

Louise made no effort to hide her cynicism. "Don't get excited until we make it out of these shoals."

"Oh, let him have his triumph." Augustus winked at Louise while trying to position himself on the raft. "The real test will be if it holds our weight."

Wilhelmina counted the volunteers as she waited. The ocean was massive. Could eight men with three small boats really find such a tiny island? Their murmurings proved it wasn't on the map. Why hadn't they brought in the Coast Guard? She strained to hear the men's discussions, praying they would continue to ignore her so she could stay in the loop.

"I will take you two and head due east." Stanley's soft baritone sounded barely above a whisper.

"We'll take young Edgar here and go southeast." A burly man pointed to a younger version of himself then clapped his hand on Astor Realty's former bookkeeper. The poor young man's shoulders collapsed under the weight of the hand.

"Great. And you can take the last boat heading northeast." Stanley pointed to two older gentlemen Wilhelmina didn't recognize.

She should be grateful anyone was willing to volunteer their time on the cool Saturday morning. If she wasn't mistaken, storm clouds were brewing, and this little search party might be delayed.

Lord, I pray these men can at least cover some ground today. Keep Louise and the guys safe until we can find them. Amen.

Wilhelmina opened her eyes from her prayer to see all the men gathering their belongings and heading out. "So, you are going now?" She addressed her question to Stanley.

"Yes." Stanley placed his hand on the former bookkeeper's back. "Edgar and I felt it best we head out this morning. The map shows five possible islands, based on our limited information. Two are but twenty miles off the coast."

"Can you communicate? How will I know if you've found them?" Wilhelmina attempted to dampen her pleading.

"The Williams brothers will search the two closer islands, since they have no radio," Edgar said.

"And Edgar and I will each be on boats that can radio back. But we must leave now to avoid trouble with storms. We will let you know. Stay close to your shop today." Stanley placed his broad hand on Wilhelmina's shoulder and ushered her out of the realty office.

"Thank you both for organizing this," she said.

"Thank us when we've found them, ma'am," Edgar said.

Stanley locked up the office as the others dispersed to the marina. "Yes. Right now, just pray we do so quickly. At this rate, we won't return until dark."

Chapter Twelve

"There's no escape, boy. Buck up and face it." Little Benny cracked his knuckles as another of Doc's goons manned the small motorboat. "Doc will get his payment one way or another."

The wind and rain tossed the feeble vessel to and fro. Remus had to get back to solid land. How did he get himself in this situation?

"B-but Astor's body is payment enough, right?"

"Doc agreed that *if* you get the inheritance, *then* yes, he'd allow that. Otherwise—"

"Of course, I'll inherit. I'm his cousin. H-his closest kin."

Little Benny let out a belly laugh, "For your sake, I hope you're right."

If Astor and the girl managed to survive this long, could they make it through this weather? Maybe his luck hadn't run out yet. Astor dying would do him a world of good. No one would be the wiser about the embezzlement, and he'd get the inheritance. Perks of rich men who had no close relatives.

The boat continued to sway, and Remus's stomach

churned. Turning away from Benny, who still laughed, Remus couldn't hold down his meager breakfast. He leaned over the edge as it returned.

How do I expect to kill someone with my bare hands if the thought alone made me lose my last meal?

Rain pelted Remus's face as he returned to his duty as scout. The next island loomed at the horizon's edge. There he *must* find Astor—dead, or soon to be.

Chapter Thirteen

"Why'd you pray for wind? We sure got it!" Louise said as the sea swells flung the raft another foot in the air. Her stomach couldn't take much more of this rocking. They must have traveled several miles by now.

"Why are you complaining?"

"Yeah. We've made it beyond the shoals to the open sea. At this rate, we'll be home by morning." Eugene's voice held excitement.

Louise was still skeptical. "Are you sure it was a good idea to leave at nightfall?"

Just then, the gusts picked up, crashing the pitiful raft into a second wave, splintering one of the boards. "Maybe this wasn't the best idea." Eugene surveyed the growing waves.

Louise peered at the distance they'd already traversed. "The island is merely a dot on the horizon. Should we turn back?"

Augustus fingered the ties holding their structure together. "If these waves continue, we'll have to. We don't have enough planks to survive many more crashes."

The once cloudless sky quickly became gray with storm clouds. This was not the time for a summer shower. Louise gnawed on the side of her cheek. Would they make it through this?

The heavens let loose, drenching the trio as a second board broke free of the raft.

"Turn back," Louise cried.

"Close the sail, it's carrying us in the wrong direction," Augustus shouted as he tried to control their propellor-turned-rudder.

Louise strained against the wind, struggling to untie their feeble sail so they could tuck their tails and return to the island. She lost her grip on the wet sail as large drops of rain pelted her face. She refused to be the weak link, holding up their progress. Finally, the sail dropped to the raft's deck. She grabbed the large piece of fabric and stuffed it down her overall flap. The massive canvas overflowed, but better to keep it tucked there than lose it in the wind.

The sky around them brightened with lightning bolts. On a normal day, she'd be enjoying the show, but today she feared for her life. Each strike was a reminder they could die in this awful place. Thunder roared, rocking their already unstable vessel.

Minutes passed, and they moved neither forward nor backward without the aid of the sail or a motor. How would they make it back?

Splash! Louise gasped as Eugene plopped into the water.

"What are you doing?" she yelled.

"We have to get back. We're sitting ducks out here." He gripped the edge of the shrinking raft and began kicking his feet up and down. "I'll push. Can you pull?"

She flattened her belly against the rough boards and stroked the water, using her arms as oars. She pulled with all her might, struggling to return to that cursed island. She noted Augustus also lay prone beside her with his arms in the water.

If they could just reach the rocky shoals, they would be able to swim-walk back, just as they had before. Could it really only have been yesterday morning that they swam out to the carnage of the GeeBee?

Several hours later, they reached the sand as the lightning flickered a faint glow in the now-dark sky.

"Grab what you can and head for the cave. I'll help Gus," Eugene called after Louise's retreating form.

If only they had thought to protect some wood from the rain, they could make another fire. Tonight would be cold, wet, and dark.

Eugene managed to half carry, half drag Augustus out of the rain. Louise felt along the cave's edges, having to go deeper to remain dry. Her skin prickled at the dampness of the walls. Why did they not fully investigate yesterday? Unfamiliar noises amplified in the hollowness. What creatures lurked in the depths?

Ignore it, Lou. You are fine. We stayed here last night. Nothing has changed.

"Well, that was fun. Miss Louise, are you sure that radio of your is shot?" With a chuckle, Augustus collapsed in a heap.

"If it wasn't earlier, it is now," Eugene said while attempting to block the entrance with a fallen branch. "This storm has been raging for hours. No way the radio stayed dry."

Louise sat, huddled on the floor, trying to regain some warmth as the wind flung rain and debris into their meager shelter. "Speaking of dry, can we use this sail as a door flap?" Her teeth chattered as she tugged the never-ending fabric from her pouch. "I don't know how much of these cold gusts I can handle."

The men stretched the canvas across the opening, tucking

the corners into crevasses. "That will have to do." Eugene said as he hunkered closer to the others.

Drenched. Defeated. And delirious. Louise prayed they'd survive the night. "Well, we'll see if that's a feat we can manage until morning."

WILHELMINA TRUDGED BACK to the shop. Two engines stared at her as if mocking her. She turned the volume of her radio up all the way, hating the static of nothingness, but knowing she couldn't dwell on it.

She busied herself, letting the work absorb her worries. After stripping a second bolt, she tossed the wrench aside and released a pent-up sigh.

Lord, give me the patience to wait and reassurance to know You are there protecting them.

Pushing off the workbench, she stretched. She needed mindless work. At this point, she could do more harm to the engines than help.

She walked the short distance to the flower garden at the cottage she and Louise rented. Something about a beautiful arrangement always set her mind at ease. They already had one at the cottage. Maybe she should make one for the shop. Colorful flowers were abundant this time of year, and it wouldn't hurt to spread some joy. Wilhelmina picked a handful and headed back to the shop. She didn't want to leave the radio unattended too long—just in case.

Once back at the empty hangar, she placed her flowers in water. Papa Krause had doted on both girls, and he often brought them handpicked bouquets. Louise's green thumb kept them in roses, zinnias, and asters. Wilhelmina had taken up the hobby of arranging and preserving bouquets, allowing the trio to enjoy their beauty for sometimes up to two weeks.

Today she needed those memories. She needed to arrange. Grabbing a handful of flowers, her favorite vase, some wire, and —she spun in a circle. Where were her cutters?

How could this be? Both Lou and Wilhelmina were obsessive about order and tidiness. The cutters belonged next to the pliers below the monkey wrench, but her workbench failed her—it held no cutters.

The radio rang out loud and clear, "Stanley, the storm is coming in sooner than we expected. Still lack half an hour to our location ... attempt it but ... waves continue ... turn ba—"

No. No. No. Edgar's voice came in choppy over the radio. He was going southeast—Lou's most recent transmission said southeast. *They're turning back too soon.*

Wilhelmina's heart sank, how could they be so close but give up now?

More spurts of garbled dialogue echoed throughout the room. Wilhelmina tried to tune the frequency, but the storms made her efforts futile. Refusing to focus on the worst, she turned off the radio and returned to her bouquet.

Where was I? Oh, right. Looking for the wire cutters.

How could she ease her mind of worry if she didn't have the tools necessary to complete her arrangement? Searching high and low, she finally found them along the wall with the extra fuel storage. Why would Lou need these? Wilhelmina shook her head and headed back to the workstation to begin a new creation.

She hummed "Georgia on my Mind," one of Papa Krause's favorite tunes. As she worked, she remembered all the times she, Louise, and Papa Krause, spent in this hangar working side-by-side. He had been cheerful as he worked. Countless hours were spent at this very workbench as she learned the trade of a mechanic. He'd spent the mornings teaching Louise to fly and the evenings here with Wilhelmina, tinkering and repairing engines and old radios. This hangar housed his treasured biplane until his fatal crash.

Work was hard, money was tight, but the bond between the three was lasting. Losing Papa Krause last year was one of the hardest things they'd had to overcome. But thankfully, he taught them well, and they were survivors.

Wilhelmina snapped out of her reverie and gazed across the room. There were five fuel tanks. Wait. Weren't there only four yesterday? Louise and her superstition with numbers had to keep everything even. Always four full and two empty, especially before a flight.

She walked over and tried to lift each to confirm that only four were full. But no, there were five full tanks, or at least five with fuel. The last wasn't as heavy as the others. Something was fishy.

Her cutters were in the wrong place. Extra fuel. Uneven tanks.

They stored the GeeBee in this hangar the night before takeoff so Lou could have some time to familiarize herself with it. Could someone have ... *No!*

She was over-reacting. Nobody would have come in here.

Hadn't Lou discovered errors in the ledgers at Astor Realty? Could someone have sabotaged the plane to stop her from sharing the information? Who knew she was looking into the books? Wilhelmina remembered Lou saying she suspected Eugene and telling Stanley of her concerns. Could he—? Not Stanley. Wilhelmina herself had told Lou not to accuse without cause or proof.

But then, who?

She determined to wait and see how today's "search" turned out. If any other suspicions arose, she just might notify the Coast Guard herself.

Chapter Fourteen

Sunday Morning, June 20

"Run!"

Louise jolted awake at the command. Where was she? Oh. On the cursed island.

Eugene and Augustus hobbled past her as if running a three-legged race, grabbing her shoulder in the process.

"We're not alone," Eugene panted.

"And our roommate isn't happy," Augustus added.

A squeal echoed throughout the cave as the trio burst from the entrance. Their makeshift door caught on Louise's heel, but she ignored it, continuing into the bright sunlight of dawn. She was not the only one trailing behind—they were followed closely by a knee-high animal.

"Climb. There. In the trees. It won't be able to get to us."

"What is it?" Louise was still confused as she scurried high into the sorry excuse for a tree.

"Doesn't matter. It's not happy." Augustus huffed, pulling himself up, and allowing his injured leg to dangle.

The beast rummaged in the mud around the tree's base. What was it doing?

Louise wedged herself between two branches, finally relaxing. She pulled the wing-turned-sail-turned-door-flap up. "Could we trap the creature?"

"Trap it? I don't want it alive. That thing looks vicious. Did you see those fangs?" Eugene shuddered.

"Tusks."

"What?" In unison, Eugene and Louise turned toward Augustus.

"It's a wild boar." Augustus pointed down. "Those are tusks, and by the length, I'd guess male." He winked at Louise. "At least it's not a momma protecting her young."

"Oh, that's great to hear." Louise rolled her eyes and turned to Eugene. "Here, hold this end. If we're lucky, we can make a noose." The two worked in silence stripping the fabric then braiding the strands together. All the while, Mr. Tusks made himself at home rooting in the leaves, apparently unaware of his impending demise.

Louise's stomach growled and her legs were going numb from sitting in such an awkward position for so long. But they finally had a decent length of rope ready. Eugene had attempted to climb down earlier, but Mr. Tusks charged him, nearly crushing his arm as he scurried back up the tree.

"Is he gone?" Louise asked, hopeful to get out of this mess.

"I think that's him there." Augustus nodded to a lump in the mud. "Eugene, you wanna give it another go?"

"Are you serious? That thing tried to—to kill me!"

"We have the rope." Louise held up the last hour's handiwork. "If it charges again ... this time we're ready."

LOUISE WAS grateful for Papa's pocketknife. Their improvised noose was no match for Mr. Tusks, yet thankfully, Augustus's aim with the tiny blade was true. She feared Mr. Tusks would gore her boss when she dropped the makeshift lariat to the ground, but Augustus flung her knife, killing the pig seconds before he reached Eugene. The only thing that suffered was Eugene's left arm, and, well, likely his pride.

Louise searched high and low for more dry wood. Soon, the reward for their efforts roasted on a spit. A feast for kings, but unfortunately it was not a celebratory meal.

"So, let's discuss our options," Augustus said as he poked the fire.

"What options?" Eugene sounded more dejected with each word.

"Well, we've exhausted the radio. And the raft was a bust. At least Mr. Tusks will give us food for a few days," Louise piped in.

"You named him? How can you eat something you named?"

Louise stuffed a large hunk of meat in her mouth. "Like this."

Chapter Fifteen

After their failed search and a restless night, the sun rose, giving Remus an unwelcome reminder that his deadline was soon approaching. He went to the marina early in hopes of procuring a boat and finding Astor's mystery island.

He would reach them first. He had to.

Much to his dismay, Little Benny anticipated his early arrival and met Remus where the small motorboat was docked.

"Thought you'd have a go alone?"

"Of course not, just wanted t-to make sure all was ready ..."

"It is." Benny made a wide swinging gesture with his arm. "Come aboard and we'll begin."

Four hours later, they spotted land in the distance. Brooding clouds from the previous day's storms still loomed above the jagged outline of a dark rock protruding above the crashing waves. Tiny outcroppings speckled the sea surrounding the single mass rising above.

From this vantage, Remus was unsure how they would make it through the outer shoals.

Chapter Sixteen

"Here, let's have a look at your 'scratch.'" Louise leaned over to Augustus.

With all they had been through in the last twenty-four hours, she feared the worst. Slowly she unwrapped the seaweed.

"Don't look so stressed," he said. "I feel fine. It barely hurts anymore, and I was able to put my full weight on it earlier."

"Why would you do that? You could reopen it or cause more damage." Louise finally placed the soiled bandage to the side and peered at the wound. No noticeable inflammation.

"Does this hurt?" She gently prodded the tissues along the edges. The seaweed bandage had worked. Most of the swelling had decreased, and new flesh was already forming.

"No, but it kind of tickles." Augustus's deep chuckle sent tingles down her spine. He reached over and covered her hand with his, and she feared her heart would stop. How could a simple touch have such an effect on her? She could not let a man change her. She would not be ruled by a man.

"Louise?"

Did he say something? She needed to get out of here. Where was Eugene? Propriety called for all three to be present. Papa may have encouraged manly hobbies, but he'd always drilled that she was a *lady* and was never to be alone with a man.

Louise rose and stepped away from Augustus.

"Where are you going?"

"I-I need to get more seaweed so we can rebandage ..." She bolted from the cave, heading for the shoreline.

"Wait. I'll come with you. A walk will do me good after eating so much."

"No. Stay here. We mustn't ..."

"What Louise?" Augustus slowly rose and took her hand in his. "What are you afraid of?"

His questions came in soft whispers mere inches from her face.

She leaned into his touch, coming up on tiptoes to be level with him.

Without hesitation, she fell into Augustus's embrace, their lips melding together as one. The kiss was quick, but tender.

Her body ached for more. *What am I doing?*

Before she realized it, his lips were once more brushing hers. She pushed off his muscular biceps, abruptly ending the heated moment.

Louise softly muttered, "We can't." She scurried away before either of them had a chance to change her mind.

Wilhelmina paced the now spacious hangar. She and Louise had cleaned out some old junk to make room for the plane. Now, without either, it felt eerily empty. Stopping just shy of the extra fuel tank, she closed her eyes. Who came for the delivery of the GeeBee? Herself and Lou, Augustus and Eugene. The delivery crew had two or three unfamiliar faces ... Was Stanley there? No ...

Didn't Eugene say his cousin and Stanley were putting in long hours at the office? He didn't mention what the men were working on. Wilhelmina walked back to her flowers. Picking up the purple aster, she twirled it and thought about the name—Astor. Eugene's name. Nearly everyone on the East Coast was familiar with the family's investments during the Depression and how they'd gained rather than failing, like Papa Krause.

Why would Stanley be working late? Who was this cousin?

Cutting the wire and shaping it around the flowers' stems, Wilhelmina puzzled as she worked.

Louise had discovered money missing. She mentioned rhythmical missing sums. Knowing her and her patterns, she'd spotted something most people would miss. If only Willie herself could have seen what Lou was talking about.

Stanley knew Lou was suspicious ...

Stanley chose not to come to the delivery because something at the office was too important. Could he ...

Stanley was the one organizing the search.

Wilhelmina let the aster slip from her fingers and ran across the room. She grabbed the phone's receiver.

No wonder he didn't want the military involved. He wanted the plane to go down—because both Lou and Eugene were on it. With them out of the way, Stanley would have full rein at Astor Realty.

"Operator? I need to speak with the Coast Guard. Now. It's an emergency."

LOUISE SLOWED HER PACE, grazing her fingers along her lips. He kissed her. Why?

Get it together, Lou. You aren't a flirt. You are not *your mother.*

Papa always told of Dorothy's wild hair and her mesmerizing beauty that had held him captive. He spoke of her with reverence, but he always left out that she abandoned him for another man less than a year after Louise was born.

How could Papa still love her and still take her back? He'd said it was the Christian thing to do.

Louise didn't think even Christ would want a woman who partied all night, flaunting her womanly figure. A woman who came crawling back only after she was sick—the Spanish Flu. On her death bed, she was left shriveled, a shell of her once glorious self. But somehow, Papa still loved her.

He cared for her until the very end. The stories of his earnest attempts at easing her pain and staying up all night to care for her were the catalyst to Louise becoming a nurse.

Thankfully, he had the foresight to call me Louise and not Dorothy.

He was so tender with her and Willie as girls too. A man forced to raise two women, both of whom managed to excel. When he came home with a cut or bruise, he would bend down asking "Papa's little nurse" to kiss it better.

She was still *not* a nurse. One day, she would make him proud. But first, to get off this dreaded island.

She wandered the jungle bordering the beach. Birds soared high above her without a care in the world. She was here. Trapped.

A faint sound echoed through the dense canopy of trees. She traipsed deeper and the noise grew louder. Less familiar. Less avian and more ... human?

Voices? But where?

There. Beyond the trees. A male voice not belonging to Eugene nor Augustus sounded in the distance. "Another empty one."

"I thought for sure this would be it. Don't those rocks look like teeth?"

Who was talking? Stanley? Louise only recognized one voice.

"Radio the others, and we'll head to the next one."

That was definitely Stanley's voice.

She sprinted up the hill calling out. "Wait!" She caught her toe on a loose root. Stumbling forward she flung out her hands, catching herself, and only faltering a moment. Pain seared. Her ankle throbbed, but she managed to hobble upright. Awkwardly dragging her right foot behind her, she continued up the incline. She must reach Stanley before he left. "We're here, don't leave!"

Louise limped to the hill's crest in time to see two men board a small boat. She wasn't dreaming. Her voice cracked, and a soft whimper released as the vessel set off. Water churned behind leaving a tail weaving in and out of the rocky coast. She had to tell the guys.

She took special care with each step as she descended. The men were looking for them, but how to get them to come back?

Chapter Seventeen

As they neared the island, Remus spotted several crags emerging from the water like teeth. No wonder it was rumored to be called Sharktooth. The jagged rocks spread out in layers, just like the jaws of a shark, but one rock stood out taller than the rest, like a lone pillar or a tooth on a necklace. The name fit either way you looked at it.

If that wasn't Sharktooth Island, it should be. No signs of movement but also no sign of a crash site. Where was the plane? Or did the girl get it wrong—they were lost at sea. Remus could hope.

He glanced back at Little Benny, unsure of his motivation for joining this rescue. Doc probably forced him to come along to keep Remus in check, but Remus wasn't happy about the situation. Little Benny made him more nervous than Doc himself. Little was the last thing Benny was. His biceps were like watermelons, and his fist was the size of a cantaloupe.

Little Benny moved to the bow of the small motorboat. "Be careful. Rocks like those will be hiding just below the surface, and I'd hate for us to end up stranded out here."

Remus shivered at the thought of having to survive with only Little Benny and another of Doc's goons for company.

"There. High on that ridge, a person is running. See them?"

Remus did it! He was the first to find them. But the scampering figure meant they did survive, or at least one did. Could he truly stomach killing them?

After an hour of tedious maneuvers, the captain managed to reach the shore with their small boat. The survivor never saw them, so Remus would have the advantage of surprise.

"Give me a chance to make this right," he gulped. "Stay here while I do them in."

Laughter rang out from Little Benny and the goon. Remus would show them. He could do this.

"Just remember, your debts will double if you fail." Benny's banana of a forefinger punctuated each word. "Doc don't want any more promises or IOUs—he wants results."

"Yeah, either two grand or two dead bodies." The goon giggled. "Ain't that right, Benny?"

"That's right." Little Benny gave Remus a shove. "Now go. Make Doc proud, or I'll have four bodies to deal with."

Remus stumbled forward, "F-four?"

"Weren't there three on that plane?"

"Oh ... I have to kill him too?" Remus's voice cracked and rose an octave with each word.

"Someone has to. Can't have any witnesses." Benny pushed harder this time, and Remus was unable to maintain his balance. "Better hurry. You never know if one of those other boats will show up. Or if we've lost your surprise element."

Remus slowly rose, making sure to move forward and out of Little Benny's reach.

Three dead bodies ... how?

Cold steel greeted him as he tucked his hands into his

jacket pocket. The revolver held six shots. He didn't have to be a good shot at close range. He could do this.

Bang bang bang! Then Doc would be out of his life for good.

Chapter Eighteen

Louise propped her swelling ankle on a rock as Eugene gathered some wood.

"Can you make it work?" She winced but looked hopefully to Augustus.

"It's still damp, but it'll have to do."

Augustus knelt beside the meager woodpile rubbing two small sticks together.

"Careful. Now I have a bum foot. We must keep you as healthy as possible."

"I'm fine. That seaweed has worked wonders." Augustus patted his torn pantleg. "It doesn't even hurt anymore. And I can all but walk normally."

"Well, don't push it," Eugene chimed in. "I'm not strong enough to carry both of you." Eugene winked at Louise then flexed his good arm emphasizing his strength.

"Aren't we a trio? A bum ankle, a sore leg, and a scraped-up arm. I just hope we make it off this island in one piece," Louise said as she repositioned on her perch.

"We will. Look! It's starting to smoke." Augustus whooped in celebration.

"Ahoy there!"

"Who said that?" Louise craned her neck around. "Am I hearing things?"

"No, I heard it too." Eugene stood and hurried up the incline. "Hello?"

Louise eased to her feet, tracking Eugene's movements up the hill just as a stranger ambled over the crest. She glanced at Augustus and raised an eyebrow.

"You're here! And you're alive!" The stranger ran toward Eugene and embraced him.

"Hey buddy, is Stanley with you?" Eugene patted the mystery man on the shoulder as he surveyed his surroundings.

"No. He's on a different boat."

"Did you hear that? Your mayday reached the Coast Guard, and they sent out a search party." Eugene called back to Louise.

Louise steadied herself and glanced to Augustus for reassurance. He nodded and made to rise himself.

"I never mentioned Coast Guard, dear cousin."

Something about the newcomer's tone sent shivers down Louise's spine. Was this truly a rescue, or something more sinister?

Eugene's question was interrupted by the echo of a gunshot.

"Wha—"

Augustus grabbed Louise's hand and yanked her in toward the cave, just as she caught sight of the gun aimed squarely at Eugene. "Run!"

What happened? Could Eugene dodge a bullet at that close range? Questions poured through Louise's mind as she and Augustus supported each other in their escape, moving deeper and deeper into the cave's dark shelter.

Louise heard shuffling of leaves outside the entrance. "That's okay, you can run, dear cousin, but you can't hide forever." The footsteps crescendoed louder, then faded. "Just think what the papers will say. Astor's mangled body found by beloved cousin. Now, I'll get to take my rightful place as head of the business."

"Rightful place, you?" Eugene's voice grew fainter with every word. "I was right to fire you and get you out of my office. I knew ..."

What? What did Eugene know, and who was this mysterious cousin?

Louise groped in the abyss. Feeling Augustus near her she whispered. "Do you know who that is?"

"I didn't get a good look, but based on his voice and way he said 'cousin,' I'd guess it's Edgar. Edgar Remus."

"He used to keep the books for Astor Realty, didn't he?"

"Yeah, Stanley hired him, but Eugene felt something was off, so gave him the boot last month. It was my idea to bring you on."

Everything was coming together for Louise. She had picked the wrong partner. Eugene was innocent.

"Something *was* off. I discovered a pattern. I told Stanley. I thought it was Eugene." Louise hung her head. "What have I done? They're trying to kill us."

LOUISE DIDN'T KNOW how much time had passed, but the scuffling was nearly non-existent by now. She took comfort in Augustus's arm around her shoulders.

"Can I pray with you?" Augustus's husky baritone caught Louise off guard.

No, I don't want him to pray. Do I?

"At this point, I guess it won't hurt." She tried to sound nonchalant, but she wanted to believe. She longed to be off this island. She knew somewhere Willie would be praying, so more voices sending up pleas for help were less likely to be ignored. Right?

"Lord, grant us patience like Job and wisdom like Solomon." He squeezed her shoulders tighter. "Show Miss Louise that You are Sovereign and have a plan to get us home. We pray in Your Son's Name. Amen."

"Amen," Louise muttered.

That wasn't so bad. Does God listen to nonbelievers?

Shifting in the uncomfortable silence, Louise peered behind them. Could it be?

"Look." She pointed at a light coming in through a crevice. "Is that a second entrance?"

Augustus took her hand. The two shuffled along the narrow passage, the light growing larger as they approached.

"What do you know, it is!" Augustus kissed her. "See, God does grant miracles, and He listens to those who ask for help."

Louise stood still in disbelief—both that his God heard their prayer and that Augustus kissed her. Granted, not a passionate kiss like the one they shared last night, but a celebratory kiss. Either way, she was speechless.

Augustus held her back, not yet crossing the threshold. "Now, I don't know where this will pop out. We haven't explored the back side of the island, so let's listen for a bit."

"Okay, but I'm ready to be done with this place. Do you think Eugene is all right?"

"I pray he is." Augustus squeezed her hand as they waited.

Chapter Nineteen

"What do you mean, you lost them?" The vein bulged in Little Benny's neck.

Remus didn't want to return empty-handed, but after three shots and an hourlong chase—he had nothing to show for his efforts. He'd tried to circle back to where the girl disappeared, but that was no luck either. Just an empty cave. He refused to explore that alone and without a light, so here he was, at Little Benny's mercy, begging for help.

"Well, I got a shot off at Astor. B-but he got the slip on me." Remus wrung his sweaty palms together. Would Benny do him in for failing so soon? "I'm pretty sure I winged him, but in the process the girl got away."

"Did you track the blood trail?"

Blood trail? Why didn't I think of that?

"Or are you exaggerating your accomplishments?" Benny smiled, suggesting Remus had overstepped in saying he winged Eugene.

"Well, he ... ah ... he stumbled as I shot, so ... I ..." Remus's palms grew stickier, and he longed to wipe them down his pants, but he remained a statue. "I winged him."

There, speak with confidence. Don't let Benny know he's won this psychological battle.

"I told him I'll be the rightful face of the company."

"We'll see about that." Benny gestured for the other goon to follow. "We'll take care of your mess. Just wait here and guard the boat in case they circle back."

"Y-yes, sir."

Remus paced. He should be out there finishing this. If Benny did all the work, Doc would still demand payment. Maybe he should take the boat himself. They motored this far. Maybe he could manage to go up the coast and escape to Savannah.

"Whatcha think yer doin'?" The awkward drawl of the second crony's voice ripped Remus from his thoughts of escape.

"N-nothing." Straightening to his full height, still several inches shy of six feet, Remus said, "Standing guard, like I was told."

"Sure ya were. Looked like you was chicken an' goin' ta run." The goon lumbered over to Remus. "Good thing Benny sent me back. Wouldn't want to lose ya too."

Remus forced a smile. So much for escaping Doc and Benny for good.

Chapter Twenty

After an eternity, Louise and Augustus agreed the coast should be clear, and they could leave the cave. She scampered out first, trying to be as silent as possible. The sun bobbed high in the sky. Was it only noon? This continual game of cat and mouse was growing tiresome. Louise preferred abandonment to being on the run.

Augustus peered out. "Any sign of them?"

"No." She cowered closer to the earth. "I'll move to the hill's crest and look about."

"Good. Stay low. I'll wander about here. If you have trouble give a hoot like an owl. You got that?"

Louise smiled. He was still trying to protect her. Didn't he know she could handle herself? She ventured higher up the incline until she reached the crest. There, on the back side of the island, was a small vessel tethered to one of the gigantic rocks protruding from the sea.

Was it Edgar's boat? Regardless—it was their escape. She stared for several minutes, studying it to see if it was guarded or lay empty. Shadows moved on the far side, Edgar himself paced back and forth in front of the small motorboat.

What was he doing?

Louise glanced back. Should she hoot to tell Augustus of her find or would that frighten him? She opted to scurry back down the mountainside. Along the way, she spotted movement to her right. Stopping behind a thin tree, she observed two men engaging in conversation. Both men were tall, but one was a beanpole, while the other was broader than a barn.

Were they friend or foe? Who was she kidding? No one could be trusted—except maybe Augustus. Yes, she could count on him. Just thoughts of him made him materialize beside her.

"What did you see?"

"Edgar is standing guard with a small motorboat, and if you look just there, two men seem to be arguing." Louise nodded rather than pointing, fearing she would bring trouble on them if she caused noise or motion. "You?" she turned to face Augustus and whispered. "Did you find Eugene?"

"Yes. The shot grazed him. He's lost some blood, but he managed to use your seaweed trick and a get it bandaged without Edgar finding him." Augustus turned her back toward their hideout. "Too much is happening out here. Let's go discuss options with Eugene in the cave."

She obediently followed. "Do you think we can ever escape this dreaded isle?"

"I do. With the Lord's help, we shall prevail." Lifting her chin he brushed her forehead with his lips. "This is but an adventure we will live to tell our grandchildren."

He was taking hold of her heart—*grandchildren.* Yes, she liked the sound of that.

Louise eased her way back through the tiny opening, "Eugene, you there?"

"Here."

"How do you fare?"

"I'll live." He gave a slight chuckle. "That is if you have a plan for us."

"I believe I do."

WILHELMINA COULD TAKE it no more. She had to know what was going on. She locked up the hangar and headed over to the Coast Guard office. If they wouldn't let her listen in, she would sit at their gates until the rescue crew returned.

Uniformed man after uniformed man rejected her and pushed her aside. Finally, one at least replied when she began to argue.

"But I'm the one who gave the tip."

"I'm sorry, ma'am, you can't be here. This area is restricted."

"Do you have somewhere I am allowed to wait?"

"At home." The officer's tone was more blunt than rude. "We will notify you immediately if there is a development on the situation."

Wilhelmina planted her feet firmly. She would get answers before she returned home. "And what of the boats pretending to search? Will there be charges against them?"

"Ma'am, please return home and let us do our jobs." He placed his hand on her shoulder guiding her toward the door. "We cannot simply arrest someone for lying to you. We have protocols and procedures. But we can aid in the search." With a final nudge he said, "If you leave and let us work."

Wilhelmina sighed as the door slammed behind her. Since they refused to let her be in on the search, she would go to the docks. Maybe there would be enough scuttlebutt to keep her in the know.

Slinking into the background along the docks, she tried to remain silent. Men talked more if no ladies were present. She'd changed before coming, so she now wore a pair of Lou's dungarees and tucked her long braid into a cap. Her petite frame and smooth skin gave the appearance of an errand boy half her age.

An hour passed, and Wilhelmina was none the wiser, but she felt less anxious here at the docks. Even though it was a Sunday afternoon, men moved and worked. There was talk of one boat having failed to report back and a second going to the last known location. A remote island, southeast, with crags jutting up from the ocean.

The elusive Sharktooth Island! Did they find Lou?

"Snares are set." Eugene and Augustus entered the cave's small opening.

"Good. And the sun? Are there enough shadows to hide us?" Louise stretched, rocking her ankle back and forth.

She needed to be stealthy as well as fast. Her bum ankle was a potential issue, but she could bear the pain if it meant they could leave this place. They had waited several hours, fine-tuning and going over the plans. All the while, she elevated and rested her foot.

The seaweed worked wonders on Augustus's gash. Now it was merely an annoying scratch. He would have no trouble maneuvering—she would be the holdup.

Edgar's shot only grazed Eugene's already banged-up shoulder, so he was no worse for wear. These men had surprised her. Only two days ago she thought them useless, but now they had defeated the boar together and were taking on three armed men. They would best this island and make it home to tell Willie their grand tale.

Their side of the island was finally in shadow. Movements would be concealed. Armed with her trusty pocketknife, Louise eased down to the motorboat. She reached the tree line as a second vessel was making its way through the shoals. Stanley.

This was not good. How many more would they be forced to face?

She hooted once signaling retreat.

"What happened?" Eugene whispered from behind Louise as they crawled back into the cave.

"Stanley."

Augustus's mud-covered body rose from the earth, "How many with him?"

"Not sure. But now it's at least four to three."

"I vote we stick to the plan." Eugene turned to Louise. "Can you disable the second boat when it docks, so they can't follow us?"

"If you two can lure them to you, I should have time." Fiddling with her knife, Louise said, "I doubt I can handle more than one without making noise. But with your distraction ..."

"Gus will take to the ground again, and I'll make some noise, hopefully bringing the men into the trees after me. We have two snares set, so if we time it right, that will leave one each for Gus and me. You disable one boat and get rid of Edgar." Augustus nodded as Eugene recounted their plan. "Then the two of us will hightail it down to the shore, and we'll motor off into the sunset."

She pocketed the knife. "I pray they leave Edgar as the guard. He is a horrible shot."

"So, you're praying now?" Augustus smiled.

"Well, your God seems to be listening, so I'll give Him a chance to get us out of here."

In unison both men said, "He will."

"Perfect. We'll be home for supper." Louise rubbed her hands together in an effort to hide her nervousness.

Chapter Twenty-One

Remus paced the sandy shoreline—where was Benny?

As he wandered back and forth, he saw movement in the trees. "Did you see that?" Remus called out to Doc's goon.

"Don't you be messin' wit me. Just stand there like Benny say," the giant said from his post.

"Whatever ..." Remus kicked the sand. "Something was there."

Twenty minutes later, Remus assumed the goon was right. Nothing had happened, and the island remained still. How long would Benny search for Astor?

Out of nowhere, a rock flew past Remus's ear, followed by a second.

What the—

Thwack! The third stone crashed into his temple. "H-hel ..." Remus attempted to call for help as the world around him faded into darkness.

Chapter Twenty-Two

One down. Two to go—for now. The second boat still had not made it to the beach. Maybe the treacherous rocks would hold it at bay.

Louise intentionally showed herself, praying the beanpole checking on Edgar was a poor shot.

She caught sight of the giant running her way as she ducked back into the trees. Telling herself to remain slow enough to be followed, but fast enough to not die was a trick. She hooted as she sprinted beyond the first snare.

Augustus was well hidden, for she herself didn't see him. He would never abandon his post.

Where was the last and largest of the three hiding?

Lord, guide Eugene and keep him safe.

There. Is that how you pray? Just talk to God? She'd ask Willie or Augustus later. For now, that should work.

Dipping into the cave's entrance, she turned back to watch the show. Precisely as they'd planned, the idiot came crashing through the trees right behind her. He stumbled. His right toe slipped into the noose snare as he adjusted his weight. In slow motion his leg flew up, sending his head and torso back. "Aaaahhhhhhh!"

Poor guy didn't know what happened until the rope settled and he rocked steadily back and forth upside down.

Louise was unsure if shock or injury caused his writhing body to go limp. Either way, he was out.

"Are you all right?" Augustus finished tying off the rope as the man swung like a pendulum.

"Yeah." Louise huffed. "You?"

"Never better." He smiled down at her.

Would he kiss her again?

Jerking his head up, he pointed back to the shore. "Did you hear that? I think we have more company."

Louise's heart sank, both at the lack of a kiss and the thought of company. Nodding to the limp form she said, "Check him for weapons, and we'll go investigate."

The two belly-crawled up the cliff and peered over. Stanley stood over Edgar's body, speaking to a group of men in uniform.

Were they here to help?

She rose and beckoned to Augustus to follow her down. Pain pierced her left side. She faltered. Louise's body hurtled forward, crashing headlong down the jungle's hillside. She flailed her arms, attempting to halt her downward progress to no avail. Her final thoughts before the world faded into darkness—*the third man.*

WILHELMINA DODGED two men sprinting toward the water's edge, but she failed to see the third and was thrown to the ground. He merely glanced down before hurrying after the first men muttering, "They've found Astor."

Astor? If Eugene was alive, surely the Lord would see fit to protect all three. She pushed her way through the gathering crowd. She spied two Coast Guard vessels escorting a third, smaller motorboat.

Where was Stanley? He was the mastermind behind this scheme.

Two officers hauled ashore three bound men. None were Stanley, but was that Edgar? And the brothers he rode with?

The guardsmen read the suspects their rights. So it wasn't Stanley after all.

Wilhelmina scanned the last vessel.

Lord, protect Lou, let her live long enough to seek You and to know You, Lord.

LOUISE WOKE. Her entire body ached. Where was she? She tried to sit up but collapsed from pain with the effort.

"There now, rest."

Was that Willie's voice? It couldn't be ... could it? Louise had to know. Her eyelids fluttered but failed her. She was unable to open them.

"What's wrong? Is she okay?" Willie's voice. She sounded frantic as monitors beeped.

"She is fine, ma'am. She will wake with time. Her body took a beating from that cliff."

Cliff? Louise wracked her brain and remembered. She got shot.

The third man. He must have come from behind and shot her in the back. She had rolled down the cliff bank. Stanley was there. And the Coast Guard.

Willie's voice broke through again. "How long before we know ... if ..."

"She'll make it."

Louise's heart warmed. She recognized Augustus's baritone, both sweet and soothing—like honey.

"Yes. Your friend will be fine. She just needs time. And rest."

Rest. Yes, that sounded good.

Louise let out a soft moan and felt her lips twitch into a smile. She would talk to Willie later—but for now, she wanted sleep.

Epilogue

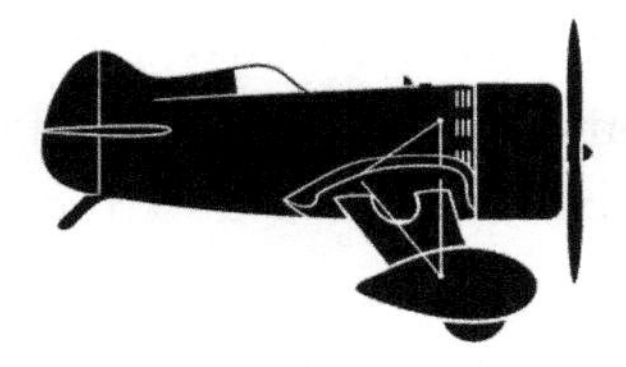

Seven Months Later

Louise had spent the summer recovering from her gunshot wound and subsequent fall down the cliff. Augustus became her nurse. Between him and Willie, Louise wanted for nothing.

Eugene opted not to buy Sharktooth Island, stating their weekend "visit" was more than enough adventure for him. Not even rumors of gold hiding in the cave were enough to lure them back. They had survived the curse. And that was enough.

Once her injuries had healed, everyone encouraged Louise to return to nursing school. Augustus was her biggest champion, stating he'd support her no matter her choice. Even if it meant she would return to Atlanta.

When she tried to use funds as an excuse, Eugene insisted on paying—stating her persistence with Astor Realty accounts had saved him thousands in the long run. Edgar and two henchmen from a big-name loan shark were rotting in jail. The embezzlement alone would have called for minimal jail time, but the district attorney was able to get three counts of attempted murder to stick.

Eugene no longer had to watch his back.

Louise ambled down the stairs of Grady Hospital School of Nursing. She still had to move slowly, but she was alive. Living her dream of becoming a nurse. Papa would be proud.

Augustus met her at the base of the stairs. "Care for a walk?"

"Don't mind if we do." Louise smiled at this wonderful man. She could spend a lifetime with him. And would. He had proposed last night.

Papa had been right. When the person was your soulmate it didn't matter—you would do anything for them.

And Augustus was her soulmate.

About Elena Hill

Elena Hill is a Christian, a wife, a dog Mom, and an optometrist. She dabbles with many hobbies including photography, painting, and most recently, writing. She has been an avid reader and supporter of Christian fiction since a young age, but in 2020 took on the title of content editor for Scrivenings Press.

Elena currently resides in northeast Arkansas, along with her husband James and fur baby Idgie. Her favorite pastime is riding around with family in their side-by-side, chasing the sunset. Many of her photos display God's handiwork—varying skyscapes and colors.

AFTER THE *Storm*

Deborah Sprinkle

Chapter One

Rain pounded on Mercedes Baxter's small house on Sharktooth Island like a giant demanding entrance. But it was the wind, howling like a thousand banshees and whipping the bushes and trees into a frenzied dance, that sent shivers down her spine.

She clutched her scruffy tomcat to her chest and stood inside her open front door, shielded from the fury of the storm by her screened porch. The windows were buttoned down, and she should secure the big door and head for shelter, but the power and sound of the hurricane at once frightened and mesmerized her.

The big tawny cat squirmed in her grasp. "Mrawr."

"Sorry, Hawkeye." She shifted her grip. "No way I'm letting you out in this. That wind will blow you off the island and you'll be shark bait."

After stuffing the protesting cat into his carrier, she went back to stand by the door. A branch from a nearby tree tore through a screen on the porch like a spear and landed at her feet. She bit back a scream. Time to head for cover.

Mercy closed the heavy oak door and lowered the solid wood beam across it. Her father built the cottage to withstand storms, water, and time. She loved it here. The only thing not crafted of wood was the beautiful silver cross over the door. He'd done that for her mother.

She grabbed Hawkeye's cage and paused before descending the ladder into the cellar. "I don't know if You're out there, but Mom and Dad thought so. For their sake, please save this house from the storm. Amen."

The cabin stood amongst the rocks halfway up the mountain. Mercy's father carved a small cellar beneath the floor for food storage and protection from the occasional storm. Sandstone boulders composed three sides of the small space below the cabin, with a solid sandstone floor. The fourth side was a wall of tightly stacked timbers. Metal shelving stood against most of the wall space.

Mercy spent as little time as possible in the cellar, coming down to grab a potato or onion for dinner. More than once she felt someone's breath on her neck as she restocked her supplies. But when she whirled around, no one was there. And one time, she heard a soft moan. She inspected the walls and floors for cracks, but never found any.

Now, in the dim glow from her flashlight, with what sounded like a war going on overhead, every nerve in her body sent a warning signal to her brain. She extracted Hawkeye from his carrier and wrapped her arms around him. Stroking his rough fur brought her some comfort.

"Hope this blasted storm doesn't last long." She peered at the cabin floor above her head. "I have a feeling we'll have a lot to report to the Conservancy when this is all over with."

Quiet settled around her. Had the storm passed?

She stood, letting Hawkeye jump to the floor. After a few

moments, she pushed the trapdoor up a crack. Hawkeye raced up the ladder and out into the house.

"Come here, you foolish cat." Mercy flung open the hatch and climbed out.

She could see the living room, dining area, and kitchen from where she stood. No windows broken in there. Some dishes shaken from the open shelves in the kitchen, and books from the cases by the fireplace. She continued her inspection.

Two bedrooms and baths okay. Only a few photos fallen over. She righted the one on her bedside table. A wiry man had his arm thrown over a petite, dark-haired woman. Both grinning as if they'd won the lottery.

"You did good, Dad. The cabin made it through the storm." Mercy touched her lips and then the glass covering their image. "I miss you guys."

But at least she had Hawkeye. Where was her cat? She raised the beam from across her front door and steeled herself for the view outside. Hawkeye appeared at her ankles.

"Oh no." She picked him up. "Let me take a look first."

Taking a deep breath, she opened the door. The bones of her porch still stood. Limbs and sticks lay in an inch of water covering the floor, and many of the screens hung in tatters. Her screen door was nowhere in sight.

"The house made it, but my poor porch." Mercy stroked her cat. "Time to see what other damage this storm did." She held Hawkeye up so she could look him in his one good eye. "Sorry. You need to stay here for now."

"Mrawr." He gave a mighty jerk and escaped her grasp.

"You little monster." Mercy shook her head. "It's wet out there."

The big cat skittered across the porch and stopped on the step to shake his soaked paws. He looked back at her.

"I warned you."

Mercy pulled on her boots and shrugged into her backpack, complete with machete. She stuffed her cellphone into her jeans pocket—no cell service, but it took great pictures. The porch felt sturdy. Clean up, new screens, a door, and it would be as if the storm never happened. She yanked her hair into a ponytail and stepped outside.

"Mrawr."

"Sorry. I'm not picking you up now, you silly cat."

The ache in her chest grew as she surveyed her once beautiful island. Bushes and ferns flattened. Trees stripped of their leaves, bent over, or uprooted. And she was on the leeward side of the island. What must the other side look like?

She pulled her machete from its sheath and began cutting her way along what used to be her normal mountainside path. Hawkeye followed at a safe distance. The banana tree her father planted ten years ago stood unharmed six feet from the house.

Tears stung the backs of her eyes. "Look, Hawkeye. Daddy's tree made it." She laid a hand on the trunk. "A good sign."

At a clearing, she peered up the mountain. Where was her transmission tower? Usually, it rose above the vegetation, and she used it as a measure for distance and time of day. Another casualty of the hurricane—a big one. Now she had no way of communicating with the outside world. A weight settled on her heart as she realized she'd have to leave her island.

Her home.

Chapter Two

She turned to scan the still unsettled seas that lay between the island and Savannah, Georgia, fifty miles away. From her perch on the side of the mountain, her twenty-eight-foot cabin cruiser seemed so small. It appeared to have weathered the storm, as it rose and fell against the dock with every swell.

She shaded her eyes. Another boat came into view. Bigger, with a more powerful engine. Someone from the Conservancy had come to check on her.

"Hawkeye, help has arrived." The pain in her chest eased. "Let's head down to meet them."

Mercy hurried along the gangway her father built over the rocks to a safe mooring place. Ten feet longer than hers, the Conservancy boat took most of the space on one side of the large rectangular docking platform at the end. Looked like one man at the helm. Maybe another sitting out of sight? She grabbed the side of the boat and secured a rope from the dock to the cleat with a practiced movement.

"I'm sure glad you're here." Mercy wiped her hands on her

pants and turned. "My tower ... Liam Stewart?" Her breath caught in her throat.

He grinned, and just like that it was ten years ago, and she was in the darkened hallway by the high school gym, waiting for her first kiss. She bit her lip. He'd changed. Taller, still thin, more muscle. But the same smile. The one that made her stomach flip.

And the same sapphire eyes with lashes to die for. Buried resentment niggled at her once more—her own being short and stubby.

"When I heard it was you stuck out here, I had to come." He finished tying off the boat.

"I didn't realize you worked for the Conservancy." She managed to keep her voice steady.

"Two years now." He surveyed the view. "You don't come off the island much, from what I hear."

"No. I moved over after my dad passed away." She led the way off the pier. "He built us a vacation cabin."

"You're lucky. It's beautiful."

"You should have seen it two days ago." Tears again. That would never do. She swiped at her cheeks. "Anyway. I just started to explore the damage. I can use your help."

"That's why I'm here." He caught up with her. "Your tower must be down. We couldn't raise you on the radio."

"The hurricane took it out." Mercedes pointed up the mountain.

"Lead the way."

Liam put his hands on his hips and sucked in air. He cut his eyes to where Mercy rummaged through her backpack. She'd walked up the mountain path like it was level ground, while he'd chugged like a steam engine behind her. What a difference ten years makes. In high school, he'd been the more athletic one. Ran track. Played basketball. While she played chess and wrote for the newspaper.

They'd dated through the last part of high school, and he was crazy about her. But Mercy had her life all planned out, and if he didn't like it, well, he could leave. So he did. He joined the Marines. But he never stopped caring about her.

Now, she scaled mountains like they were nothing, gathered data on the flora and fauna of her island, and he wrote reports on the data she gathered. He worked out and swam, but not enough, if today was any indication.

The girl he knew was now a woman. Her compact frame moved with grace and assurance, and he couldn't keep his eyes off her.

"I'm not sure how we're going to fix this." Mercy took a photo of the bent metal toppled on its side.

Liam forced himself to study the scene. Bushes, ferns, and branches broken from nearby trees lay beneath it.

"Line's damaged. I brought the stuff to fix that." He worked his way around to the base of the tower. "Getting the tower standing again is the problem. Need a block and tackle." He looked at Mercy. "Didn't bring one of those."

She shook her head.

"Looks like I'll need to make another trip." He'd get to see her again. Joy shot through him.

"How long will that take?" she said. "I'll be stuck out here without a way of getting help if I need it."

"Be back within a day. Promise." His joy lessened at the anxiety on her face. "Why don't you come back with me to the mainland?"

"No." She backed away. "I'll be fine here. As long as it's only a day or two." She looked at the sun. "Let's have some lunch and make a quick tour of the rest of the island before you leave."

A terrible howl echoed through the trees.

Chapter Three

Mercy resisted as Liam thrust her behind him.

"What are you doing?" She stepped around to face him.

"Protecting you."

There was a time when she would have swooned at those words, but now they only annoyed her. What was he thinking? She lived on the island. If anyone needed protecting, it would be him.

But she stifled her snarky remark. After all, he'd come to help her.

"That's my cat. Hawkeye." Mercy gave him a brief smile. "He does that when he wants me to let him in the house."

"A cat made that noise?" Liam raised an eyebrow. "A house cat? Not a bobcat or a lynx?"

"No." Mercy shook her head. Bobcat? Lynx? Why would they be on her island? "I rescued him from an alley in Savannah, and he likes to think he's rough and tough. But ... well, you'll meet him."

"Whatever you say." Liam sheathed his machete. "You mentioned lunch?"

Liam followed Mercy down the hill. Lots easier, and it gave him time to look around. The storm had pulled the moisture out of the air, leaving them with one of those rare perfect days. He took a deep breath. A good day to be outside and not stuck behind his desk. Even better to be spending it with a woman like—

"Watch where you're going." Mercy grabbed his arm. "You almost stepped on some wild pig droppings. Talk about smelly." She shook her head. "You don't want that on your shoes."

"So you do have some dangerous animals on your island."

"They're not dangerous." She threw a glance over her shoulder at him. "As long as you don't get between a sow and her shoats, or a boar and his mate."

They crested a rise, and to the left of the path Liam caught sight of a cottage that seemed to grow from the rocks and trees. He slowed. Mercedes's father had chosen the site for his cabin well.

"Are you coming or not?" Mercy stood on the porch holding the ugliest cat he'd ever seen.

To his surprise, when he came close, the animal squirmed from her grasp and jumped into his arms. Liam wrapped his arms around the scruffy thing, which proceeded to nestle against him and purr.

"Hawkeye's never done that before." Mercy gave him a perplexed look. "I guess he likes you."

Liam didn't know whether to smile or apologize—so he went with a smile. "I'm a likable guy."

Mercy turned her back on him with a huff and opened the door.

Maybe he should have apologized.

"I can see why you love it here." Liam gently disengaged the cat from his shirt and set him on the floor. "This place is terrific."

"It is." Mercy's tone softened. "I can't imagine living anywhere else." She opened the refrigerator. "We have ham and cheese—or cheese and ham."

"Either will do." Liam chuckled. "Let me help." He reached for the cheese, and their hands touched. Warmth traveled up his arm to his entire body in a flash. Old feelings surfaced in a rush. She was close enough to kiss. He turned his head ...

"My kitchen's too small for two people." She pulled away.

"Got it."

"You can feed Hawkeye. His dish is by the door." She handed him an open tin and a spoon.

No eye contact.

Idiot. He'd gotten carried away and assumed she felt the same way. "Be glad to."

As he finished spooning the food into Hawkeye's dish, he raised his eyes to the cross above the door. He touched his chest where his simple cross hung under his shirt.

"That's a beautiful cross over the door."

"My dad made that for my mom." Mercy glanced at it before setting a plate on the table.

"Are you a believer?"

"I used to be, until my mom got so sick." Mercy sat. "Everyone told me if I prayed hard enough, God would heal her. I prayed and prayed, but He didn't. I figured if He's not going to hold up His end of the bargain, why should I have anything more to do with Him?"

"Don't you think ..." Liam stopped. Not the right time. He felt it in his spirit. "Never mind. I'm sure you've heard it all before."

"I have." Mercy rolled her eyes.

"Maybe you can show me some of the plants I keep reading about in your reports."

"Sure." Mercy's shoulders relaxed. "I'll point them out as we inspect the island for more damage."

And maybe they could be friends again. He'd like that.

Chapter Four

"Once we get my communications tower fixed, next on my list of projects is to repair my screened porch." As she stepped through her front door, Mercy picked up a branch from the porch floor and tossed it aside.

"I'd be glad to help you with that." Liam surveyed the damage.

"Maybe. I'm used to taking care of myself."

"I understand, but this is a big job. I could bring some screening and a new door over when I come back with the block and tackle."

Her forehead creased into a frown. It was hard for her to accept help from anyone. What did she know about Liam anyway? It had been ten years since she last saw him. Now, all of a sudden, he showed up and acted like he wanted to pick up where they left off in high school. No way that was going to happen. She slid him a guarded look. Although he was good-looking and nice and . . . Get a grip, girl.

"We need to get moving if we're going to check out the island before you have to leave." She stepped off the porch onto the path. "These are maidenhair ferns." Mercy pointed to a cluster of low plants ahead of her. "They're found all over the island."

"What about the banana tree? Is it native?"

"No." Mercy ran a hand along its trunk. "My dad planted it when we first started coming here."

"What are some of the other trees?"

"There's the Bermuda palmetto." Mercy pointed to a tree with large leaves. "This one is a yellowwood or West Indian satinwood."

"Wow. A big guy." Liam tilted his head back to peer into the tangle of leaves and branches.

"Along the rocky shore, there's a tree called the buttonwood or sea mulberry. And then there's the Bermuda cedar." Mercy turned to Liam, unable to contain her enthusiasm. "Did you know the Bermuda cedar— indigenous to Bermuda of course—was wiped out on Bermuda by insects? But I found it here on Sharktooth Island. Seeds must have been carried by birds. How exciting is that?"

"Very exciting." He winked at her.

"You asked." She narrowed her gaze. "Remember?"

"Sorry. I couldn't resist teasing you a little." He smiled at her, his deep blue eyes pulling her in. She took a step in his direction. The raucous cry of a sea bird broke the spell.

"At this rate, we'll never get anywhere." She turned her back on him and took off down the path at a brisk pace, her heart beating in her throat.

What a mistake. She should have let him leave and checked the rest of the island on her own. By asking him to go with her, she'd encouraged him—given him reason to think she liked him—was attracted to him. And nothing could be further from the truth.

She would have to be brutally honest with him. Better to

tell him how she felt now and not drag this out any longer. She stopped and pivoted to face him.

But instead of looking at her, his gaze was fixed on something over her shoulder, his eyes wide in a pale face.

"What—" She swiveled around to see what caused such a reaction.

And froze.

The beady eyes of a massive feral pig glared at her from about six feet away.

"Back up slowly." Mercy withdrew her machete. "To your right is a yellowwood tree. Climb it. I'll come up after you. We only need to get about five feet off the ground."

One step. Two steps. Grunt. The pig tracked them with his eyes. He pawed the ground. The scrape of Liam's shoes on the bark of the tree sounded behind her. Mercy took another step back.

The boar exploded in her direction. She reached for the tree. Liam grabbed her arm and yanked her upward. She dropped her machete, gripped Liam's arm with both hands, and pulled her legs up and in against her chest. The pig barreled under her with inches to spare. Liam helped her climb to a low-hanging branch.

"That was a close one." Mercy ran the back of her hand across her brow. "Never had one charge before."

"Good thing I was with you."

"Hmm." She threw him a brief smile. The man saved her. So why was she having such a hard time thanking him?

"What were you going to say back there?"

"Say?" She averted her eyes. "Nothing important." This was not going the way she'd planned.

"I like it up here," Liam said. "You can see more of the island."

She lifted her eyes above the canopy of green. It was a great view. She would have enjoyed it more if it weren't for her constant awareness of the warmth radiating from the man sitting so close beside her.

"Time to get down," Mercy said. "You need to get back to your boat."

"Yes, ma'am." Liam saluted her. "But there's time to go a little farther."

The branch bounced under Mercy as Liam grasped the limb with his hands, pushed off so he hung a few feet from the ground, and dropped to his feet.

"Do what I did, and I'll help you down." Liam reached his arms up to catch her.

"I don't need any help." But before she could fall on her own, his strong hands were at her waist, lowering her to the ground.

"That wasn't so bad. Was it?"

Was he smirking at her? "You can take your hands off me now."

"Just making sure you had your balance."

Definitely smirking. She retrieved her machete and marched off. Feral pig or Liam. It was a toss-up.

"Mercy."

"Now what?" She rounded on him.

"What's that?" He pointed up the slope of the mountain.

A dark hole appeared in the sea of green. Where did that come from?

Chapter Five

"It looks like a cave." Mercy had heard rumors of caves on her island, but she'd never seen one. With machete in hand, she hacked a path through the vegetation toward the black void. "Stay behind me. I don't want any valuable plants damaged."

"You got it."

Mercy's whole body hummed with excitement the closer they came to the hole in her mountain. What a find. But why hadn't she seen it before?

She broke through into the clearing surrounding the cave entrance. A stately Bermuda palmetto lay on its side, broken off at ground level by the hurricane, no longer concealing the opening into the mountain.

"Liam, look." She dropped to her knees at the cave entrance, her pulse racing. "Governor Laffan's fern."

"And that's more exciting than a cave because ...?" Liam squatted beside her.

"It's another threatened species. Found only in caves and rock crevices."

When she looked at him, his smile reflected her joy. He stood and offered his hand to help her up. Maybe it wasn't so bad having him along after all.

"Want to see what's inside?" He indicated the yawning darkness with a tilt of his head.

"Maybe a little ways in." Goosebumps rose on her arms. Enclosed spaces. Especially caves. She rustled around for a flashlight in her backpack.

Liam extracted a small light from his pocket. "I'll go first."

The dank earth smell hit her as soon as they stepped inside, like being buried alive. Her pulse raced. And the clammy cold temperature. Why did it always have to feel like she was breathing underwater?

The farther in they went, the more rapid her breathing. Beads of sweat formed on her upper lip. She reached for Liam.

"Are you okay?" He took her hand.

"Yeah." She took a deep breath. "Just a touch of claustrophobia."

"We can go back."

Concern resonated in his voice, and a ripple of joy ran through her.

"No. We've come this far. We can go a little farther." She squared her shoulders but kept hold of his hand.

As the cave sloped deeper into the mountain, boulders pressed closer together.

"We'll need to walk single file," Liam said. "You sure you want to continue?"

"Yes." Something in her urged Mercy to continue.

The narrow passage turned left and widened.

Liam stopped short.

"What is it?" Mercy played the beam of her flashlight around his arm. On the walls, the ceiling, the floor. She gasped and squeezed his hand tighter. "Is that a ...

"Skeleton? Yes."

Liam loved the feel of Mercy's small, warm hand in his—not the way he preferred it to happen, but he'd take it. Until they stumbled upon the skeleton. He never liked dead people—in any way, shape, or form.

"It's time we go back and call the authorities," Liam said.

He turned and expected Mercy to do the same. Instead, she shook off his hand and approached the bones, squatting down for a closer look. His stomach churned.

"Look at this." She pulled gloves from her back pocket and picked something up.

He was going to be sick.

"I think it's a doubloon." The light from her flashlight reflected off the object in her hand. "I'm sending it back with you—along with photos of the skeleton—for the director of the Conservancy."

"Fine." Photographs he could handle.

She snapped several shots with her camera, wrapped one of the coins in a latex glove, and joined him. To his dismay, she didn't hold his hand going out.

"I can't believe it." Mercy propped against the fallen tree trunk and removed the old coin. "All those stories about pirate treasure may have been true."

"What stories?" Liam leaned next to her.

Shadows stretched across the clearing as the sun set over the trees. He should be going if he expected to get back to Savannah by nightfall. But he was reluctant to leave.

"We know pirates stopped here or were wrecked here at some point. That's how the pigs got here. Ships in those days carried pigs for food. When a ship landed or wrecked, some would make it to shore." Mercy gazed at the coin. "But the stories also said pirates buried a treasure here."

"Did you and your dad ever look for treasure?"

She shook her head. "He didn't believe the stories. One of my dad's rich ancestors bought the island, came here, and realized it wasn't good for what they wanted—partying mostly. Then in the 1930s, an airplane crashed on the island." She handed the doubloon to Liam. "None of them ever mentioned finding any treasure."

"What if they were wrong? What if there are piles of doubloons somewhere in that cave?" Liam gave her a soft smile. "What would you do with all that money?"

A yearning filled Mercy's eyes that arrowed straight to his heart.

"I'd quit working for the conservancy and start my own non-profit conservation business, studying the flora and fauna of my island and others the way I think it should be done."

"You don't like your job?"

She stiffened. "No—I mean—I'm grateful for my job. It's allowed me to live on my island." She gave an awkward shrug. "I just meant it would be nice to have my own business—be my own boss one day."

"You don't have to worry," Liam said. "Your dream is safe with me." He sighed. "It's late."

Mercy led him down the side of the mountain to his boat. He tossed his pack onto a seat and turned to face her. She gazed across the water deep in thought, hands shoved into her pants pockets. What was she thinking?

She roused. "Do you have a computer on board? I can transfer the pictures of the bones from my phone to it, for you to take back."

"Good idea." He helped her onto the boat and retrieved the computer.

As she worked, she absentmindedly tugged the scrunchie from her long hair and let it spill to her shoulders. Liam's fingers itched to touch it.

A small animal hurried along the pier. "Mrawr." Hawkeye leapt into the boat and rubbed against his legs.

"How'd you find us?" Liam picked the cat up and ran a hand down its back.

"You monster." Mercy closed the computer and joined them, scratching her cat on top of his head. "Come on. Time to go home."

But Hawkeye had other ideas.

"Ow." Liam pushed the cat away from him, bowing his back. "Sharp claws. I don't think he's ready to go."

"Stop that." Mercy pulled at her cat's legs. At the sound of tearing cloth, Hawkeye retracted his talons. Mercy grabbed him and her backpack and stepped onto the dock. She glanced back. "Liam, keep the discovery of the doubloon between you, me, and the director until we can investigate the cave further. If any treasure hunters get a whiff of our find, my life will be a living nightmare."

"You have my word."

She was right. The scoundrels would overrun her island, and there'd be nothing she could do about it. He toyed with the idea of throwing the coin overboard. No coin, no chance of disrupting Mercy's life.

Maybe he could look for the treasure himself and not involve the Conservancy. But when? And how? He'd never searched for pirates' treasure before, and he wasn't crazy about the idea of encountering more dead bodies in the cave.

The sea air stung his chest. He looked down at his torn shirt and the blood oozing from the scratches Hawkeye left. He probed his pack for a first-aid kit and a clean shirt.

Chapter Six

Liam grasped his coffee in one hand and swiped his key card with the other. In a practiced movement, he yanked the employees' entrance door open, stuck his foot out to hold it, and grabbed his backpack off the concrete next to him. Inside, he placed his pack on the table to be inspected.

"Good morning, Liam." A large woman in uniform peered at him over her glasses. "You know it would be a lot easier on you if you'd put that pack on your back."

"Rose, you know how it wrinkles my shirt." He smirked at her.

"Mmmhmm." Her eyes did a slow up-and-down over his creased short-sleeved shirt. "Whatever." She unzipped the front pocket of his backpack.

"Watch out for my gun. It's loaded."

"You're going to say that to the wrong person someday and get yourself thrown in jail."

He laughed. "I don't even own a gun."

"I thought you were in the service. Afghanistan or something."

"I was." He felt that familiar knot in his belly. "That's why."

"Gotcha." She finished her inspection and motioned Liam through the metal detector. "Here you go. And Liam, thanks for your service, buddy."

He nodded and hustled down the long hallway of the Land and Sea Conservancy. Liam, unlike other employees of the Conservancy, didn't mind all the security. Not since the incident next door, where a disgruntled employee decided to settle his grievances with an AR-15. Seven dead and ten more injured. He grimaced as pain shot through his stomach.

The door to his office came into sight. He'd drop his pack and head for Carl Roberts's office. The sooner he reported to his boss, the sooner he could return to the island—and Mercedes Baxter.

"Liam." Carl appeared in the hall next to him. "I expected you back yesterday. What happened?"

"Sorry. I got back too late to call." Liam swiped his card to open his office door. "Give me a minute. I've got a lot to report. We found a skeleton."

"Old or new?" Carl's tone sharpened.

"Old. No need for police."

"Good." The director's face relaxed. "I'll wait for you in my office."

Images of Mercy continued to distract him. What was she doing right now? Liam grabbed his laptop and the coin. He had to get back to fix her communication tower and help repair her porch.

He entered Carl's office and opened his computer. "I've sent you my report and the photos of the bones we found in the cave."

"Are those coins I see on the ground?" Carl grunted as he squinted at his screen.

"Yes." Liam pulled the glove holding the doubloon from his pocket. "I brought one for examination."

Carl shook the piece of dull gold metal out onto a clean white cloth.

Dirt encrusted the surface, but Liam made out a figure stamped into the metal. Not a perfect circle. A true doubloon wouldn't be. Each was handmade. Something different appeared on the reverse side. A pyramid?

"It certainly seems to be a gold doubloon, but not like any I've seen before," Carl said. "We need an expert opinion, and I know just the man."

"Wait a minute." Liam held up a hand. "I promised Mercy you and I would be the only other people to know about the coins. She's concerned about treasure hunters, and so am I."

"I understand her concern, but Dr. Alton Ewing is a reputable British expert on all things pirate and their treasure." Carl placed the coin in a small clear bag. "And we're in luck. He's in Savannah giving a talk at the university."

"Can he be trusted to keep this quiet?"

"I'll have our lawyers draw up a non-disclosure agreement for him to sign," Carl said.

"I don't like it." Liam pressed his lips together in a grim line. "More people will be involved. What if news of the treasure gets out anyway?"

"The Conservancy will take on the responsibility for hiring protection for Ms. Baxter and her island."

Liam vowed to make sure the Conservancy kept that promise. "What about the bones?"

"We'll have to get a forensic anthropologist out to the island to look at them. Let me think about who to call."

"I need to get back there ASAP. Mercedes's communications tower requires a block and tackle to get it up and functioning again. Until then, she can't get in touch with anyone in case of an emergency. I'm heading back this afternoon." Liam stood. "If it's okay with you."

"Of course." Carl nodded. "We must be able to let her know when the anthropologist is coming, once I get that arranged."

"I may be there a couple of days. She has some other repairs she needs help with." He studied his boss's face for resistance, but Carl seemed absorbed in his thoughts.

"Fine. No problem."

Liam grabbed his computer and left before Carl could change his mind. A list of supplies formed in his brain as he hurried to his office. Once there, he allowed himself to smile. Another chance to be around Mercy. Another chance to see her beautiful face. Another chance to win her affection.

Dr. Alton Ewing had heard all the stories about pirates stopping at Sharktooth Island—named for the black rock rising out of the sea on the north end. Some said it was cursed because so many ships wrecked against its jagged coastline.

An isle surrounded by rocky shores that offered no natural harbor. Ewing found it hard to believe that a pirate ship would have chanced a landing on such an inhospitable spit of land. But he found it best to keep an open mind. After all, it would be the perfect place to secure a treasure. Who would be willing to risk their vessel to look for it there?

Now he'd been asked to consult about an artifact found on Sharktooth Island. Entering through the front door of the Land and Sea Conservancy building, he approached the guards. "I'm Dr. Alton Ewing. I have an appointment with Carl Roberts."

The man peered at his computer screen. "Yes. Dr. Ewing.

Here's a visitor's badge. If you'll please put your briefcase on the belt and step through there."

"A great deal of security for a non-profit organization." Ewing felt his neck grow hot. He hated being treated like a potential terrorist.

"Yes, sir." The guard handed him his case, his tone polite but weary. "Take the first right. Mr. Roberts's office is at the end of the hall."

Ewing wished he'd made Carl Roberts come to him. He only hoped this meeting would be worth his time. Photos of plants and sea animals lined the walls of the hallway. Nothing of interest to Ewing.

Until he approached the end of the hall. An aerial photo of Sharktooth Island caught his eye with its distinctive rock formation. A high ridge ran north to south, and a silver thread of water shimmered through the green on the south end of the mountain range.

He'd been told someone owned and lived on the island now. A woman. That could prove to be a problem if this meeting was about treasure. But he'd dealt with more difficult obstacles before. He knocked on the door labeled Carl Roberts and opened it.

"Dr. Ewing. Please come in." Carl stood and indicated a leather armchair in front of a mahogany desk, then returned to his chair. "Thank you for coming."

Ewing glanced around. Bookshelves with specimens of sea creatures. A second chair next to his. Plants on the windowsill. The only thing out of place was the safe. Three feet high and two feet deep. What could be so valuable in Roberts's line of work? Maybe Ewing had misjudged him and his business.

"I know your time's as valuable as mine, so I'll get right to the business at hand." Carl spread a clean cloth on the desk between the two men and pulled on gloves. He handed a pair to Ewing. "This is the artifact I contacted you about."

As Roberts extracted the piece of metal, Ewing fought to contain his excitement. This could prove to be the evidence he sought—that many sought. If so, he'd have to remain cool until he could figure out a way to possess it and the others no doubt buried somewhere close by. He fixed a jeweler's loupe to his right eye and examined the coin. He pressed his hands on the table to keep them from trembling.

"Poor condition." A lie, but ... Ewing flipped the gold piece over and covered his exclamation with a cough. After regaining his inner composure, he replaced the coin and removed his eyepiece. "Possibly genuine. Unfortunately, there are many excellent reproductions."

Ewing struggled to maintain his blasé attitude. A cursory examination proved to him that this was indeed a Brasher Doubloon. And where there was one, there could be more. The stories of pirate treasure on Sharktooth Island were true.

And what a treasure it was.

"I would need to take this to the lab space I'm using at the University for authentication. Are you willing to allow that?"

"Of course. After all, you're the expert."

"Very well," Ewing said. "I'm very busy, but I'll try to return the piece along with my report to you in two weeks. Will that suffice?"

"Yes. That should be fine." Carl Roberts placed the coin in its bag and handed it to Ewing. "There is just one thing. The owner of the island is concerned—and rightly so—about treasure hunters. I'll need your signature on this document before you take the coin."

Ewing glanced through the typewritten pages. "This is preposterous. I've never been required to sign such a thing before in my life."

"I am sorry." Roberts gave him a tight smile. "However, those are the terms I agreed to."

Ewing took a deep breath. He didn't intend for anyone else to know about the treasure anyway. "The coin is most likely a forgery, so why not."

Alton Ewing couldn't control the slight shake of his hand as he signed his name. This could be the biggest discovery of his career—of the decade—of the century.

And to think, when Carl Roberts called, he almost turned him down.

Chapter Seven

Mercy opened the door to her small storage closet. Pushing aside what she called her mainland clothes, she reached for a small box on a shelf tucked against the back wall. In the kitchen, she ran a rag over the top and sides before carrying it to the sofa.

"Haven't looked in here for years." She took the lid off and peered inside.

A photo album, greeting cards, and a pair of her mother's favorite earrings sat next to a package wrapped in yellowed linen and tied with a velvet ribbon. Mercy lifted the parcel from the box and set it on her lap.

Bits of the cloth wrap crumbled in her hands. She had no idea how old it was, but she'd replaced the ribbon several years ago when the original disintegrated. Inside this simple covering was a diary started in the 1800s that might contain clues to a treasure.

Mercy had never read it. She'd never believed a treasure existed before now, and history bored her. People who kept diaries from that time usually wrote about the weather and other everyday things. Who cared about that stuff?

But with the discovery of the body, and more importantly, the doubloons, maybe it was time she took a look at this thing.

Hawkeye landed on the couch next to her.

"No you don't." Mercy circled her arms around the fragile parcel. "Don't even think about touching this."

The cat turned his back on her and flicked his tail. He marched to the other end of the couch and, after circling a few times, curled into a ball and closed his eyes.

"You don't fool me, monster." Mercy glared at him. "You're over there planning your attack."

She peered at the clock over the stove. The best use of her time would be to finish her surveying during daylight and look at the diary tonight. She rose, went to her bedroom, and placed the package in the drawer of her bedside table.

"Come on, cat. Let's go outside."

Hawkeye jumped off the couch and stretched.

Turning left outside her house, she headed for a section she hadn't checked yet. There appeared to be more damage in this direction. She cleared the path and made notes, but her progress was slow.

Mercy stopped on the trail by yet another downed tree. The loss of every plant the hurricane destroyed was like a stab to her heart. She'd spent the last five years of her life recording and mapping out the flora and fauna of the island. Logical or not, this small expanse of rock in the middle of the ocean meant more to her than just a place to live and work.

Every day her home offered her a gift—a new plant species or flower ... or a cave. The scientist part of her brain itched to go back and explore. However, the less rational part said, "*Caves are dark and closed-in spaces, and you know how you feel about those.*"

She lifted her eyes and gazed through a break in the trees toward the mainland. Liam promised to return either today or tomorrow. Her chest rose and fell in a heavy sigh. Why did he have to be the one to come help her?

Feelings she'd packed away long ago had burst out of their box at the sight of him, and she looked forward to his next visit. That would never do. She'd carved out a perfect life for herself on the island. Uncomplicated. Simple.

Lonely?

Scratch that. She had her cat and her work. Mercy made a note in her book about the downed tree. Hawkeye jumped from a nearby branch onto the path in front of her.

"Hey, monster." Mercy scooped up the tomcat and rubbed his scraggly head with her chin. "What have you been doing?"

He answered with a loud purr.

"I love you too." She blinked back tears. Where did those come from? She must be hungry. "How about some lunch?"

She found a shaded spot to sit and opened her backpack. "Get your nose out of there, cat. I'll share."

A welcome breeze drifted up the side of the mountain, bringing with it the smell of the sea. Once again Mercy scanned the horizon. She shook her head, needing to get her mind off Liam.

"After lunch, we're going for a boat ride around the island." She stroked the rough fur along Hawkeye's spine. "See what damage the hurricane did to the ocean side of home." She stood. "Let me clean up here and—"

Something dropped on her shoulder. She shrieked and swatted it to the ground. A large Bermuda toad landed on the path, and before she could react, Hawkeye pounced.

"No." Mercy grabbed for her cat. "Don't touch it." Too late. Her heart pounded in her chest as she yanked her backpack on and rushed down the path toward home, Hawkeye wrapped in her arms.

At a break in the vegetation, she spied Liam's boat pulling in to the dock. Relief flooded through her. She changed direction and raced down the side of the mountain.

"Get the boat started. We need to get Hawkeye to the vet. Now." She leaped into his boat. Was he deaf? "Go." She stared at him. "It's an emergency."

LIAM BLINKED. Emergency. He tossed the rope aside, jumped into his boat, and fired her up. Within seconds, he was headed back the way he'd come. He glanced at his passengers. Mercy sat on the floor, her back braced against the bench seat across the rear. Hawkeye lay lethargic across her lap.

"What happened?" he said.

"He bit a Bermuda toad."

Mercy's tawny-colored mane whipped around in the wind. Tears streamed from her eyes, across her cheeks, and into her hairline. Liam waited for more explanation.

"The toads carry a neurotoxin that's only an irritant to humans but can be deadly to small animals."

Hawkeye shook his head. Saliva flung from the corners of his lips. Mercy forced his mouth open and wiped the inside of the cat's mouth with a dry paper towel from her pack. She poured water from a bottle onto another one and wiped around her pet's eyes.

"If we can get him to the vet soon enough, there's a slim chance he can survive."

A vise closed around Liam's heart. "Hang on." He pushed the handle forward, and the big motor responded. The seas were calm and there weren't many boats out today. He'd never driven over water this fast before. For a time, he forgot about his passengers and concentrated on getting to his destination as soon as possible.

When he came to the no-wake zone, Liam reluctantly slowed the boat to a crawl. He found an open spot at the dock and pulled in. Before he could tie up, Mercy and her cat were on the pier and headed for town.

"Where are you going?" Liam watched her weave through the people.

"I'll call you."

But how? She didn't have his number. He wished he was with her, especially if something happened to Hawkeye. Frustration flooded his soul. What could he do?

The answer was simple.

Pray.

MERCY HAILED A TAXI, gave the driver an address, and piled into the backseat. "Please hurry. My cat is really sick."

"He's not going to throw up, is he?"

"No." She glared at the man. "Drive. Please?"

At the veterinarian's office, Mercy threw money at the driver and bolted for the door. Hawkeye's limbs stiffened as a seizure hit his body. Fear stabbed her chest. She pushed through the door into the waiting room and ran for the reception desk.

"My cat's been poisoned. I need your help now."

The lady pressed a button to unlock the door into the back.

"What happened?"

"He bit into a Bermuda toad. They release bufotoxin." Mercy thrust Hawkeye into the nurse's arms. "He's had one seizure already."

"We'll take it from here. Give your information to the desk." The nurse hurried into a surgery room with Hawkeye and closed the door.

Mercy swiped her hands across her cheeks. She'd gotten him to the vet—she and Liam. She ached to have him here.

Was that her phone? It'd been so long since she'd heard it ring. She dug it out of her backpack and looked at it. One missed call. It rang again and she almost dropped it.

"Hello?"

"Where are you?"

Liam. Joy flooded through her. "At the vet's. Can you come?"

"Sure. As soon as you tell me where the office is."

She gave him the address and dropped into the nearest chair. A woman with a Labrador puppy sat next to her.

"I heard what happened to your cat," the woman said. "I'll pray for you and your sweet pet."

"Thank you." Mercy forced the words out around the lump in her throat.

The woman had such a kind face. Mercy didn't have the heart to tell her that praying didn't work. Tears spilled over her eyelids and coursed down her cheeks. If prayer wasn't enough to keep her mom from dying, it sure wouldn't be enough to keep a cat alive. She covered her face with her hands.

"Mercy?" Liam touched her shoulder.

As she turned into his embrace, all the grief she'd held inside for her mother and her father poured from her soul. Wave after wave rushed through her and beat against Liam's chest—and she was incapable of stopping it.

Chapter Eight

Liam held on to Mercy as she sobbed, her misery crashing against him. *Father, give me the strength to absorb her pain.* He murmured comforting words to her, unsure if she even heard them.

After several moments, Mercy's wails became slow tears punctuated by shuddering breaths. She lay against him as if her spine wouldn't support her.

The woman next to Mercy rocked gently, eyes closed in prayer. An elderly couple across the room held hands while tears coursed down their faces.

The nurse opened the door into the reception area. "Mercedes Baxter."

Mercy pushed away from Liam and touched his shirt where she'd drenched it with her tears. "Sorry."

Her eyes and nose were a mess. Liam grabbed a box of tissues and offered it to her.

"We'll be right there." Liam held up a hand. "Give her a sec."

Mercy blew her nose a couple of times and wiped her eyes. She straightened her shoulders and faced the nurse.

"No need to be so upset." The nurse pivoted on her heel and led them into a room with cages floor to ceiling. "Your cat has a good chance of recovering." She stopped in front of a large Plexiglas door at about chest height. "Although I'll admit at first it didn't look that way. Then about a half hour ago, everything changed." She shook her head. "Maybe cats do have nine lives."

Mercy frowned and glanced over her shoulder at the waiting room.

"We've got him sedated so he won't seize again, and to give his liver time to get rid of the toxin." The nurse made some notes on her pad. "The IV's simply to keep him hydrated."

Hawkeye lay inside the compartment with an IV tube in his paw and a ventilator tube in his mouth.

"Get well, monster." Mercy laid her forehead against the clear door. "I can't lose you too."

Liam's heart squeezed.

Dr. Alton Ewing replaced the gold coin in its protective case. A near-perfect specimen of a Brasher doubloon. Worth close to a million dollars by itself. He swallowed at the thought of a whole treasure chest of these waiting to be found on a rocky island off the coast.

He'd searched the internet for everything he could find on Mercedes Baxter and Sharktooth Island. Disappointingly little. And no social media presence. Didn't she have friends or relatives that she kept up with?

But Ewing had friends—connections—in all the right places, and they told him enough. Well before Mercy's father inherited the island, there were several lean years when the family failed to pay the property taxes. The governor pardoned the debt, but Ewing doubted if Ms. Baxter knew about it. In fact, he counted on her ignorance.

Time to go treasure hunting. He folded the copies of the tax documents obtained from his friend and placed them in his briefcase. The gleam of gold caught his eye, and he reached a trembling hand to touch the object of his desire.

"Soon you will be mine." He sighed. "And all the rest as well." A tear escaped his eye and ran down his face. "No more guest lectures for a pittance or consulting for inane salvage companies. I will be free to pursue my research."

MERCEDES SCOOPED her last spoonful of oatmeal and stared out the window of the café. She envied the sun, with its head buried beneath a blanket of clouds. Sleeping on a friend's sofa and worrying about Hawkeye robbed her of any rest the night before.

"You look—" Liam eyed her before taking a seat. "—in need of another cup of coffee." He motioned for the waitress. "Have you talked to the vet's office?"

Mercy shook her head. "It's tea."

"What?"

"Not coffee." She held up her cup. "Hot tea."

In truth, she was afraid to call the vet. She wasn't sure she could handle it if her cat ... She squared her shoulders and picked up her cell phone.

"This is Mercedes Baxter. I'm calling about—"

"Hawkeye," the woman said. "Yes, Ms. Baxter. Let me get the nurse."

Mercy's breakfast turned to cement in her stomach. She

raised her eyes to Liam. He lowered his cup and gave her a reassuring smile.

"Ms. Baxter? Your cat's resting comfortably. Still sedated, but all his vital signs are good." A rustling of paper. "We'd like to keep him here for a couple of days to be sure the toxin is out of his body. Is that all right with you?"

Mercy smiled into the phone. "Yes. Do whatever you need to." She paused. "Thanks. He's not much to look at, but he means a lot to me."

"I understand."

After ending the call, Mercy took a drink of her tea, grown cold by now. Liam sliced into a stack of pancakes dripping with syrup. Relief filled her with nervous energy. She was ready to go home.

"When you finish breakfast, would you take me back to the island? Maybe we can at least get my tower up and working."

"What about Hawkeye?"

"He's good. He'll be here for a few days of rest and recuperation." She caught the eye of their waitress. "I've got lots to do back home." When the young woman arrived at their table, Mercy gave her a big smile. "Would you make us a tea and a coffee to go, please?"

"Certainly."

The good news about Hawkeye energized her. She eyed Liam's plate of food. "You going to eat all that?"

"I planned on it."

"Okay." She gazed out the window, but she was having trouble sitting still. Soon her fingers were tapping a rhythm on the table.

Liam took another bite and pushed his plate of half-eaten flap-jacks across the table with a sigh.

Chapter Nine

Mercy stood at the helm next to Liam, searching the horizon for a glimpse of her island. At last, the dark rock in the shape of a giant tooth came into view. Her pulse quickened. Home. Another half hour, and the boat slowed as it approached the dock.

"I'll get the cart to carry everything." She headed for a small shed at the land end of the pier.

A stab of sadness. No bedraggled cat running to greet her. Liam unloaded supplies from the boat. For the first time in five years, she wasn't sure about her future. The storm uprooted her like one of the trees on her island. She'd been so anxious to get back to her home, but now that the cart was loaded and they were ready to make the trek up the hill, uncertainty threatened to keep her from moving forward.

"That's it." Liam wiped his forehead with the back of his hand. "It's heavy. I'll push it." He started off ahead of her.

"It's better to pull it," Mercy said. "I'll help."

"I got this."

"Don't be so stubborn." She grabbed the handle. "I do this all the time."

"*You're* calling *me* stubborn?" Liam raised an eyebrow at her.

She narrowed her eyes at him. He had a point. But so did she.

"We'll work together. Okay?"

"On one condition." Liam grinned at her.

"What?" If he asked for a kiss, she'd let him push the stupid thing up the mountain on his own.

"I cook dinner for you."

Relief—tinged with a tiny bit of disappointment. "Deal."

By the time they arrived at the cabin huffing and puffing, the sun brushed the tops of the trees. Much of the porch and surrounding vegetation lay in shadow. Mercy opened the solid front door and grabbed a lantern. She led Liam around to the generator on the side of the cabin.

"Hope this works. I left without shutting it down." She filled the gas and pressed the button. The engine growled into life. "Success."

In the cabin, she opened the refrigerator door. "Luckily, I didn't have much in here." Yuck. "Hand me a trash bag."

"Need help?"

"Nope." Mercy pointed to a shelf over the sink. "Why don't you get started on that dinner you're making for me? You can use one of those bowls for salad."

"Will do."

HAMBURGER PATTIES FRIED IN A PAN, salad, and applesauce. Simple, but tasty. Especially since she didn't have to make it herself. And he cleaned up after. She glanced at him.

Best not to get used to this treatment. Pretty soon it would be her and the monster again. Alone on her island. But wasn't that how she liked it? Then why this ache in her chest?

"What do you usually do in the evenings on your island?" Liam plopped on the couch next to her.

"Write up my notes for the day. If it's a nice evening, go for a boat ride." She gazed around her living room, her eyes landing on her bookshelves. "Read."

The journal. She jumped up.

"Excuse me a sec." She rushed into her bedroom and opened the nightstand drawer. The muslin-wrapped book rested there undisturbed.

"What's that?" Liam stood in the doorway.

"A journal passed down through my family." Mercy touched the fabric covering. "I'm hoping it has a clue to the possible treasure in the cave." She maneuvered past Liam back to her spot on the sofa, where he joined her.

She untied the ribbon and lifted the linen wrapping with care until the journal lay exposed on her lap. A small leather book, maybe four inches by six inches, once most likely a rich red color, the cover now a faded pink. Worn gold filigree embossing along each edge, with matching embossed letters in the center that read Day to Day.

Mercy opened the diary with the greatest of care. The old dry paper snapped and crinkled in protest.

"The pages are lined." Liam sounded surprised.

So was she. And the handwriting—all loops and swirls. She could barely make it out. This wasn't going to be easy.

"Can you read this?" She studied the first page.

"I think it says something about this being the diary of Laura Bryant recording her voyage from Maine aboard the *Anindol*—or *Arundel*—with her father, Captain Bryant."

"To where?" Mercy leaned closer to Liam. The warm spicy scent of his cologne tickled her nose.

He frowned in concentration as he ran a finger down the page. "The Caribbean islands?"

"Let me see if I can read any of it." She shifted the book so light from the lamps fell directly on the pages. "It looks like the first pages are about life at sea. Nothing more exciting than spotting a whale or a pod of dolphins."

"Here's where it gets interesting." Liam pointed to an entry several pages in. "They're fighting a storm and see a pirate ship bearing down on them."

Excitement pulsed through her. "You read the rest. Were they near my island?"

"The description fits." Several minutes of quiet as Liam deciphered a few pages. "It seems the schooner braved the storm to get away from the pirates and crashed on the rocks on the leeward side. Somehow, they got ashore and set up a rough camp."

"What about the pirates?" Mercy's hopes of learning anything from this book dimmed.

"Nothing." Liam flipped a couple of pages ahead. "She doesn't say anything more about the pirates. But if they spotted them headed for the island, they may have landed on the ocean side."

"That seems almost impossible."

"Hey. Look on the bright side." Liam handed her the diary. "At least we know there were pirates in the vicinity of your island."

Chapter Ten

"She doesn't mention any treasure." Liam read the disappointment in her eyes. "Doesn't mean there wasn't one."

"I know." She slumped against the back of the sofa. "But ..."

"Near the end, she talks about a cave." A picture of the black hole amongst a sea of green flitted through his mind. "I think it may be the same one we discovered." He nudged her. "Look at her drawing."

Mercy leaned close to him once more. Her hair brushed his cheek, and he fought the urge to touch it.

"This cave looks very similar," she said.

"We need to explore it further."

She turned to him. "You would do that?"

"Of course. I ... you're my friend." The gratitude in her eyes took his breath away. Was that scruffy cat the only friend Mercedes had?

She rose and hurried from the room.

Now what? He placed the book on a nearby table and went

after her. Mercy sat on the edge of her bed with her face in her hands.

"Was it something I said?" Liam stopped at the doorway.

She shook her head.

"Did?"

Another head shake.

"Then I give up." He let frustration tinge his voice. "Good night."

At the door, he heard a noise behind him. He turned. Mercy stood so close he thought he could hear her heart beating.

"I'm sorry." She lowered her gaze. "It's been so long since I've let myself rely on anyone. Trust anyone."

"You can trust me." He smoothed loose hairs behind her ears.

She raised her lips to his, her hands on his shoulders. Slowly, she slid her arms around his neck.

He pulled her in tighter and deepened their kiss. Warmth flooded his body.

"I'd forgotten what it was like." She pushed away.

"I've never forgotten."

She laid a hand on his chest. "I can't decide if seeing you again is the best thing that's happened to me—or the worst."

"You'll have to decide that for yourself." He grinned. "As for me, it's the best." However, he knew better than to hang his hopes on one kiss. Time to leave. "But it's late. See you in the morning." He planted a kiss on her nose. "Sweet dreams. I'll be on the boat."

MERCY CLOSED the sturdy wood door and pressed her forehead against its rough surface. The storm that battered her island several days ago didn't compare with the one raging inside her at that moment. She paced the room.

Light glinted off the silver cross above the door. She paused and gazed at it.

"What do You want from me?" She lifted her hand. "I felt the cross under his shirt." She turned her back to the door and crossed her arms over her chest. Tears poured from her eyes and dripped from her chin. A reflection of the cross shone in the mirror in front of her.

"The woman prayed and Hawkeye ..." Mercy cut her eyes to the ceiling. "I guess I owe You for that one." She scrubbed her face with her hands. "But what about Liam? If You sent him into my life again, how can I trust You won't take him away again, like You have all the other people I've cared about?" She shook her head. "No. I can't go through that again."

She collapsed onto the sofa, and her gaze fell on the diary once more. When she picked it up, it fell open to an entry in a different hand, later in the book, written by another young woman wrecked on the island. A distant relative from a time when wealth and greed ruled. But Mercy's wild island with its rocky shores got the best of them, and they gave up the idea of building an ocean resort here.

Her smile stopped cold as she read the entry. They'd found the cave. The same one described earlier. But there'd been an altercation, and a man died. Could he be the man she and Liam had found? She stared at the diary. That could only mean one thing.

The cave in the book and her cave had to be the same.

Which still left the question, where did he get the doubloons? Did he already have them when he went into the cave? Or did he find a treasure somewhere deep inside?

Mercy took the book and its wrappings into the bedroom

with her. No way she'd get any sleep until she'd read some more.

In what seemed like a matter of minutes, Mercy woke to a knock on her door. Weak sunlight filtered through her curtains and reflected off the mirror over her dresser. She winced.

"Hang on a sec." She located the open journal unharmed on the bed to her left, rolled to her right, and stood.

Running a hand through her hair and straightening her clothes, she padded into the living room and opened the door. Liam raised a hand in greeting. All clean-shaven, combed dark brown hair, unwrinkled, six feet of male. How had he managed that after sleeping on his boat?

Mercy shut the door in his face.

"Give me to the count of five and come in." She hurried for her room and adjoining bath, closing the bedroom door behind her.

"Too late." Liam opened the front door as she disappeared into her bedroom. "I've already seen you." He strolled to the closed bedroom door and leaned an ear close. "Whatever you're doing, you don't have to."

A muffled answer.

"What?" He turned the knob on the door like he was going to open it and smirked to himself.

"Come in here and you're a dead man, Liam Stewart."

"Fine. I'll make coffee." He headed for the kitchen. No coffeemaker or pot. Instant? He rummaged through the shelves.

"You won't find any." Mercy's voice sounded behind him a few minutes later. "I don't drink coffee. Only tea." She reached for the teakettle, filled it with water, and set it on the stove to heat. “If you wanted coffee, you should have brought some from your boat.”

Her damp hair smelled good. Like the bush with purple flowers his grandmother had outside her front door. He inhaled again, and memories of his granny filled his mind.

“Liam.” Mercy tapped his arm. “Do you want tea or not?”

“Yes. But first ...” He leaned in for a kiss.

She shied away.

“It’s only a kiss, Mercy.” He touched her cheek. “I don’t expect anything. I’ll never push you.”

“I don’t know what I want.” Her brown eyes searched his as if for answers.

“I understand. You’ve been on your own for a long time.” He smiled, praying she felt all the reassurance and love he strived to transmit.

She touched her lips to his in a sweet kiss. “Thank you.”

Better. “What’s on the agenda today? Fix the antennae, and then what?” He took his cup to the table.

Her face lit up. “I read some more of the diary last night. Someone else wrote in it later. They skipped a few pages after Laura left off, and guess what?” She hurried on without giving him time to answer. “Our ancestors from around the turn of the century discovered the same cave as Laura.”

“No kidding.”

“There’s more. According to the journal, a man died in the cave, and I think it may be our skeleton.” She thumped the table. “What do you think of that?”

His stomach clenched. The thought of trying to find his way in the pitch dark only to die yards from another entrance ... He sighed.

“Antennae and cave exploring it is.” *Please Lord, no more dead bodies.*

Chapter Eleven

F*ix the antennae and explore the cave.* Mercy breathed a sigh of relief. Having tasks to focus her energy made it easier to ignore her internal turmoil.

"I'll get the sled." She headed out the door.

"Can't we use the cart?"

"Too wide for the mountain trail. You'll see."

She crossed to a sturdy shed sheltered between two rocks. A heavy-duty plastic toboggan stood inside the door. Four feet long by about a foot and a half wide. Perfect for her trails. She pulled a can of wax from a shelf and carried both to the porch.

"I get it. A toboggan." Liam stood on the porch with his cup in one hand.

"Get me a rag from the bottom drawer in the kitchen." Mercy sat on the top step. "I need to wax this thing before we drag it up the mountain."

"Can I help?" Liam handed her a couple of stained cloths.

"No. I ..." She stopped. It was nice to have help, and before long, she'd be back to doing things by herself. "On second thought, why not? You take the back end, and I'll take the front."

"I see how you secure stuff to the sled, but how do you pull it up the trail?" Liam said.

"Dad made a leather harness that fits over the shoulders and attaches across the chest. The rope at the front of the sled hooks onto the back of the harness."

"Like a dog sled." Liam laughed.

Mercy stopped rubbing. "I never thought of it that way." She pointed at him. "But don't get any ideas about riding in the back."

"Wouldn't dream of it." He grinned.

"SHOULD'VE LET you pull on this part of the trail." Liam's eyes stung from sweat pouring off his forehead. "How much longer?"

"We're close."

The steady whack, whack of Mercy's machete stopped, and Liam raised his head. Four feet to the summit. He leaned into the traces once more. His right calf twitched. Not a good sign for later.

"Take a break." Mercy handed him a sport drink and a towel.

"Thanks." He took a drink and surveyed the area at the top.

They needed to cut the vegetation away from the tower. Could use those two trees to attach guy wires. Shouldn't take too long.

"Let's get started." Liam got the ropes in place while Mercy cleared the pad.

An hour later, the tower stood tall again. A little bent, but in working order. Liam patched the break in the wires to complete the process.

"Now to check if it works." He threw extra rope on the sled. "Back to the cabin to make a call."

"Great." Mercy shaded her eyes to admire her tower. "Thanks for this. I'll pull the sled."

"You would. It's all downhill." He shook his head and took off down the trail, but felt the rock slide out from under him too late. "Ow!" A sharp pain lanced his ankle, and he ended up on his rear end.

"What happened?" Mercy squatted next to him.

"Stepped on a rock. Turned my ankle." Good thing he'd put on his boots, or it would have been worse. "I'm okay."

"Can you walk?" She stood and placed her hands on her hips. "I told you, no riding in the sled."

Was she smirking at him? "I think I can manage. Help me up."

Pain. Step. Pain. Step. He gritted his teeth. Not good.

"Use this." Mercy handed him a stout branch to use as a walking stick. "Is that better?"

He nodded. Took some getting used to, but it did help. A sigh escaped his lips when the cabin came into view.

Mercy dragged the sled to a spot by the porch. *Guess I'll have to search the cave on my own.*

"I made it," Liam said with a growl.

Mercy rushed to help him with the steps. "Let me get you settled, and I'll make us a fresh pot of tea." Memories of taking care of her dad flitted through her mind.

"I'd like to make that call to the director." He scanned the room. "Where's your radio?"

"Why do want to call the director?" Mercy led Liam to the rear of her cabin, where an older model shortwave radio sat on a desk.

"I just want to let him know your tower is up and working again and check on ... stuff at work."

What a mess. Papers and charts pinned to the cork board above the radio overlapped in a haphazard array. The pencil holder on its side spilled its contents over more papers, and two old mugs from who-knew-when sat atop all the clutter.

"Sorry." She righted the pencil holder and gathered all the pens and pencils as Liam pulled out the rolling chair and sat. "Hawkeye enjoys knocking things over."

"No problem. You should see my desk."

She shook her head and grabbed the cups. Who did he think he was kidding? She'd sat on the floor of his boat. Clean enough to eat off. No doubt his office was pristine. She dropped the mugs into the sink and swiped at her eyes. Stupid cat. She missed that monster. Why'd he have to attack that toad?

"Mercy? How do you work this thing?"

"Let me do it." Mercy strode across the room and pushed Liam aside. Like any machine, her radio had its quirks, and Mercy knew them all. The sticky frequency knob. The exact spot to slap when it acted up.

And the right words to use to coax it into life. Satisfied that her prima donna was cooperating, she relinquished the spot to Liam.

"You can make the call to Carl," he said.

"Oh no." She waved her hands at him. "I've only talked to him maybe two times in five years. You talk to him almost every day."

"Fine."

"Good." Mercy stood next to him. "It's ready."

Liam drew the mike closer and pressed the button. "Station 496, this is 498 calling. Over."

"Station 498, this is 496. Good to hear you're back online. Who am I speaking with? Over."

"Liam Stewart."

"Is anyone with you, Liam?"

"Yes, Mercedes Baxter."

"Please put her on to verify."

"Hello, 498." Mercy bent to the mike. "Mercedes here."

"What is your code please?"

Mercy glanced at the calendar overhead. "5197. Over."

"Thank you, Mercy. What can I do for you?"

She pushed the mic in Liam's direction.

"We'd like to talk to the director, Carl Roberts, if possible. Please tell him Liam Stewart is calling from this location."

"One moment."

After a few moments, they heard a man's voice. "Is it ready for me to talk now?"

"Yes sir," the woman said.

"Liam? Can you hear me?"

"Yes sir." Liam rolled his eyes at Mercy.

She put a hand over her mouth to suppress a giggle.

"So glad you were able to get communications restored to the island."

"Yes, sir. We got the tower back on its pad, and I was able to repair the break in the line." Liam looked at Mercy. "I added more guy wires to secure it so when the next storm blows through, Mercy should be okay."

"Good. As for the other business, I haven't heard from the forensics pathologist about when he can come examine the bones. Nor have I heard from Dr. Ewing about the doubloon."

Who was Dr. Ewing, and what did he have to do with her

doubloon? Mercy took a step away from the desk and from Liam.

Liam turned, and the look on his face confirmed her fears. He'd broken his promise.

Her chest hurt and she was having trouble breathing. She backed toward the door.

"Liam?" Carl said. "Did you hear me?"

"Have to go." He swiveled back to the mic. "I'll call later. Over and out."

She hurried outside and leaned her back on the banana tree. "First mom. Then dad. Now just when I was beginning to believe again, hope again, You snatch that away too? What kind of God are you?"

"Don't blame Him for my weakness." Liam stood six feet away leaning on his walking stick. "I tried to stop Carl from calling in Dr. Ewing, but ..." He scrubbed a hand down his face. "I almost threw the stupid coin overboard on my way back. Now I wish I had."

"Why would you do that?"

"I had this crazy idea I could find the treasure on my own, so you wouldn't have to get anyone else involved." He shook his head. "I'm so sorry, Mercy."

Something inside her shifted. She walked over and lifted his face until she could see his eyes. He was telling the truth, but there was more. Pain mingled with unbridled desire and love poured from his gaze, taking her breath away.

"It's okay." She stroked his cheek. "But I'll need your help dealing with these experts."

"I'm not going anywhere." He took her hand in his. "Except, I need a doctor." He looked at his ankle and sighed. "It hurts bad."

"Let me get the sled." She kissed him on the cheek.

"You can't—"

"Yes. I can. It's how I got my dad to and from our boat at the end."

At least she hoped she could. Liam was quite a bit heavier than her dad had been. She paused. *Okay, look. I may not believe like I should, but Liam does. So, for his sake, please help me get him down to his boat. Amen. Safely. Amen.*

THE TIDE WAS GOING OUT, and his boat rode low in the water. Maybe her idea would work. Mercy positioned the sled parallel to the pier and stepped into the gently swaying boat.

"I'm going to help you swing your legs in." She brought the sled closer to the edge of the pier.

"Not sure I can stand on my own."

"You don't have to." She retrieved his walking stick. "I'll help."

"If you get me to the captain's chair, I can make it back." Liam winced as his foot hit the deck of the boat. "I'll call for help once I get there."

Mercy shook her head. "I'm coming with you."

"You can't." He plopped into the chair and reached for the laces on his boot.

"Don't." Mercy put a hand on his. "Leave the boot on until you get to the doc's office. Trust me."

He sat back. "Stay here and keep watch over your island." A pained look crossed his face. He grabbed her hand and kissed it. "I'll be back as soon as I can."

The storm inside raged again. Her eyes searched the hills of her island for an answer and came to rest on Liam's chest, where his simple gold cross lay against his T-shirt.

What should she do?

"Mercy, pray with me before I go."

It was a simple prayer asking for protection and healing. But as he spoke the words, her face lifted toward the sky as peace flooded through her like a warm ocean wave.

She squeezed his hand and stepped onto the dock.

"I love you," she said.

But the engine roared to life and she was sure he hadn't heard. Just as well.

She lingered there until he disappeared beyond the horizon. Movement to the right caught her attention. She shaded her eyes with her hand. Was that another boat plowing through the waves?

Chapter Twelve

Dr. Alton Ewing eased the throttle back until the yacht came off plane. Setting the motor to idle, he reached for his binoculars. Waves rocked the boat as he scanned the island about a half mile away.

According to the map, the line of hills reached about one thousand feet in elevation. Hardly mountains, but from the water, the steep-sided ridge, lush with vegetation, appeared much higher than he expected. Too much vegetation to see a cave entrance from his vantage point.

What about the woman, Mercedes Baxter?

"Where are you, my dear?" He swept the binoculars over the sea of green.

The steel lattice of a communications tower stood on the highest point, its upper half visible above the trees. No sign of a cabin. A twenty-five-foot cabin cruiser bobbed in the swells next to the dock. He followed the gangway to the land and then up the path cut into the hillside.

Movement among the trees. A woman. With binoculars.

Looking his way.

He jerked the field glasses away from his eyes and stepped back into the shadows, uttering a mild expletive. Not how he'd planned their first encounter.

Ewing pushed the throttle forward, bringing the big boat up to speed, and headed for Mercy's dock.

Time to properly introduce himself.

MERCY LOWERED THE BINOCULARS. "GA3716ZQ" She repeated the boat registration to herself as she rushed to the cabin. Once inside, Mercy jotted the number on a pad by her radio and adjusted the frequency dial with a trembling hand.

"This is Sharktooth Island calling the Coast Guard. Come in, Coast Guard. Over."

"This is Coast Guard Air Station Savannah. What is your emergency, Sharktooth? Over."

"No emergency, but there's a yacht approaching my island that—worries me. The registration numbers are GA3716ZQ. Could you check it out for me?"

"What is it about the vessel that worries you?"

"I live alone. I don't know him. And when he saw me with his binoculars, he headed my way." She shuddered.

"One moment."

Mercy left the desk and fitted the beam across the door. When she returned, the man from the Coast Guard spoke again.

"The boat's a rental. A Dr. Alton Ewing paid for a week, starting today. Does that name mean anything to you?"

Ewing. She should have known. "Yes. Unfortunately. I didn't invite him."

"Would you like us to send someone out?"

Once when her dad was still alive, two men came to the

island. When they discovered the cabin, they decided to rob it. But as they came in the door, she and her dad sneaked out a window. They boarded their boat, untied the men's boat, and took both away from the dock.

The thieves returned to the dock only to find their boat drifting out to sea. And a Coast Guard cutter steaming toward them.

If the professor was there to rob her, could she find some equally clever way to handle him on her own?

But what if he wasn't alone?

"I hate to ask you to do that ..." she said.

"We've got a boat on patrol. I'll have him stop by."

"Thanks." Her shoulders dropped as tension bled from her body.

She changed the dial on her radio. In the meantime, she'd call the Conservancy and give them a piece of her mind.

Ewing nudged the yacht against the dock and tied it off. He doubted she'd come meet him, but he took his time fussing over his pack anyway. Papers showing the back taxes owed. Research on the coin. Latest auction values for a Brasher doubloon. All there.

Along with a few other items that might come in handy.

He glanced at his watch and sighed. No sign of Ms. Baxter. He would have to find the house on his own. Knotting a red scarf around his neck, Ewing donned a safari hat and marched toward the island.

The path followed a couple of switchbacks up the side of the hill until it dead-ended in another trail. Ewing stopped to wipe his neck and face. Why did this treasure have to be on an island? With hills and heat? And which way did he go now?

"Ms. Baxter, you are trying my patience." He closed his eyes.

Of course, he'd spotted her to the right. Headed home. He replaced his scarf and hat and swung his pack over his shoulder.

"Here I come. Ready or not."

Chapter Thirteen

Mercy pushed her chair back and buried her face in her hands. What had she done? Maybe the third or fourth time she'd spoken to Director Roberts, and she'd let him have it for sharing the doubloon with Ewing.

That was it. He was sure to fire her. No job, no money. No money, no more living on her island. She jumped to her feet and paced around her living space. A flash of light caught her eye—the beautiful cross above her door.

"I need Your help." She folded her hands. "I know I don't deserve it. I've done nothing but yell at You or ignore You for years—and I'm sorry. Please help me. I don't want to lose my job and have to leave my island." She used the neckline of her T-shirt to soak up her tears. "Amen."

A knock on her door. Tears shut off, and her heart rate increased as she crossed the room.

"And protect me, Lord. Amen."

A change of shirt, a scrub of her face, and she stood at her front door.

"Who is it?" She made her voice gruff and unwelcoming on purpose.

"I'm Dr. Alton Ewing. I'm here to talk to you about your doubloon. May I come in?" Pause. "Or you could come out?"

"Why did you come here without letting Director Roberts know?"

"I think you'll want to see what I've found before anyone else does. I'm doing this as a service to you." Pause. "But if you'd rather I go through the director, I'll leave and ..."

She opened the door and stepped outside. "What is it you found that you think I should know about first?"

Ewing set his pack on the floor of the porch and withdrew some papers. "Your doubloon is rare. A Brasher doubloon." He handed her a print-out. "At auction, the latest price for one was 9.36 million dollars." Another piece of paper.

Mercy scanned the information. The lowest bid for a Brasher was seven hundred and twenty-five thousand. She stumbled inside to a chair.

"Of course, that coin was almost perfect." Ewing sat by her. "Yours has some flaws, but ..."

She raised her eyes to him. "Is this real? Because if you're pulling my leg—"

"No." He placed his finger on the document. "You can see for yourself. Look on your computer."

"What's your angle, Dr. Ewing?" She peered at him. Silver hair swept back from a smooth, tan face. One of those men difficult to pin an age on. Could be anywhere from forty to sixty.

"Angle?" he said. "I have no angle. I'm here to offer my services as a professional."

"You want to help me find the treasure." She crossed her arms over her chest. Of course he did. "And what do you get out of it?"

"We would settle on a fee. Say, ten percent of the value? Plus expenses."

"Let me think about it." Mercy rose. "Do you have my coin with you?"

"No. It's back at the lab." His voice was clipped. "Ms. Baxter—"

"Coast Guard calling Sharktooth Island. Come in. Over."

Mercy hurried to her radio. "Sharktooth Island here. Over."

"We're at your pier. Do you want us to come to the house?"

"Not necessary. We're on our way down to you. Please wait." She keyed the mike off.

"Roger. Out."

Mercy turned to face Ewing. "Time to go, Doctor. If you have a shortwave radio, we can communicate through that, or you can get to me through the director. Please let me know next time you plan on visiting."

"There's just one more thing before I go." He withdrew another sheet of paper. "During the Depression, your family failed to pay the taxes on the island. For some reason, this fact went unnoticed. I happened across it in my research."

"What does that have to do with anything?" She narrowed her eyes at him.

"If you find a treasure, and if the state of Georgia gets wind of those back taxes, they could decide to seize the island and the treasure." He laid a finger against his nose. "Something to think about."

Anger flashed through her. "Are you threatening me, Dr. Ewing?"

"No. In fact, I have a friend in the tax office who could make this whole thing go away if you want it to. Just say the word, and I'll be glad to see to it."

And then she'd owe this creep big time. No, thank you.

"I'll look into it. Thanks for letting me know." She shut the door behind her and led the way toward the dock.

When they reached the gangway, one man in a Coast Guard uniform stood near the beginning of the trail while another waited next to the professor's boat.

"Ms. Baxter?" the first man said.

"Yes. Thanks for coming out."

"No problem, ma'am." He fell into line behind Dr. Ewing.

At the yacht, Ewing turned to Mercy. "It was a pleasure meeting you, Ms. Baxter. Hopefully, you won't feel the need to call the Coast Guard next time." He bowed in her direction and boarded his boat.

Mercy rubbed her arms against a sudden chill.

"We'll stay with you until he's gone." The men stepped to either side of her as Ewing's yacht gunned away from the dock. His wake slammed the other vessels against the bumpers attached to the dock. The Guardsmen shook their heads.

After Ewing's vessel disappeared from sight, Mercy scanned the dark clouds on the horizon. "Are we due for a storm?"

"Some rain and wind later. Nothing bad. You should be fine." The men hopped into their boat. "If he comes back, you let us know. We'll send someone out."

"Thank you. I will."

But could they get to her before it was too late?

Chapter Fourteen

Liam slid his backpack off his shoulder onto the table with a grunt. The security guard leaned over and eyed the orthopedic boot on his left foot and his cane.

"Mm, mm, mmm. What have you done to yourself?"

"Twisted my ankle kicking a shark in the mouth while saving a child from certain death?" He grinned at her. "You didn't see it on the news?"

She quirked an eyebrow and handed him his pack. "What really happened?"

"I slid on a rock." He looked at his new footwear. Bad sprain, but not broken. *Thank You, Jesus.* "I'll need this thing for a while." He brandished his cane in the air.

"I'll keep you in my prayers."

"Thanks."

Liam hobbled along the hallway to his office. He had a few things to catch up on, and then back to Sharktooth and Mercy.

"I'm glad I caught you." Carl Roberts stepped in front of him. "Come inside. I'll take that for you."

Liam relinquished his pack to the director and lowered

himself into a chair across the desk from Roberts. So much for a quick trip into the office. He glanced at his watch.

"Ms. Baxter called yesterday evening and she ..." Roberts frowned at his clasped hands. "Let's say she wasn't happy. She told me about your accident, and your argument." He raised his eyes to Liam's. "It seems you and Ms. Baxter were right. I never should have let Dr. Ewing see that gold piece." Roberts ran a hand through his sparse hair. "I had no idea he'd show up without telling me."

"Ewing went to the island?" Anger crashed through Liam.

"Apparently, and he tried to make some sort of deal with her about finding the treasure and ended up threatening her. She had to call the Coast Guard to remove him."

Liam jumped to his feet. Pain stabbed his ankle, and he grabbed Robert's desk for support. Deep breaths.

"I thought you knew."

"How could I? I need to get back there." He pinned the director with his gaze. "You need to arrange for private security like you promised."

The throb in his ankle didn't compare to the misery in his heart. Liam headed for the exit with a lurching gait. What if Ewing decided to return to the island before he could get there? The whiff of treasure brought out the shark in some men. And Professor Ewing sounded like a great white.

He threw his cane into his car and peered at the sky. A storm building to the south. Two stops before he could head for the island. He'd need to hurry.

Mercy paced through her small house. Nobody ever bothered her. In all the years she'd been on the island, she'd never had to defend herself. She stopped and pressed her fingers to her temples.

"Think, woman." What did she have that could be used as a weapon?

The machete. She strode to her pack and pulled it out. But she needed something smaller. Something she could carry on her person. A knife? She opened a drawer and selected a paring knife. Too small. A steak knife. But where to put it?

She changed into shorts with cargo pockets. The knife fit. She practiced taking it out a few times. Then she sat down. Ouch. Back to the paring knife. She settled for hiding larger knives around the house, and the machete next to her bed.

Tears pricked her eyes. How could she have let herself get so complacent? So vulnerable? She'd never felt so alone.

"Liam, I miss you."

What was she thinking? It was his fault she feared for her life. Anger canceled desire in a heartbeat. If he'd stopped the director from sharing the doubloon, none of this would have happened. No professor. No threats.

No paring knife in her pocket.

A ripple of unease traveled from her head to her toes, but she shook herself. The island was her home. No one messed with her home without a fight. She glanced at the cross above the door.

"Lord, I'm new at this prayer thing. You know the situation. I need Your help." She dropped her voice to a whisper. "Please."

Bang. Something hard hit the metal roof above her. Mercy flinched, her nerves tingling. She should check to see what it was. At the door, she hesitated to let the pounding in her ears subside. Nothing or no one on the porch. She clutched the knife in her pocket and stepped onto the path.

A limb from a nearby tree lay on her roof. Poor timing, but

at least it gave her something else to think about. She collected her chainsaw and ladder from near the shed. The trick would be to cut the tree branch into manageable pieces without damaging the roof. She pulled on gloves and got to work, tossing the chunks of wood onto the ground to pile later.

As she finished, she turned toward the mainland and the magnificent view. The blue and gray waves of the sea wore white hats. A line of dark clouds on the southern horizon inched north toward the island. The storm last evening had dispersed, but this one looked more serious.

She drew in a deep breath. The panoramic scene before her never failed to put things in perspective. To bring her peace. Was this what it felt like to connect to God?

A boat appeared on the horizon. She stiffened.

Chapter Fifteen

Liam winced as the boat slammed over another wave. The wind picked up, pushing against the tide. About a mile from the island, the rain came. Needles pelted his skin. The only good thing about it was it took his mind off the pain in his ankle.

He slowed and peered through the downpour. Wouldn't do to wreck on the rocks. The dock came into sight. Tension eased from his body. No boats except Mercy's. He'd made it back before Ewing.

After securing his boat, Liam sat the package he'd brought on the dock.

"I'm in no shape to carry you up the trail." He opened the pet carrier, and Hawkeye glared at him with his good eye. "I got you this far. You're going to have to make it to the cottage on your own, big guy."

Liam grabbed his backpack and limped up the gangway through the storm. The cat streaked by him. He prayed the animal headed for the cabin.

A stream of water ran down the middle of the mountain

path, and the sides were slick. Rain plastered his hair to his head and soaked his clothes. Mud covered his orthopedic boot and his knees and hands. Exhausted, he made it to the cover of her porch.

Mercy flung open the door and pulled him inside, mud and all. Hawkeye lay in a nest of towels before the fire.

"I'd hug you, but I'll wait till you clean up." She walked him to the guest bathroom. "Do you have dry clothes? If not, I think I have some left of Dad's that might fit you."

"In my pack." He faced her. "Mercy, I'm ..."

"Yeah, me too." The corners of her mouth lifted in a brief smile. "Leave your dirty clothes in the tub. I'll deal with them later."

"I'm glad it was only a sprain." Mercy finished scrubbing the mud off Liam's boot and handed it back to him. "How much longer do you have to wear this?"

"One more week." Liam strapped his foot and ankle into the sturdy black boot. "It's a real pain."

"Does it help?" Mercy plopped next to him on the couch. The joy she experienced seeing him at her door made her happy and unhappy at the same time. She scooted away from him.

"It does—help I mean." Liam's brow furrowed. "What's wrong, Mercy? Are you still mad at me? Because I'm really sorry. I'll never break a promise to you again." He moved closer.

"No, I'm not mad."

"Then what?" He reached for her hand.

At his touch, the walls of resolve she'd built around her heart crumbled. Tears came unbidden. She grabbed a handful of tissues and stabbed at her eyes, trying to stem the flow.

"For years I've led a peaceful, simple life." She stuttered the words out between sobs. "Then a hurricane hits my island and upsets everything."

What was wrong with her? She couldn't stop.

"My sweet Mercy." Liam pulled her into his arms. "Whatever is upsetting you, we'll fix together."

"Will we?" She pushed away from him. "That's part of the problem. I was used to taking care of myself, but then you came along. Now I—I rely on you. I want to rely on you. But I'm afraid. Afraid you'll disappear like everyone else in my life."

He studied her with his sapphire blue eyes. "I want to be more than just someone you rely on—a glorified handyman."

Was he telling her he loved her? *Dear Lord, do I love him?* Her heart quickened in her chest.

"You ..." She placed a hand on his cheek. "I think I'm falling in love with you."

"I've loved you since high school." He stood and pulled her into an embrace. His mouth covered hers in a kiss that took her breath away. "I tried to get you out of my mind, but nothing worked. And when I saw you on the dock that first day, I knew you were the one."

She wanted to dance. To laugh. To twirl around.

And so she did.

Liam filled a hole in her life that she'd ignored all these years—skirted, closed her eyes to, pretended didn't exist.

The sound of rain and wind grew louder as they tumbled to the sofa. Hawkeye arched his back and hissed.

"How sweet." A man's sarcastic tone slithered through the air.

She pulled away from Liam, and they sat up.

Dr. Alton Ewing stood in the doorway with a gun in his hand.

Chapter Sixteen

"Stay where you are." Ewing dragged a kitchen chair over so he had a good line of sight on them both. "What happened to your foot?" He nodded at Liam's boot.

"I twisted my ankle."

Sprained ankle and concern for the girl. He should be easy to handle.

"What do you want?" Mercy said. "I told you I'm not interested in your help the last time you were here."

"I remember. You called the Coast Guard to throw me off your island." His trigger finger tensed ever so slightly before he relaxed it. Mustn't harm her. She knew where the cave was.

The man was a different story. Maybe he could use this fellow to his advantage.

"What's your name?" Ewing stared at the younger man.

"Liam."

"Here's my plan. Ms. Baxter is going to show me where the cave is that contains the remains she found and possibly the treasure." Ewing tilted his head slightly. "But I hadn't counted on you. What do you suggest I do with you?"

"I know where the cave is." Liam took a step toward Ewing. "Take me and leave her here tied up."

Mercy gasped and reached for Liam's hand. The fright on her face sent a thrill down Ewing's spine. Better than any drug he'd ever tried.

"Why would I do that? She's a lot smaller." Ewing pulled Mercy close. "Easier to handle." The air bristled with the younger man's rage and Ewing tensed for what he knew was about to happen.

With a roar, Liam lowered his head and rushed straight for Ewing. The older man stepped to one side like a bullfighter playing with a charging bull and slammed the gun into the back of the younger man's skull. Liam dropped to the floor and Ewing pointed the gun at his head.

"No."

The panic in Mercy's voice brought a smile to his face.

"There's a cellar under the house. No exit," Mercy said. "Put him in there. When you finish with me, you can bring me there too."

"Open it." He released Mercy.

She lifted the hatch to the cellar. "It's cut into the limestone. This is the only entrance."

Ewing glanced at the dark hole. He shined a light around the space. It would be a good temporary solution. Was he relieved or sad? He'd never killed anyone before. Could he have shot Liam in cold blood? Now, it seemed, he'd never know.

"Your boyfriend goes in the cellar. Time to wake him up."

Liam stumbled across the living room to the hole in the floor. He turned, hands tied in front of him. Mercy hugged him.

"Don't worry. I'll be fine." He brought his lips to her ear.

"Do what he says. Don't argue. I'll see you later." He gave her a smile filled with promise. "How about untying my hands so I can climb down?"

"You'll manage."

His eyes found the cross above the door as he descended the ladder into darkness. At the last minute, his backpack flew past him and landed on the cellar floor.

A yell from Mercy, and the hatch slammed shut. His chest tightened with fear.

Lord, keep her safe.

Liam searched for his flashlight.

More sounds of a struggle. Talking, but he couldn't make out the words. Then came the screech of furniture dragging across the floor. He needed to free his hands. Metal shelving. He found a rough edge and began to rub his bindings against it. Five minutes and his hands popped apart.

Liam climbed the ladder and pushed on the hatch. No give.

"Mrawr." Hawkeye appeared at his feet.

He started. "Hey buddy. I thought you were a ghost or something. How'd you get down here?"

The cat rubbed against his leg and purred.

"Glad to see you, too, but you picked a bad place to hide out." Liam shined his light around the small space. "We're stuck here."

"First thing is to check supplies." Liam found three flashlights with batteries, a sack of potatoes, a bag of onions, some cans of small sausages, and bottled water. "We're okay for eats."

One shelf held a propane lantern and matches.

"No sense in running my flashlight down." Liam struck a match.

The flame flickered as if in a breeze. But the air was still. Or was it? He lit the lantern and struck another match. Same thing. He moved around the room striking matches.

And then the butterfly wings of a breeze fluttered on his cheek. So slight he might have imagined it, if it weren't for the quiver of the flame. He stood in front of the wall of stacked timbers.

"Now load it with books." Ewing ordered after the steamer trunk was in place over the hatch.

Mercy did as she was told, then shoved her hand into her pocket, clenched it around the paring knife, and pushed off the wall behind her.

Ewing sidestepped her attack and grabbed her by the left arm. The barrel of his gun pressed into her neck.

"Don't be daft, girl." He leaned close. "If you cause me too much trouble, I'll simply kill you and find the cave on my own." He pushed her away from him. "I was a Tactics and Weapons Training Instructor in the British Army. I'm a very good shot." He eyed her. "What's in your pocket?"

She withdrew the paring knife.

"Toss it across the room."

The rage inside her turned from red hot to ice. Ewing would let down his guard at some point, and when he did ... In the meantime, she would follow Liam's advice and do what Ewing said.

Chapter Seventeen

Liam moved the shelving away from the wall of stacked timbers and examined it closely. Along the right side, something was barely visible.

Hinges. Hope coursed through him. The wall was a door. But how did it open? He scoured the opposite edge with his fingers but found nothing but an odd octagonal-shaped hole on the third log.

"Mrawr." Hawkeye swatted at his leg.

"Not now, buddy."

The cat leapt onto his shoulder. "Mrawr."

His stomach growled. Liam looked at his watch. Six o'clock. "I get it." He opened a can of sausages and lay one before Hawkeye.

The cat sniffed it and looked at Liam.

"It's that or nothing." Liam took a bite of one and grimaced.

He poured some water into a depression in the stone floor. Hawkeye crouched and took a drink.

"After dinner, I'm getting us out of here." At least, he hoped so.

He pondered the wall of timbers. Was another limestone room behind the wall? But then where was the air coming from?

It was clear the wall of logs hadn't been opened in a decade or longer. Liam gulped the last bite of sausage and slugged the last of his water. He'd need help.

The dull green of a bottle of olive oil shone in the beam of Liam's flashlight. Maybe pour it on the disused hinges? Work it into the wood and metal. He continued his search.

"If only I had a pry bar or a shovel." Liam shined his light into the darkest corners of the room and behind the shelves.

His beam gleamed off something shiny behind some paint cans. A butcher knife. What was it doing here? It looked new. He picked it up. Might come in handy if he couldn't get the door open. Or even if he could.

Old tools lay in a heap in a corner. Hammers, screwdrivers, a hacksaw with a broken blade, other items he didn't recognize. Liam squatted to rummage through them. He selected the largest screwdriver and hammer.

He rose and stretched his cramped legs—and then his mind caught up with his eyes. He'd been staring at it without realizing what it was. Maybe a hand drill or something. He picked it up. The wrought iron object was shaped like a *T* with a wooden handle across the top.

But what drew his eye—what made him drop the other tools back on the pile—was the octagonal shape on the end of the stem.

"It's late." Mercy took a step toward the kitchen. "The cave is far from here, and the jungle's dangerous after dark." How much did Ewing know about her island?

The professor eyed her. She willed her face to show no emotion.

"What do you have to eat?"

"Salad." She inclined her head toward the refrigerator. "Fruit. Leftover chicken."

"Bring it to the table along with plates." He waved the barrel of his gun at her. "I will shoot you if you try anything."

"What about forks and knives?"

"Where are they? I'll get them."

Mercy pointed to the silverware drawer. Scenarios raced through her mind where she attacked the man standing across the room, but none ended well. She sniffed and blinked back tears of frustration.

When the table was ready, Ewing motioned her to sit. He took the chair opposite. The seed of a plan grew in her mind as she ate. One small bite at a time, to give her plan time to blossom.

A spasm of coughing. She couldn't breathe. Gasping for air.

At first, Ewing watched, a bemused look on his face. But soon he rose. "Stop. It won't work."

But she saw the uncertainty in his eyes. Mercy fell from her chair onto the floor clutching her throat with her hand.

A look of bewilderment flashed across his face. He rushed to her side. She had him.

She grasped for him. The terror in her eyes real.

"What can I do?" He bent closer.

She brought the fork down into his hand with as much force as she could muster. He screamed, and the gun clattered to the floor. Mercy jumped to her feet and leaped over his kneeling form.

"No." He grabbed her ankle with his undamaged hand.

She hit the floor hard, but instinct took over and she kicked out. A satisfying crunch of bone as her foot found its target.

Ewing released her leg and shrieked again as blood erupted from his broken nose. She scrambled to her feet and ran once more for the door. This time she made it.

The darkness soon provided all the cover she needed. Would he come after her? Probably not. He had his wounds to tend to, and he didn't know the island. She slowed and looked back the way she'd come.

Ewing didn't need to chase after her. He had Liam.

Despair crushed her to the ground.

Chapter Eighteen

After the scream from above, rage roared through Liam. He glanced at his backpack. His second stop before coming to the island was to get a gun from his dad. For the first time in his civilian life, he had a gun, and he would use it without hesitation. But first, he had to get out of this hole.

He fit the octagonal end of the tool into the place he'd found on the timber. Grabbing the wooden handle, he tried turning it first clockwise, then counterclockwise. Nothing.

Angry shouts from above. Urgency filled his soul. He tried again. Had it been too long? He banged on the end of the tool in frustration. It moved inward. He put is weight on it and turned. Something clicked. He pulled.

The wall of stacked logs swung open three feet. Hawkeye rushed through the opening into the darkness.

"Wait up, cat."

Liam grabbed his backpack and the lantern and took a step inside. He stopped. The key. He'd take it with him so Ewing couldn't follow.

As Liam removed the odd key, the door began to close. He squeezed through as the log door shut with a resounding thud and prayed he hadn't traded a prison for a grave. The light from his lantern played off a narrow passage of limestone walls and ceiling, with a floor made of rock and dirt.

The flame in the lantern danced as the breeze grew stronger. He was headed for an opening. The question was where? Would he be able to find his way back to the cabin in time to help Mercy?

Ewing may have already taken her to the cave. Then what? Could he find his way there in the dark? Their encounter with the wild boar played through his mind.

But memories of her screams pushed aside all other thoughts. Mercy needed him.

EWING CURSED as he flung pill bottles and makeup on the floor of Mercy's bathroom. Where did she keep her first aid things? He needed more than an adhesive bandage. Gauze and tape. Some sort of antibiotic cream. Surely she had that around here somewhere.

He tore through her linen closet. Nothing. Maybe the kitchen. He found it under the sink. *What an insane place to put it.* He bandaged his hand first. Then he went into the guest bedroom to see about his nose.

Bruising around his eyes had already begun. He cleaned his poor nose as best he could. Then he sat on the floor in case he fainted and, using both hands, reset the cartilage with a quick snap. The pain brought tears to his eyes. Gauze and tape to hold it in place.

Dirty clothes in the bathtub made the corners of his lips lift in a smile. He didn't have to go after the girl. She would come to him. After all, he still had something she wanted. Something she loved.

He picked up his gun. A red-hot poker of pain shot through his injured hand. The pistol clattered to the floor. He retrieved it with his other hand. Not as accurate, but doable. He gazed at the trunk sitting atop the hatch in the floor. What to do with the man?

If he could just get some sleep. His nose throbbed and he closed his eyes. Maybe there was a way. Ewing dropped the heavy oak beam across the door and moved to the couch. A few minutes' rest. Nothing more.

Mercy retraced her steps. Almost to the cabin, she hid and waited. No movement at the windows or outside. She sprinted for the shed—and the butcher knife hidden there. This time, she would be the hunter and he would be the prey.

Once armed, she crossed the open ground from the shed to the porch. She avoided the boards that squeaked, inched the latch open, and gently pressed on the door. No give. She pressed harder. It wouldn't move.

Ewing had barred the door. She released the latch with slow movements and backed off the porch. Why? Mercy retreated to the shed. Whatever the reason, there was nothing she could do tonight. She'd wait until first light and examine the cabin more closely.

The shed had no windows and only one door. She moved a portable generator to block the entrance. A pile of old boat cushions made a reasonable couch. Tears burned her eyes.

The thought of Liam trapped in her cellar ... but then a worse thought crossed her mind.

Lord, please. Keep him safe.

She let her head fall back onto her makeshift couch, her eyelids suddenly very heavy.

Chapter Nineteen

Liam yelped as he felt something touch his leg.

"Mrawr."

"Monster." Liam stooped to pet the cat. "Don't do that. Got it?"

The scruffy animal rubbed his head against Liam's leg and purred.

"Yeah. I like you too." He set the lantern down and switched on his flashlight. "That's better. Now let's get out of here and find Mercy."

The passageway narrowed and took a sharp turn to the right. Liam moved through sideways. He was glad Mercy didn't have to do this. What seemed like a hundred feet later, it widened and angled upward. Was he getting to the end?

A whisper of a breeze dried the sweat on his arms and face as he stopped to rest. He looked at his watch. Still nighttime. The stars and the moon would be shining above in an endless sky. Time to get out of here. He'd been too long underground.

He shrugged into his backpack and started off with

renewed energy. Another one hundred feet by his estimate and he found himself at the bottom of some steps cut into the limestone.

MERCY WOKE WITH A START. Had she heard Hawkeye? She flipped her flashlight on and scanned the interior of the shed. How had he gotten in here? A moment of joy, but no cat. She must have been dreaming. She sighed and sank onto the cushions once more.

The shelving against the back wall moved. Every muscle in her body tensed. She leaped to her feet and brandished the knife in front of her. Hawkeye ran through the opening and wrapped around her legs. Was she still asleep? She bent to pick him up.

"Mercy?" Liam stepped inside the shed, a bewildered look on his face.

"Liam." She started. "How did you get in here?"

"There's an escape tunnel from the storage cellar to here." He indicated the opening in the far wall with his hand.

"I thought I'd never see you again." She crossed the floor in two strides and put a hand on his arm. "I—" Her throat closed around her words.

"Me too." He lifted the cat from her arms and took the knife from her hand. "But here we are."

He drew her into his embrace, and hope mixed with joy filled her once more. She tilted her head and pressed her lips to his in an urgent kiss that turned into several.

"Time for this later." Liam gently pushed her away. "We need to get out of here. When Ewing discovers I'm gone, he'll come after us."

"We'll take your boat and get help." Mercy grabbed her cat.

WHEN ALTON EWING AWOKE, the first light of day filtered through the trees. He jumped to his feet. A mistake. He fell back onto the couch, his head pounding.

The girl had escaped. How had his plan gone so terribly wrong? Anger flooded his system and he stood once more. He grabbed a bottled water from the refrigerator and sat at the table. A new plan emerged.

He would kill the man. Find the cave on his own. Then deal with the woman.

Ewing unloaded the books from the trunk and yanked it to one side.

"Open the hatch," he said in a loud voice.

Nothing.

Should he try to bluff? "Do it or I'll kill the girl."

Nothing.

Ewing threw the hatch cover back. Darkness. Now what? He removed the flashlight from his bag and shone it into the hole.

"I'm coming down with a gun. Don't try anything." Ewing jumped from the ladder into a crouch and spun his light around illuminating the small space.

No Liam. Ewing straightened. He had to be there. But where? A curious smell drew him to an empty can next to a puddle of water.

"You managed to find something to eat. But where are you now?" Ewing played his flashlight along the rock floor.

A faint footprint. Then another. And paw prints? Leading to the wall of stacked timbers. Of course. A secret exit. He shoved with all his might. It didn't budge. Anger roared through him. He dropped his gun and the flashlight and grabbed an ax leaning against the wall nearby.

After several swings, sweat plastered his shirt to his back, and his hand throbbed. No use. Better to go out and find the cave. He'd deal with the girl and her boyfriend later. After all, this was an island, and he'd already taken care of their boats.

Chapter Twenty

The first light of day greeted Mercy and Liam as they cracked the door to the shed. She peered at the cabin.

"We'll stay off the path for a while through the brush to our right." Mercy hugged the side of the shed. "Follow me." Her heart beat so loudly in her ears she couldn't hear if Liam answered.

When they were out of sight of the cabin, Mercy led him to the trail. "It'll be faster going now." She smiled at Liam. "Let's get out of here."

Hawkeye jumped from her arms and ran ahead.

They came to the break in the trees where the path started down to the dock. Mercy stopped dead. Their boats were gone. In fact, there were no boats at the dock at all. Not even Ewing's. How did he expect to get off the island?

"What now?" Tears pooled in her eyes. Her beautiful island, once her sanctuary, had become her trap.

"We regroup." Liam put his arm around her. "Let's head for the cave. He doesn't know where it is, and we can think up there."

She nodded and set off along the path. The cave. A shiver ran down her spine. And yet, despite her fear of small spaces, she knew that was where she would be safe.

As they approached the cave entrance, they heard a rustle in the ferns to the left. Mercy and Liam froze. Hawkeye appeared, a small rodent in his mouth. A collective sigh.

"Are you planning on sharing, buddy?" Liam said.

"I'll pass." Mercy scanned the area and listened but heard only leaves moving in the wind and the cries of sea birds overhead. "Let's get inside."

"How far do you want to go in?"

"To where I can still see the entrance but be in the shadows." Mercy found a rock to sit on. "Like here?"

Liam went outside and looked back into the cave. "That's good." He joined Mercy. "Tell me what went on last night. All I heard were screams." He rubbed her arm. "Did he hurt you?"

"Not really." She shook her head. "But I stabbed him in the hand with a fork and broke his nose."

"Whoa. So it was his screams I heard."

"Probably. Although he did slam me to the floor once." She rubbed the back of her head. "But it's okay. Do you think he'll find us?" His sapphire eyes were black in the shadows.

"Yes. He's determined."

"He has a gun."

"So do I." Liam rummaged in his backpack. "I stopped by my dad's on the way here and borrowed his service pistol."

A chill went through her. Instead of bringing her peace, the news that Liam had a gun only made her more anxious.

"Please promise me you won't use it unless it's absolutely necessary."

"I promise."

She placed a finger against his lips. She'd heard humming.

EWING PACKED his backpack and left the cabin when the sun was well above the trees. Since the more mountainous part of the island lay to the north—to the right of the cabin—he'd decided to go in that direction first.

The path along the side of the hill proved level and an easy walk. He kept his head down, not wanting to trip on any roots or rocks in the path. Every once in a while, he stopped to survey the hillside with his binoculars.

And then he saw it. A boot print on the trail like the one in the cellar.

"Well, well," he muttered under his breath.

Maybe he would be able to take care of two problems at once. He watched for another print. There. He followed the prints to a place where they disappeared. Humming to himself, he withdrew his binoculars and scanned the vegetation above him.

There it was. Almost invisible. A darker place amidst the dark plants and trees. He'd found the cave.

Chapter Twenty-One

Mercy drew back from the cave's entrance and sucked in her breath. Ewing stood on the path below her.

"We need to hide." She grabbed Liam's sleeve. "He's seen the cave." She was barely able to breathe. Fear twisted her stomach.

"Calm down. We'll find a place." Liam took her by the arm and led her farther into the cave.

The walls narrowed, and the dank smell assailed her nostrils. Panic threatened to paralyze her. She concentrated on Liam's touch. They passed the skeleton and found a cleft between two rocks that offered a natural hiding place. If only she could get control of her emotions. She closed her eyes and reached for Liam's hand. *Lord, help me.*

How HAD Ewing found them so fast? Liam shone his light briefly on the floor of the cave and saw his footprints in the dust. The orthopedic boot had a distinctive tread. His heart sank. Once Ewing entered the cave, all he had to do was follow the footprints straight to their hiding place. He needed to do something.

"I need to take care of something." He pried Mercy's hand from his. "I'll be back."

"Don't go."

"I need to get rid of our tracks." His heart ached at the fear in her voice.

He removed his shirt and swept his tracks from the dirt until he got to the skeleton. Then he ran past where Mercy hid and around another corner before stopping at another hidey hole. Carefully, he removed his shoe and the supportive boot and came back to Mercy in his socks, leaving almost no perceptible prints in the dirt.

"Take your shoes off." Liam offered his arm for support. "You won't leave any prints when we get out of here."

With a nod, she untied her right boot, and slipped her foot out.

"Liam. I know you're in here." Alton Ewing's British accent echoed off the limestone walls.

Liam and Mercy swiveled their heads toward the voice that held the chill of death.

"Do not make me hunt you down." Ewing drew closer.

No doubt he followed Liam's footprints. Would he pass them by?

"This must be the skeleton you found." A grunt. "I'll just relieve the poor fellow of his other doubloon. You know, my boy, you could be a very rich man if you chose to help me instead of resist."

Silence.

"There's more where these two came from." Ewing was very close. "And I could use a strong back to help get the treasure from here to my boat."

Ewing's voice sounded right outside their hiding place. Mercy stiffened and Liam placed a hand on her mouth.

"I've found your hidey hole, my boy. Might as well come out and give me your answer."

Liam's trick had worked. The professor had followed his footprints around to the other break in the rocks. Time to get out of the cave. He grabbed Mercy's hand and they stepped from the cleft in the wall.

"Not so fast."

Liam swiveled to see Ewing's gun pointed at his chest.

"Clever, but not clever enough." Ewing motioned for the two of them to go ahead of him deeper into the cave. "We'll find the treasure together. Then Ms. Baxter will sign it over to me, and there will be an unfortunate accident in which you will both be killed."

Liam squeezed Mercy's hand and they led the way deeper inside the cave. Another one hundred yards and the cave ended. Liam examined the sides and ceiling with his light. "It looks like there was a cave-in a long time ago." He shone his beam upward. "And the roof doesn't look too stable. I say we get out of here."

"Of course you would." Ewing waved his pistol at them. "Sit on your hands over there while I take a look myself."

The professor kicked at the pile of stones to one side and muttered to himself.

"Inch away when he's not paying attention." Liam whispered. "When I give the signal, jump and run. Got it?"

Mercy gave a small nod, but she was shaking all over.

"There must be another entrance." Ewing grew more agitated. "It has to be here."

"Now." Liam jumped to his feet, pulling Mercy up with him. "Run."

Shots rang out. The pair ducked and rounded the corner. A

rock chip caught Liam on the cheek, but he kept running, pushing Mercy ahead of him. Hawkeye streaked by them in the shadows.

It was the other sound that caused his chest to tighten with fear—the sound immediately after the gunshots. A rumble deep within the cave that sent a vibration through the floor and up his spine.

Chapter Twenty-Two

Mercy bit back a scream. "That sounded like a cave-in. We have to go back."

"It's too dangerous." Liam held onto her. "There's nothing we can do. The area will be filled with smoke and debris."

"I don't care." She pinned him with her eyes. "Ewing is still a human being. He deserves our help. And I haven't seen Hawkeye." Fear tore through her. "What if he's back there? Trapped under the rubble?"

"I saw Hawkeye pass us in the tunnel. He's fine." Liam put his hands on her arms. "As for Ewing, you're right. We need to go back." Liam gave her a grim look and tore his shirt into pieces. "Cover your mouth and nose."

It was difficult to breathe even with the mask. Her throat and her eyes stung from the dust that hung in the air. The beam from her flashlight was so diffused by the floating particles that she could hardly see as they made their way back toward where they'd left the professor.

It wasn't until her foot struck something soft that she realized she'd found Alton Ewing's body.

"Over here." She bent to see if he was still alive.

The lower half of his torso lay crushed beneath a giant boulder and his eyes stared at her devoid of life. Weariness infused her body. The cave and its promise of treasure had claimed another soul.

"Looks like his shot caused the roof to cave in on him." Liam put a hand on her shoulder.

The dust was settling, and a large void appeared where there once was a wall. Mercy stood. Another cavern? She walked around Ewing and found a pathway into a different room.

"Liam." Her voice came out as a croak. She cleared her throat and tried again. "Come here."

"What?" He hurried to her side.

She pointed with a shaky finger. "Do you see what I see?"

Liam gawked at the two trunks whose wooden sides, old and rotten, had split open revealing the treasure inside. Jewels sparkled in the beams of their flashlights. They lay among tarnished pieces of copper, silver, and gold. And coins. Lots of coins.

"Seems the stories were true." He led Mercy over for a closer look.

She nodded.

"How does it feel to be rich?" He looked at her.

She wrapped her arms around her waist. "It scares the liver out of me." She raised her eyes to his. "Let's get out of here. I need my cat."

"Yeah. And, we need to let the authorities know what happened." Liam glanced once more at the treasure. "Also get you some help with this. Someone you can trust."

Back at the cabin, Hawkeye sat at the front door waiting. Mercy swept him into her arms and gave him a big hug, and for once, he didn't squirm.

"You monster. I thought you were dead." Tears filled her eyes.

She opened the door, handed Hawkeye to Liam, and crossed to her radio. "This is Sharktooth Island calling the Coast Guard. Come in Coast Guard. Over." She glanced at Liam sitting beside her, Hawkeye curled against his chest.

"This is Coast Guard Air Station Savannah. What is your emergency Sharktooth? Over."

"A man got caught in a cave-in. He's dead, and we need your help."

Chapter Twenty-Three

One Week Later

"All these years, Dad struggled to make a good living for Mom and me." Mercy laid her head back on the couch. "When Mom got sick, he used up all his savings to pay for her hospital bills. And all the time, the treasure sat right here on our island."

"When your mom was sick, why didn't he sell the island?" Liam brought her a cup of tea and sat beside her.

"He was about to, but then she passed away." Mercy raised her cup to her lips, but she couldn't swallow. Remembered pain froze her in place. She didn't resist when Liam took the cup from her and placed it on the coffee table.

"Dad could have used that money." She turned to Liam. "And I could have used it when Dad was ill."

"It does no good looking back." Liam took her face in his hands. "Your parents would want you to look forward—to put the money to good use."

She searched his eyes. How did he get so wise? She ran a

finger down his cheek. "If I start my own company, will you come work for me?"

"No."

She gasped, his answer like a knife to her heart.

"But I will be your partner. For life." Liam dropped to one knee and took her hand. "Mercedes Baxter, will you marry me? I promise to be with you through thick and thin. In sickness and in health. In good times and in bad. Whether you keep the treasure or give it all away."

"Yes. The answer is yes, I'll marry you." She pulled him into her arms and pressed her lips to his.

After a while, she nibbled his ear. "What if I offer you a vice-presidency?" she whispered.

"I'll think about it," he murmured.

Hawkeye rubbed against them and purred louder than he had ever purred before.

THE END

About Deborah Sprinkle

When Debbie Sprinkle retired from teaching in 2004, she had a plan for keeping busy. Attend the women's Bible study at her church, join a local book club, and write a mystery novel. She began going to Bible study on Wednesday mornings, and when her local library started a book club, she was one of the charter members.

One thing led to another—as they usually do—and pretty soon she was a Bible study leader and facilitating the book club. (She says it's because she has the biggest mouth!)

In 2009, she was asked to attend the She Speaks Christian Writers' Conference put on by Proverbs 31 Ministry, where she met Kendra Armstrong. It was their friendship that led to her first book written in collaboration with Kendra, *Common Sense and an Uncommon God*, published in 2012 by Lighthouse of the Carolinas. The second edition was later released under the title of *Exploring the Faith of America's Presidents*.

After attending lots of conferences, taking many classes, and sitting at the feet of a plethora of experienced writers, Debbie wrote her first novel. And, in 2019, her dream came true when *Deadly Guardian* made its debut. Two more novels rounded out the Trouble in Pleasant Valley series, and Debbie is now working on a new set of romantic suspense novels set in a small town in Missouri.

Originally from St. Louis, Debbie received her bachelor's degree in chemistry from the University of Missouri-St. Louis. She worked as a research chemist for many years at both St. Louis University Medical School and Washington University Medical School. In 1991, she and her family moved to Memphis, where Debbie taught chemistry for ten years at a private girls' school before retiring.

More Novella Collections from Scrivenings Press

Love in Any Season

Four Seasons—Each with its own love story.

Coming September 2022.

This contemporary romance collection includes:

Spring Has Sprung **– by Regina Rudd Merrick**

Spring has sprung, the grass is riz... Laurel Pascal, Assistant City Manager of Spring, Kentucky, is tasked with organizing the town's beloved Dogwood Festival, and she's not happy. An allergy sufferer all her life, she dreads the season from the first Daffodil bloom in the yard to the last coat of pollen on her car. Newcomer Dr. Owen Roswell volunteers to help, and soon finds that not only does Laurel need his expertise as an allergist, but help in appreciating the season she's obligated to celebrate.

What does he want more—for Laurel to fall in love with his favorite season? Or him?

The Missing Piece **– by Amy R. Anguish**

Beth Norton and Tommy England grew up together with best-friend moms who had a love of quilting and a business celebrating the craft. When high school ended, though, so did Beth and Tommy's friendship. When Tommy moves back after seven years and his mother's death, he can't understand why Beth is so angry with him. Helping Beth and her mother stabilize the finances of the business, they're forced to work together. As Tommy sorts through his mother's things, he finds an unfinished quilt, and it turns into a joint project. With each stitch taken, they work toward more than just a completed blanket.

A Sweet Dream Come True **– by Sarah Anne Crouch**

Isaac Campbell is living his dream of running an ice cream shop but fears he won't last past the first difficult year. Mel Wilson is a busy single mother who longs to be a chocolatier but is too afraid to turn her dreams into reality. When Mel and Isaac meet at Bestwood, Tennessee's fall festival, it seems like divine providence. But once Mel agrees to help Isaac bring in customers by selling her chocolates at his shop, she realizes how challenging running a business can be. Can Mel and Isaac trust in God's provision and make a leap of faith? Will their partnership end in disaster, or will it be a sweet dream come true?

Sugar and Spice **– by Heather Greer**

Emeline Becker, owner of Sugar and Spice Bakery, loves New Kuchenbrünn, except for the gingerbread. As the only bakery, she supplies the annual Gingerbread Festival with the one treat she can't stand. It's gingerbread everywhere. Things get worse when Ryker Lehmann is hired as the festival photographer. He was her secret teen crush, her sister's boyfriend, and witness to her worst humiliation. Plus, he broke her sister's heart and bruised hers when he left town after graduation. Now, he's back in town, determined to fix their friendship before the festival ends. With gingerbread and Ryker together, can Emmie make it through the festival with her mind and heart intact?

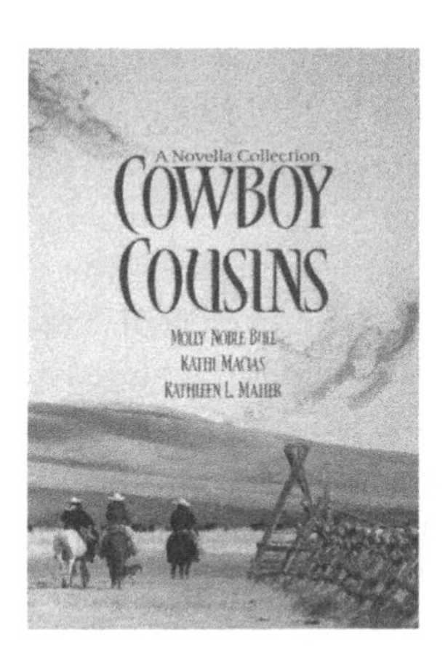

Cowboy Cousins

Saddle Up ... for the fastest reading ride of your life as three cowboys become cattlemen.

This novella collection includes:

Lucy and the Lawman by Molly Noble Bull: While on a business trip to Colorado in 1890, Sheriff Caleb Caldwell stops to inform Miss Lucy Gordan and her widowed mother of property they inherited in Texas, land coveted by a rich and powerful man—willing to do anything to get his hands on what is rightfully theirs, and Caleb feels obligated to protect them. However, he cannot reveal his attraction for Lucy. To do so would mean disaster for all of them.

The Meddlesome Maverick by Kathleen L. Maher: A new job as a bronco buster on a Lincoln, Nebraska ranch offers Boyd Hastings a fresh start. Cured of romance after a kiss-and-tell flirt falsely accused him, he must flee his hometown and cousins who have been like brothers. Banjo picking for a music show would lure him to the big city, but an opinionated tomboy with a heart of gold makes grand plans for him. Can he trust a meddlesome maverick to steer him true, or will she lead him into a briar patch of trouble?

A Panhandle Sunrise by Kathi Macias: Thirty-one year old Jake Matthews, newly appointed foreman of the Double Bar-J Ranch, is deeply attracted to the ranch owner's daughter, Anabelle, but he can't work up the nerve to approach her father, Jasper Floyd, and ask for permission to court her. But when tall, handsome, longtime Jasper-family friend, Clint Jordan, gets hired on, it seems Clint doesn't have the same insecurities and begins pursuing Anabelle immediately. Jake now accepts that his dreams of a life with Anabelle are hopeless—until a near life-and-death situation changes everything.

Candy Cane Wishes and Saltwater Dreams

A collection of Christmas beach romances

by five multi-published authors.

***Mistletoe Make-believe* by Amy Anguish** – Charlie Hill's family thinks his daughter Hailey needs a mom–to the point they won't get off his back until he finds her one. Desperate to be free from their nagging, he asks a stranger to pretend she's his girlfriend during the holidays. When romance author Samantha Arwine takes a working vacation to St. Simon's Island over Christmas, she never dreamed she'd be involved in a real-life romance. Are the sparks between her and Charlie real? Or is her imagination over-acting ... again?

***A Hatteras Surprise* by Hope Toler Dougherty** –Ginny Stowe spent years tending a childhood hurt that dictated her college study and work. Can time with an island visitor with ties to her past heal lingering wounds and lead her toward a happy Christmas ... and more? Ben Daniels intends to hire a new branch manager for a Hatteras Island bank, then hurry back to his promotion and Christmas in Charlotte. Spending time with a beautiful local, however, might force him to adjust his sails.

***A Pennie for Your Thoughts* by Linda Fulkerson** –When the Lakeshore Homeowner's Association threatens to condemn the cabin Pennie Vaughn inherited from her foster mother, her only hope of funding the needed repairs lies in winning a travel blog contest. Trouble is, Pennie never goes anywhere. Should she use the all-expenses paid Hawaiian vacation offered to her by her ex-fiancé? The trip that would have been their honeymoon?

***Mr. Sandman* by Regina Rudd Merrick** – Events manager Taylor Fordham's happily-ever-after was snatched from her, and she's saying no to romance and Christmas. When she meets two new friends—the cute new chef at Pilot Oaks and a contributor on a sci-fi fan fiction website who enjoys debate—her resolve begins to waver.

Just when she thinks she can loosen her grip on thoughts of love, a crisis pulls her back. There's no way she's going to risk her heart again.

***Coastal Christmas* by Shannon Taylor Vannatter** – Lark Pendleton is banking on a high-society wedding to make her grandparent's inn at Surfside Beach, Texas the venue to attract buyers. Tasked with sprucing up the inn, she hires Jace Wilder, whose heart she once broke. When the bride and groom turn out to be Lark's high school nemesis and ex-boyfriend, she and Jace embark on a pretend romance to save the wedding. But when real feelings emerge, can they overcome past hurts?

Scrivenings
PRESS
Quench your thirst for story.
www.ScriveningsPress.com

The Meaning of Addiction

The Meaning of Addiction

An Unconventional View

Stanton Peele

Jossey-Bass Publishers
San Francisco

FIRST JOSSEY-BASS EDITION PUBLISHED IN 1998
THIS BOOK WAS ORIGINALLY PUBLISHED BY D.C. HEATH AND COMPANY

Manufactured in the United States of America on acid-free paper.

Library of Congress Cataloging-in-Publication Data

Peele, Stanton.
The meaning of addiction : an unconventional view / Stanton Peele.
p. cm.
Originally published: Lexington, Mass. : Lexington Books, 1985.
Includes bibliographical references and index.
ISBN 0-7879-4382-7 (pbk.)
1. Substance abuse—Social aspects—United States. 2. Alcoholism—Social aspects—United States. 3. Compulsive behavior.
4. Substance abuse—Treatment—United States. 5. Substance abuse—Government policy—United States. I. Title.
RC564.P45 1998
616.86—dc21 98-19896

FIRST EDITION

printing number:
25 24 23 22 21 20 19 18

To Isidor Chein and David McClelland—
two who showed the way

Contents

Updated Preface ix

First Edition Preface xi

Acknowledgments xiii

1. The Concept of Addiction 1

Opiate Addiction in the United States and the Western World 3

Divergent Evidence about Narcotic Addiction 6

Nonbiological Factors in Addiction 12

The Nature of Addiction 17

2. The American Image of Alcohol: Does Liquor Have the Power to Corrupt and Control? 27

The Disease of Alcoholism 28

Historical, Social, Ethnic, and Economic Factors in Alcoholism in the United States 30

The Social Science Challenge to the Disease Theory 32

Controlled-Drinking Therapy for Alcoholism 37

3. Theories of Addiction 47
Stanton Peele and Bruce K. Alexander

Genetic Theories 48

Exposure Theories: Biological Models 56

Exposure Theories: Conditioning Models 62

Adaptation Theories 69

The Requirements of a Successful Theory of Addiction 72

4. Adult, Infant, and Animal Addiction 73
Bruce K. Alexander, Stanton Peele, Patricia F. Hadaway, Stanley J. Morse, Archie Brodsky, and Barry L. Beyerstein

The Effect on the Infant of Mother's Drug Use 73

The Addicted Animal 77

Animal Narcotics Use in Rat Park 79

What Causes Animals to Accept Narcosis? 88

The Implication of Infant and Animal Research for Conceptions of Addiction 94

5. Addiction to an Experience 97

Elements of the Addictive Experience 97

Susceptibility to Addiction and the Choice of Addictive Object: Social and Cultural Factors 104

Susceptibility to and Choice of Addiction: Situational Factors 110

Susceptibility to and Choice of Addiction: Individual Factors 113

Susceptibility to and Choice of Addiction: Developmental Factors 122

The Nature of Addiction: The Addiction Cycle 128

6. The Impaired Society 133

The Narcotic Connection—Supply and Demand 135

The Negative Effects of the Belief in Chemical Dependence 140

Can We Treat Away the Drug Problem? 142

The Alcoholism and Chemical Dependence Industry 145

Spreading Diseases 150

The Cure for Addiction 154

References 159

Author Index 187

Subject Index 193

About the Author 205

Updated Preface

I have been gratified to see *The Meaning of Addiction* become the classic expression of the extensive research that shows addiction cannot be resolved biologically—lived human experience and its interpretation are central to the incidence, course, treatment, and remission of addiction. The data presented in this book indicate this is permanently the case. The idea, on the other hand, that new genetic and neurochemical discoveries will eliminate this irrefutable truth is the greatest of all myths about addiction.

The compulsion to bypass human experience in creating models of addiction is stronger than ever. The director of the National Institute on Alcohol Abuse and Alcoholism (NIAAA), Enoch Gordis (1990: 1), believes that biological and genetic sources of alcoholism will be discovered and medical cures developed so that we can cease what he finds to be the pointless effort of understanding why people drink and why they drink too much:

> For treatment to be most effective, a strong, long-term commitment is required to conducting research on the causes and consequences of disease. For example, sanitoria were widely available for the treatment of tuberculosis in the early 20th Century and provided the best treatment known at the time for this disease. However, it was not until medical scientists identified the tubercle bacillus and discovered useful antibacterial agents that the treatment for tuberculosis became effective.

Thus, the head of the NIAAA misunderstands the fundamental nature of the problem he has been addressing in that capacity for over a decade. Gordis believes we will cure alcoholism the way we did tuberculosis. As this book shows, he is demonstrably wrong.

The leading U.S. government official charged with understanding addiction is the director of the National Institute of Mental Health, Steven Hyman, who was formerly director of the Harvard Medical School Division of Addictions. Hyman (1996), writing in the prestigious journal *Science,* described how researchers are "shaking out the cause of addiction" in terms of specific brain mechanisms. Actually, Hyman discusses research that describes how opiates and other drugs act on the brain. But, as this book describes, most opiate users are not addicts, and most addicts give up or reduce their use of opiates as dictated by their life needs. The effects of drugs on the brain are a small, variable contributor to addiction that are always mediated by social and personal interpretation.

The best indicator of the highly situationalized nature of addiction is the research overwhelmingly demonstrating that addicts in Vietnam, even when they used narcotics stateside, did not return to addiction. Lee Robins, John Helzer, and their colleagues (1980) described the research on the Vietnam veteran heroin experience that indicates treatment isn't necessary for recovery from heroin addiction (in fact veterans rarely required it), that reuse of narcotics by former addicts only occasionally and temporarily led to readdiction, and so on.

These prominent American scientists, who have conducted addiction research for decades, indicated that all of their previous notions of heroin—exactly the ones to which Hyman and others are currently addicted—were simply and fundamentally wrong. However, a few years later Helzer, Robins, and their colleagues (1985) wrote an article in the *New England Journal of Medicine* which concluded that alcoholics cannot resume moderate drinking (even though earlier they had found that the "highly addictive" drug heroin does not have such invariably addicting effects). *The Meaning of Addiction* ties together this myth of alcoholism with the other myths of addiction.

Ultimately, this book presents a systematic, seamless model of addiction that makes sense of the natural history of addiction for individuals, cultural variations in addictive experience, and the wide range of addictive experiences for different individuals with different involvements at different times and places. This is the meaning of addiction—something that cannot bypass real people in real settings in all their experiential and cultural richness. The effort to do otherwise is strange and misguided, scientifically and therapeutically, and will eventually die away—but meanwhile doing horrible mischief.

Morristown, New Jersey
February 1998

References

Gordis, E. 1990. Confronting alcohol abuse and dependence: Treatment research fortifies front lines. *ADAMHA News Supplement* (January/February):1–2.

Helzer, J. E.; Robins, L.N.; Taylor, J.R.; Carey, K.; Miller, R.H.; Combs-Orme, T.; and Farmer, A. 1985. The extent of long-term moderate drinking among alcoholics discharged from medical and psychiatric treatment facilities. *New England Journal of Medicine* 312:1678–1682.

Hyman, S.E. 1996. Shaking out the cause of addiction. *Science* 273:611–612.

Robins, L. N.; Helzer, J.E.; Hesselbrock, M.; and Wish, E. 1980. Vietnam veterans three years after Vietnam: How our study changed our view of heroin. In *The yearbook of substance use and abuse*, eds. L. Brill and C. Winick, vol. 2:213–230. New York: Human Sciences Press.

First Edition Preface

The conventional idea of addiction—that a substance or activity can produce a compulsion to act that is beyond the individual's self-control—is a powerful one. In *The Meaning of Addiction*, I explore the social and personal meanings of this idea and its relevance to human behavior. This exploration includes histories of narcotic addiction (chapter 1) and alcoholism (chapter 2) in the United States, histories that explain recent theoretical developments in these fields. I judge the efficacy of prominent theories of drug and alcohol addiction—along with current models of overeating, smoking, and even running and love addictions—and analyze their flaws in a larger intellectual and psychological context (chapter 3).

In the course of this book I review a large body of epidemiological, historical, experimental, life-span, and clinical research about human drug use. I also address the literature on animal drug use studies, along with ideas about infant addiction, because these hold such a large place in contemporary views of addiction (chapter 4). In addition, I present the results of systematic experimentation on animal opiate use conducted by Dr. Bruce Alexander and his colleagues, which correct inaccurate popular notions about how animals respond to drugs. The purpose of these animal data, in common with much of the material in this book, is to puncture simplistic, often magical visions about the nature of addiction.

My major endeavor, after establishing a suitable level of analysis for addiction, is to create a framework for understanding addictive behavior (chapter 5). I evaluate the factors that cause addiction and describe the nature of self-perpetuating, self-destructive behavior. I construct a model of the relationships among cultural, social, psychological, pharmacological, and other components of addictive motivation, based on the idea that addiction is a response to socially and individually conditioned needs for specific psychophysiological, or experiential, states. This model is designed to apply equally well to *all* areas of repetitive, compulsive behavior, from self-destructive running to narcotic addiction.

I draw further implications from my analysis (chapter 6), including an understanding of the current high levels of addiction and of the failures of

treatment and public policies for addiction, and I propose a direction for reasonable therapeutic and prevention efforts. Moreover, my analysis offers insights into the process of scientific definition and into some core social and psychological themes of our times: namely, the designation of new categories of psychic disease and their impact on our image of the sources of human conduct. The idea of addiction, I make clear, has always expressed central cultural conceptions about motivation and behavior. Now, in an age when science and health magazines have become our bibles, ill-founded psychological generalizations presented as scientific wisdom dictate our collective decisions about children, criminals, and ourselves.

Our conventional view of addiction—aided and abetted by science—does nothing so much as convince people of their vulnerability. It is one more element in a pervasive sense of loss of control that is the major contributor to drug and alcohol abuse, along with a host of other maladies of our age. We feel we must warn people against the dangers of the substances our society has banned, or attempted to curtail, but cannot eradicate. This book argues that our best hope is to convey these dangers realistically, by rationally pointing out the costs of excess and, more importantly, by convincing people of the benefits of health and of positive life experience. Otherwise, the idea of addiction can only become another burden to the psyche. Science cannot increase our understanding of ourselves and our world—nor can it show us the way to freedom—if it is held captive by our fears.

Acknowledgments

Beginning any book is a daunting project. I found the work on this book—extending over three years—to be particularly so. Although I was well familiar with and in constant touch with much of the material, organizing and expressing my ideas to achieve the force I hoped proved a formidable task. To the extent that I accomplished my goal, I am indebted to Archie Brodsky for the assistance he gave in discussing ideas, restructuring chapters, contributing original insights (chapter 4), and correcting phraseology and syntax. Bruce Alexander, as well as contributing original material to chapter 3 and (along with his colleagues Patricia Hadaway and Bruce Beyerstein) conducting, analyzing, and presenting the animal research in chapter 4, commented on drafts of chapters 1 and 5 and made available to me reference materials used throughout this book. Stanley Morse, as he has so often done before, selflessly read and critiqued several of these chapters, making particularly invaluable contributions to chapters 1 and 4. Without the help of any of these people, I would not have been able to give the book the form it has.

In addition, a number of people over the years made me aware of information and ideas that have helped shape this book. These people include John Falk, Nick Heather, Alan Marlatt, Harold Kalant, William Miller, Norman Zinberg, Peter Nathan, Griffith Edwards, James Woods, Harriet Braiker, Mark and Linda Sobell, Robin Room, Constance Weisner, Dan Waldorf, Martha Sanchez-Craig, Larry Gaines, David Funder, David McClelland, Robert Allen, and Judd Allen. Needless to say, although this book has been enriched by my contact with all these people, the responsibility for the ideas I express is strictly my own. I have also received great assistance in retrieving source materials from the staffs of the libraries of Fairleigh Dickinson University, Drew University, Sandoz Corporation, and the Institute for the Study of Drug Dependence (particularly the ISDD's ever-helpful information officers, Mike Ashton and Harry Shapiro). Paula Ives, for her typing, and Paula Cloutier, for her help in duplicating my manuscripts, get my special thanks. Finally, Dan Barmettler of the Institute for

Integral Development enabled me to present and sharpen my ideas during these years by offering me a continuing forum at the conferences he organized around the United States, and Mary Arnold, my wife, provided the financial support needed to complete this work.

1
The Concept of Addiction

The conventional concept of addiction this book confronts—the one accepted not only by the media and popular audiences, but by researchers whose work does little to support it—derives more from magic than from science. The core of this concept is that an entire set of feelings and behaviors is the unique result of one biological process. No other scientific formulation attributes a complex human phenomenon to the nature of a particular stimulus: statements such as "He ate all the ice cream because it was so good" or "She watches so much television because it's fun" are understood to call for a greater understanding of the actors' motivations (except, ironically, as these activities are now considered analogous to narcotic addiction). Even reductionist theories of mental illness such as of depression and schizophrenia (Peele 1981b) seek to account for a general state of mind, not specific behavior. Only compulsive consumption of narcotics and alcohol—conceived of as addictions (and now, other addictions that are seen to operate in the same way)—is believed to be the result of a spell that no effort of will can break.

Addiction is defined by tolerance, withdrawal, and craving. We recognize addiction by a person's heightened and habituated need for a substance; by the intense suffering that results from discontinuation of its use; and by the person's willingness to sacrifice all (to the point of self-destructiveness) for drug taking. The inadequacy of the conventional concept lies not in the identification of these signs of addiction—they do occur—but in the processes that are imagined to account for them. Tolerance, withdrawal, and craving are thought to be properties of particular drugs, and sufficient use of these substances is believed to give the organism no choice but to behave in these stereotypical ways. This process is thought to be inexorable, universal, and irreversible and to be independent of individual, group, cultural, or situational variation; it is even thought to be essentially the same for animals and for human beings, whether infant or adult.

Observers of addictive behavior and scientists studying it in the laboratory or in natural settings have uniformly noted that this pure model of

addiction does not exist in reality, and that the behavior of people said to be addicted is far more variable than conventional notions allow. Yet unexamined, disabling residues of this inaccurate concept are present even in the work of those who have most astutely exposed the inadequacy of conventional models for describing addictive behavior. Such residues include the persistent view that complex behaviors like craving and withdrawal are straightforward physiological reactions to drugs or are biological processes—even when they appear with nondrug involvements. Although these beliefs have been shown to be unfounded in the context in which they first arose—that of heroin use and heroin addiction—they have been rearranged into new notions such as drug dependence, or used as the basis for conditioning models that assume that drugs produce invariant physiological responses in humans.

It is the burden of this book to show that exclusively biological concepts of addiction (or drug dependence) are ad hoc and superfluous and that addictive behavior is no different from all other human feeling and action in being subject to social and cognitive influences. To establish how such factors affect the dynamics of addiction is the ultimate purpose of this analysis. In this reformulation, addiction is seen not to depend on the effects of specific drugs. Moreover, it is not limited to drug use at all. Rather, addiction is best understood as an individual's adjustment, albeit a self-defeating one, to his or her environment. It represents an habitual style of coping, albeit one that the individual is capable of modifying with changing psychological and life circumstances.

While in some cases addiction achieves a devastating pathological extremity, it actually represents a continuum of feeling and behavior more than it does a distinct disease state. Neither traumatic drug withdrawal nor a person's craving for a drug is exclusively determined by physiology. Rather, the experience both of a felt need (or craving) for and of withdrawal from an object or involvement engages a person's expectations, values, and self-concept, as well as the person's sense of alternative opportunities for gratification. These complications are introduced not out of disillusionment with the notion of addiction but out of respect for its potential power and utility. Suitably broadened and strengthened, the concept of addiction provides a powerful description of human behavior, one that opens up important opportunities for understanding not only drug abuse, but compulsive and self-destructive behaviors of all kinds. This book proposes such a comprehensive concept and demonstrates its application to drugs, alcohol, and other contexts of addictive behavior.

Since narcotic addiction has been, for better or worse, our primary model for understanding other addictions, the analysis of prevailing ideas about addiction and their shortcomings involves us in the history of narcotics, particularly in the United States in the last hundred years. This his-

tory shows that styles of opiate use and our very conception of opiate addiction are historically and culturally determined. Data revealing regular nonaddictive narcotic use have consistently complicated the effort to define addiction, as have revelations of the addictive use of nonnarcotic drugs. Alcohol is one drug whose equivocal relationship to prevailing conceptions of addiction has confused the study of substance abuse for well over a century. Because the United States has had a different—though no less destructive and disturbing—experience with alcohol than it has had with opiates, this cultural experience is analyzed separately in chapter 2. This emphasis notwithstanding, alcohol is understood in this book to be addictive in exactly the same sense that heroin and other powerful drug and nondrug experiences are.

Cultural and historical variations in ideas about drugs and addiction are examples of the range of factors that influence people's reactions to drugs and susceptibility to addiction. These and other salient nonpharmacological factors are outlined and discussed in this chapter. Taken together, they offer a strong prod to reconceive of addiction as being more than a physiological response to drug use. Drug theorists, psychologists, pharmacologists, and others have been attempting such reconceptualizations for some time; yet their efforts remain curiously bound to past, disproven ideas. The resilience of these wrongheaded ideas is discussed in an effort to understand their persistence in the face of disconfirming information. Some of the factors that explain their persistence are popular prejudices, deficiences in research strategies, and issues of the legality and illegality of various substances. At the bottom, however, our inability to conceive of addiction realistically is tied to our reluctance to formulate scientific concepts about behavior that include subjective perceptions, cultural and individual values, and notions of self-control and other personality-based differences (Peele 1983e). This chapter shows that any concept of addiction that bypasses these factors is fundamentally inadequate.

Opiate Addiction in the United States and the Western World

Contemporary scientific and clinical concepts of addiction are inextricably connected with social developments surrounding the use of narcotics, especially in the United States, early in this century. Before that time, from the late sixteenth through the nineteenth centuries, the term "addicted" was generally used to mean "given over to a habit or vice." Although withdrawal and craving had been noted over the centuries with the opiates, the latter were not singled out as substances that produced a distinctive brand of dependence. Indeed, morphine addiction as a disease state was first noted

in 1877 by a German physician, Levenstein, who "still saw addiction as a human passion 'such as smoking, gambling, greediness for profit, sexual excesses, etc.'" (Berridge and Edwards 1981: 142–143). As late as the twentieth century, American physicians and pharmacists were as likely to apply the term "addiction" to the use of coffee, tobacco, alcohol, and bromides as they were to opiate use (Sonnedecker 1958).

Opiates were widespread and legal in the United States during the nineteenth century, most commonly in tincturated form in potions such as laudanum and paregoric. Yet they were not considered a menace, and little concern was displayed about their negative effects (Brecher 1972). Furthermore, there was no indication that opiate addiction was a significant problem in nineteenth–century America. This was true even in connection with the enthusiastic medical deployment of morphine—a concentrated opiate prepared for injection—during the U.S. Civil War (Musto 1973). The situation in England, while comparable to that in the United States, may have been even more extreme. Berridge and Edwards (1981) found that use of standard opium preparations was massive and indiscriminate in England throughout much of the nineteenth century as was use of hypodermic morphine at the end of the century. Yet these investigators found little evidence of serious narcotic addiction problems at the time. Instead, they noted that later in the century, "The quite small number of morphine addicts who happened to be obvious to the [medical] profession assumed the dimensions of a pressing problem—at a time when, as general consumption and mortality data indicate, usage and addiction to opium in general was tending to decline, not increase" (p.149).

Although middle-class consumption of opiates was considerable in the United States (Courtwright 1982), it was only the smoking of opium in illicit dens both in Asia and by Chinese in the United States that was widely conceived to be a disreputable and debilitating practice (Blum et al. 1969). Opium smoking among immigrant Asian laborers and other social outcasts presaged changes in the use of opiates that were greatly to modify the image of narcotics and their effects after the turn of the century. These developments included:

1. A shift in the populations using narcotics from a largely middle-class and female clientele for laudanum to mostly male, urban, minority, and lower-class users of heroin—an opiate that had been developed in Europe in 1898 (Clausen 1961; Courtwright 1982);
2. Both as an exaggerated response to this shift and as an impetus to its acceleration, the passage in 1914 of the Harrison Act, which was later interpreted to outlaw medical maintenance of narcotic addicts (King 1972; Trebach 1982); and

3. A widely held vision of narcotic users and their habits as being alien to American lifestyles and of narcotic use as being debased, immoral, and uncontrollable (Kolb 1958).

The Harrison Act and subsequent actions by the Federal Bureau of Narcotics led to the classification of narcotic use as a legal problem. These developments were supported by the American Medical Association (Kolb 1958). This support seems paradoxical, since it contributed to the loss of a historical medical prerogative—the dispensing of opiates. However, the actual changes that were taking place in America's vision of narcotics and their role in society were more complex than this. Opiates first had been removed from the list of accepted pharmaceuticals, then their use was labeled as a social problem, and finally they were characterized as producing a specific medical syndrome. It was only with this last step that the word "addiction" came to be employed with its present meaning. "From 1870 to 1900, most physicians regarded addiction as a morbid appetite, a habit, or a vice. After the turn of the century, medical interest in the problem increased. Various physicians began to speak of the condition as a disease" (Isbell 1958: 115). Thus, organized medicine accepted the loss of narcotic use as a treatment in return for the rewards of seeing it incorporated into the medical model in another way.

In Britain, the situation was somewhat different inasmuch as opium consumption was a lower-class phenomenon that aroused official concern in the nineteenth century. However, the medical view of opiate addiction as a disease arose as doctors observed more middle-class patients injecting morphine later in the century (Berridge and Edwards 1981: 149–150):

> The profession, by its enthusiastic advocacy of a new and more "scientific" remedy and method, had itself contributed to an increase in addiction. . . . Disease entities were being established in definitely recognizible physical conditions such as typhoid and cholera. The belief in scientific progress encouraged medical intervention in less definable conditions [as well] . . . . [S]uch views were never, however, scientifically autonomous. Their putative objectivity disguised class and moral concerns which precluded a wider understanding of the social and cultural roots of opium [and later morphine] use.

The evolution of the idea of narcotic—and particularly heroin—addiction was part of a larger process that medicalized what were previously regarded as moral, spiritual, or emotional problems (Foucault 1973; Szasz 1961). The idea central to the modern definition of addiction is that of the individual's inability to choose: that addicted behavior is outside the realm

of ordinary consideration and evaluation (Levine 1978). This idea was connected to a belief in the existence of biological mechanisms—not yet discovered—that caused the use of opiates to create a further need for opiates. In this process the work of such early heroin investigators as Philadelphia physicians Light and Torrance (1929), who were inclined to see the abstaining addict wheedling for more drugs as a malcontent demanding satisfaction and reassurance, was replaced by deterministic models of craving and withdrawal. These models, which viewed the need for a drug as qualitatively different from other kinds of human desires, came to dominate the field, even though the behavior of narcotic users approximated them no better than it had in Light and Torrance's day.

However, self-defined and treated addicts did increasingly conform to the prescribed models, in part because addicts mimicked the behavior described by the sociomedical category of addiction and in part because of an unconscious selection process that determined which addicts became visible to clinicians and researchers. The image of the addict as powerless, unable to make choices, and invariably in need of professional treatment ruled out (in the minds of the experts) the possibility of a natural evolution out of addiction brought on by changes in life circumstances, in the person's set and setting, and in simple individual resolve. Treatment professionals did not look for the addicts who did achieve this sort of spontaneous remission and who, for their part, had no wish to call attention to themselves. Meanwhile, the treatment rolls filled up with addicts whose ineptitude in coping with the drug brought them to the attention of the authorities and who, in their highly dramatized withdrawal agonies and predictable relapses, were simply doing what they had been told they could not help but do. In turn, the professionals found their dire prophecies confirmed by what was in fact a context–limited sample of addictive behavior.

Divergent Evidence about Narcotic Addiction

The view that addiction is the result of a specific biological mechanism that locks the body into an invariant pattern of behavior—one marked by superordinate craving and traumatic withdrawal when a given drug is not available—is disputed by a vast array of evidence. Indeed, this concept of addiction has never provided a good description either of drug-related behavior or of the behavior of the addicted individual. In particular, the early twentieth-century concept of addiction (which forms the basis of most scientific as well as popular thinking about addiction today) equated it with opiate use. This is (and was at the time of its inception) disproven both by the phenomenon of controlled opiate use even by regular and heavy users

and by the appearance of addictive symptomatology for users of nonnarcotic substances.

Nonaddicted Narcotics Use

Courtwright (1982) and others typically cloud the significance of the massive nonaddicted use of opiates in the nineteenth century by claiming local observers were unaware of the genuine nature of addiction and thus missed the large numbers who manifested withdrawal and other addictive symptomatology. He struggles to explain how the commonplace administration of opiates to babies "was unlikely to develop into a full-blown addiction, for the infant would not have comprehended the nature of its withdrawal distress, not could it have done anything about it" (p. 58). In any case, Courtwright agrees that by the time addiction was being defined and opiates outlawed at the turn of the century, narcotic use was a minor public health phenomenon. An energetic campaign undertaken in the United States by the Federal Bureau of Narcotics and—in England as well as the United States—by organized medicine and the media changed irrevocably conceptions of the nature of opiate use. In particular, the campaign eradicated the awareness that people could employ opiates moderately or as a part of normal lifestyle. In the early twentiety century, "the climate . . . was such that an individual might work for 10 years beside an industrious law-abiding person and then feel a sense of revulsion toward him upon discovering that he secretly used an opiate" (Kolb 1958: 25). Today, our awareness of the existence of opiate users from that time who maintained normal lives is based on the recorded cases of "eminent narcotics addicts" (Brecher 1972: 33).

The use of narcotics by people whose lives are not obviously disturbed by their habit has continued into the present. Many of these users have been identified among physicians and other medical personnel. In our contemporary prohibitionist society, these users are often dismissed as addicts who are protected from disclosure and from the degradation of addiction by their privileged positions and easy access to narcotics. Yet substantial numbers of them do not appear to be addicted, and it is their control over their habit that, more than anything else, protects them from disclosure. Winick (1961) conducted a major study of a body of physician narcotic users, most of whom had been found out because of suspicious prescription activities. Nearly all these doctors had stabilized their dosages of a narcotic (in most cases Demerol) over the years, did not suffer diminished capacities, and were able to fit their narcotic use into successful medical practices and what appeared to be rewarding lives overall.

Zinberg and Lewis (1964) identified a range of patterns of narcotic use, among which the classic addictive pattern was only one variant that appeared in a minority of cases. One subject in this study, a physician, took

morphine four times a day but abstained on weekends and two months a year during vacations. Tracked for over a decade, this man neither increased his dosage nor suffered withdrawal during his periods of abstinence (Zinberg and Jacobson 1976). On the basis of two decades of investigation of such cases, Zinberg (1984) analyzed the factors that separate the addicted from the nonaddicted drug user. Primarily, controlled users, like Winick's physicians, subordinate their desire for a drug to other values, activities, and personal relationships, so that the narcotic or other drug does not dominate their lives. When engaged in other pursuits that they value, these users do not crave the drug or manifest withdrawal on discontinuing their drug use. Furthermore, controlled use of narcotics is not limited to physicians or to middle-class drug users. Lukoff and Brook (1974) found that a majority of ghetto users of heroin had stable home and work involvements, which would hardly be possible in the presence of uncontrollable craving.

If life circumstances affect people's drug use, we would expect patterns of use to vary over time. Every naturalistic study of heroin use has confirmed such fluctuations, including switching among drugs, voluntary and involuntary periods of abstinence, and spontaneous remission of heroin addiction (Maddux and Desmond 1981; Nurco et al. 1981; Robins and Murphy 1967; Waldorf 1973, 1983; Zinberg and Jacobson 1976). In these studies, heroin does not appear to differ significantly in the potential range of its use from other types of involvements, and even compulsive users cannot be distinguished from those given to other habitual involvements in the ease with which they desist or shift their patterns of use. These variations make it difficult to define a point at which a person can be said to be addicted. In a typical study (in this case of former addicts who quit without treatment), Waldorf (1983) defined addiction as daily use for a year along with the appearance of significant withdrawal symptoms during that period. In fact, such definitions are operationally equivalent to simply asking people whether they are or were addicted (Robins et al. 1975).

A finding with immense theoretical importance is that some former narcotics addicts become controlled users. The most comprehensive demonstration of this phenomenon was Robins et al.'s (1975) research on Vietnam veterans who had been addicted to narcotics in Asia. Of this group, only 14 percent became readdicted after their return home, although fully half used heroin—some regularly—in the United States. Not all these men used heroin in Vietnam (some used opium), and some relied on other drugs in the United States (most often alcohol). This finding of controlled use by former addicts may also be limited by the extreme alteration in the environments of the soldiers from Vietnam to the United States. Harding et al. (1980), however, reported on a group of addicts in the United States who had all used heroin more than once a day, some as often as ten times a day, who were now controlled heroin users. None of these subjects was cur-

rently alcoholic or addicted to barbiturates. Waldorf (1983) found that former addicts who quit on their own frequently—in a ceremonial proof of their escape from their habit—used the drug at a later point without becoming readdicted.

Although widely circulated, the data showing that the vast majority of soldiers using heroin in Vietnam readily gave up their habits (Jaffe and Harris 1973; Peele 1978) and that "contrary to conventional belief, the occasional use of narcotics without becoming addicted appears possible even for men who have previously been dependent on narcotics" (Robins et al. 1974: 236) have not been assimilated either into popular conceptions of heroin use or into theories of addiction. Indeed, the media and drug commentators in the United States seemingly feel obligated to conceal the existence of controlled heroin users, as in the case of the television film made of baseball player Ron LeFlore's life. Growing up in a Detroit ghetto, LeFlore acquired a heroin habit. He reported using the drug daily for nine months before abruptly withdrawing without experiencing any negative effects (LeFlore and Hawkins 1978). It proved impossible to depict this set of circumstances on American television, and the TV movie ignored LeFlore's personal experience with heroin, showing instead his brother being chained to a bed while undergoing agonizing heroin withdrawal. By portraying heroin use in the most dire light at all times, the media apparently hope to discourage heroin use and addiction. The fact that the United States has long been the most active propagandizer against recreational narcotic use—and drug use of all kinds—and yet has by far the largest heroin and other drug problems of any Western nation indicates the limitations of this strategy (see chapter 6).

The failure to take into account the varieties of narcotic use goes beyond media hype, however. Pharmacologists and other scientists simply cannot face the evidence in this area. Consider the tone of disbelief and resistance with which several expert discussants greeted a presentation by Zinberg and his colleagues on controlled heroin use (see Kissin et al. 1978: 23–24). Yet a similar reluctance to acknowledge the consequences of nonaddictive narcotics use is evident even in the writings of the very investigators who have demonstrated that such use occurs. Robins (1980) equated the use of illicit drugs with drug abuse, primarily because previous studies had done so, and maintained that among all drugs heroin creates the greatest dependency (Robins et al. 1980). At the same time, she noted that "heroin as used in the streets of the United States does not differ from other drugs in its liability to being used regularly or on a daily basis" (Robins 1980: 370) and that "heroin is 'worse' than amphetamines or barbiturates only because 'worse' people use it" (Robins et al. 1980: 229). In this way controlled use of narcotics—and of all illicit substances—and compulsive use of legal drugs are both disguised, obscuring the personality and social

factors that actually distinguish styles of using any kind of drug (Zinberg and Harding 1982). Under these circumstances, it is perhaps not surprising that the major predictors of illicit use (irrespective of degree of harmfulness of such use) are nonconformity and independence (Jessor and Jessor 1977).

One final research and conceptual bias that has colored our ideas about heroin addiction has been that, more than with other drugs, our knowledge about heroin has come mainly from those users who cannot control their habits. These subjects make up the clinical populations on which prevailing notions of addiction have been based. Naturalistic studies reveal not only less harmful use but also more variation in the behavior of those who are addicted. It seems to be primarily those who report for treatment who have a lifetime of difficulty in overcoming their addictions (cf. Califano 1983). The same appears true for alcoholics: For example, an ability to shift to controlled drinking shows up regularly in field studies of alcoholics, although it is denied as a possibility by clinicians (Peele 1983a; Vaillant 1983). (See chapter 2.)

Nonnarcotic Addiction

The prevailing twentieth-century concept of addiction considers addiction to be a byproduct of the chemical structure of a specific drug (or family of drugs). Consequently, pharmacologists and others have believed that an effective pain-reliever, or analgesic, could be synthesized that would not have addictive properties. The search for such a nonaddictive analgesic has been a dominant theme of twentieth-century pharmacology (cf. Clausen 1961; Cohen 1983; Eddy and May 1973; Peele 1977). Indeed, heroin was introduced in 1898 as offering pain relief without the disquieting side effects sometimes noted with morphine. Since that time, the early synthetic narcotics such as Demerol and the synthetic sedative family, the barbiturates, have been marketed with the same claims. Later, new groups of sedatives and narcotic-like substances, such as Valium and Darvon, were introduced as having more focused anti-anxiety and pain-relieving effects that would not be addictive. All such drugs have been found to lead to addiction in some, perhaps many, cases (cf. Hooper and Santo 1980; Smith and Wesson 1983; Solomon et al. 1979). Similarly, some have argued that analgesics based on the structures of endorphins—opiate peptides produced endogenously by the body—can be used without fear of addiction (Kosterlitz 1979). It is hardly believable that these substances will be different from every other narcotic with respect to addictive potential.

Alcohol is a nonnarcotic drug that, like the narcotics and sedatives, is a depressant. Since alcohol is legal and almost universally available, the possibility that it can be used in a controlled manner is generally accepted. At the same time, alcohol is also recognized to be an addicting substance.

The divergent histories and differing contemporary visions of alcohol and narcotics in the United States have produced two different versions of the addiction concept (see chapter 2). Whereas narcotics have been considered to be universally addictive, the modern disease concept of alcoholism has emphasized a genetic susceptibility that predisposes only some individuals to become addicted to alcohol (Goodwin 1976; Schuckit 1984). In recent years, however, there has been some convergence in these conceptions. Goldstein (1976b) has accounted for the discovery that only a minority of narcotic users go on to be addicts by postulating constitutional biological differences between individuals. Coming from the opposite direction, some observers oppose the disease theory of alcoholism by maintaining that alcoholism is simply the inevitable result of a certain threshold level of consumption (cf. Beauchamp 1980; Kendell 1979). (See chapter 3.)

Observations of the defining traits of addiction have been made not only with the broader family of sedative-analgesic drugs and alcohol but also with stimulants. Goldstein et al. (1969) have noted craving and withdrawal among habitual coffee drinkers that are not qualitatively different from the craving and withdrawal observed in cases of narcotics use. This discovery serves to remind us that at the turn of the century, prominent British pharmacologists could say of the excessive coffee drinker, "the sufferer is tremulous and loses his self-command. . . . As with other such agents, a renewed dose of the poison gives temporary relief, but at the cost of future misery" (quoted in Lewis 1969: 10). Schachter (1978), meanwhile, has forcefully presented the case that cigarettes are addicting in the typical pharmacological sense and that their continued use by the addict is maintained by the avoidance of withdrawal (cf. Krasnegor 1979).

Nicotine and caffeine are stimulants that are consumed indirectly, through their presence in cigarettes and coffee. Surprisingly, pharmacologists have classified stimulants that users self-administer directly—such as amphetamines and cocaine—as nonaddictive because, according to their research, these drugs do not produce withdrawal (Eddy et al. 1965). Why milder stimulant use like that manifested by coffee and cigarette habitués should be more potent than cocaine and amphetamine habits is mystifying. In fact, as cocaine has become a popular recreational drug in the United States, severe withdrawal is now regularly noted among individuals calling a hot line for counseling about the drug (Washton 1983). In order to preserve traditional categories of thought, those commenting on observations of compulsive cocaine use claim it produces "psychological dependence whose effects are not all that different from addiction" because cocaine "is the most psychologically tenacious drug available" ("Cocaine: Middle Class High" 1981: 57, 61).

In response to the observation of an increasing number of involvements that can lead to addiction-like behavior, two conflicting trends have

appeared in addiction theorizing. One, found mainly in popular writing (Oates 1971; Slater 1980) but also in serious theorizing (Peele and Brodsky 1975), has been to return to the pre-twentieth-century usage of the term "addiction" and to apply this term to all types of compulsive, self-destructive activities. The other refuses to certify as addictive any involvement other than with narcotics or drugs thought to be more or less similar to narcotics. One unsatisfactory attempt at a synthesis of these positions has been to relate all addictive behavior to changes in the organism's neurological functioning. Thus biological mechanisms have been hypothesized to account for self-destructive running (Morgan 1979), overeating (Weisz and Thompson 1983), and love relationships (Liebowitz 1983; Tennov 1979). This wishful thinking is associated with a continuing failure to make sense of the experiential, environmental, and social factors that are integrally related to addictive phenomena.

Nonbiological Factors in Addiction

A concept that aims to describe the full reality of addiction must incorporate nonbiological factors as *essential ingredients* in addiction—up to and including the appearance of craving, withdrawal, and tolerance effects. Following is a summary of these factors in addiction.

Cultural

Different cultures regard, use, and react to substances in different ways, which in turn influence the likelihood of addiction. Thus, opium was never proscribed or considered a dangerous substance in India, where it was grown and used indigenously, but it quickly became a major social problem in China when it was brought there by the British (Blum et al. 1969). The external introduction of a substance into a culture that does not have established social mechanisms for regulating its use is common in the history of drug abuse. The appearance of widespread abuse of and addiction to a substance may also take place after indigenous customs regarding its use are overwhelmed by a dominant foreign power. Thus the Hopi and Zuni Indians drank alcohol in a ritualistic and regulated manner prior to the coming of the Spanish, but in a destructive and generally addictive manner thereafter (Bales 1946). Sometimes a drug takes root as an addictive substance in one culture but not in other cultures that are exposed to it at the same time. Heroin was transported to the United States through European countries no more familiar with opiate use than was the United States (Solomon 1977). Yet heroin addiction, while considered a vicious social menace here,

was regarded as a purely American disease in those European countries where the raw opium was processed (Epstein 1977).

It is crucial to recognize that—as in the case of nineteenth-and twentieth-century opiate use—addictive patterns of drug use do not depend solely, or even largely, on the *amount* of the substance in use at a given time and place. Per capita alcohol consumption was several times its current level in the United States during the colonial period, yet both problem drinking and alcoholism were at far lower levels than they are today (Lender and Martin 1982; Zinberg and Fraser 1979). Indeed, colonial Americans did not comprehend alcoholism as an uncontrollable disease or addiction (Levine 1978). Because alcohol is so commonly used throughout the world, it offers the best illustration of how the effects of a substance are interpreted in widely divergent ways that influence its addictive potential. As a prime example, the belief that drunkenness excuses aggressive, escapist, and other antisocial behavior is much more pronounced in some cultures than in others (Falk 1983; MacAndrew and Edgerton 1969). Such beliefs translate into cultural visions of alcohol and its effects that are strongly associated with the appearance of alcoholism. That is, the displays of antisocial aggression and loss of control that define alcoholism among American Indians and Eskimos and in Scandinavia, Eastern Europe, and the United States are notably absent in the drinking of Greeks and Italians, and American Jews, Chinese, and Japanese (Barnett 1955; Blum and Blum 1969; Glassner and Berg 1980; Vaillant 1983).

Social

Drug use is closely tied to the social and peer groups a person belongs to. Jessor and Jessor (1977) and Kandel (1978), among others, have identified the power of peer pressure on the initiation and continuation of drug use among adolescents. Styles of drinking, from moderate to excessive, are strongly influenced by the immediate social group (Cahalan and Room 1974; Clark 1982). Zinberg (1984) has been the main proponent of the view that the way a person uses heroin is likewise a function of group membership—controlled use is supported by knowing controlled users (and also by simultaneously belonging to groups where heroin is not used). At the same time that groups affect *patterns* of usage, they affect the way drug use is *experienced*. Drug effects give rise to internal states that the individual seeks to label cognitively, often by noting the reactions of others (Schachter and Singer 1962).

Becker (1953) described this process in the case of marijuana. Initiates to the fringe groups that used the drug in the 1950s had to learn not only how to smoke it but how to recognize and anticipate the drug's effects. The

group process extended to defining for the individual why this intoxicated state was a desirable one. Such social learning is present in all types and all stages of drug use. In the case of narcotics, Zinberg (1972) noted that the way withdrawal was experienced—including its degree of severity—varied among military units in Vietnam. Zinberg and Robertson (1972) reported that addicts who had undergone traumatic withdrawal in prison manifested milder symptoms or suppressed them altogether in a therapeutic community whose norms forbade the expression of withdrawal. Similar observations have been made with respect to alcohol withdrawal (Oki 1974; cf. Gilbert 1981).

Situational

A person's desire for a drug cannot be separated from the situation in which the person takes the drug. Falk (1983) and Falk et al. (1983) argue, primarily on the basis of animal experimentation, that an organism's environment influences drug-taking behavior more than do the supposedly inherently reinforcing properties of the drug itself. For example, animals who have alcohol dependence induced by intermittent feeding schedules cut their alcohol intake as soon as feeding schedules are normalized (Tang et al. 1982). Particularly important to the organism's readiness to overindulge is the absence of alternative behavioral opportunities (see chapter 4). For human subjects the presence of such alternatives ordinarily outweighs even positive mood changes brought on by drugs in motivating decisions about continuing drug use (Johanson and Uhlenhuth 1981). The situational basis of narcotic addiction, for example, was made evident by the finding (cited above) that the majority of U.S. servicemen who were addicted in Vietnam did not become readdicted when they used narcotics at home (Robins et al. 1974; Robins et al. 1975).

Ritualistic

The rituals that accompany drug use and addiction are important elements in continued use, so much so that to eliminate essential rituals can cause an addiction to lose its appeal. In the case of heroin, powerful parts of the experience are provided by the rite of self-injection and even the overall lifestyle involved in the pursuit and use of the drug. In the early 1960s, when Canadian policies concerning heroin became more stringent and illicit supplies of the drug became scarce, ninety-one Canadian addicts emigrated to Britain to enroll in heroin maintenance programs. Only twenty-five of these addicts found the British system satisfactory and remained. Those who returned to Canada often reported missing the excitement of the street scene. For them the pure heroin administered in a medical setting

did not produce the kick they got from the adulterated street variety they self-administered (Solomon 1977).

The essential role of ritual was shown in the earliest systematic studies of narcotic addicts. Light and Torrance (1929) reported that addicts could often have their withdrawal symptoms relieved by "the single prick of a needle" or a "hypodermic injection of sterile water." They noted, "paradoxic as it may seem, we believe that the greater the craving of the addict and the severity of the withdrawal symptoms the better are the chances of substituting a hypodermic injection of sterile water to obtain temporary relief" (p. 15). Similar findings hold true for nonnarcotic addiction. For example, nicotine administered directly does not have nearly the impact that inhaled nicotine does for habitual smokers (Jarvik 1973) who continue to smoke even when they have achieved their accustomed levels of cellular nicotine via capsule (Jarvik et al. 1970).

Developmental

People's reactions to, need for, and style of using a drug change as they progress through the life cycle. The classic form of this phenomenon is "maturing out." Winick (1962) originally hypothesized that a majority of young addicts leave their heroin habits behind when they accept an adult role in life. Waldorf (1983) affirmed the occurrence of substantial natural remission in heroin addiction, emphasizing the different forms it assumes and the different ages when people achieve it. It does appear, however, that heroin use is most often a youthful habit. O'Donnell et al. (1976) found, in a nationwide sample of young men, that more than two-thirds of the subjects who had ever used heroin (note these were not necessarily addicts) had not touched the drug in the previous year. Heroin is harder to obtain, and its use is less compatible with standard adult roles, than most other drugs of abuse. However, abusers of alcohol—a drug more readily assimilated into a normal lifestyle—likewise show a tendency to mature out (Cahalan and Room 1974).

O'Donnell et al. (1976) found that the greatest continuity in drug use among young men occurs with cigarette smoking. Such findings, together with indications that those seeking treatment for obesity only rarely succeed at losing weight and keeping it off (Stunkard 1958; Schachter and Rodin 1974), have suggested that remission may be unlikely for smokers and the obese, perhaps because their self-destructive habits are the ones most easily assimilated into a normal lifestyle. For this same reason remission would be expected to take place all through the life cycle rather than just in early adulthood. More recently, Schachter (1982) has found that a majority of those in two community populations who attempted to cease smoking or to lose weight were in remission from obesity or cigarette addiction.

While the peak period for natural recovery may differ for these various compulsive behaviors, there may be common remission processes that hold for all of them (Peele 1983d).

Personality

The idea that opiate use caused personality defects was challenged as early as the 1920s by Kolb (1962), who found that the personality traits observed among addicts preceded their drug use. Kolb's view was summarized in his statement that "The neurotic and the psychopath receive from narcotics a pleasurable sense of relief from the realities of life that normal persons do not receive because life is no special burden to them" (p. 85). Chein et al. (1964) gave this view its most comprehensive modern expression when they concluded that ghetto adolescent addicts were characterized by low self-esteem, learned incompetence, passivity, a negative outlook, and a history of dependency relationships. A major difficulty in assessing personality correlates of addiction lies in determining whether the traits found in a group of addicts are actually characteristics of a social group (Cahalan and Room 1974; Robins et al. 1980). On the other hand, addictive personality traits are obscured by lumping together controlled users of a drug such as heroin and those addicted to it. Similarly, the same traits may go unnoted in addicts whose different ethnic backgrounds or current settings predispose them toward different types of involvements, drug or otherwise (Peele 1983c).

Personality may both predispose people toward the use of some types of drugs rather than others and also affect how deeply they become involved with drugs at all (including whether they become addicted). Spotts and Shontz (1982) found that chronic users of different drugs represent distinct Jungian personality types. On the other hand, Lang (1983) claimed that efforts to discover an overall addictive personality type have generally failed. Lang does, however, report some similarities that generalize to abusers of a range of substances. These include placing a low value on achievement, a desire for instant gratification, and habitual feelings of heightened stress. The strongest argument for addictiveness as an individual personality disposition comes from repeated findings that the same individuals become addicted to many things, either simultaneously, sequentially, or alternately (Peele 1983c; Peele and Brodsky 1975). There is a high carry-over for addiction to one depressant substance to addiction to others—for example, turning from narcotics to alcohol (O'Donnell 1969; Robins et al. 1975). Alcohol, barbiturates, and narcotics show cross-tolerance (addicted users of one substance may substitute another) even though the drugs do not act the same way neurologically (Kalant 1982), while cocaine and Valium addicts have unusually high rates of alcohol abuse and frequently have family histories of alcoholism ("Many addicts . . ." 1983; Smith 1981). Gilbert

(1981) found that excessive use of a wide variety of substances was correlated—for example, smoking with coffee drinking and both with alcohol use. What is more, as Vaillant (1983) noted for alcoholics and Wishnie (1977) for heroin addicts, reformed substance abusers often form strong compulsions toward eating, prayer, and other nondrug involvements.

Cognitive

People's expectations and beliefs about drugs, or their mental set, and the beliefs and behavior of those around them that determine this set strongly influence reactions to drugs. These factors can, in fact, entirely reverse what are thought to be the specific pharmacological properties of a drug (Lennard et al. 1971; Schachter and Singer 1962). The efficacy of placebos demonstrates that cognitions can *create* expected drug effects. Placebo effects can match those of even the most powerful pain killers, such as morphine, although more so for some people than others (Lasagna et al. 1954). It is not surprising, then, that cognitive sets and settings are strong determinants of addiction, including the experience of craving and withdrawal (Zinberg 1972). Zinberg (1974) found that only one of a hundred patients receiving continuous dosages of a narcotic craved the drug after release from the hospital. Lindesmith (1968) noted such patients are seemingly protected from addiction because they do not see themselves as addicts.

The central role of cognitions and self-labeling in addiction has been demonstrated in laboratory experiments that balance the effects of expectations against the actual pharmacological effects of alcohol. Male subjects become aggressive and sexually aroused when they incorrectly believe they have been drinking liquor, but not when they actually drink alcohol in a disguised form (Marlatt and Rohsenow 1980; Wilson 1981). Similarly, alcoholic subjects lose control of their drinking when they are misinformed that they are drinking alcohol, but not in the disguised alcohol condition (Engle and Williams 1972; Marlatt et al. 1973). Subjective beliefs by clinical patients about their alcoholism are better predictors of their likelihood of relapse than are assessments of their previous drinking patterns and degree of alcohol dependence (Heather et al. 1983; Rollnick and Heather 1982). Marlatt (1982) has identified cognitive and emotional factors as the major determinants in relapse in narcotic addiction, alcoholism, smoking, overeating, and gambling.

The Nature of Addiction

Studies showing that craving and relapse have more to do with subjective factors (feelings and beliefs) than with chemical properties or with a person's history of drinking or drug dependence call for a reinterpretation of

the essential nature of addiction. How do we know a given individual is addicted? No biological indicators can give us this information. We decide the person is addicted when he acts addicted—when he pursues a drug's effects no matter what the negative consequences for his life. We cannot detect addiction in the absence of its defining behaviors. In general, we believe a person is addicted when he says that he is. No more reliable indicator exists (cf. Robins et al. 1975). Clinicians are regularly confused when patients identify themselves as addicts or evince addicted lifestyles but do not display the expected physical symptoms of addiction (Gay et al. 1973; Glaser 1974; Primm 1977).

While claiming that alcoholism is a genetically transmitted disease, the director of the National Institute on Alcohol Abuse and Alcoholism (NIAAA), a physician, noted there are not yet reliable genetic "markers" that predict the onset of alcoholism and that "the most sensitive instruments for identifying alcoholics and problem drinkers are questionnaires and inventories of psychological and behavioral variables" (Mayer 1983: 1118). He referred to one such test (the Michigan Alcohol Screening Test) that contains twenty questions regarding the person's concerns about his or her drinking behavior. Skinner et al. (1980) found that three subjective items from this larger test provide a reliable indication of the degree of a person's drinking problems. Sanchez-Craig (1983) has further shown that a single subjective assessment—in essence, asking the subject how many problems his or her drinking is causing—describes level of alcoholism better than does impairment of cognitive functioning or other biological measures. Withdrawal seizures are not related to neurological impairments in alcoholics, and those with even severe impairment may or may not undergo such seizures (Tarter et al. 1983). Taken together, these studies support the conclusions that the physiological and behavioral indicators of alcoholism do not correlate well with each other (Miller and Saucedo 1983), and that the latter correlate better than the former with clinical assessments of alcoholism (Fisher et al. 1976). This failure to find biological markers is not simply a question of currently incomplete knowledge. Signs of alcoholism such as blackout, tremors, and loss of control that are presumed to be biological have already been shown to be inferior to psychological and subjective assessments in predicting future alcoholic behavior (Heather et al. 1982; Heather et al. 1983).

When medical or public health organizations that subscribe to biological assumptions about addiction have attempted to define the term, they have relied primarily on the hallmark behaviors of addiction, such as "an overpowering desire or need (compulsion) to continue taking the drug and to obtain it by any means" (WHO Expert Committee on Mental Health 1957) or, for alcoholism, "impairment of social or occupational functioning such as violence while intoxicated, absence from work, loss of job, traffic

accidents while intoxicated, arrested for intoxicated behavior, familial arguments or difficulties with family or friends related to drinking" (American Psychiatric Association 1980). However, they then tie these behavior syndromes to other constructs, namely tolerance (the need for an increasingly high dosage of a drug) and withdrawal, that are presumed to be biological in nature. Yet tolerance and withdrawal are not themselves measured physiologically. Rather, they are delineated entirely by how addicts are observed to act and what they say about their states of being. Light and Torrance (1929) failed in their comprehensive effort to correlate narcotic withdrawal with gross metabolic, nervous, or circulatory disturbance. Instead, they were forced to turn to the addict—like the one whose complaints were most intense and who most readily responded to saline solution injections—in assessing withdrawal severity. Since that time, addict self-reports have remained the generally accepted measure of withdrawal distress.

Withdrawal is a term for which meaning has been heaped upon meaning. Withdrawal is, first, the cessation of drug administration. The term "withdrawal" is also applied to the condition of the individual who experiences this cessation. In this sense, withdrawal is nothing more than a homeostatic readjustment to the removal of any substance—or stimulation—that has had a notable impact on the body. Narcotic withdrawal (and withdrawal from drugs also thought to be addictive, such as alcohol) has been assumed to be a qualitatively distinct, more malignant order of withdrawal adjustment. Yet studies of withdrawal from narcotics and alcohol offer regular testimony, often from investigators surprised by their observations, of the variability, mildness, and often nonappearance of the syndrome (cf. Jaffe and Harris 1973; Jones and Jones 1977; Keller 1969; Light and Torrance 1929; Oki 1974; Zinberg 1972). The range of withdrawal discomfort, from the more common moderate variety to the occasional overwhelming distress, that characterizes narcotic use appears also with cocaine (van Dyke and Byck 1982; Washton 1983), cigarettes (Lear 1974; Schachter 1978), coffee (Allbutt and Dixon, quoted in Lewis 1969: 10; Goldstein et al. 1969), and sedatives and sleeping pills (Gordon 1979; Kales et al. 1974; Smith 1983). We might anticipate the investigations of laxatives, antidepressants, and other drugs—such as L-Dopa (to control Parkinson's disease)—that are prescribed to maintain physical and psychic functioning will reveal a comparable range of withdrawal responses.

In all cases, what is identified as pathological withdrawal is actually a complex self-labeling process that requires users to detect adjustments taking place in their bodies, to note this process as problematic, and to express their discomfort and translate it into a desire for more drugs. Along with the amount of a drug that a person uses (the sign of tolerance), the degree of suffering experienced when drug use ceases is—as shown in the previous section—a function of setting and social milieu, expectation and cultural

attitudes, personality and self-image, and, especially, lifestyle and available alternative opportunities. That the labeling and prediction of addictive behavior cannot occur without referring to these subjective and social-psychological factors means that addiction exists fully only at a cultural, a social, a psychological, and an experiental level. We cannot descend to a purely biological level in our scientific understanding of addiction. Any effort to do so must result in omitting crucial determinants of addiction, so that what is left cannot adequately describe the phenomenon about which we are concerned.

Physical and Psychic Dependence

The vast array of information disconfirming the conventional view of addiction as a biochemical process has led to some uneasy reevaluations of the concept. In 1964 the World Health Organization (WHO) Expert Committee on Addiction-Producing Drugs changed its name by replacing "Addiction" with "Dependence." At that time, these pharmacologists identified two kinds of drug dependence, physical and psychic. "Physical dependence is an inevitable result of the pharmacological action of some drugs with sufficient amount and time of administration. Psychic dependence, while also related to pharmacological action, is more particularly a manifestation of the individual's reaction to the effects of a specific drug and varies with the individual as well as the drug." In this formulation, psychic dependence "is the most powerful of all factors involved in chronic intoxication with psychotropic drugs . . . even in the case of most intense craving and perpetuation of compulsive abuse" (Eddy et al. 1965: 723). Cameron (1971a), another WHO pharmacologist, specified that psychic dependence is ascertained by "how far the use of drugs appears (1) to be an important life-organizing factor and (2) to take precedence over the use of other coping mechanisms" (p. 10).

Psychic dependence, as defined here, is central to the manifestations of drug abuse that were formerly called addiction. Indeed, it forms the basis of Jaffe's (1980: 536) definition of addiction, which appears in an authoritative basic pharmacology textbook:

> It is possible to describe all known patterns of drug use without employing the terms *addict* or *addiction.* In many respects this would be advantageous, for the term *addiction,* like the term *abuse,* has been used in so many ways that it can no longer be employed without further qualification or elaboration. . . . In this chapter, the term *addiction* will be used to mean *a behavioral pattern of drug use, characterized by overwhelming involvement with the use of a drug (compulsive use), the securing of its supply, and a high tendency to relapse after withdrawal.* Addiction is thus viewed as an extreme on a continuum of involvement with drug use . . .

> [based on] the degree to which drug use pervades the total life activity of the user. . . . [*T*]*he term* addiction *cannot be used interchangeably with* physical dependence. [italics in original]

While Jaffe's terminology improves upon previous pharmacological usage by recognizing that addiction is a behavioral pattern, it perpetuates other misconceptions. Jaffe describes addiction as a pattern of drug use even though he defines it in behavioral terms—that is, craving and relapse—that are not limited to drug use. He devalues addiction as a construct because of its inexactness, in contrast with physical dependence, which he incorrectly sees as a well-delineated physiological mechanism. Echoing the WHO Expert Committee, he defines physical dependence as "an altered physiological state produced by the repeated administration of a drug which necessitates the continued administration of the drug to prevent the appearance of . . . withdrawal" (p. 536).

The WHO committee's efforts to redefine addiction were impelled by two forces. One was the desire to highlight the harmful use of substances popularly employed by young people in the 1960s and thereafter that were not generally regarded as addictive—including marijuana, amphetamines, and hallucinogenic drugs. These drugs could now be labeled as dangerous because they were reputed to cause psychic dependence. Charts like one titled "A Guide to the Jungle of Drugs," compiled by a WHO pharmacologist (Cameron 1971b), classified LSD, peyote, marijuana, psilocybin, alcohol, cocaine, amphetamines, and narcotics (that is, every drug included in the chart) as causing psychic dependence (see figure 1–1). What is the value of a pharmacological concept that applies indiscriminately to the entire range of pharmacological agents, so long as they are used in socially disapproved ways? Clearly, the WHO committee wished to discourage certain types of drug use and dressed up this aim in scientific terminology. Wouldn't the construct describe as well the habitual use of nicotine, caffeine, tranquilizers, and sleeping pills? Indeed, the discovery of this simple truism about socially accepted drugs has been an emerging theme of pharmacological thought in the 1970s and 1980s. Furthermore, the concept of psychic dependence cannot distinguish compulsive drug involvements—those that become "life organizing" and "take precedence over . . . other coping mechanisms"—from compulsive overeating, gambling, and television viewing.

The WHO committee, while perpetuating prejudices about drugs, claimed to be resolving the confusion brought on by the data showing that addiction was not the biochemically invariant process that it had been thought to be. Thus, the committee labeled the psychic-dependence-producing properties of drugs as being the major determinant of craving and of compulsive abuse. In addition, they maintained, some drugs cause physical dependence. In "A Guide to the Jungle of Drugs" and the philosophy it rep-

A GUIDE TO THE JUNGLE OF DRUGS

	Drug	Medical use	Dependence		Tolerance
			Physical	Psychic	
1	Hallucinogenic cactus (mescalin, peyote)	None	No	Yes	Yes
2	Hallucinogenic mushrooms (psilocybin)	None	No	Yes	Yes
3	Cocaine (from coca bush)	Anaesthesia	No	Yes	No
	Amphetamines* (synthetic, not derived from coca)	Treatment of narcolepsy and behavioural disorders	No	Yes	Yes
4	Alcohol (in many forms)	Antisepsis	Yes	Yes	Yes
5	Cannabis (marihuana, hashish)	None in modern medicine	Little if any	Yes	Little if any
6	Narcotics (opium, heroin, morphine, codeine)	Relief of pain and cough	Yes	Yes	Yes
7	LSD (synthetic, derived from fungus on grain)	Essentially none	No	Yes	Yes
8	Hallucinogenic morning glory seeds	None	No	Yes	Uncertain

* Taken intravenously, cocaine and amphetamines have quite similar effects.

Source: Cameron 1971b. With acknowledgments to *World Health.*

Figure 1–1. A Guide to the Jungle of Drugs

resented, two drugs were designated as creating physical dependence. These drugs were narcotics and alcohol. This effort to improve the accuracy of drug classifications simply transposed erroneous propositions previously associated with addiction to the new idea of physical dependence. Narcotics and alcohol do not produce qualitatively greater tolerance or withdrawal—whether these are imputed to physical dependence or addiction—than do other powerful drugs and stimulants of all kinds. As Kalant (1982) makes clear, physical dependence and tolerance "are two manifestations of the same phenomenon, a biologically adaptive phenomenon which occurs in all living organisms and many types of stimuli, not just drug stimuli" (p. 12).

What the WHO pharmacologists, Jaffe, and others are clinging to by retaining the category of physical dependence is the idea that there is a purely physiological process associated with specific drugs that will describe the behavior that results from their use. It is as though they were saying: "Yes, we understand that what has been referred to as addiction is a complex syndrome into which more enters than just the effects of a given drug. What we want to isolate, however, is the addiction-like state that stems from these drug effects if we could somehow remove extraneous psychological and social considerations." This is impossible because what are being identified as pharmacological characteristics exist only in the drug user's sensations and interactions with his environment. Dependence is, after all, a characteristic of people and not of drugs.

The Persistence of Mistaken Categories

While there has been some movement in addiction theorizing toward more realistic explanations of drug-related behavior in terms of people's life circumstances and nonbiological needs, old patterns of thought persist, even where they don't agree with the data or offer helpful ways of conceptualizing drug abuse problems. This is nowhere more apparent than in the writing of investigators whose work has effectively undermined prevailing drug categorizations and yet who rely on categories and terminology that their own iconoclastic findings have discredited.

Zinberg and his colleagues (Apsler 1978; Zinberg et al. 1978) have been among the most discerning critics of the WHO committee's definitions of drug dependence, pointing out that "these definitions employ terms that are virtually indefinable and heavily value-laden" (Zinberg et al. 1978: 20). In their understandable desire to avoid the ambiguities of moral categories of behavior, these investigators seek to restrict the term "addiction" to the most limited physiological phenomena. Thus they claim that "physical dependence is a straightforward measure of addiction" (p. 20). However, this retrenchment is inimical to their purpose of satisfactorily conceptualizing

and operationalizing addictive behavior. It is also irreconcilable with their own observation that the effort to separate psychological habituation and physical dependence is futile, as well as with their forceful objections to the idea that psychic dependence is "less inevitable and more susceptible to the elements of set and setting" than is physical dependence (p. 21). At the same time that they complain that "The capacity of different individuals to deal with different amounts of substances without development of tolerance is sufficiently obvious . . . [that] one must question how the complexity of this phenomenon could have been missed" (p. 15), they trumpet "the inevitable physical dependence which occurs following the continued and heavy use of substances such as the opiates, barbiturates, or alcohol, that contain certain pharmacological properties" (p. 14). They then contradict this principle by citing the case, described earlier by Zinberg and Jacobson (1976), of the doctor who injected himself with morphine four times a day for over a decade but who never underwent withdrawal while abstaining on weekends and vacations.

Zinberg et al. (1978) find that "the behavior resulting from the wish for a desired object, whether chemical or human," is not the result of "differentiation between a physiological or psychological attachment. . . . Nor does the presence of physical symptoms per se serve to separate these two types of dependence" (p. 21). Yet they themselves maintain exactly this distinction in terminology. While noting that people may be just as wedded to amphetamines as to heroin, they claim that the former are not "psychologically addicting." (Probably the authors meant to say that amphetamines are not "physiologically addicting." They employ "psychological addiction" elsewhere in this article to describe nondrug or nonnarcotic involvements and "physiological addiction" to describe heavy heroin use characterized by withdrawal. Their use of both phrases, of course, adds to the confusion of terms.) Zinberg et al. claim without supporting citations that "if naloxone, a narcotic antagonist, is administered to someone who is physically dependent on a narcotic, he will immediately develop withdrawal symptoms" (p. 20). It is puzzling to compare this declaration with their statement that it "is now evident many of the symptoms of withdrawal are strongly influenced by expectations and culture" (p. 21). In fact, many people who identify themselves in treatment as narcotic addicts do not manifest withdrawal even when treated by naloxone challenge (Gay et al. 1973; Glaser 1974; O'Brien 1975; Primm 1977).

The Zinberg et al. formulation leaves unexplained the hospital patients Zinberg (1974) studied who, having received greater than street level dosage of narcotics for ten days or more, almost never reported craving the drug. If these people are physically dependent, as Zinberg et al. (1978) seem to suggest they would be, it amounts to saying that people can depend on what they can't detect and don't care about. Surely this is the reductio ad absurd-

um of the concept of physical dependence. That amphetamines and cocaine are labeled as not physical-dependence inducing or addictive (see discussion above), despite the fact that users can be wedded to them in ways that are indistinguishable from addiction, invalidates these distinctions among drugs from the opposite direction. Apparently, those pharmacological effects of a given drug that *are* unique and invariant are irrelevant to human functioning. Here scientific terminology approaches the mystical by identifying distinctions that are unmeasurable and unrepresented in thought, feeling, and action.

Finally, Zinberg et al.'s illustrations of the "difficulty of separating physical dependence from psychic dependence and of differentiating both from overpowering desire" (p. 21) go to show the futility of using different terms to describe drug-related and nondrug-related variants of the same process. A primitive logic dictates that a chemical introduced into the body should be conceived to exert its effects biochemically. However, any other experience a person has will also possess biochemical concomitants (Leventhal 1980). Zinberg et al. emphasize that craving and withdrawal associated with intimate relationships are substantial and unmistakable. In detecting withdrawal symptoms on the order of those reported for barbiturates and alcohol among compulsive gamblers, Wray and Dickerson (1981) noted that "any repetitive, stereotyped behavior that is associated with repeated experiences of physiological arousal or change, *whether induced by a psychoactive agent or not,* may be difficult for the individual to choose to discontinue and should he so choose, then it may well be associated with disturbances of mood and behavior" (p. 405, italics in original). Why do these states and activities not have the same capacity to produce physical dependence?

The Science of Addictive Experiences

What has held science back from acknowledging commonalities in addiction and what now impedes our ability to analyze these is a habit of thought that separates the action of the mind and the body. Furthermore, it is for concrete physical entities and processes that the label of science is usually reserved (Peele 1983e). The mind–body duality (which long antedates current debates about drugs and addiction) has hidden the fact that addiction has always been defined phenomenologically in terms of the experiences of the sentient human being and observations of the person's feelings and behavior. Addiction may occur with any potent experience. In addition, the number and variability of the factors that influence addiction cause it to occur along a continuum. The delineation of a particular involvement as addictive for a particular person thus entails a degree of arbi-

trariness. Yet this designation is a useful one. It is far superior to the relabeling of addictive phenomena in some roundabout way.

Addiction, at its extreme, is an overwhelming pathological involvement. The object of addiction is the addicted person's experience of the combined physical, emotional, and environmental elements that make up the involvement for that person. Addiction is often characterized by a traumatic withdrawal reaction to the deprivation of this state or experience. Tolerance—or the increasingly high level of need for the experience—and craving are measured by how willing the person is to sacrifice other rewards or sources of well-being in life to the pursuit of the involvement. The key to addiction, seen in this light, is its persistence in the face of harmful consequences for the individual. This book embraces rather than evades the complicated and multifactorial nature of addiction. Only by accepting this complexity is it possible to put together a meaningful picture of addiction, to say something useful about drug use as well as about other compulsions, and to comprehend the ways in which people hurt themselves through their own behavior as well as grow beyond self-destructive involvements.

2
The American Image of Alcohol: Does Liquor Have the Power to Corrupt and Control?

Alcohol is the substance, along with heroin, with which addiction is most strongly associated. Yet addiction has been studied separately for the two substances because of their disparate cultural histories. The concepts of addiction for each do have commonalities—perhaps more now than at any time previously in this century. However, cultural perceptions of the drugs and of their abuse still differ widely. This book approaches both substances as being addictive in the same way, although the process of addiction in each case is influenced by distinct cultural attitudes toward its use.

It seems strange to us today that in the nineteenth century, narcotics use was legal and accepted, while strong movements arose to ban all consumption of alcohol. In the early nineteenth century, problem drinking was rampant in the United States, while opium and morphine addiction presented a negligible problem. Even as heroin came to be regarded as the most sinister drug of abuse in the United States in the 1910s and 1920s and public officials claimed narcotics addicts numbered in the millions, there were probably no more than 100,000 such addicts in the United States (Clausen 1961; Courtwright 1982). Concepts of drug use as a disease first appeared in the eighteenth century in the United States and concerned alcoholism (Levine 1978). Early versions of the disease theory of alcoholism were predicated solely on the idea of exposure to the drug. That is, alcoholism appeared in the individual who drank habitually and chronically became intoxicated. This kind of exposure model eventually was applied to narcotics addiction; today heroin is viewed as being inherently addicting—independent of the physical and psychological make-up of the person using the drug—both popularly and by addiction theorists (see chapter 3).

Conceptions of alcoholism meanwhile took a different direction following the repeal of Prohibition in 1933. The failure of national temperance led the alcoholism movement instead to propose that alcoholics were a special group of people with an inbred susceptibility to alcohol's effects (Beauchamp 1980). The differences in the views of narcotic and alcohol addiction

are inextricably entwined with the social realities of their use. Controlled users of heroin form a distinct majority of those taking the drug (Lukoff and Brook 1974; Robins et al. 1975; Zinberg and Lewis 1964)—Trebach (1982) reported 500,000 regular users or addicts compared to 3.5 million occasional users. Yet such users, by definition, keep their illegal drug use hidden and are not part of public consciousness. It is obvious, on the other hand, that most people drink liquor—many regularly—without becoming addicted. What the prevailing disease notions of alcoholism and heroin addiction have in common is their physiological determinism and the belief in a stereotypical addiction syndrome that rules out controlled or variable use by the addict.

That prejudice and misinformation have formed the basis for much of what we think about heroin addiction can partially be explained by the minimal involvement most people have with the drug. Alcohol, on the other hand, is everywhere present in our society and is widely consumed. The emotional component of attitudes toward alcohol is thus more deeply engrained in people's experience and intrudes more into treatment policies. The American approach to drinking has indeed been deeply contentious and problematic and has continued to distort our understanding of alcoholism (Room 1983). The cultural history of American drinking practices in the United States provides an immediate example of the ways in which larger social attitudes influence not only the views of addiction to a drug but a drug's very addictive potential.

The Disease of Alcoholism

Approximately 80 percent of the Americans responding to a Gallup poll conducted in August 1982 said that they thought alcoholism was a disease. This was the highest figure recorded since the question was first asked by Gallup in 1955. A collation of public surveys indicated that about one-fifth of the general population agreed that alcoholism was an illness in the 1946–1951 period, that about three-fifths thought so in 1955–1960, and that by the early 1960s the percentage agreeing with this view had risen to sixty-five percent (Room 1983). As Room pointed out, those who endorse this position simultaneously often hold many nondisease ideas, such as that the alcoholic is morally deficient. Yet the almost universal medical, public, and treatment community acceptance of the outlines of a disease theory and of the appropriateness of medical treatment for alcoholism, forged largely over the last thirty to forty years, represents a transition in cultural attitudes of formidable dimensions.

As the continued moralism in many people's conceptions of the disease of alcoholism indicates, the disease theory is broad and inclusive. Crit-

ics of the disease theory are often required to specify the theory's elements in order to dispute them (Pattison et al. 1977). The key element that emerges in the disease theory of alcoholism is the alcoholic's *loss of control,* or the inability to drink moderately that leads some regularly to drink until they become intoxicated. Only the true—or "gamma"—alcoholic manifests this inability, unlike some others who get drunk as a matter of "choice" (Alcoholics Anonymous 1939; Jellinek 1952; Mann 1970). At the same time, alcoholism is seen to be a progressive disease, meaning that it inexorably proceeds from its early stages to its ultimate true form. A contradiction appears here: How is it possible to know whether an individual who displays drinking problems is a true alcoholic at an early stage of the disease or whether the person simply has a mild or passing drinking problem?

The actual empirical basis for the current disease model was Jellinek's (1946) analysis of ninety-eight questionnaires from a mailing sent to about 1,600 Alcoholics Anonymous members. Certain uniformities in the experiences of this highly self-selected group led Jellinek (1952, 1960) to formulate a typology of alcoholism. However, practically every independent effort to test these categories has found that alcoholism does not necessarily follow any particular path in its development and is not a unitary entity (cf. Miller 1983b; Pattison et al. 1977; Room 1983). Of even greater import are studies showing that no internal mechanism (nor the failure of any such mechanism) accounts for the alcoholic's loss of control. Instead, laboratory studies in which priming dosages of liquor are given to alcoholics or in which alcoholics are simply observed while drinking find that alcoholics typically *do* regulate their drinking (Mello and Mendelson 1971; Nathan and O'Brien 1971; Heather and Robertson 1981: 122). Finally, contrary to the idea of an inevitable progression, alcoholics with every degree of severity of drinking problem have been found to recover without treatment and to return to nonproblematic drinking (Heather and Robertson 1981; Knupfer 1972; Polich et al. 1981).

The nonempirical basis of the disease concept of alcoholism is actually most apparent in a recent, widely heralded defense of the disease approach to alcoholism. In his study of both treated and untreated alcoholics, Vaillant (1983) presented data showing that alcoholism occurs along a continuum and includes a range of drinking disorders, that alcohol problems regularly reverse themselves without medical intervention or the support of Alcoholics Anonymous (AA), that a genetic basis for alcoholism is doubtful, and that alcoholics generally drink again without endangering their sobriety. As a result of such findings, Vaillant concluded that "in our attempts to *understand* and to *study* alcoholism, it behooves us to employ the models of the social scientist and of the learning theorist. But in order to *treat* alcoholics effectively we need to invoke the model of the medical

practitioner" (p. 20). Compare this, however, with Vaillant's evaluation of his own success in treating alcoholics in a medical setting and requiring that they attend AA: "our results were no better than the natural history of the disorder" (p. 285).

Historical, Social, Ethnic, and Economic Factors in Alcoholism in the United States

The cultural variations in attitudes toward a substance—and particularly its addictiveness (see chapter 1)—are especially relevant to the history and variety of American drinking patterns. Both because of the ethnic diversity in the United States and because of changes in this ethnic balance and in other social factors, attitudes toward alcohol have undergone considerable historical shifts and have been the object of major social disagreements and conflict (Lender and Martin 1982). In the ethnically homogeneous American colonies, where the community and family were the major forces in regulating drinking, drinking problems were minimal. Although per capita consumption was several times its contemporary levels in the United States, excessive drinking was not regarded as a social problem, alcoholism rates were lower, and heavy drinkers did not report experiencing a compulsion to drink (Zinberg and Fraser 1979; Levine 1978).

In this cultural setting, alcohol was seen as a benign, even positive force (Lender and Martin 1982). The current idea of alcoholism did not exist and the person who became drunk was thought of as having chosen this state (Levine 1978). The idea of drunkenness as an uncontrollable disease was introduced late in the colonial period by the physician Benjamin Rush. It grew rapidly between 1790 and 1830 when expanding frontiers and new waves of immigration broke down the traditional social regulation of drinking. Instead of taking place in a family-oriented tavern, most drinking was now done in saloons where the only women likely to be present were prostitutes. Alcohol took on a new image—drinking became a male prerogative that symbolized assertive independence and high spiritedness. Simultaneously liquor began to be seen by many as "demon rum."

Alcoholism rates rose precipitously during this period, and the temperance movement was born and flourished in response. Many former drunkards took the pledge of abstinence, forming self-help groups such as the Washingtonians to assist their resolve. The concept of alcoholism and the behavior of alcoholics reinforced each other, with the new kind of inebriate swearing that it was only by dint of total abstinence that he could forestall drunkenness. Meanwhile, the entire nation became polarized around the issue of temperance. Wet and dry forces began a century-long battle that ended when national Prohibition went into effect in 1920 (at a point, para-

doxically, when drinking patterns had moderated substantially compared to the first half of the nineteenth century). The dry and wet sides of the issue divided up variously (cf. Gusfield 1963) according to region (the South and the Midwest versus the East and the West), religion (Protestant versus Catholic), sophistication (the less-well educated versus the better educated), and ethnicity (older versus newer Americans).

When Prohibition was repealed in 1933, the goal of national temperance was permanently laid to rest. In its place grew the modern disease theory of alcoholism, as defined and defended by the Alcoholics Anonymous self-help fellowship. Both the disease theory and AA achieved prominence in the late 1930s and early 1940s with the assistance of researchers at the Yale University Center of Alcohol Studies (most notably Jellinek and Keller), and through the energetic efforts of several recovered alcoholics who formed the progenitor of the National Council on Alcoholism (NCA) and its many state and local chapters (Beauchamp 1980; Room 1983; Wiener 1981). Whereas the nineteenth-century version of the disease theory focused on the substance itself, claiming that the disease befell anyone who drank regularly and who frequently became intoxicated, the modern version of the theory emphasized that only a small group of habitual inebriates had the disease. This group of people was characterized by a peculiar sensitivity or allergy to alcohol that caused them to crave it without bounds—that is, to lose control of their drinking—once they began to drink (cf. Alcoholics Anonymous 1939: 55).

Nonetheless, the AA vision of alcoholism had important commonalities with the temperance vision of demon rum. The chief of these was the utter necessity of abstinence (Roizen 1978). This point of view was forwarded by AA adherents with a religious fervor strongly reminiscent of the temperance movement. AA borrowed much in style from the nineteenth-century temperance brotherhoods like the Washingtonians. As they did in the earlier organization, reformed drinkers in AA meet in a highly charged atmosphere to relate their struggles with alcohol and to support each other's continued abstinence (as well as to convince others to join them). Both types of groups descend from the Protestant revival meeting, where the sinner seeks salvation through personal testimony, public contrition, and submission to a higher power (Trice and Roman 1970). The issue of abstinence for the alcoholic has thus always been a deeply emotional one in the United States, not one that has rested on a body of evidence.

AA-based groups and recovered alcoholics have been involved in formulating treatment policy in the United States in a way unmatched by any other Western nation (Miller 1983b). However, the current dominance of the disease model rests on more than the outlook of such groups and individuals. It has been supported by the general trend toward the medicalization of emotional and moral problems that has occurred in Western socie-

ties (Foucault 1973; Levine 1978). When it was formally endorsed by the American Medical Association in 1956, the disease model was given biomedical legitimacy. At the same time, the alliance between grass-roots self-help movements and the medical profession is often uneasy. A typical treatment apparatus will be under nominal medical supervision, while actual contact and counseling with clients is carried out by paraprofessionals who are themselves recovered alcoholics.

The identification and treatment of alcohol abusers who are not gamma alcoholics has always presented a problem for the disease model. In practice, the same abstinence orientation and overall approach to alcoholism have been utilized for all those who manifest drinking problems (cf. Hansen and Emrick 1983). The group of people for whom the disease approach has been applied seems consistently to have expanded as acceptance of the disease theory has grown. Room (1980) estimated that there was a twentyfold increase in the number of alcoholics in treatment between 1942 and 1976. The rate of growth has accelerated dramatically in the last fifteen years, as changes in the financing of treatment have placed a premium on the aggressive marketing of alcohol services (Weisner 1983; Weisner and Room 1984).

The result has been an explosion in the scope of alcohol services and those deemed to need it. These developments have included: (1) the proliferation of private treatment facilities, (2) the definition of new populations as requiring special attention, such as the young, women, minorities, (3) the creation of compulsory treatment referrals through such agencies as employee-assistance programs and the traffic court system, (4) the designation of certain social problems or crimes as being inescapably linked to alcohol abuse—including wife battering and child abuse and other crimes against people and property, (5) the identification of families of alcoholics as a whole new group with problems equivalent to the alcoholic's, and (6) the encouragement of confrontational interventions to reach those who do not recognize their own drinking problems. A theme for the alcoholism movement in the United States since the 1940s has been the public's lack of awareness of the nature and the extent of the alcohol problem. The ascendance of the disease theory has changed our entire culture's concept of the nature of its problems with alcohol. (The implications of these developments are treated in chapter 6.)

The Social Science Challenge to the Disease Theory

Psychological and other social scientific studies refuting the disease theory are of four types: (1) laboratory studies showing that alcoholics' patterns of drinking do not conform to the loss-of-control model (Marlatt et al. 1973;

Merry 1966; Paredes et al. 1973), (2) clinical research demonstrating the efficacy of techniques aimed at moderating problem drinking and alcoholism (Miller and Hester 1980; Sobell and Sobell 1973, 1976), (3) longitudinal studies both of the natural course of alcoholism and of outcomes for treated populations (Cahalan and Room 1974; Gerard and Saenger 1966; Polich et al. 1981; Vaillant 1983), (4) cross-ethnic and cultural studies demonstrating that social and belief systems are a principal component in alcoholism (Blum and Blum 1969; MacAndrew and Edgerton 1969; McClelland et al. 1972).

The last category of study has special relevance in America where so many divergent drinking traditions are present. Greeley et al. (1980) continued a tradition of finding distinct "ethnic drinking subcultures" in the United States with Irish, Slavic, and Protestant populations having a high incidence of drinking problems among white ethnic groups, while Jews and Italians have a low incidence. Perhaps even more noteworthy is the dichotomy among Oriental groups' drinking habits in the United States: the widespread chronic disabling alcoholism of Native Americans and Eskimos and the deeply engrained moderate drinking of Chinese and Japanese Americans (Stewart 1964). These data seem to indicate how readily culturally inculcated patterns of drinking overcome genetic differences in the rate of metabolizing alcohol (Mendelson and Mello 1979a). (See chapter 3.) The mechanisms by which moderate drinking is socialized in the young and maintained by the social group have been studied for Italians (Lolli et al. 1958), Jews (Glassner and Berg 1980), Chinese (Barnett 1955), and Greeks (Blum and Blum 1969). In these groups, children are gradually introduced to drinking in the family setting, where alcohol is not made to seem a rite of passage into adulthood or associated with masculinity and power. Adult drinking is also controlled by group attitudes about both the proper amount of drinking and the person's behavior when drinking. Strong disapproval is expressed when an individual violates these standards and acts in an antisocial manner. Wilkinson (1970) reported very similar dimensions to characterize the different ways alcoholics and nonproblem drinkers were taught to drink at home, regardless of their cultural heritage.

Group differences in alcoholism rates run counter to the emphasis of disease theorists on inbred and unalterable alcoholic mechanisms. There seems little reason why groups should differ in terms of biological susceptibility. Thus the movement in the field of alcoholism has been toward revealing greater-than-suspected numbers of alcoholics among such groups as women and Jews on the assumption that their apparently lower alcoholism rates are due simply to underreporting. Yet even studies conducted to substantiate hidden numbers of Jewish and women alcoholics continue to turn up distinctly lower rates for them than for the society at large (Efron et al. 1974; Glassner and Berg 1980). Moreover, the studies of general or community populations (cf. Cahalan and Room 1974) have revealed that drink-

ing problems vary (increase) with such traditional demographic traits as age (younger), socioeconomic status (lower), ethnicity and race (black and hispanic). Not only drinking problems, but actual diagnoses of alcohol dependence or alcoholism are strongly associated with such demographic factors. Vaillant (1983) found his working-class, core-city sample had three times the percentage of alcoholics that his college sample had. Similarly, Irish-Americans in Vaillant's study were seven times as likely to be alcohol dependent as were those from Mediterranean backgrounds.

Cahalan and Room (1974) found the most important factor in predicting drinking problems for both a national and a community sample was an individual's immediate social context: how much his companions drank and how much of his social life revolved around drinking. A contextual framework for drinking is supported by a number of studies that find that people imitate the type of drinking going on around them (Caudill and Marlatt 1975; Jessor and Jessor 1975; Harford 1979). These findings strongly suggest the value (in both prevention and treatment) of creating moderate-drinking atmospheres for both young people and adults (Kraft 1982; Wilkinson 1970; Zinberg and Fraser 1979). The elements in these settings generally reproduce the ones found in moderate-drinking ethnic groups: serving wine and beer rather than distilled spirits, drinking where food is served and where those of all ages and both sexes participate, explicitly presenting values for responsible drinking. This approach conflicts with the growing trend in the alcoholism movement to identify young people with drinking problems as being alcohol dependent—an allegedly permanent condition like alcoholism—or to label those from families in which there is alcohol abuse as having a high risk for alcoholism. In both these cases, the proposed remedy is enrollment in abstinence-oriented groups to prevent the likely or inevitable development of alcoholism (see chapter 6).

The concept of problem drinking that Cahalan and Room (1974) employed is fundamentally different from the disease idea of alcoholism because it sees alcohol abuse as a function of time and situation rather than as a clinical problem; that is, it focuses on the ground rather than the figure in problem drinking. This viewpoint is supported by the observation that problem drinking is an extremely changeable and complicated behavior (Clark and Cahalan 1976; Room 1977). Various measures of alcohol abuse show little connection to each other (Clark 1976; Miller and Saucedo 1983) and seem instead to be situation-specific. Not only do young people often grow out of their drinking problems, but even older drinkers with long histories of abuse frequently abstain or drink without problems. Indeed, laboratory studies of diagnosed alcoholics support this view of drinking as a highly situation-specific behavior (Mello and Mendelson 1972).

This social-setting or sociological perspective is most at odds with the disease model when it regards alcoholism itself as a social construct (Beau-

champ 1980; Gusfield 1981; Room 1983; Shaw 1979). What is defined as alcoholism at any time or place is a social convention at the same time that social policies have a great impact on the amount of alcohol abuse in a society. Keller, (1981, quoted in Room 1983: 53) directed a particularly pointed attack on this point of view:

> [If] it is a social problem, . . . the social scientists are the ones to take charge of it! . . . They freely use words they have invented—like medicalization, clinicization, with obvious implications that these are bad—socially undesirable—practices. . . . It is no accident but a logical coincidence that the proponents of legal measures to combat alcohol problems are the same people who decry, deny and denigrate the disease concept of alcoholism. . . . The solution of the problem should not be left to the medicalists—biologists. The solution should be put into the hands of us all-knowing social scientists, the expert formulators of social policy.

Although the social constructivist point of view is totally incompatible with disease notions, the full fury of the disease movement has been reserved for findings that alcoholics can control their drinking. It is here that disease advocates and social scientific researchers and clinicians clash over issues of treatment. Prior to 1960, controlled drinking was often regarded matter of factly as one potential outcome of therapy for alcoholism in the United States (Miller 1983a; see Wallerstein et al. 1957). In some European countries, such as Norway, this attitude still holds, and clinicians do not even consider the question of controlled drinking versus abstinence to be a primary one in treatment, but focus simply on the reduction of an individual's drinking problems (Duckert, cited in "The Behaviorists," 1984). This outlook is so foreign to current policies in the United States that we must comprehend contemporary attitudes toward controlled-drinking treatment as having undergone a culturewide shift induced by disease conceptions.

The first research to be attacked for uncovering a return to social drinking by alcoholics was by Davies (1962) in England. Davies was a clinician who found safely moderated drinking among seven of a group of ninety-three alcoholics who had been followed up for about ten years following treatment. The challenge to these findings appeared principally in the pages of the American *Quarterly Journal of Studies on Alcohol.* That disease adherents felt the capability and necessity of attacking this research was due to the consolidation of their power over the treatment of alcoholism at this time. Numerous confirmations of the possibility of a return to controlled drinking by a range of alcoholics appeared in the years following the Davies study. These are documented and summarized in detail in Heather and Robertson's (1981) thorough review, *Controlled Drinking* (these authors

also point out studies prior to Davies's that uncovered controlled drinking outcomes). It thus requires some explanation to account for the uproar raised by the Rand Reports, the first of which appeared in 1976 (Armor et al. 1978).

The Rand investigators were under contract to the National Institute on Alcohol Abuse and Alcoholism (NIAAA) to evaluate the results of NIAAA treatment programs. They did so for 2,339 alcoholics at six months and for 597 at eighteen months. At the eighteenth-month point, 24 percent of the treated alcoholics were abstaining while 22 percent were drinking normally. Among those the investigators identified as definitely alcoholic, the figures were 25 percent abstaining and 16 percent drinking normally. The report was immediately assailed, principally by the National Council on Alcoholism, which made an effort to have the report delayed and its results reinterpreted (see Roizen 1978). Amidst many wild and unfounded allegations about the report, there were genuine methodological criticisms raised (although none that would obviate the thrust of the results). In response to these, the investigators conducted a follow-up study (Polich et al. 1981) in which they extended the period over which treated patients were observed to four years, checked self-reports of drinking with breathalyzer tests, carefully divided the subjects into groups based on how severely dependent on alcohol they were at admission, and toughened their definitions of controlled drinking—which was called nonproblem drinking. Nonproblem drinking was defined as the absence of any alcohol dependence symptoms (e.g., tremors, blackout, morning drinking) or negative consequences from drinking (e.g., arrest, missing work). The second of the Rand Reports found that nearly 40 percent of the subjects who were free from drinking problems were drinking, including a distinct portion of those most severely alcoholic initially.

Opposition to the second Rand Report continued to be both substantial and emotional. Despite the success of its authors in affirming and solidifying their results (see Beauchamp et al. 1980), most practitioners in the field and disease researchers have felt safe in simply ignoring the Rand data (see Vaillant 1983). The directors of the NIAAA at the time of both of the reports reiterated that abstinence remained the "appropriate goal in the treatment of alcoholism" (see Armor et al. 1978: 230; "Drinking Problem Dispute" 1980). Thus the ultimate significance of the reports rests in the cultural response to them rather than their actual findings. Ernest Noble, the director of the NIAAA, solicited reviews from impartial scientific sources when the first Rand Report was issued. While the comments were inherently reasonable, they appear ironic in light of the current atmosphere toward alcoholism in America. From Gerald L. Klerman, Professor of Psychiatry, Harvard Medical School (in Armor et al. 1978: 223):

> This is a very important document. I think the conclusions are highly justified. I understand you are under great political pressure. . . . I would strongly urge you and the NIAAA to stand firm wherever possible.

From Samuel B. Guze, Head of the Department of Psychiatry, Washington University School of Medicine (in Armor et al. 1978: 221):

> What the data do demonstrate is that remission is possible for many alcoholics and that many of these are able to drink normally for extended periods. These points deserve emphasis, because they offer encouragement to patients, to their families, and to relevant professionals.

Controlled-Drinking Therapy for Alcoholism

The reaction to the Rand Reports indicated that rejection of the idea of controlled drinking for alcoholics was beyond questions of evidence. The Rand investigators, in reporting these outcomes, were attempting to describe how clients at NIAAA treatment centers behaved following treatment. They were not advocates or practitioners of controlled-drinking therapy nor were their subjects encouraged to become moderate drinkers at the abstinence-oriented NIAAA centers where they were treated. The Rand Reports were in fact a part of a different tradition in alcoholism research, one that has repeatedly emphasized how variable and responsive to life and situational cues drinking of any kind is (Polich et al. 1981: 214):

> We found a great deal of change in individual status, with some persons continuing to improve, some persons deteriorating, and most moving back and forth between relatively improved and unimproved statuses.

Another body of work has applied behavioral modification techniques to the task of teaching alcoholics to drink moderately. Success for this approach was reported in the early 1970s by several research teams (Lovibund and Caddy 1970; Schaefer 1972; Vogler et al. 1975). In 1982, a study published in the prestigious journal *Science* by Pendery et al. attacked one of these seminal studies, by Sobell and Sobell (1973, 1976), which had found that alcoholics who received behavior therapy aimed at moderating drinking patterns fared better than did a comparable group who underwent standard hospital abstinence treatment. In their reinvestigation of the controlled-drinking subjects from the original study, Pendery et al. reported that most had difficulty moderating their drinking years later and that nearly all had reported instances of relapse very soon after treatment. The

Science study was highly publicized, usually accompanied by accusations by the investigators that the Sobells had falsified their results. Media depictions of the case generally assumed that abstinence had been shown to be the only possible alternative for alcoholics (see Peele 1984c).

The Pendery et al. investigation was by any standards an unusual one. It focused solely on the experimental, controlled-drinking group without reporting any follow-up on the comparison, abstinence group. The data were primarily recollections by subjects, in some cases nine years after the events, and descriptions of individual episodes of relapse. The only summary data in the paper were in the form of the amount of hospitalization controlled-drinking subjects underwent after treatment. The Addiction Research Foundation of Toronto, which at the time of the *Science* article employed the Sobells, convened an investigation of the controversy by an independent panel of distinguished academics not previously involved in alcoholism policy. The panel's report (Dickens et al. 1982) found that Pendery et al. had presented no new data, since the Sobells' published papers had already noted more hospitalizations for the experimental subjects than were reported in the *Science* article. Moreover, the committee chastized the Pendery group for failing to reexamine the subjects treated with abstinence techniques and to take into account the body of evidence about controlled drinking (Peele 1983f).

It is impossible to understand this controversy without considering, as all the media failed to do, the history of the debate about alcoholism in the United States. For example, the senior author of the *Science* article was a prominent critic of the Rand Reports and a spokesperson for the National Council on Alcoholism in its effort to suppress the first report (Roizen 1978: 266). That the Pendery et al. article does not present a balanced perspective on alcoholism research has gone unrecognized by the public; indeed, the article has been invested with importance beyond its dubious value precisely because it is one of the few answers to an avalanche of studies contradicting disease notions. As such, however, it fits in with dominant views about alcoholism that trace back to nineteenth-century America and that are buttressed by effective control of public information about alcoholism by medical, AA, and other disease proponents.

One consequence of this near-unanimity in the United States has been the almost complete extinction of controlled drinking as a treatment goal. The director of the Rutgers Center of Alcohol Studies, who has himself endorsed controlled-drinking treatment, announced: "There is no alcoholism center in the United States using the technique as official policy" ("Debate Rages . . ." 1982). This certainly contrasts with other countries, such as Britain, where a survey of treatment centers revealed that 93 percent consider controlled drinking an appropriate goal and 76 percent offer it as one alternative (Robertson and Heather 1982). What may be more impor-

tant than the erosion in controlled-drinking therapy in the United States is that the assault on the idea has influenced approaches to and theories of alcoholism even among those who explicitly oppose the disease viewpoint.

Clinical Approaches to Controlled-Drinking Therapy

The Pendery et al. (1982) attack on one controlled-drinking study for alcoholics paradoxically occurred at a time of retrenchment for those practicing the approach. In nearly all cases, behavior therapists have indicated that the goal of controlled drinking should be employed with problem drinkers rather than alcoholics or alcohol-dependent clients (Marlatt 1983). This new consensus began to emerge in the mid-1970s after the publication of the first Rand Report. Thus, controlled-drinking studies and books authored before that time are less guarded or more optimistic about the prospects for treating alcoholics (Miller and Muñoz 1976; Sobell and Sobell 1976; Steiner 1971; Vogler et al. 1975), while later works by the same authors tred that ground cautiously or even deny the possibility (Miller and Muñoz 1982; Sobell and Sobell 1982; Vogler and Bartz 1982). No clinician in the United States today actively speaks for the controlled-drinking option for alcoholics. This is again in contrast with Britain, where some observers "regret the tendency to relegate the new methods to a minor and ancillary role . . . as being applicable, for example, to *only* those with less serious problems" (Heather and Robertson 1981: viii).

The evidence for taking into account the level of alcoholism when applying controlled-drinking goals is that the more severe a person's drinking problems the more likely are abstinence outcomes relative to moderation outcomes (Miller 1983a). However, the investigations of clinical psychologists agree with survey researchers in finding no distinct point where a line between alcoholics and others with drinking problems can be drawn. Instead, drinking problems occur along a continuum to which a number of factors contribute (Clark and Cahalan 1976; Miller and Saucedo 1983), and some drinkers at even the most severe levels of alcohol dependence successfully adopt controlled drinking. While fewer of the most dependent subjects (those with eleven or more signs of dependence on admission) in the Rand Study were drinking without problems at four years than were those who had been less dependent, still over one-quarter of those in remission were doing so.

Longitudinal studies likewise find it uncommon for heavily alcoholic subjects to become normal social drinkers. The Davies finding of between 5 and 10 percent who did so over a period from seven to eleven years appears typical (Vaillant 1983). However, only about the same 5 to 10 percent range of alcoholics achieve complete abstinence following treatment (Emrick and Hansen 1983; Polich et al. 1981). For the 80 to 90 percent of alco-

holics who do not abstain totally or return to normal drinking, the issue is the relative frequency of the person's drunken binges. Thus clearcut outcome categories have little meaning for the majority of alcoholics. Vaillant (1983) observed that among 110 alcohol abusers in his study who were tracked for over thirty years, 20 percent became moderate drinkers (no signs of dependence in the previous year) and 34 percent became abstinent. However, Vaillant assigned to the abstinence category those *drinking less than once a month* as well as those who had *drinking binges of less than a week's duration once a year.*

There seems quite a bit of leeway in the definition of controlled drinking and abstinence. Some, unlike Vaillant, might call a person who drank only occasionally to be a controlled rather than an abstinent drinker. Some (including, paradoxically, the Rand investigators, whom Vaillant derided for their leniency in defining controlled drinking) would label those who had drinking binges of any duration to be problem drinkers. In noting that occasional drinkers may for all intents and purposes be considered abstinent, Vaillant identified a crucial issue in therapy: how an alcoholic who has had one drink avoids a full-blown alcoholic relapse. Marlatt (1982) has developed an overall strategy for relapse prevention that includes teaching the alcoholic that a single slip is not necessarily a precursor to an episode of drunkenness. Alcoholics given practice in relapse prevention abstained no less than a comparison group of treated alcoholics (almost two-thirds of all subjects drank within a year), but they did show significantly less drunkenness (Chaney et al. 1978).

Abstinence philosophers argue that the danger of relapse is overwhelming for the alcoholic who is told he may take another drink. Yet there is an equivalent danger that those trying to adhere to strict abstinence will be more likely to abandon self-control entirely when they have a single drink (Heather et al. 1982; Marlatt 1978; Peele and Brodsky 1975; Schaefer 1971). This occurs because they believe they are powerless after they taste alcohol, as AA teaches them. The Rand Reports found relapses between eighteen months and four years had occurred for both those abstaining and those drinking without problems. In general, lower levels of dependence favored efforts to limit drinking and higher levels favored abstinence. However, other factors such as age and marital status were also important in this equation: For example, highly alcohol-dependent single men under age 40 were more likely to relapse if they were abstaining at eighteen months than if they were drinking moderately. It would seem that these alcoholics confront more drinking opportunities that may break their resolve to abstain, after which they are likely to drink excessively.

An understanding of the concept of relapse and a recognition of its frequency are necessary to make sense out of the Sobells' study and its cri-

tique by Pendery et al. The central finding in the original study was that abstinence subjects relapsed more than did controlled-drinking subjects. Pendery et al. pointed out that debilitating drinking was not uncommon for the controlled-drinking group following treatment. In the absence of any information about the abstinence group, it is possible to imagine that abstinence treatment successfully eliminated relapse. In fact, Pendery et al. (1982) noted about this group that "all agree (they) fared badly" (p. 173). Vaillant (1983) found a 95 percent relapse rate for a comparable group of patients he treated with hospital detoxification, compulsory AA attendance, and an active follow-up program.

Vaillant's strenuous insistence on the value of such medical and abstinence treatment is remarkable considering his own treatment group showed no better progress at two and eight years than did comparable groups of untreated alcoholics. This finding reflects a general absence of definitive results from therapeutic interventions for alcoholism (cf. Emrick 1975; Orford and Edwards 1977). On what grounds, then, have psychologists come to agree with medical practitioners that controlled-drinking approaches are not feasible for more seriously alcoholic clients? Miller (1983a, 1983b) maintains this position while reporting that twenty-three out of twenty-four studies have found reduced drinking techniques superior to other treatments for a range of alcohol abuse and "no study has demonstrated moderation training to be less effective than abstinence overall [that is, for any group of alcoholics]" (Miller 1983b: 15). It is not the evidence that has led to the total rejection of this technique for alcoholics. Rather, it is the current cultural climate toward alcoholism, one in which an alcoholism expert is quoted in a national magazine as saying "the suggestion that an alcoholic might be able to return to social drinking safely is 'a serious ethical problem, because at least 97% of alcoholics, if you let them drink, could die'" ("New Insights into Alcoholism" 1983: 69). Compare this with Vaillant's forlorn finding for his clinical sample that, "Tragically, abstinence does little to reduce the increased mortality of alcoholics" (1983: 164). Still, the risk to the therapist whose client fails at controlled drinking—since sooner or later nearly all alcoholics will relapse under any treatment condition—is that he or she will be accused of causing the client's death.

In this vein, several of the media depictions of the Sobells–Pendery et al. case visited graves or sites where controlled-drinking clients died. Yet the Addiction Research Foundation investigation actually found fewer deaths among subjects in the controlled-drinking group than in the abstinence group. The Sobells (1984) reported a detailed analysis of all subject deaths. They found the death rate for controlled-drinking subjects was lower than that regularly reported in alcoholism studies (none of these subjects died in the first six years following treatment and the last two died ten

years later, while intoxicated, shortly after leaving abstinence treatment clinics). In their rebuttal to Pendery et al., the Sobells (1984: 413) concluded that reinvestigations of their work "actually strengthen the validity of our original reports and conclusions." In the strange environment of controlled-drinking research, the publication of the Rand Reports—which found non-problem drinking among those with the most severe alcoholism—contributed to the rejection of controlled-drinking approaches for alcoholics in the United States. Then a fervid attack on a study of controlled-drinking therapy for severe alcoholics by researchers who no longer maintained this position reopened the question, at least for those interested in the truth.

Given that the two principal parties in the controlled-drinking debate had agreed by the late 1970s that this therapy was inapplicable to gamma (physically dependent) alcoholics, there seems little reason for argument. In the area of controlled drinking for alcoholics, however, broad outward agreement fails to obviate mutual suspicion and antagonism. There is, in addition, a practical side to the continuing battle: the competition over the less severely alcoholic person, labeled the problem drinker by psychologists (cf. Marlatt 1983). Every available comparative study has found that controlled-drinking therapy is the superior treatment for such clients (Miller and Hester 1980). Yet therapy with a goal of moderating drinking is just as unavailable for these types of drinkers as for those termed alcoholics. While abstinence proponents painstakingly evaluate whether those who return to social drinking were ever genuine alcoholics (see discussion of such a case in Pendery et al. 1982: 173), in practice abstinence treatment is offered to anyone with a noticeable drinking problem. In one highly publicized study in Denver, subjects who reported to alcoholism clinics with any type of concern about their drinking were invariably welcomed for treatment as alcoholics (Hansen and Emrick 1983).

The theoretical loophole in the disease approach that permits abstinence to be urged for all is the putative progressive nature of the disease. A more important Catch-22 concept in disease treatment is "denial." Alcoholics are defined as having an innate proclivity for denying their true condition, and this provides a justification for coercing clients to acknowledge that they are alcoholics and that therefore they need to abstain (see chapter 6). In fact, the second Rand Report discovered alcoholics were very aware of the negative consequences of their drinking (Polich et al. 1981). Those whose drinking problems obviously do not qualify them as alcoholic frequently refuse this label and with it, treatment (Miller 1983c). A Canadian study that offered stable, employed problem drinkers an abstinence therapy found that two-thirds rejected this goal at the outset while nearly all of a comparable group accepted treatment aimed at moderation (Sanchez-Craig 1980).

The Self-Selection of Treatment and Treatment Goals

It is clear, however, that not only those with milder drinking problems reject the idea that they are alcoholic, the need for lifelong abstinence, or both. All the Rand subjects underwent traditional alcoholism treatment, and yet very many of them, including a portion of those displaying a large number of symptoms of dependence, chose moderation as their own standard for improvement. These clients were not likely to be ones who enrolled in AA as an adjunct to treatment. Still, quite a few of them *were* able to demonstrate improved functioning and the elimination of drinking problems. A similar process occurred for the less severely impaired subjects who were told to abstain in the Canadian study. A solid majority of these actually moderated their drinking, so that there were not differences in the diminution of drinking problems between this group and those taught controlled drinking after two years (Sanchez-Craig et al. 1984). The finding that just as many people moderate their drinking no matter how extensive—or nonexistent—the controlled-drinking therapy they receive suggests that the primary determinant of moderation as a treatment outcome is a client's motivation to control his drinking (Nathan 1980).

Miller (1983a), Heather and Robertson (1981), Hodgson et al. (1979), and other behavior therapists have emphasized the need to classify alcoholics for treatment according to how potentially able they are to control their drinking. The primary criterion used is the severity of the individual's dependence on alcohol. A drinker's self-conception of being alcoholic also plays a role, however (Skinner et al. 1982). For example, subjects who believe that they are alcoholic and that abstinence is the only possible answer for their problem do better with an abstinence regimen (Miller 1983a). They are more likely to relapse following treatment after having had just one drink (Heather et al. 1983). These are examples of clients for whom abstinence is undoubtedly the preferred treatment modality. On the other hand, there may be just as much risk in contradicting the alcoholic who believes he can control his drinking as there is in convincing an alcoholic who believes abstinence will work that he should drink.

The more basic issue is in assuming an alcoholic's self-diagnosis is unreliable and that instead the therapist should determine the goal of treatment. It is not surprising that, as in the Rand Reports, we find human beings defiantly pursuing their own agendas for improvement. Alcoholics may avoid not only disease treatments but therapy of any kind. Tuchfeld (1981) interviewed people who had had significant drinking problems (e.g., blackout, tremors) and who had quit or moderated drinking on their own. These people often explicitly rejected the value of therapy for them. Instead, they changed their behavior when their drinking patterns became

intolerable in line with other values, relationships, or desires (Peele 1983d). Untreated alcoholics and problem drinkers are often identified by both disease theorists and psychologists as needing their attention. However, those who refuse to seek treatment for their abuse of alcohol remain in the majority. Vaillant (1983), while championing the effectiveness of AA, found that only about one-fifth of the 54 percent of alcohol abusers in his sample who were in remission were assisted by AA. Nor did many turn to other therapies. Not only did the 20 percent of those drinking without problems go it on their own, but so too did the majority of the 34 percent who were abstaining. One wonders if those Vaillant defined as abstinent but who continued to drink less than once a month were those who did not attend AA and who were thus less dogmatic about abstinence. In their national and community surveys, Cahalan (1970) and Roizen et al. (1978) uncovered large percentages of their samples whose drinking problems mitigated in the natural course of their lives, hardly any of whom became abstinent.

We have no evidence that those people who eschew treatment would be better off to admit their problem openly to others and to enlist in therapy (see chapter 5). Even when alcoholics show improvement through therapy the impetus is often provided by events outside the therapy setting (Gerard and Saenger 1966; Moos and Finney 1982). The kind of change involved in becoming a social drinker would seem especially to entail a substantial change in environment and outlook (Peele 1983a). For this reason, young drinkers show the greatest capacity to outgrow drinking problems (Cahalan and Room 1974), even when they have manifested symptoms of serious alcoholism (Fillmore 1975).

The disease theory of alcoholism—with its emphasis on lifelong abstinence, the need to confront people actively about their denial, and the treatable nature of alcoholism—has become firmly ensconced in American lore and social services. At the same time, success rates from typical abstinence programs seem to center in the 5 to 10 percent range (Emrick and Hansen 1983), with one massive study of a hospital-based program reporting less than 10 percent abstaining by the end of a year (Gordis et al. 1981). Treatment of any type strains to demonstrate a clearcut improvement in prognosis over the natural course of alcoholism (Baekeland et al. 1975; Emrick 1975; Orford and Edwards 1977; Vaillant 1983). Perhaps of most concern, the number of those with active alcohol problems does not seem to have decreased along with the ascendance of the disease theory, but rather has increased alarmingly (see chapter 6).

The growth of the disease theory is not due to its demonstrated efficacy, but instead represents the dominance of a set of attitudes about drinking. These attitudes paradoxically characterize those groups that are *most* likely to have alcohol problems. Vaillant found that not only were Irish-Americans in his sample seven times as likely to be alcoholic as those of

Mediterranean descent but that, in order to deal with a drinking problem, they were more likely to abstain. He notes that "It is consistent with Irish culture to see the use of alcohol in terms of black and white, good or evil, drunkenness or complete abstinence, while in Italian culture it is the distinction between moderate drinking and drunkenness that is most important" (1983: 226). This former view, from which the disease theory springs, is coming increasingly to inform our entire culture's conception of drinking. In noting the increasing incidence of drunkenness among U.S. high school students (by the end of the 1970s and the beginning of the 1980s, 40 percent of high school seniors reported having five drinks in one sitting at least once in the prior two weeks), Johnston et al. (1981) found a parallel rise in the acceptance of binge drinking on weekends in preference to mild daily consumption.

Theories about alcoholism reflect the same cultural influences. The strict version of the disease theory endorsed by AA and some physicians has found next to no empirical support. Meanwhile, however, medical investigators continue to emphasize genetic influences in alcoholism (cf. Schuckit 1984). More tellingly, the psychologists who most actively contest the disease theory have begun to formulate the problem in terms very reminiscent of those with whom they are arguing. Even within sociology today, the dominant view is that alcohol problems are solely a function of consumption (Room 1984).

3
Theories of Addiction

Stanton Peele and Bruce K. Alexander

In many cases, addiction theorists have now progressed beyond stereotyped disease conceptions of alcoholism or the idea that narcotics are inherently addictive to anyone who uses them. The two major areas of addiction theory—those concerning alcohol and narcotics—have had a chance to merge, along with theorizing about overeating, smoking, and even running and interpersonal addictions. Yet this new theoretical synthesis is less than meets the eye: It mainly recycles discredited notions while including piecemeal modifications that make the theories marginally more realistic in their descriptions of addictive behavior. These theories are described and evaluated in this chapter as they apply to all kinds of addictions. They are organized into sections on genetic theories (inherited mechanisms that cause or predispose people to be addicted), metabolic theories (biological, cellular adaptation to chronic exposure to drugs), conditioning theories (built on the idea of the cumulative reinforcement from drugs or other activities), and adaptation theories (those exploring the social and psychological functions performed by drug effects).

While most addiction theorizing has been too unidimensional and mechanistic to begin to account for addictive behavior, adaptation theories have typically had a different limitation. They do often correctly focus on the way in which the addict's experience of a drug's effects fits into the person's psychological and environmental ecology. In this way drugs are seen as a way to cope, however dysfunctionally, with personal and social needs and changing situational demands. Yet these adaptation models, while pointing in the right direction, fail because they do not directly explain the pharmacological role the substance plays in addiction. They are often considered—even by those who formulate them—as adjuncts to biological models, as in the suggestion that the addict uses a substance to gain a specific effect until, inexorably and irrevocably, physiological processes take hold of the individual. At the same time their purview is not ambitious enough (not nearly so ambitious as that of some biological and conditioning models) to incorporate nonnarcotic or nondrug involvements.

They also miss the opportunity, readily available at the social-psychological level of analysis, to integrate individual and cultural experiences.

Genetic Theories

How Is Alcoholism Inherited?

Cigarette smoking, alcoholism, and overweight—like divorce, child abuse and religion—run in families. This addictive inheritance has been most studied in the case of alcoholism. Studies endeavoring to separate genetic from environmental factors, such as those in which adopted-away offspring of alcoholics were compared to adopted children with nonalcoholic biological parents, have claimed a three to four times greater alcoholism rate for those whose biologic parents were alcoholic (Goodwin et al. 1973). Vaillant (1983) approvingly cited the Goodwin et al. and other research indicating genetic causality in alcoholism (see especially Vaillant and Milofsky 1982), but his own research did not support this conclusion (cf. Peele 1983c). In the inner-city sample that formed the basis for Vaillant's primary analysis, those with alcoholic relatives were between three and four times as likely to be alcoholic as those without alcoholic relatives. Since these subjects were reared by their natural families, however, this finding does not distinguish effects of alcoholic environment from inherited dispositions. Vaillant did find that subjects with alcoholic relatives they did not live with were twice as likely to become alcoholic as subjects who had no alcoholic relatives at all.

Yet further nongenetic influences remain to be partialed out of Vaillant's results. The chief of these is ethnicity: Irish Americans in this Boston sample were seven times as likely to be alcohol dependent as were those of Mediterranean descent. Controlling for such large ethnicity effects would surely reduce the 2 to 1 ratio (for subjects with alcoholic relatives compared to those without) in alcoholism substantially even as other potential environmental factors that lead to alcoholism (besides ethnicity) would still remain to be controlled for. Vaillant reported two other tests of genetic causality in his sample. He disconfirmed Goodwin's (1979) hypothesis that alcoholics with alcoholic relatives—and hence a presumed inherited predisposition to alcoholism—inevitably develop problems with drinking earlier than do others. Finally, Vaillant found no tendency for the choice of moderate drinking versus abstinence as a resolution for drinking problems to be related to number of alcoholic relatives, although it was associated with the drinker's ethnic group.

Proposing genetic mechanisms in alcoholism on the basis of concordance rates does not provide a model of addiction. What are these mechanisms through which alcoholism is inherited and translated into alcoholic

behavior? Not only has no biological mechanism been found to date to underlie alcoholism, but research on alcoholics' behavior indicates that one cannot be found in the case of the loss of control of drinking that defines alcoholism. Even the most severely alcoholic individuals "clearly demonstrate positive sources of control over drinking behavior" so that "extreme drunkenness cannot be accounted for on the basis of some internally located inability to stop" (Heather and Robertson 1981: 122). Intriguingly, controlled-drinking theorists like Heather and Robertson (1983) propose exceptions to their own analyses: Perhaps "some problem drinkers are born with a physiological abnormality, either genetically transmitted or as a result of intrauterine factors, which makes them react abnormally to alcohol from their first experience of it" (Heather and Robertson 1983: 141).

While it is certainly a fascinating possibility, no research of any type supports this suggestion. Vaillant (1983) found that self-reports by AA members that they immediately succumbed to alcoholism the first time they drank were false and that severe drinking problems developed over periods of years and decades. The exceptions to this generalization were psychopaths whose drinking problems were components of overall abnormal lifestyles and behavior patterns from an early age. However, these kinds of alcoholics showed a greater tendency to outgrow alcoholism by moderating their drinking (Goodwin et al. 1971), indicating they also do not conform to a putative biological model. Prospective studies of those from alcoholic families also have failed to reveal early alcoholic drinking (Knop et al. 1984).

Findings like these have led genetic theorists and researchers instead to propose that the inherited vulnerability to alcoholism takes the form of some probabilistically greater risk of developing drinking problems. In this view a genetic tendency—such as one that dictates a drinker will have an overwhelming response to alcohol—does not cause alcoholism. The emphasis is instead on such biological abnormalities as the inability to discriminate blood alcohol level (BAL), which leads alcoholics to show less effect from drinking and to drink more without sensing their condition (Goodwin 1980; Schuckit 1984). Alternately, Schuckit (1984) proposed that alcoholics inherit a different style of metabolizing alcohol, such as producing higher levels of acetaldehyde due to drinking. Finally, Begleiter and other theorists have proposed that alcoholics have abnormal brain waves prior to ever having drunk or that drinking creates unusual brain activity for them (Pollock et al. 1984; Porjesz and Begleiter 1982).

All these theorists have indicated that their results are preliminary and require replication, particularly through prospective studies of people who become alcoholics. Negative evidence, however, is already available. Several studies have found that sensitivity to BAL, peak BAL after drinking, and elimination of blood alcohol are unrelated to family histories of alco-

holism (Lipscomb and Nathan 1980; Pollock et al. 1984). Other negative evidence for both BAL discrimination *and* metabolic hypotheses is provided by the case of American Indians and Eskimos. These groups are hyperresponsive to alcohol's effects (that is, they respond immediately and intensely to the alcohol in their systems) and yet have the highest alcoholism rates in the United States. The claim of inheritance of alcoholism from the opposite theoretical direction—that these groups succumb to alcoholism so readily because they metabolize alcohol so quickly—likewise does not succeed. Groups that share the hypermetabolism of alcohol that Eskimos and Indians display (called Oriental flush), such as the Chinese and Japanese, have among the lowest alcoholism rates in America. The disjunctive connection between obvious metabolic characteristics and drinking habits actually contraindicates significant biological determinism in alcoholism (Mendelson and Mello 1979a).

The basic problem with genetic models of alcoholism is the absence of a reasonable link to the drinking behaviors in question. Why do any of the proposed genetic mechanisms lead people to become compulsive imbibers? For example, in the case of an insensitivity to alcohol's effects, why wouldn't an individual who can't reliably detect that he has drunk too much simply learn from experience (in the absence of any proposed genetic compulsion to drink) to limit himself to a safer number of drinks? Do such drinkers simply choose to drink at unhealthy levels and to experience the extreme negative consequences of drinking that, after years, may lead to alcoholism (Vaillant 1983)? If so, why? That is the question.

On the other hand, the proposed differences in metabolizing alcohol and changes in brain functioning due to drinking are extremely subtle when compared with the gross effects of Oriental flush. Yet even groups characterized by Oriental flush, like the Indians and the Chinese, can show diametrically opposite responses to the same intense physiological changes. If a given individual did indeed have an extreme reaction to alcohol, why would he not become the type of drinker who announces, "I only have a drink or two because otherwise I become giddy and make a fool of myself"? For those drinkers for whom alcohol might produce a desirable change in brain waves, why does the person prefer this state over others or other ways of gaining the same effect? The variation in behavior that is left unaccounted for in the most optimistic of these models is such as to discount the potential gain from the pursuit of as yet unestablished links between genetically inherited reactions to alcohol and alcoholic behavior. Finally, since all studies have found that it is sons and not daughters who most often inherit the risk of alcoholism (Cloninger et al. 1978), in what comprehensible ways can any of the genetic mechanisms thus far suggested for alcoholism be sex-linked?

The Endorphin-Deficiency Explanation of Narcotic Addiction

Since the primary assumption about narcotics has been that the drugs are equally and inevitably addictive for everyone, pharmacological theories of narcotic addiction have rarely stressed individual biological proclivities to be addicted. It was only a matter of time, however, before pharmacological and biological theorists began to hypothesize inherited mechanisms to account for differences in addictive susceptibility. When Dole and Nyswander (1967) introduced the ideas that narcotic addiction was a "metabolic disease" and that the tendency to become addicted outlived the actual dependence on a drug, the way was opened to suggest that "metabolic disorder could precede as well as be precipitated by opiate use" (Goldstein, cited in Harding et al. 1980: 57). That is, not only might habitual narcotic use cause a chronic and residual need for drugs, but people conceivably might already have had such a need when they started taking drugs and came to rely on them.

The discovery that the body produces its own opiates, called endorphins, presented a plausible version of this mechanism. Endorphin theorists like Goldstein (1976b) and Snyder (1977) speculated that addicts may be characterized by an inbred endorphin deficiency that leaves them unusually sensitive to pain. Such people would then especially welcome—and might even require—the elevation of their pain threshhold brought on by narcotics. Heroin addicts have not yet been demonstrated to show unusual levels of endorphins. Moreover, this type of theorizing is badly strained—as are all metabolic theories of addiction—by the commonplace observations of drug abuse and addiction that were noted in chapter 1. Addicts do not in fact indicate a chronic, habitual need for narcotics. They regularly alter the type and amount of drug they use, sometimes abstaining or quitting altogether as they age. Most of the Vietnam veterans who were addicted in Asia and who then used narcotics in the United States did not become readdicted. Noting that almost none of the patients introduced to a narcotic in the hospital indicate a prolonged desire for the drug, we may wonder why so small a percentage of the general population displays this endorphin deficiency.

Endorphin deficiency and other metabolic models suggest a course of progressive and irreversible reliance on narcotics that actually occurs in only exceptional and abnormal cases of addiction. Those with inbred metabolic defects could conceivably account for only a small percentage of those who become addicted over their lifetimes. Why would the narcotic addiction that disappeared for most Vietnam veterans (or for the many other addicts who outgrow it) differ fundamentally from all other kinds of

addiction, such as the kind that persists for some people? To accept this dichotomous view of addiction violates the basic principle of scientific parsimony, by which we should assume that the mechanisms at work in a large portion of cases are present in all cases. This is the same error made by psychologists who concede (without empirical provocation) that some alcoholics may indeed have constitutional traits that cause them to be alcoholic from their first drink even as research shows all alcoholics to be responsive to situational rewards and to subjective beliefs and expectations.

Preprogrammed Obesity

In his influential internal–external model of obesity, Schachter (1968) proposed that fat people had a different style of eating, one that depended on external cues to tell them when to eat or not. Unlike those of normal weight, Schachter's overweight subjects apparently could not rely on internal physiological signs to decide whether they were hungry. As a social psychologist, Schachter originally emphasized cognitive and environmental stimuli that encouraged the obese to eat. However, his model left open the question of the source of this insensitivity to somatic cues, suggesting the probability that this was an inherited trait. Schachter's (1971) view of the sources of overeating became increasingly physiological in nature when he began comparing the behavior of ventromedial-lesioned rats with obese humans. Several of Schachter's prominent students followed his lead in this direction. For example, Rodin (1981) eventually rejected the internal–external model (as most researchers have by now) with an eye toward locating a neurological basis for overeating. Meanwhile Nisbett (1972), another Schachter student, proposed an extremely popular model of body weight based on an internal regulatory mechanism, called set-point, which is inherited or determined by prenatal or early childhood eating habits.

Peele (1983e) analyzed Schachter's evolution into a purely biological theoretician in terms of biases Schachter and his students had shown all along against personality dynamics; against group, social, and cultural mechanisms; and against the role of values and complex cognitions in the choice of behavior. As a result, the Schachter group consistently failed to pick up discrepant indicators in their obesity research, some of which led eventually to the jettisoning of the internal–external model. For example, Schachter (1968) noted that normal-weight subjects did not eat more when they were hungry (as predicted) because they found the type of food and the time of day inappropriate for eating. In another study that had important implications, Nisbett (1968) discovered that formerly overweight subjects who were no longer obese behaved similarly to obese subjects in an eating experiment. That is, they ate more after having been forced to eat earlier

than when they had not eaten before. Nisbett interpreted these results as showing that these subjects were unable to control their impulses to overeat and could therefore not be expected to keep excess weight off.

This line of thinking was solidified in Nisbett's set-point hypothesis, which held that the hypothalamus was set to defend a specific body weight and that going below this weight stimulated a greater desire to eat. The idea that obese people could not lose weight, based on laboratory studies and the performance of clients in weight-loss programs, had been the central tenet in all of the Schachter group's work on obesity (cf. Schachter and Rodin 1974; Rodin 1981). Yet such pessimism seems an unlikely deduction from a study like Nisbett's (1968), in which subjects who had been obese and who continued to display an external eating style had indeed lost weight. When Schachter (1982) actually questioned people in the field about their weight-loss histories, he found remission was quite common in obesity: of all those interviewed who had ever been obese and who had tried to lose weight, 62.5 percent were currently at normal weight.

Schachter's serendipitous finding disputed the entire thrust of over a decade's research—namely, that people were locked into obesity by biological forces. The idea would not die easily, however. Another Schachter student and his colleague recorded Schachter's (1982) finding but dismissed its significance by indicating it was probably only those obese subjects who were above their set-points who had been able to lose weight in this study (Polivy and Herman 1983: 195–96). Polivy and Herman based this calculation on the estimate that from 60 to 70 percent of obese people were not obese in childhood. Their assertion requires that we believe that nearly all of the people in the Schachter study who have been overweight for reasons other than biological inheritance (and only these) had lost weight. Yet undoubtedly many in this category would remain fat for whatever presumably nonset-point reasons had caused them to become obese in the first place. Rather than being the underlying source of obesity its adherents had painted it to be, set-point now seemed not to be a major factor in most cases of overweight.

Polivy and Herman's (1983) description of their outlook did not reflect this understanding about set-point and obesity. Instead, they argued that "for the foreseeable future, we must resign ourselves to the fact that we have no reliable way to change the natural weight that an individual is blessed or cursed with" although "perhaps, as research progresses, we will be able to imagine such biological interventions—including even genetic manipulations" that will enable people to lose weight (p. 52). Polivy and Herman furthermore attributed binge overeating—the extreme of which is bulimia—to people's attempts to restrain their eating in the effort to go below their natural weight (see chapter 5). These researchers' work agrees with that of popular writers (Bennett and Gurin 1982) and the dominant

research approaches in the field (Stunkard 1980) in maintaining a view of human eating and overeating that is essentially the same as that held by biological theorists of alcoholism and drug addiction toward drinking and drug consumption. In all cases, people are seen to be under the sway of invariant forces that, in the long run, they cannot hope to contravene.

Meanwhile, Garn and his coworkers (1979) have shown that similarities in weight levels among people who live together are a result of similar eating habits and energy expenditure. This "cohabitational effect" holds for husbands and wives and is the largest factor in weight similarities between parents and adopted offspring. People who live together who *become* fat do so together (Garn et al. 1979). The longer parents and their children live together (even when the children are age 40) the more they resemble each other in fatness. The longer parents and children live separately, the less pronounced such similarities become until they approach 0 at the extremes of separation (Garn, LaVelle, and Pilkington 1984). Garn, Pilkington, and LaVelle (1984), observing 2,500 people over two decades, found "those . . . who were lean to begin with generally increased in fatness level. Those who were obese to begin with generally decreased in fatness level" (pp. 90–91). "Natural weight" may be a very variable thing, influenced by the same social values and personal coping strategies that affect all behavior (Peele 1984a).

Interpersonal Addiction

The enormity of the implications of the genetic transmission of addictive impulses is driven home by several theories claiming that people are compelled by chemical imbalances to form unhealthy, compulsive, and self-destructive interpersonal relationships. Tennov (1979) maintained that such "limerent" people, who are in every other way indistinguishable from other people, have a biological propensity to fall head-over-heels in love and create disastrous romantic attachments. Liebowitz (1983) proposed that a failure in neurochemical regulation—similar to that hypothesized to cause manic-depressive reactions—leads people (almost exclusively women) to fall heatedly in love, often with inappropriate partners, and to become inordinately depressed when the relationships fail. These theories illustrate mainly the temptation to believe that compelling motivations must have a biological source and the desire to mechanize human differences, imperfections, and mysteries.

Global Biologic Theories of Addiction

Peele and Brodsky (1975), in the book *Love and Addiction,* also described interpersonal relationships as having addictive potential. The thrust of their version of interpersonal addiction, however, was exactly the opposite

of that in Liebowitz (1983) and Tennov (1979): Peele and Brodsky's aim was to show that any powerful experience can form the object of an addiction for people predisposed by combinations of social and psychological factors. Their approach was antireductionist and rejected the deterministic force of inbred, biological, or other factors outside the realm of human consciousness and experience. Their work signaled a burst of addiction theorizing in areas other than substance abuse, the bulk of which—paradoxically—sought to analyze these phenomena at a biological level. The result has been the proliferation of biologic theories to account both for the range of compulsive involvements people form and for the tendency some people show to be addicted to a host of substances.

Smith (1981), a medical clinician, has posited the existence of an "addictive disease" to account for why so many of those who become addicted to one substance have prior histories of addiction to dissimilar substances (cf. "The Collision of Prevention and Treatment" 1984). It is impossible to explain—as Smith attempts to do—how innate, predetermined reactions could cause the same person to become excessively involved with substances as disparate as cocaine, alcohol, and Valium. In examining the generally strong positive correlations among tobacco, alcohol, and caffeine use, Istvan and Matarazzo (1984) explored the possibilities both that these substances are "linked by reciprocal activation mechanisms" and that they may be linked by their "pharmacologically antagonistic . . . effects" (p. 322). The evidence here is rather that substance abuse exceeds biological predictability. The fact of multiple addictions to myriad substances and nonsubstance-related involvements is *primary evidence against genetic and biological interpretations of addiction.*

Nonetheless, neuroscientists put forward biological theories of just this degree of universality. One researcher (Dunwiddie 1983: 17) noted that

> drugs of abuse such as opiates, amphetamine, and cocaine can pharmacologically stimulate many of the brain centers identified as reward centers. . . . On the other hand, there is considerable evidence that certain individuals have an enhanced liability for drug abuse, and frequently misuse a variety of seemingly unrelated drugs. It is interesting to speculate that for various reasons, perhaps genetic, perhaps developmental or environmental, the normal inputs to these hypothetical "reward pathways" function inadequately in such individuals. If this were the case, there may be a biological defect underlying poly-drug abuse.

While piling hypothesis upon hypothesis, Dunwiddie's description presents no actual research findings about drug abusers, nor does it present a specific hypothetical link between deficient "reward pathways" and "polydrug abuse." It would seem the author thinks people who get less reward from drugs are more likely to abuse them.

Milkman and Sunderwirth's (1983) neurological model of addiction is not limited to drug abuse (as nothing in Dunwiddie's account would so limit it). These authors believe that addiction can result from any "self-induced changes in neurotransmission," where the more neurotransmitters that are involved "the faster the rate of firing," leading to the "elevated mood sought by cocaine users, for example" (p. 36). This account is actually a social-psychological one masquerading as neurological explanation, in which the writers introduce social and psychological factors such as peer influence and low self-esteem into their analysis by suggesting "that the enzyme produced by a given gene might influence hormones and neurotransmitters in a way that contributes to the development of a personality potentially more susceptible to . . . peer group pressure" (p. 44). Both Dunwiddie's and Milkman and Sunderwirth's analyses cloak experiential events in neurological terminology without reference to any actual research that connects biological functioning to addictive behavior. These models represent almost ritualistic conceptions of scientific enterprise, and while their analyses are caricatures of contemporary scientific model building, they come unfortunately close to mainstream assumptions about how the nature of addiction is to be interpreted.

Exposure Theories: Biological Models

The Inevitability of Narcotic Addiction

Alexander and Hadaway (1982) referred to the prevailing conception of narcotic addiction among both lay and scientific audiences—that it is the inevitable consequence of regular narcotics use—as the exposure orientation. So entrenched is this viewpoint that Berridge and Edwards (1981)—while arguing that "Addiction is now defined as a disease because doctors have categorized it thus" (p. 150)—refer readers to an appendix in which Griffith Edwards declared "anyone who takes an opiate for a long enough period of time and in sufficient dose will become addicted" (p. 278). This view contrasts with conventional beliefs about alcohol that would reject the same statement with the word "alcohol" substituted for "an opiate."

Underlying the exposure model is the assumption that the introduction of a narcotic into the body causes metabolic adjustments that require continued and increasing dosages of the drug in order to avoid withdrawal. No alteration in cell metabolism has yet been linked with addiction, however. The most prominent name in metabolic research and theory, Maurice Seevers, characterized efforts during the first sixty-five years of this century to create a model of addictive narcotic metabolism to be "exercises in semantics, or plain flights of imagination" (cited in Keller 1969: 5). Dole and

Nyswander (1967; cf. Dole 1980) are the modern champions of heroin addiction as a metabolic disease, although they have provided no explicit metabolic mechanism to account for it. Endorphin theorists have suggested that regular use of narcotics reduces the body's natural endorphin production, thus bringing about a reliance on the external chemical agent for ordinary pain relief (Goldstein 1976b; Snyder 1977).

This version of the relationship between endorphin production and addiction—like the one suggesting addicts inherit an endorphin deficiency (see above)—does not fit the data reviewed in chapter 1. Put baldly, exposure to narcotics does not lead to addiction, and addiction does not require the metabolic adjustments claimed for it. Those given the most reliable and purest supplies of narcotics, hospital patients, display—rather than an escalating need for the drug—a reduced desire for it. In an experimental trial of self-administration of morphine by hospitalized postoperative patients, subjects in the self-administration condition employed moderate, progressively declining doses of the drug (Bennett et al. 1982). That even infants and animals do not manifest an acquired hunger for opiates is the subject of chapter 4. On the other hand, compulsive street users of narcotics often do not show the expected hallmarks of addiction, such as withdrawal.

Endorphins and Nonnarcotic Addiction

Although unsubstantiated in the case of narcotic addiction, endorphin-related explanations have proved irresistible to those considering other addictive behavior. In particular, discoveries that food and alcohol—as well as narcotics—can affect endorphin levels have prompted speculation that these substances create self-perpetuating physical needs along the lines of those the narcotics supposedly produce. Weisz and Thompson (1983) summarized these theories while noting that "At this time there is not sufficient evidence to conclude that endogenous opioids mediate the addictive process of even one substance of abuse" (p. 314). Harold Kalant (1982), a distinguished neuroscientist, was more conclusive in his rejection of the idea that alcohol and narcotics could act according to the same neurological principles. "How do you explain . . . in pharmacological terms," he queried, that cross-tolerance occurs "between alcohol, which does not have specific receptors, and opiates, which do" (p. 12)?

To date, the most active speculation by clinicians about the role of endorphins has been in the area of compulsive running and exercising (cf. Sacks and Pargman 1984). If running stimulates endorphin production (Pargman and Baker 1980; Riggs 1981), then compulsive runners are presumed to undergo narcotic-like physical states to which they become addicted. Research on the relationship between endorphin levels, mood

swings, and running motivation has failed to turn up regular relationships (Appenzeller et al. 1980; Colt et al. 1981; Hawley and Butterfield 1981). Markoff et al. (1982) and McMurray and his colleagues (1984) reported that exercising subjects treated with the narcotic-blocking agent naloxone reported no differences in perceived exertion and other physiological measures from those not treated. Addicted running—defined by inflexibility and insensitivity to internal and external conditions, running until the point of harming oneself, and being unable to quit without experiencing withdrawal—is no better explained by endorphin levels than is the self-destructiveness of the heroin addict (Peele 1981a).

Cigarette Addiction

Schachter (1977, 1978) has been the most vigorous proponent of the case that cigarette smokers are physically dependent on nicotine. They continue to smoke, in Schachter's view, in order to maintain habitual levels of cellular nicotine and to avoid withdrawal. Interestingly, Schachter (1971, 1977, 1978; Schachter and Rodin 1974) has proposed that different *types* of factors determine obesity and smoking: the former is due to an inbred predilection while the latter is due to an acquired constraint (avoidance of withdrawal). This is the same distinction drawn in traditional theories of alcohol and narcotic addiction. The distinction is necessary in order to defend biological causality in the case of excessiveness both in activities that are common to most people (eating and drinking alcohol) and activities that only some indulge in (smoking and narcotics use).

As with alcohol and narcotic use (see below), there is no prima facie reason why destructive eating and smoking habits need necessarily be dictated by separate classes of factors. Indeed, studies Schachter (1978) and his students conducted with cigarette smokers replicated results of Schachter and Rodin's (1974) work with the obese. For example, both smokers (while not smoking) and the obese were more distractible and more sensitive to negative stimuli like pain than were nonsmokers or normal-weight people. Both smokers and the obese apparently found their habits allayed anxieties and cushioned them against unpleasant stimulation (see Peele 1983e for further discussion). Furthermore, the apparent uniformity in the addictive use of cigarettes that Schachter's model suggests is illusory. Different smokers consume different amounts of tobacco and inhale different levels of nicotine; Best and Hakstian (1978) found such variations to reflect different motivations and settings for smoking and to suggest different circumstances under which smokers can quit.

Leventhal and Cleary (1980) have pointed out how inexact the regulation of nicotine intake is in Schachter's studies: Schachter (1977) found that a 77 percent reduction in nicotine level produced only a 17 to 25 percent

increase in cigarette consumption. More tellingly, these authors reflected, "Schachter's model and studies . . . assume a direct and automatic step from changes in plasma nicotine level to craving and [separately] smoking and say nothing about the mechanisms and experience that give rise to either" (p. 390). For example, Schachter (1978) himself noted that Orthodox Jews regularly withstood withdrawal to give up smoking during the sabbath. People's values do not cease to operate in the face of physiological forces. Later, in the same study in which he detected a high remission rate for obesity, Schachter (1982) discovered that over 60 percent of those in two communities who had tried to quit smoking had succeeded. They had ceased smoking on the average for 7.4 years. Heavier smokers—those consuming three or more packs of cigarettes a day—showed the same remission rate as lighter smokers. It would seem that Schachter's nicotine regulation model, which he designed primarily to explain why habitual smokers cannot quit, does not take the measure of the behavior in question. Whereas his formulation of nicotine addiction had emphasized the ineluctable, overwhelming nature of withdrawal from cigarettes, he now found the ability to overcome such withdrawal "to be relatively common" (p. 436). In other words, there needs to be some additional level of explanation for why people persist in smoking as well as for why they can give it up (Peele 1984a).

Alcohol Dependence

As narcotic addiction theorists have been forced by the recognition of individual variations in addiction to postulate innate neurochemical differences among people, alcoholism specialists have increasingly put forward the claim that alcohol problems are simply a function of excessive drinking. It might be said that conceptions of alcoholism and narcotic addiction not only are meeting on common ground but are passing each other going in opposite directions. The change in emphasis in alcoholism is in good part a result of the desire of psychologists and others to achieve rapprochement with disease theories (see chapter 2). It has led controlled-drinking clinicians to assert that a return to moderate drinking is impossible for the physically dependent alcoholic. Intriguingly, behaviorists have thus adopted Jellinek's (1960) formulation of the disease theory of alcoholism, in which he claimed that true (gamma) alcoholics could not control their drinking due to their physical dependence. (In his 1960 volume Jellinek was ambiguous about the extent to which this disability was inbred and irreversible, the traditional claims made by AA.)

The concept of alcohol dependence has been elaborated by a group of British researchers (Edwards and Gross 1976; Hodgson et al. 1978). In the same breath, it attempts to replace the disease theory (whose defects are

more broadly agreed upon in Great Britain than in the United States) while rescuing important disease notions (see critique by Shaw 1979). The alcohol-dependence syndrome resembles the disease of alcoholism in conceiving of drinking problems as a condition that can be identified in isolation from the drinker's psychological state and situation and as one that endures beyond the alcoholic's active drinking. Severity of dependence is assessed purely in terms of how much people habitually drink and the physical consequences of this drinking (Hodgson et al. 1978), without regard for their reasons for drinking or cultural, social, and other environmental factors. Thus, those who are heavily dependent are thought to have a stable condition that makes their return to moderate drinking unlikely.

The alcohol-dependence syndrome suffers from the tension of acknowledging the complexity of alcoholic behavior. As its supporters note, "the control of drinking, like any other behavior, is a function of cues and consequences, of set and setting, of psychological and social variables; in short, control, or loss of it, is a function of the way in which the alcoholic construes his situation" (Hodgson et al. 1979: 380). Within this framework, Hodgson et al. regard withdrawal symptoms to be a strong cue for alcoholics to return to heavy drinking. However, the appearance of withdrawal in alcoholism is itself variable and subject to drinkers' subjective constructions. Moreover, such symptoms are regularly overcome by alcoholics in their drinking careers and in any case are limited in duration. Avoidance of withdrawal simply cannot account for continued drinking (see Mello and Mendelson 1977). There is a more basic objection yet to the alcohol dependence concept. In his critique of "the concept of drug dependence as a state of chronic exposure to a drug," Kalant (1982) remonstrated that dependence concepts have "ignored the most fundamental question—why a person having experienced the effect of a drug would want to go back again and again to reproduce that chronic state" (p. 12).

Whereas speculation about human drug dependence has been influenced greatly by generalizations from animal research (generalizations that are largely incorrect, see chapter 4), the alcohol-dependence syndrome has had to fly in the face of animal research. It is difficult to get rats to drink alcohol in the laboratory. In his seminal research, Falk (1981) was able to induce such drinking through the imposition of intermittent feeding schedules that the animals find highly uncomfortable. In this condition, the rats drink heavily but also indulge in excessive and self-destructive behavior of many kinds. All such behavior—including drinking—depends strictly on the continuation of this feeding schedule and disappears as soon as normal feeding opportunities are restored. Thus, for rats that had been alcohol-dependent, Tang et al. (1982) reported "a history of ethanol overindulgence was not a sufficient condition for the maintenance of overdrinking" (p. 155).

On the basis of animal research, at least, alcohol dependence seems to be strongly state-dependent rather than a persistent characteristic of the organism. Rather than being contradicted by human behavior, this phenomenon may be even more pronounced for humans. The supposed biological basis of drinking behavior in the alcohol dependence model is thus unable to deal with major aspects of alcoholism. As one of the authors (Gross 1977: 121) of the alcohol-dependence syndrome observed:

> The foundation is set for the progression of the alcohol dependence syndrome by virtue of its biologically intensifying itself. One would think that, once caught up in the process, the individual could not be extricated. However, and for reasons poorly understood, the reality is otherwise. Many, perhaps most, do free themselves.

Control of Alcohol Supply

Sociological theory and research has been the main counterpoint to disease theories of alcoholism (Room 1983) and has made decisive contributions in depicting alcoholism as a social construction, in discrediting the idea that drinking problems can be organized into medical entities, and in disproving empirical claims regarding such bedrock disease notions as inevitable loss of control and reliable stages in the progress of alcoholism (see chapter 2). Yet some sociologists have also been uncomfortable with the idea that social beliefs and cultural customs affect levels of drinking problems (Room 1976). In place of such sociocultural interpretations of alcoholism, sociology as a field has now largely adopted a supply-of-alcohol perspective based on findings that alcohol consumption in a society is distributed in a unimodal, lognormal curve (Room 1984).

Since a large proportion of the alcohol available is drunk by those at the extreme end of this skewed curve, increases or decreases in alcohol availability are believed to push many drinkers above or below what might be considered a heavy and dangerous drinking level. Alcohol supply policy recommendations thus include raising taxes on liquor to lower overall consumption. The alcohol supply model is most certainly not a biological theory and does not itself lead to theoretical derivations about alcohol metabolism. Yet as Room (1984: 304) has pointed out, it can be rationalized with the disease-theory view that those at the extreme of the curve have lost control of their drinking. In fact, the model fits best with the alcohol-dependence syndrome, where alcoholic behavior is conceived principally to be the result of excessive consumption.

At the same time, the alcohol-supply view violates a number of sociologically based findings. Beauchamp (1980), for example, propounded the alcohol-supply argument while reporting that Americans consumed from

two to three or more times as much alcohol per capita in the late eighteenth century as they do today and yet had fewer alcohol problems in the colonial period. Nor does the supply model make good sense of discontinuities in consumption within a given region. Alcohol problems in France are centered in the nonwinegrowing regions that must import more expensive alcoholic beverages (Prial 1984). In the United States, fundamentalist Protestant sects consume less alcohol per capita because many of these groups abstain. However, these groups—and the relatively dry regions of the South and Midwest—also have higher alcoholism rates and incidences of binge drinking (Armor et al. 1978; Cahalan and Room 1974). How also do the Jews, located principally in the highest consumption areas in the country (urban and Eastern), maintain an alcoholism rate one-tenth or less than the nationwide rate (Glassner and Berg 1980)? On the policy side, Room (1984) noted that efforts to curtail supplies have often backfired and led to greater binges in consumption.

At a psychological level, the idea that people incur the costs of alcoholism simply because they have more alcohol available to them makes little sense. For example, what exactly is the impact on the alcoholic of making supplies harder to obtain? The result of limiting the ready medical supply of narcotics was to turn many men into alcoholics (O'Donnell 1969). Vaillant (1983) found that abstaining alcoholics were highly prone to abuse other substances or to form alternate compulsive involvements. Here the sociological level of analysis, like the metabolic, suffers from a lack of a grasp of the individual's overall addictive ecology. The popularity of alcohol-supply ideas within a community noted for its opposition to disease ideas may make one pessimistic about whether there still can remain any intellectual resistance to metabolic theories of alcoholism and addiction.

Exposure Theories: Conditioning Models

Conditioning theories hold that addiction is the cumulative result of the reinforcement of drug administration. The central tenet of conditioning theories is that (Donegan et al. 1983: 112):

> To say that a substance is used at a level considered to be excessive by the standards of the individual or society and that reducing the level of use is difficult is one way of saying that the substance has gained considerable control over the individual's behavior. In the language of behavior theory, the substance acts as a powerful reinforcer: behaviors instrumental in obtaining the substance become more frequent, vigorous, or persistent.

Conditioning theories offer the potential for considering all excessive activities along with drug abuse within a single framework, that of highly

rewarding behavior. Originally developed to explain narcotic addiction (cf. Woods and Schuster 1971), reinforcement models have been applied to most popular psychoactive drugs and to nondrug addictions like gambling and overeating (Donegan et al. 1983). Solomon (1980), in a broadly influential approach he calls the opponent-process model of motivation, has extended conditioning principles to every pleasurable and compulsive activity. The complex processes that characterize learning also allow increased flexibility in describing addictive behavior. In classical conditioning, previously neutral stimuli become associated with reactions brought on in their presence by a primary reinforcer. Thus an addict who relapses can be conceived to have had his craving for the addiction reinstated by exposure to the settings in which he previously used drugs (Wikler 1973; S. Siegel 1979, 1983).

The Myth of the Universal Reinforcer: The Inherent Pleasurableness of Narcotics

Conditioning theories leave open one critical question: What is a reinforcing activity? The assumption in narcotic addiction is usually that the drug provides an inherent, biologic reward and/or that it has strong reinforcement value due to its prevention of withdrawal pain (Wikler 1973). This assumption is part of a wide range of theories of addiction (cf. Bejerot 1980; Dole 1972; Goldstein 1976a; McAuliffe and Gordon 1974; Wilker 1973). Indeed, the belief that narcotics are irresistible to any organism that, once having tried them, has free access to drugs is the epitome of the exposure model of addiction. The body of work thought best to demonstrate the truth of this belief is the observation that laboratory animals can readily be induced to ingest narcotics and other drugs. Chapter 4 shows this view to be unfounded: drug use is no more self-perpetuating for animals than it is for humans. No less a biological determinist than Dole (1980) has now declared that "most animals cannot be made into addicts. . . . Although the pharmacological effects of addictive substances injected into animals are quite similar to those seen in human beings, animals generally avoid such drugs when they are given a choice" (p. 142).

If the behavior of laboratory animals is not locked in by drug action, how is it possible for human beings to become addicted and lose the possibility of choice? One proposal to account for the feverish pursuit of drugs and other human involvements has been that these experiences bring inordinate pleasure, or euphoria. The idea that pleasure is the primary reinforcement in addiction is present in several theories (Bejerot 1980; Hatterer 1980; McAuliffe and Gordon 1974) and most especially has a central role in Solomon's (1980) opponent-process model. The ultimate source of this idea has been the supposedly intense euphoria that narcotics, particularly heroin, produce, a euphoria for which normal experience offers no near coun-

terpart. In the popular image of heroin use and its effects, euphoria seems the only possible inducement for using a drug that is the ultimate symbol of self-destructiveness.

Some users describe euphoric experiences from taking heroin, and McAuliffe and Gordon's (1974) interviews with addicts revealed this to be a primary motivation for continuing to use the drug. Other research contests this notion vigorously. Zinberg and his colleagues have interviewed a large number of addicts and other heroin users over several decades and have found the McAuliffe and Gordon work to be extremely naive. "Our interviews have revealed that after prolonged heroin use the subjects experience a 'desirable' consciousness change induced by the drug. This change is characterized by increased emotional distance from external stimuli and internal response, but it is a long way from euphoria" (Zinberg et al. 1978: 19). In a survey of British Columbian addicts (cited in Brecher 1972: 12), seventy-one addicts asked to check their mood after taking heroin gave the following responses: Eight found the heroin experience to be "thrilling" and eleven found it "joyful" or "jolly," while sixty-five reported it "relaxed" them and fifty-three used it to "relieve worry"

Applying labels such as "pleasurable" or "euphoric" to addictive drugs like alcohol, barbiturates, and narcotics seems paradoxical, since as depressants they lessen intensity of sensation. For example, narcotics are antiaphrodisiacs whose use frequently leads to sexual dysfunction. When naive subjects are exposed to narcotics, usually in the hospital, they react with indifference or actually find the experience unpleasant (Beecher 1959; Jaffe and Martin 1980; Kolb 1962; Lasagna et al. 1955; Smith and Beecher 1962). Chein et al. (1964) noted the very special conditions under which addicts found narcotic effects to be pleasurable: "It is . . . not an enjoyment of anything positive at all, and that it should be thought of as a 'high' stands as mute testimony to the utter destitution of the life of the addict with respect to the achievement of positive pleasures and of its repletion with frustration and unresolvable tension" (in Shaffer and Burglass 1981: 99). Alcoholics' drinking does not conform any better to a pleasure model: "The traditional belief that alcoholism is maintained primarily as a function of its rewarding or euphorigenic consequences is not consistent with the clinical data" as "alcoholics become progressively more dysphoric, anxious, agitated and depressed during chronic intoxication" (Mendelson and Mello 1979b: 12–13).

The opposite picture—the rejection of positive drug rewards by those in a position to pursue more lasting satisfactions—is evident in a study of volunteer subjects' reactions to amphetamines (Johanson and Uhlenhuth 1981). The subjects originally reported the drug elevated their moods and preferred it to a placebo. After three successive administrations of the drug over several days, however, the subjects' preference for the amphetamine

disappeared even though they noted the same mood changes from its use. "The positive mood effects, which are usually assumed to be the basis of the reinforcing effect of stimulants, . . . were not sufficient for the maintenance of drug taking, probably because during the period of drug action these subjects were continuing their normal, daily activities." The drug state interfered with the rewards they derived from these activities, and thus, "in their natural habitat these subjects showed by their preference changes that they were uninterested in continuing to savor the mood effects" (Falk 1983: 388).

Chein et al. (1964) noted that when ordinary subjects or patients find narcotics pleasurable they still do not become compulsive drug users and that a percentage of addicts find heroin to be extremely unpleasant at first but nonetheless persist in taking drugs until they became addicted. All these examples make clear that drugs are not inherently rewarding, that their effects depend on the individual's overall experience and setting, and that the choice of returning to a state—even one experienced as positive—depends on the individual's values and perceived alternatives. Reductionist models have no hope of accounting for these complexities in addiction, as illustrated by the most widely deployed of such models, Solomon's (1980) opponent-process view of conditioning.

Solomon's model draws an elaborate connection between the degree of pleasure a given state produces and its subsequent capacity to inspire withdrawal. The model proposes that any stimulus leading to a distinct mood state eventuates in an opposite reaction, or opponent process. This process is simply the homeostatic function of the nervous system, much the same way that presenting a visual stimulus leads to an after-image of a complementary color. The stronger and the greater the number of repetitions of the initial state, the more powerful the opponent reaction and the more rapid its onset after the first stimulus ceases. Eventually, the opponent reaction comes to dominate the process. With narcotics and other powerful mood-arousing involvements such as love, Solomon proposes, an initial positive mood is replaced as the individual's primary motivation for re-experiencing the stimulus by the desire to avoid the negative, or withdrawal state.

Solomon and Corbit (1973, 1974) constructed this model from experimental evidence with laboratory animals. As we have seen, neither the positive feelings it posits from narcotics use nor the traumatic withdrawal it imagines can account for human drug taking. Moreover, the model's mechanistic version of neurological sources of motivation creates a Platonic ideal of pleasure as existing independent of situation, personality, or cultural milieu. The model likewise holds that a person's response to this objective degree of pleasure (or else equally specifiable withdrawal pain) is a predetermined constant. People in fact display all sorts of differences in

how ardently they pursue immediate pleasure or how willing they are to endure discomfort. For example, people vary in their willingness to delay gratification (Mischel 1974). Consider that most people find hot fudge sundaes and devil's food cake to be extremely enjoyable and yet only a very few people eat such foods without restraint. It simply isn't plausible that the main difference between compulsive and normal eaters is that the former enjoy the taste of food more or suffer greater withdrawal agony when not stuffing themselves.

Solomon uses the opponent-process model to explain why some lovers cannot tolerate the briefest of partings. Yet this separation anxiety seems less a measure of depth of feeling and length of attachment than of the desperation and insecurity of a relationship, which Peele and Brodsky (1975) called addictive love. For example, Shakespeare's Romeo and Juliet prefer to die rather than be parted. This state does not result from accumulated intimacies that were eventually replaced by negative sensations, as Solomon's model predicts. Shakespeare's lovers cannot bear to part from the start. At the time when they both commit suicide, they have met only a handful of times, with most of their meetings having been brief and without physical contact. The kinds of relationships that lead to the withdrawal extremes of murder and suicide when the relationship is threatened rarely coincide with notions of ideal love affairs. Such couplings usually involve lovers (or at least one lover) who have histories of excessive devotion and self-destructive affairs and whose feeling that life is otherwise bleak and unrewarding has preceded the addictive relationship (Peele and Brodsky 1975).

Associative Learning in Addiction

Classical conditioning principles suggest the possibilities that settings and stimuli associated with drug use either become reinforcing in themselves or can set off withdrawal and craving for the drug that lead to relapse. The first principle, secondary reinforcement, can explain the importance of ritual in addiction, since actions like self-injection acquire some of the reward value of the narcotics they have been used to administer. Conditioned craving leading to relapse would appear when the addict encountered settings or other stimuli that were previously connected with drug use or withdrawal (O'Brien 1975; S. Siegel 1979; Wikler 1973). For example, Siegel (1983) applied conditioning theory to explain why the Vietnam soldier addicts who most often relapsed after their return home were those who had abused drugs or narcotics before going to Asia (Robins et al. 1974). Only these men would be exposed to familiar drug-taking environments when they returned home that set off the withdrawal that in turn required them to self-administer a narcotic (cf. O'Brien et al. 1980; Wikler 1980).

These ingenious conditioning formulations of human drug use have been inspired by laboratory studies of animals and human addicts (O'Brien 1975; O'Brien et al. 1977; Siegel 1975; Wilker and Pescor 1967). For example, Teasdale (1973) demonstrated that addicts showed greater physical and emotional responses to opiate-related pictures than to neutral ones. However, the conditioned craving and withdrawal such studies uncover are by the evidence minor motivations in human relapse. In the laboratory, Solomon has been able to create negative opponent-process states that last for seconds, minutes, or at most days. O'Brien et al. (1977) and Siegel (1975) have found that responses associated with narcotic injections in humans and rats that can be conditioned to neutral stimuli are extinguished almost immediately when the stimuli are presented on unrewarded trials (that is, without a narcotic).

What is more important, these laboratory findings do not appear relevant to addicted street behavior. O'Brien (1975) reported a case of an addict just out of prison who became nauseated in a neighborhood where he frequently had experienced withdrawal symptoms—a reaction that led him to buy and inject some heroin. This case has been described so often that, in its repetition, it seems a typical occurrence (see Hodgson and Miller 1982: 15; Siegel 1983: 228). Yet it is actually a novelty. McAuliffe and Gordon (1974) reported that "We have interviewed 60 addicts concerning their many relapses, and we could find only one who had ever responded to conditioned withdrawal symptoms by relapsing" (p. 803). In their thorough study of the causes of relapse, Marlatt and Gordon (1980) found heroin addicts rarely reported postaddiction withdrawal to be the reason they relapsed. None of the cigarette smokers or alcoholics Marlatt and Gordon interviewed listed withdrawal symptoms as the cause of their relapse.

Conditioned responses are particularly unlikely to account for relapse, since most former addicts do not relapse to addiction after they use a drug again. Schachter (1982) found that former smokers would smoke at a party but not return to regular smoking. Vaillant (1983) noted that "relatively few men with long periods of abstinence had never taken another drink" (p. 184). Half of the addicted Vietnam soldiers used a narcotic at home, but only a minority became readdicted (Robins et al. 1975). Waldorf's (1983) investigation of heroin addicts who quit on their own found ex-addicts typically injected themselves with heroin after licking the habit to prove to themselves and others that they were no longer hooked. All these data point out that the unconditioned stimulus (actual drug use) is not sufficient provocation for a return to addiction. It is impossible that the weaker conditioned stimuli could provide sufficient motivation.

For Siegel and others who have analyzed the Vietnam remission data in conditioning terms, the crucial variable is simply situational change. All situational changes are equivalent in terms of this model as long as drugs

have been taken in one environment and not the other, since then the new environment does not evoke conditioned withdrawal symptoms. This has prompted Siegel et al. to recommend a fresh setting as the best remedy for addiction. Yet it would certainly seem that other features of this new setting would be at least as important as familiarity for affecting addiction. Rats habituated to morphine in a diverse, social environment refused the drug in the same environment when offered a choice, while caged, isolated rats on the same presentation schedule continued to consume the morphine (Alexander et al. 1978). Zinberg and Robertson (1972) reported that addicts' withdrawal symptoms disappeared in a treatment environment where withdrawal was not accepted, while their withdrawal was exacerbated in other environments, such as prison, where it was expected and tolerated.

The Role of Cognition in Conditioning

Addicts and alcoholics—whether treated or untreated—who achieve remission often do experience important changes in their environments. These changes frequently result, however, from self-initiated attempts to escape the addiction and other life problems. There are also those who modify addictive habits without drastically rearranging their lives. This is especially true for those addicted to less socially disapproved substances like cigarettes but also holds for a distinct minority of former alcoholics and heroin addicts. Modification of the addict's enviornmental stimuli appears in these cases to be an entirely internal, or psychological process. Siegel (1979) recognized this role for cognitive stimuli when he explained why some Vietnam veterans relapsed without returning to old drug haunts. He cited Teasdale (1973) and O'Brien (1975) to indicate men experienced withdrawal and craving when "talking about drugs in group therapy," "seeing pictures of drugs and 'works,'" or just "imaginging themselves injecting drugs in their customary setting" (p. 158).

The conditioned responses that occur with regard to subjective experience and as a result of environmental changes that addicts themselves bring about cast conditioning theories in a whole new light, where these responses seem an adjunct to individual self-control and motivation to change rather than the sources of such change. Moreover, conditioning theories in addiction are limited by their inability to convey the meaning the individual attaches to his or her behavior and environment. As a result, conditioning theories must be made so complex and ad hoc to explain the complexities of human drug taking that they lose the precision and predictive power that are their supposed scientific assets. They seem destined to suffer the same fate as did the U.S. intervention in Vietnam, the event that has prompted so much speculation about the role of conditioning in drug use. In both cases rationales become so cumbersome and counterproduc-

tive in the effort to respond to information from the field that they must collapse of their own weight.

Siegel's utilization of cognitive variables to account for conditioning anomalies observed in heroin use is part of a venerable tradition. The first explicitly cognitive conditioning model in addiction was Lindesmith's (1968, originally published in 1947), which contended that to be addicted the heroin user must be aware that the withdrawal pain he suffers is due to cessation of drug use and that readministering the drug will alleviate this pain. Thus so many nineteenth century narcotic users may have failed to become addicted because they simply didn't know that narcotics were addicting! Lindesmith elaborated how cognitions affect addiction in connection with hospital patients. Patients do realize they are taking a narcotic and understand the drug's effects, but they associate these effects with their illness. When they leave the hospital (or later when their prescription for painkillers runs out) they know any discomfort will be temporary and a necessary part of convalescence and thus they do not become addicted.

We may wonder why Lindesmith reserved the role of cognition in his model for this very limited number of ideas. For example, would not a hospital patient's belief that continued narcotic use was harmful or that other opportunities outweighed the option of giving in to the drug's effects be a part of the decision not to continue using narcotics? Such matters as self-conception, perceived alternatives, and values against drug intoxication and illicit activity would naturally seem to influence the individual's choices. It is not only the decision whether to continue using a drug that cognitions, values, and situational pressures and opportunities determine, however. They also determine how the drug's effects and withdrawal from these effects will be experienced. Contrary to Lindesmith's scheme, people who recover from illnesses almost never acknowledge craving narcotics outside the hospital (Zinberg 1974).

Adaptation Theories

Social Learning and Adaptation

Conventional conditioning models cannot make sense of drug behavior because they circumvent the psychological, environmental, and social nexus of which drug use is a part. One branch of conditioning theory, social-learning theory (Bandura 1977b), has opened itself to the subjective elements of reinforcement. For example, Bandura described how a psychotic who continued his delusional behavior in order to ward off invisible terrors was acting in line with a reinforcement schedule that was efficacious despite its existing solely in the individual's mind. The essential insight that reinfor-

cers gain meaning only from a given human context enables us to understand (1) why different people react differently to the same drugs, (2) how people can modify these reactions through their own efforts, and (3) how people's relationships with their environments determine drug reactions rather than vice versa.

Social-learning theorists have been especially active in alcoholism, where they have analyzed how alcoholics' expectations and beliefs about what alcohol will do for them influence the rewards and behaviors associated with drinking (Marlatt 1978; Wilson 1981). Yet it has also been social-learning theorists who have launched the alcohol-dependence syndrome and who seem to feel subjective interpretation is far less important than the pharmacological effects of alcohol in causing drinking problems (Hodgson et al. 1978, 1979). This lacuna in their theorizing is most noticeable in the inability of modern social-learning theorists to make sense out of cultural variations in drinking styles and experiences (Shaw 1979). Whereas McClelland et al. (1972) offered an experiential bridge between individual and cultural conceptions about alcohol (see chapter 5), behaviorists have regularly rejected this kind of synthesis in favor of direct observations and objective measurements of alcoholic behavior (embodied by Mendelson and Mello 1979b).

In another area of social-learning theory, Leventhal and Cleary (1980) proposed "that the smoker is regulating emotional states and that nicotine levels are being regulated because certain emotional states have been conditioned to them in a variety of settings" (p. 391). In this way they hoped to "provide a mechanism for integrating and sustaining the combination of external stimulus cues, internal stimulus cues, and a variety of reactions including subjective emotional experience . . . with smoking" (p. 393). In other words, any number of levels of factors, from past experience to current setting to idiosyncratic thoughts, can influence the person's associations with smoking and subsequent behavior. In creating a conditioning model as complex as this one in order to account for behavior, however, the authors may have been putting the cart before the horse. Instead of conceiving of cognition and experience as components of conditioning, it seems easier to say that addiction involves cognitive and emotional regulation to which past conditioning contributes. In this view, addiction is an effort by an individual to adapt to internal and external needs, an effort in which a drug's effects (or some other experience) serve a desired function.

Social-Psychological Adaptation

Studies that have questioned users about their reasons for continued drug-taking or that have explored the situations of street users have revealed crucial, self-aware purposes for drug use and a reliance on drug effects as an

effort to adapt to internal needs and external pressures. Theoretical developments based on these investigations have focused on the psychodynamics of drug reliance. Such theories describe drug use in terms of its ability to resolve ego deficiencies or other psychological deficits—brought on, for example, by lack of maternal love (Rado 1933). In recent years theorizing of this sort has become broader: less wedded to specific child-rearing deficits, more accepting of a range of psychological functions for drug use, and including other substances besides narcotics (cf. Greaves 1974; Kaplan and Wieder 1974; Khantzian 1975; Krystal and Raskin 1970; Wurmser 1978).

These approaches developed in response to the clearcut finding that very few of those exposed to a drug, even over extended periods, came to rely on it as a life-organizing principle. What they failed to explain adequately is the great variability of reliance on drugs and addiction in the same individuals over situations and life span. If a given personality structure led to the need for an specific kind of drug, why then did the same people wean themselves from the drug? Why did others with comparable personalities not become wedded to the same substances? What was obvious in the case of narcotic addiction was its strong association with certain social groups and lifestyles (Gay et al. 1973; Rubington 1967). Efforts to incorporate this level of social reality led to higher-order theories that went beyond purely psychological dynamics to combine social and psychological factors in drug use (Ausubel 1961; Chein et al. 1964; McClelland et al. 1972; Winick 1962; Zinberg 1981).

Such social-psychological theories addressed the function of drug use in adolescent and postadolescent life stages as a way of preserving childhood and avoiding adult conflicts (Chein et al. 1964; Winick 1962). They also dealt with the availability of drugs in certain cultures and the predisposing social pressures toward their use (Ausubel 1961; Gay et al. 1973). Finally, they presented the impact of social ritual on the meaning and style of use that a person in a given setting adopted (Becker 1963; Zinberg et al. 1977). What ultimately limited these theories was their lack of a formulation of the nature of addiction. While nearly all of them minimized the role of physiological adjustments in the craving and response to withdrawal that signify addiction (Ausubel 1961; Chein et al. 1964; Zinberg 1984), they provided little in the way of basic mechanisms to account for the dynamics of addiction.

As a result, the social-psychological literature exists in almost total isolation from the pharmacological and learning literature on addiction. Because they do not confront laboratory-based models directly, social-psychological theorists are forced to rely on biological concepts that their own data and ideas contradict (as illustrated by the discussion, in chapter 1, of Zinberg et al. 1978). This exaggerated deference to pharmacological constructs makes these theorists reluctant to incorporate a cultural dimension as a

basic element in addiction or to explore the meaning of nonsubstance addictions—surprisingly so, given that their own emphasis on the socially and psychologically adaptive functions of drugs would seem to apply equally well to other involvements. What may curtail the social and psychological analysis of addiction most is the inappropriate meekness and limited scientific aspirations of those best suited to extend the boundaries of addiction theory in this direction. Such meekness certainly does not characterize modern conditioning and biological theorizing.

The Requirements of a Successful Theory of Addiction

A successful addiction model must synthesize pharmacological, experiential, cultural, situational, and personality components in a fluid and seamless description of addictive motivation. It must account for why a drug is more addictive in one society than another, addictive for one individual and not another, and addictive for the same individual at one time and not another (Peele 1980). The model must make sense out of the essentially similar behavior that takes place with all compulsive involvements. In addition, the model must adequately describe the cycle of increasing yet dysfunctional reliance on an involvement until the involvement overwhelms other reinforcements available to the individual.

Finally, in assaying these already formidable tasks, a satisfactory model must be faithful to lived human experience. Psychodynamic theories of addiction are strongest in their rich explorations of the internal, experiential space of their subject matter. Likewise, disease theories—while seriously misrepresenting the nature and constancy of addictive behavior and feelings—are based on actual human experiences that must be explained. This last requirement may seem the most difficult of all. One may wonder whether models built on social-psychological and experiential dynamics make any sense when confronted with the behavior of laboratory animals or newly born infants.

4
Adult, Infant, and Animal Addiction

Bruce K. Alexander
Stanton Peele
Patricia F. Hadaway
Stanley J. Morse
Archie Brodsky
and Barry L. Beyerstein

The idea that organisms lacking complex cognitions and social environments—namely, caged animals and human infants—become addicted when exposed to narcotics has been a primary argument for the purely physiological genesis of addiction. The data on fetuses born to mothers using narcotics and other drugs and on laboratory animals that are administered such drugs are complicated and conflicting: primarily they show that the appearance of addiction in these cases depends on a range of psychological and situational variables. These facts tend to disprove a basic irreducible concept of biological addiction. This chapter attempts both to formulate a realistic model of the factors that play a role in addiction for organisms other than adult human beings and to make clear just how profound a phenomenon human addiction really is. There is no exact equivalent among animals or newborn babies to either the addiction, or the resistance to it, that appear in a fully developed human being.

The Effect on the Infant of Mother's Drug Use

Infant Narcotic Withdrawal

The idea of the addiction of the fetus to narcotics and the appearance of postpartum withdrawal is an unquestioned fact for the public and most addiction professionals and researchers. The appearance of infant withdrawal has been regularly observed since the 1970s under a very specific set of research conditions. Only women known to be addicts (and who often label themselves as such), whose drug use and lifestyle are clearly aberrant, and who might themselves be undergoing withdrawal in the hospital alert investigators to the possibility of addicted newborns. By definition, con-

trolled narcotics users would be excluded from this group. Once identified, high-risk subjects (mothers and children) are evaluated carefully for any signs of abnormality. Once observed, to what might these symptoms be attributed? Mothers' drug abuse tends to be global and indiscriminate, involving many licit and illicit substances. Moreover, addicts are less aware of and concerned about health maintenance in general. The women whose children are observed are thus likely to be only those whose overall lifestyle is degraded and marked by multiple drug abuse and a lack of regard for health.

Yet even under such conditions, withdrawal rarely constitutes a distinct pathological entity. The popular portrayal of infant addiction is invariably of a severe and life-threatening condition; Cummings (1979) in his presidential address to the American Psychological Association claimed, without citation, that 92 percent of the children born to heroin-addicted mothers manifested severe withdrawal. In fact, in 75 to 90 percent of cases withdrawal is nonexistent or difficult to detect with such mothers (Kron et al. 1975). Ostrea et al. (1975) did not find a single case of convulsions in 198 cases they studied. What is labeled as infant withdrawal is instead a variable syndrome defined as a "generalized disorder characterized by signs and symptoms of central nervous system excitation" (Desmond and Wilson 1975: 113). Typical indicators are undue crying and ineffective feedings followed cyclically by restless periods of sleep.

There is little or no direct evidence for attributing this distress to narcotic withdrawal. It does not vary in occurrence or severity with the heroin dosage intake reported by the mother (Zelson 1975) or the drug level measured in the infant's or mother's urine or in the cord blood (Ostrea et al. 1975). Rather than comprising a pronounced medical entity, "there are difficulties in diagnosing the narcotic withdrawal syndrome in the absence of prior knowledge of maternal addiction" (Kron et al. 1975: 258). Desmond and Wilson (1975) observed the severity of infant narcotic withdrawal to vary with other metabolic disturbances and particularly with low birth weight. Furthermore, the symptoms they found tended to persist or reappear, indicating more permanent damage rather than withdrawal. These investigators saw the problems of the newborn of heroin addicts to include damage from drug impurities and the cumulative effects of their mothers' lifestyles (many of the mothers of these infants were prostitutes, for whom infection is a danger along with polydrug use and other unhealthy habits).

Emotional factors have been shown to play a role in severity of neonatal withdrawal. Davis and Shanks (1975) found that—along with protein malnutrition, neglected health, and self-destructive behavior—addicted mothers' guilt and depression contributed to the problematic behavior of their infants. Mothers in this study were especially distressed by nonnutritive sucking, a major symptom of infant withdrawal. Yet ineffective feed-

ings are frequently reported by nonaddicted mothers and the anxiety and personal problems manifested by the addicted women would be especially likely to produce this problem. Infants are also more likely to be separated from addicted mothers in the hospital. Maternal contact has been shown to have a reassuring and beneficial impact for the baby and to exacerbate behaviors that could be described as withdrawal (Klaus and Kennell 1981). A conventional research design involving blind observation of narcotics- and nonnarcotics-using mothers would thus not only allow most infants of using mothers to pass undetected (as in Kron et al. 1975) but would label as undergoing withdrawal at least some babies of nonnarcotics users (see below).

It is true, for a host of reasons that are difficult to separate, that both narcotics-using mothers and their offspring are likely to experience greater-than-average amounts of postpartum trauma. Coppolillo (1975) suggested an interactive model of what has been labeled withdrawal based on disturbances in addicted mothers' relationships with their newborn. Addicted mothers in this study were unusually likely to be upset by their children and to derive less than ordinary amounts of maternal gratification, creating a cycle of abnormal and nonnurturing behavior. Such a complex model of withdrawn neonate functioning is a far cry from the specific biological addiction syndrome claimed to exist independent of infant (or adult) social and psychological setting. We may even recall that infants were commonly dosed with paregoric and other opium preparations in the nineteenth century in the United States and England (Berridge and Edwards 1981; Courtwright 1982) without parents' being aware of the phenomenon of infant withdrawal. Nonetheless, all public accounts of infant withdrawal depict it in the most monochromatic, lurid light possible, as if to recognize its frequent mildness or its complexity would encourage more pregnant women to take illicit narcotics (see, for a recent account, "Addicted Mothers and Babies" 1984).

Fetal Alcohol Syndrome

Desmond and Wilson's (1975) analysis of neonate withdrawal as a misidentification of more basic damage to the fetus from a variety of causes has proved prescient for later developments in the field. In the mid 1970s and increasingly into the 1980s there was a shift in concern from neonatal narcotic withdrawal to the effects of alcohol on the fetus. The term "fetal alcohol syndrome" (FAS) was applied to abnormalities in offspring of alcoholic women, most of whom had serious alcohol-related health problems (Hanson et al. 1976; Jones and Smith 1973). FAS incorporates a large number of observed deficits in such infants, including increased mortality, birth defects, and smaller size to "failure to thrive, hyperirritability and motor

dysfunction" (Cushner 1981: 202). The syndrome has been conceived from the beginning as involving long-term organic damage, even though reported symptoms are often similar to those attributed to heroin withdrawal. Also from the onset of this research, complications have been noted in separating the factors contributing to the appearance of FAS, particularly because heavy drinking and heavy smoking are strongly correlated (Ouellette et al. 1977).

Research on FAS has advanced to include a more general, multivariate framework where other factors—such as time during the woman's pregnancy when drinking occurred—are taken into account. In addition, earlier dramatic reports about FAS have been replaced by more modulated accounts of the nature of the syndrome. Chernick et al. (1983) called the current definition of FAS inadequate because among heavy drinking mothers (who were typically also heavy smokers), the extreme morphology that had been reported for FAS was infrequent. Wright et al. (1983) found *no* cases of FAS among 903 women even though some were very heavy drinkers, causing the chief investigator to remark that FAS "is a rare disease . . . associated with pathologically heavy drinking" ("Drink/Smoke Combo . . ." 1983). The only difference due to drinking found by these investigators was in birthweight, with moderate drinking (50 to 100 grams of alcohol weekly) being associated with a slightly higher risk of delivering a lightweight baby (Chernick et al. 1983 did not note moderate drinking to be a risk). Greater drinking and smoking increased this likelihood, with mothers who were heavy drinkers and smokers being about four times as likely as moderate drinkers to produce lightweight offspring.

Perhaps the most comprehensive study of fetal alcohol syndrome to date was conducted at Boston City Hospital, employing 1,690 mothers and their infants. Hingson et al. (1982) approached the question by reviewing a range of studies that both have reported the appearance of FAS and have failed to find it. Their own data revealed "neither level of drinking prior to pregnancy nor during pregnancy was significantly related to infant growth measures, congenital abnormality, or features compatible with the fetal alcohol syndrome" (p. 544), although the number of seriously alcoholic mothers in the study was limited. What did predict infant size at birth and other features representing FAS were lower maternal weight gain, maternal illnesses, cigarette smoking, and marijuana use. "The results underline the difficulty in isolating and proclaiming single factors as the cause of abnormal fetal development. . . . In this study the quantitative impact of each behavior was relatively minor, whereas the impact of a lifestyle that combines smoking, drinking, marijuana use, etc., is more marked" (p. 545).

At this point, a fair summary might be that introducing any of a (large) variety of foreign substances during pregnancy is potentially risky, the more so when this reflects an overall lack of concern for health, heavy al-

cohol or licit or illicit drug use, and other problematic maternal behavior. To connect serious and clear-cut abnormalities, either short-lived or more enduring, to use of specific substances by mothers has not been possible. Once again, in the case of fetal alcohol syndrome as with infant narcotic withdrawal, the focus and magnitude of attention directed at a cause of fetal distress or defect has been determined more by external social forces than by the evidence at hand. In the early 1970s, when infant withdrawal was discovered, concern was focused on narcotics epidemics (see chapter 6), while in the late 1970s and the 1980s, coinciding with FAS publicity, we have had a concerted campaign against drinking (see chapter 2). Predictably, in the current climate toward alcohol use, early discoveries of dangers from drinking by pregnant women were built into the recommendation from the U.S. Surgeon General that prospective mothers abstain entirely, a claim from which investigators whose study prompted the recommendation have dissented (Kolata 1981).

The Addicted Animal

The fact that laboratory animals, under the right conditions, will persistently ingest opiates and other drugs has been generalized by many drug commentators to a belief that human beings, along with other mammals, find such drugs inherently rewarding and their use self-perpetuating. This generalization has led to the proposal of metabolic and conditioning theories that support the concept of an inexorable, pharmacological addiction process (see chapter 3). As with other data on drug use and addiction, experimentation with animals yields far more complex results than has been recognized. In particular, research indicates that animals consume opiates only under very limited circumstances. Moreover, research that takes the *setting* of the animal's drug use into account strongly suggests that many of the same environmental and even psychological mechanisms that play a role in human drug use in fact also do so for animals.

Opiates have generally been at the forefront of the attention of animal researchers in the United States. Studies of animal narcotic self-administration were pioneered by Seevers (1936), who showed that morphine-habituated monkeys willingly submitted to continued injections. Subsequently, Nichols et al. (1956) demonstrated that rats could be made to drink morphine solutions in preference to water. In the 1960s, investigators at the University of Michigan developed a technique whereby restrained animals were able to inject themselves with drug infusions through a permanently implanted catheter (see Weeks and Collins 1968, 1979; Woods and Schuster 1971). This led to a profusion of studies of the self-administration of such substances as cocaine, amphetamines, and other CNS stimulants; heroin,

morphine, methadone, and other narcotics; and alcohol, tobacco, and hallucinogenic drugs. Overall, the quantity and regularity of self-dosing were highest for the stimulants but were also high for the narcotics. Tobacco, alcohol, and hallucinogenics were taken less consistently, although this may result from difficulties in administering these substances (Kumar and Stolerman 1977).

Aided by the self-administration apparatus, researchers investigated such pharmacological areas as the effects of physiological states on self-administration rates and different schedules of drug reinforcement. However, the most prominent result from this work has been the idea that drugs (particularly narcotics) are powerfully reinforcing—even irresistible—to the organism with free access to them. This conclusion has regularly been put forward (see Bejerot 1980; Dole 1972; Goldstein 1972, 1976a; Jaffe 1980; McAuliffe and Gordon 1980; Wikler and Pescor 1967), one version of which is as follows (Goldstein 1972: 291–92):

> Extensive studies on self-injection of opiates by monkeys show that any animal, having discovered that pressing a lever injects a narcotic intravenously, will inject itself repeatedly, raise the frequency to maintain drug effects . . . and develop full-blown addiction. It seems, therefore, that becoming addicted requires nothing more than availability of the drug, opportunity for its use, and (in man) willingness to use it.

Such conclusions have provided the major scientific support for popular conceptions about heroin addiction in the United States, including the belief that there is a biological and neurological underpinning for addictive behavior (Peele 1977). The nature of this putative mechanism in addiction—whether a metabolic process, cellular adjustment, or chemical change in the brain—has never been established, as Seevers (1963) made clear. Currently, the endorphins and opiate receptors in the brain are being investigated to find the key to addiction. Pharmacologists express caution and appropriate scientific modesty about this search (Goldstein 1976b), a restraint not apparent in writing by popularizers of work in the neurosciences (Restak 1979).

Biological and neurological theory have had notable difficulty in explaining basic data from animal psychopharmacology studies: for example, the large range of dissimilar chemicals that animals have been found to self-administer chronically. No single physiological mechanism seems likely to be triggered by such a diverse array of substances, each with its individual molecular structure. Moreover, animal researchers and pharmacologists have been forced to create elaborate, abstract conceptions to fit laboratory results. When Wikler and Pescor (1967) found some rats relapsed to morphine use months after having been withdrawn, they hypothesized

that withdrawal symptoms had been conditioned to appear in response to cues associated with the animals' previous drug use (see chapter 3). Keller (1969) described these researchers' hypothesis to be an "arbitrary pronouncement—remembering that they had not demonstrated any biochemical changes in the delayed withdrawal symptoms of their post-addicted rats, but only a behaviorial syndrome." Keller suggested "that these investigators are addicted to the physicalist-pharmacological explanation of anything that involves drugs" (p. 13).

A potentially more important issue for evaluating theories about drug use derived from the observation of laboratory animals is that the animals that are studied are deprived of normal social life, environmental richness, and mobility. The investigation of drug self-injection by animals has taken place for the most part with animals who are encaged and harnessed to an implanted catheter, conditions that may well be painful and that certainly prohibit the normal activity of a healthy animal. Animal researchers like Yanagita (1970) have declared strong reservations about generalizing from behavior under these conditions—in which social inhibitions are absent, drugs are constantly available and require next to no effort to obtain, and the organism is deprived of stimulation and is under constant stress—to the behavior of human beings.

Furthermore, the behavior of these laboratory animals may not generalize *to animals in natural environments.* Animals, even in laboratory environments, do not readily self-administer hallucinogenic drugs (Griffiths et al. 1979). The study of hallucinogen behavior has been extended to animals in the field, where similarly most herbivores do not self-administer the drugs, except episodically (R. Siegel 1979). Yet when placed in sensory isolation chambers for several days, rhesus monkeys were found continually to self-administer the hallucinogen DMT (Siegel and Jarvik 1980). This study indicates that the restrictiveness of the animal's environment is a crucial determinant of its drug-taking behavior. To what extent is this also true of the use of narcotics by animals in the laboratory, a phenomenon on which pharmacologists have built the notion of the inherent addictiveness of narcotics?

Animal Narcotics Use in Rat Park

An ongoing body of research at the Simon Fraser University Drug Addiction Research Laboratory (conducted by Patricia Hadaway, Robert Coambs, Barry Beyerstein, and Bruce Alexander) has addressed the question of how physical and social environment affects opiate use among rats. Rats—along with mice, monkeys, and apes—are the usual subjects in drug experiments. The Simon Fraser experiments utilized Wistar strain albino rats, which are

easy to obtain and are extremely gregarious, curious, and active. Their progenitors, wild Norway rats, are intensely social animals (Lore and Flannelly 1977) whose social responses remain largely intact even after hundreds of generations of laboratory breeding (Grant 1963). The opiate used in the experiments was morphine hydrochloride (MHCI) a salt of morphine manufactured by ICN Canada and used in morphine tonics for oral consumption. Both popular and clinical experience indicate that morphine and heroin are readily interchangeable (Zentner 1979), and Lasagna (1981) has made a clear case that there are no important differences in the relative analgesic efficacy of the two drugs for humans.

The purpose of the Simon Fraser studies was to determine whether and how laboratory housing conditions influenced the animals' consumption of the morphine solution. The hypothesis was that animals in isolated, constrained housing—that typical for the University of Michigan and other laboratories in which animal research has been conducted—would ingest more morphine than animals in more nearly natural surroundings. To test this initial, basic idea, a housing environment was constructed that differed radically from the typical cage and that mimicked the rats' natural environment as much as possible. This laboratory environment was dubbed Rat Park. It was more spacious than a standard cage (about 200 times as large in square footage), was more stimulating (with painted walls and objects rats seem to enjoy such as tin cans strewn about), and contained a rat colony (groups of sixteen to twenty rats of both sexes).

Measuring each rat's consumption of morphine solution is a straightforward matter in a cage. In these experiments, a drinking bottle of the solution was fastened next to the animal's regular water bottle on the side of the cage. Weighing both bottles daily provided a measure of drug solution and of water (or other inert substance) that was consumed. The rats in Rat Park required a more elaborate mechanism to measure individual consumption. Accordingly, a short tunnel was built which allowed one rat at a time access to two drop dispensers. One dispenser contained the drug solution and the other the inert control substance; a device automatically recorded how many times each rat activated each drop dispenser, while a photoelectrically activated camera recorded an identifying dye mark on the back of the animal (see Coambs et al. 1980 for a full description). Raw consumption data were converted into three measures of each rat's daily morphine consumption: grams of morphine solution, mg morphine/kg body weight, and proportion of morphine solution to total fluid consumption.

Morphine solutions are unpleasantly bitter to human taste and also, apparently, to rats, since they reject it with the same signs of distaste as they show towards extremely bitter nonnarcotic solutions. Offered a simple choice between water and morphine solution, rats take only a drop or two of the drug solution and ignore it thereafter. Khavari et al. (1975) found

concentrations of morphine and sucrose that were sweet enough that rats would drink them in preference to water in quantities great enough to produce signs of withdrawal when the solution was removed.

An early Rat Park experiment was designed to measure differences in the consumption of sweetened morphine solution between eighteen individually caged rats (nine of each sex) and eighteen rats (also nine of each sex) living in a Rat Park colony (see Hadaway et al. 1979). In order to discover any differences that the two housing environments produced in attraction to the taste of sugar, an initial phase in the experiment offered the rats a choice between tap water and sugar solution without morphine. The second phase offered rats a choice between water and morphine (no sugar) solution. In five subsequent phases of the experiment, the solution contained both sugar and morphine. The morphine was made increasingly palatable to the rats in each successive phase by either raising the concentration of sugar or lowering the concentration of morphine compound. In a final phase, sugar solution alone was again presented.

The results show clearly that the caged rats ingested more morphine than the animals in Rat Park (see Figure 4–1). There was no housing effect on preference for the plain sugar water in the initial phase, and the Rat Park animals actually drank more of the sugar solution in the last phase. In the first couple of phases in which morphine–sugar solution was used, few of the rats in either environment drank any morphine solution. As the flavor improved, caged rats increased their consumption of morphine dramatically, while those in Rat Park increased theirs by only a small amount. The differences in morphine consumption were large and highly significant in the last three morphine–sugar solution phases. Alexander et al. (1981) replicated this experiment with a second pretest in addition to the one offering rats a choice between water and a sugar solution. This additional phase presented rats with water and a bittersweet quinine–sugar solution that was, to the human palate, almost indistinguishable from one of the morphine–sugar solutions. The purpose of this pretest was to rule out the possibility that the differences in morphine consumption were due to an aversion to the bitterness of the morphine solution. There were no significant housing effects on either pretest in the replication, and the differences in the subsequent morphine phases were about as large as those in the first Rat Park experiment.

Habituating the Animals in Rat Park

Rats in Rat Park were less likely to be lured into drinking a sweetened morphine solution than were caged rats. Would this same difference in susceptibility to narcotic effects also hold for animals that had first been habituated to the drug? In other words, would Rat Park animals ingest less

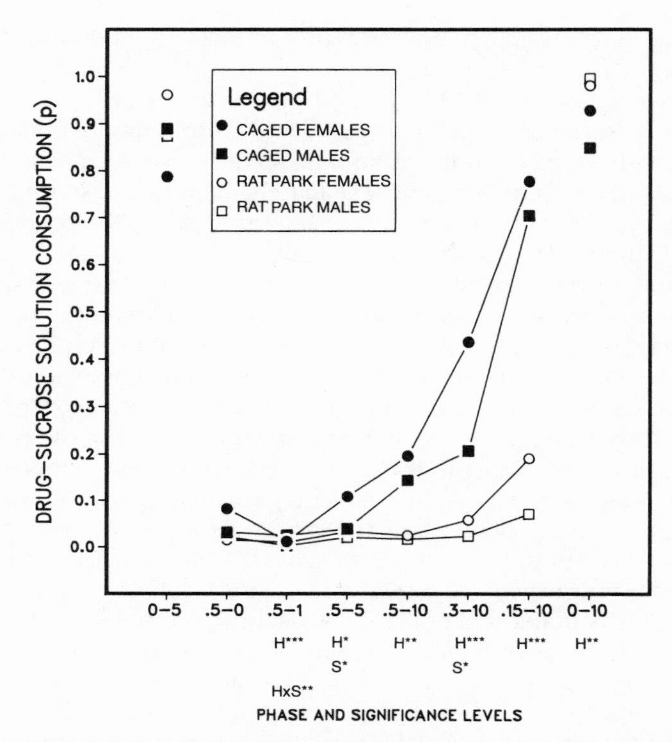

Morphine–sucrose solution consumption as proportion of total fluid consumed. Numbers identifying phases are mg MHCl per ml followed by percentage of sucrose in solution. Significance levels from analyses of variance for each phase use following symbols: H = housing effect, S = sex effect, H × S = housing by sex interaction; * = $p < .05$, ** = $p < .01$, *** = $p < .001$.

Figure 4–1. First Rat Park Experiment

narcotic than caged animals when both groups were being withdrawn from narcotics use?

To test the housing effect under these conditions, Alexander et al. (1978) habituated caged and Rat Park rats to narcotics by making morphine solution (0.5 mg morphine hydrochloride/ml water) their only source of fluid for fifty-three days. A number of prior experiments indicated that the amount of narcotic these animals ingested was more than enough to cause withdrawal symptoms (e.g., Fuentes et al. 1978). Interspersed in this forced consumption phase were four choice days during which the rats in both environments were given access both to water and to morphine solution. At the end of this fifty-seven-day period, in the second phase of the experiment, the rats were put on a training regimen developed by Nichols et al.

(1956) to teach rats that drinking morphine solution would relieve their withdrawal symptoms. The Nichols phase of the experiment consisted of repeated three-day cycles comprising one day of no fluids, one of only morphine solution, and one of only water. This cycle was repeated eight times interspersed with four morphine–water choice days. In the final, abstinence phase of the experiment, all morphine was withdrawn except for two morphine–water choice days, one each at two weeks and five weeks after the Nichols cycle phase.

Again results were highly significant. In all these phases of the experiment, caged rats consumed more morphine; during the Nichols phase, caged rats consumed about eight times as much morphine solution during the four choice days as did Rat Park rats (see figure 4–2). Figure 4–3 examines the changes in morphine consumption that took place during the Nichols cycle. The training regimen apparently achieved the purpose of

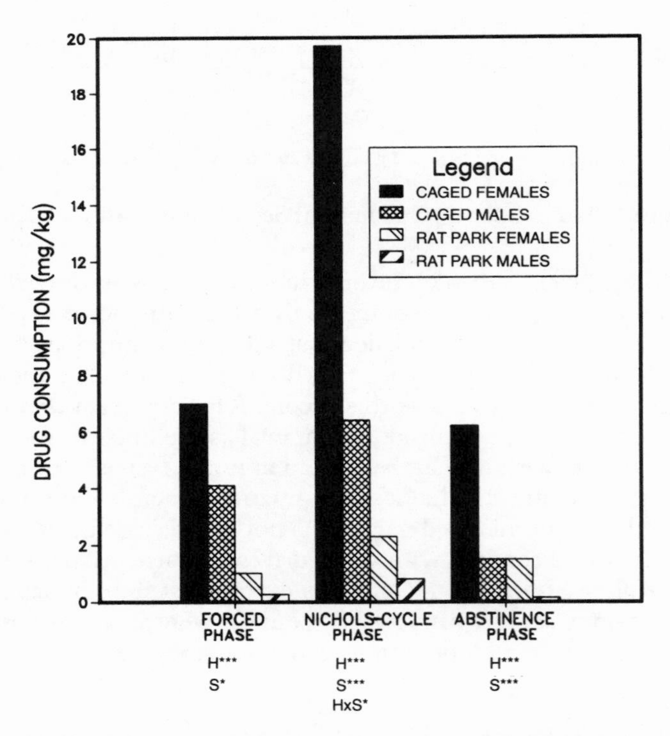

Morphine consumption on choice days in three phases as mg MHCl/kg body weight. Significance levels indicated as in figure 4–1.

Figure 4–2. Second Rat Park (Forced Consumption) Experiment

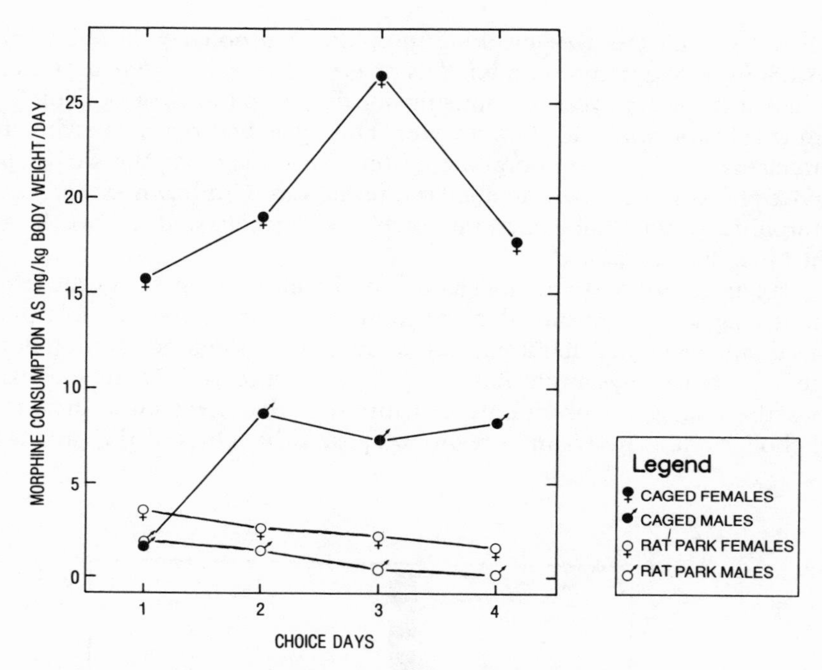

Morphine consumption as mg MHCl/kg body weight/day on choice days during Nichols-cycle phase.

Figure 4–3. Nichols-Cycle Phase of Second Rat Park Experiment

teaching the caged rats to take the drug in response to withdrawal, and they increased their morphine consumption over the four choice days. The Rat Park animals, on the other hand, decreased their consumption slightly over the same period, as if learning about the drug's effects *reduced* their willingness to ingest it. The results of this second Rat Park experiment call into question conventional notions of withdrawal as the impetus to opiate consumption. Just as with human beings, an animal's response to being withdrawn from a narcotic is influenced by situational factors. Withdrawal from even a regularly administered narcotic is not so overwhelming as to eliminate the creature's concern with other drives and attractions. When given reasonable alternatives, animals in this experiment did *not* act as though the motivation to avoid withdrawal discomfort were an all-purpose reinforcer with which ordinary motivations could not compete.

What Factor(s) Cause the Rat Park Housing Effect?

The Rat Park data that have been reviewed so far had an essentially negative purpose: to disprove an ill-founded generalization from previous re-

search on caged animals. The data clearly show that the readiness to consume opiates displayed by caged animals does not hold for rats living in an environment that resembles the animals' natural setting, even after the rats have been habituated to drug use. While these data show that differences in housing conditions can produce a considerable difference in the amount of morphine rats consume, the many distinctions between Rat Park and a standard cage make it impossible to pinpoint the specific factors that affect the animals' morphine intake. This section reports studies that explored these factors in an attempt to cast light on the reasons for continued morphine consumption in animals and in human drug addiction.

Social interaction, which is known to be a powerful factor in animal and human behavior, was the first environmental feature tested for its effect on morphine consumption. A group-size experiment was devised that placed one, two, and four rats in single cages about two-and-a-half times the size of a standard cage. Some of the duos and quads were all female, some all male, and some mixed. The animals were then exposed to the same sequence of solutions used in the first Rat Park experiment and their consumption of morphine measured by weighing the bottles in their cages. The results of this experiment clearly supported the null hypothesis—that group size per se did not affect morphine consumption. Groups of four rats (whatever the sexual composition) ingested about four times as much morphine as one rat and twice as much as two.

Space was taken as the next most obvious environmental feature to be explored. Twelve pens, each five-feet square (making them one-third the size of Rat Park but still more than sixty-five times as large as standard cages), were constructed. Four of the pens contained single males, four single females, and four male-female pairs. A comparison group of twelve rats (six male and six female) were housed in individual cages. Both a quinine solution pretest and posttest were employed along with the presentation of three increasingly sweet morphine solutions. No significant differences were found between the caged and the penned singles in the pretest or posttest or in any of the morphine-intake phases. However, as figure 4–4 shows, the *penned pairs* drank *less* morphine than both the penned and the caged singles. The housing difference for the .3–10 phase was significant for the proportion data.

The last result suggested that it is neither space nor the presence of other rats taken alone but rather the *combination* of space and companionship that brings about the housing effect noted in Rat Park. To test this possibility directly, rats in an experiment with four housing conditions—caged singles (six male and six female caged single rats), caged duos (six caged male–female pairs), penned singles (five male and five female penned single rats), and penned duos (five penned male–female pairs)—were exposed to morphine according to the standard design. The results of this

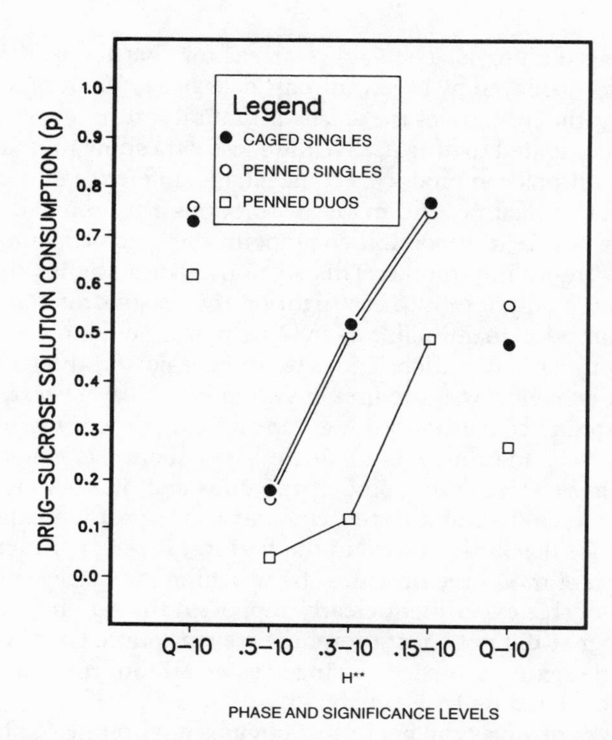

Morphine consumption as proportion of total fluid consumed. All abbreviations same as for figure 4–1, with the addition of Q-10 to represent 0.06 mg quinine sulfate/ml water + 10 percent sucrose.

Figure 4–4. Morphine Consumption by Individual Rats in Cages and Individual and Paired Rats in Pens

study corroborated the important finding in the earlier study: rats that have both space and a companion ingested significantly less morphine in the .3–10 phase than those lacking either or both of these assets (see figure 4–5). In this experiment space alone did seem to make a difference, with both penned singles and duos consuming less morphine than rats in either of the two caged conditions. No such effect was found for the social condition alone. In fact, the caged duos ingested more morphine than the penned *or* caged singles.

Unfortunately, in this case alone among the experiments reported here, there was a significant quinine phase pretest difference in the same direction as the difference in morphine consumption. It is thus possible that differences in morphine consumption among the groups could have resulted from an aversion to bittersweet solutions somehow produced by the differ-

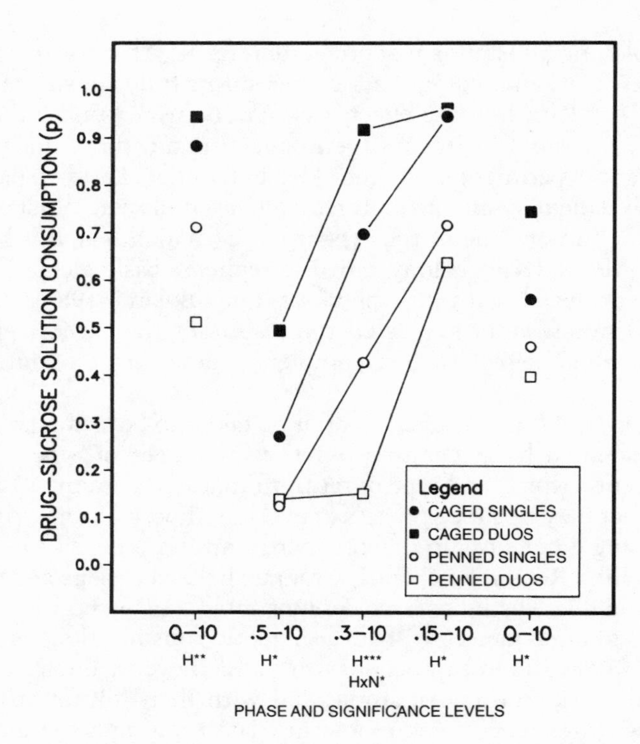

Morphine consumption as proportion of total fluid consumed. H represents housing factor (cage vs. pen) and H × N is interaction between housing and number of rats (one or two).

Figure 4–5. Morphine Consumption by Individual and Paired Rats in Cages and Pens

ent housing conditions. Still, the differences in the .3–10 phase were larger than the quinine pretest differences, even though the bittersweet taste of the quinine– and morphine–sucrose solutions were matched for these phases. An analysis of covariance yielded a significant housing effect for this phase when the initial taste preference was partialled out. Because it is not possible to test all the assumptions about these data required for analysis of covariance (see Ferguson 1981: 370–73), these results can only indicate trends in the data rather than establishing a firm level of significance.

Complications in Rat Park

In order to resolve the possibility of taste preference differences suggested by the experiment combining the housing and social factors, the Simon Fraser Drug Addiction Research Laboratory investigators ran an experi-

ment employing a tasteless narcotic, etonitazene. At the same time, they utilized new computer equipment for measuring fluid consumption in Rat Park. The Rat Park housing effect was *not* confirmed under these conditions, nor with two subsequent experiments utilizing morphine in the original Rat Park experimental designs (Alexander et al. 1978; Hadaway et al. 1979). Subsequently, an alcohol researcher employing Wistar rats announced that a new line of the Wistar strain, which had also been introduced into the Rat Part colony, failed to replicate basic alcohol consumption data achieved with the previous line (Boland 1983). Lastly, the laboratory investigators replicated the results of the earliest experiment (Alexander et al. 1978) with a completely new strain of rats: Sprague Dawleys.

The Rat Park housing effect cannot be taken to be as robust as it originally appeared to be. Separating out the influences of type of narcotic, measurement system, and type of rat from that of environment in producing this effect may be a long process or even an impossible one. At the same time, housing differences in narcotic consumption were also found at the Drug Addiction Research Laboratory for rats housed in pens and cages. The Rat Park and related studies have demonstrated, under specific conditions, that environmental factors will affect narcotic consumption, as Siegel and Jarvik (1980) have found to occur with hallucinogens. Environmental effects in Rat Park and related studies, all with their limitations, must be analyzed with reference to corroborating data from both the Drug Addiction Research Laboratory and other investigators. More important than the specific housing effect in these data may be some overriding results concerning the likelihood of rats consuming narcotics under all conditions.

What Causes Animals to Accept Narcosis?

Not only the rats in Rat Park but the comparison animals in cages failed to consume opiates with the avidity that Goldstein (1972) described or that seems typical for animals studied at the University of Michigan and elsewhere. In the current studies, rats only took a drug when it was presented in a highly sweetened solution and then only irregularly—with high day-to-day variation in consumption. These results suggest a need to reevaluate the extant hypotheses for why caged animals seek narcotic effects.

Relief of stress and pain. The Rat Park and similar data on the impact of isolation and being caged could be explained by the stress that constrained housing causes the animals and that narcotics relieve. Working against this interpretation is the surprising absence of independent evidence that stress or pain induces opiate consumption in rats. In several experiments, Chipkin (1976) found that intermittent electric shocks spread over periods as

long as fourteen days failed to increase methadone consumption in caged rats. In the Drug Addiction Research Laboratory at Simon Fraser, Brunke et al. (1980) found no increase in the oral self-administration of morphine for caged rats that underwent surgical implantation of venous catheters.

Constitutional differences. Panksepp (1980) has presented evidence that brief isolation makes young rats more sensitive to pain. Such sensitivity could be caused by an inability to maintain normal endorphin levels or by other physiological deficits that enhance the utility of the pain relief provided by narcotics. Some support for this idea comes from reports that long-term isolation can increase the effectiveness of morphine for relieving pain (DeFeudis et al. 1976; Kostowski et al. 1977). However, some of the same studies have also shown that long-term isolation does *not* make animals more sensitive to pain (Adler et al. 1975; DeFeudis et al. 1976) and that isolation makes animals *less* sensitive to the analgesic effects of morphine (Katz and Steinberg 1970; Kostowski et al. 1977). The latter data suggest an alternative physiological hypothesis that partially contradicts the first. If morphine has less of an analgesic effect on rats in isolation, then it could be that isolated rats need to consume more morphine than those living with other rats to achieve the same level of pain relief.

Both of these arguments bear an obvious affinity to those that trace human addiction to inherited or acquired endorphin deficiencies (cf. Goldstein 1976b). Both also fit with animal research showing that quality of the early postweaning environment for rats has major effects on the anatomy and physiology of the developing nervous system (cf. Greenough 1975; Horn et al. 1979; Rosensweig 1971), some of which have been related to later drug use (Prescott 1980). To the extent that isolation has its effect through permanent or long-term changes in the animal's nervous system, isolation early in life should be more influential than later isolation in the consumption of morphine. This possibility was explored at the Simon Fraser Laboratory. Thirty-two rats (sixteen of each sex) were divided between individual cages and Rat Park at weaning (age 21 days). At age 65 days, half the rats in each setting were moved to the other, creating four housing conditions: C-C, or caging both early and late; C-RP, or caging early and Rat Park late; RP-C, Rat Park early and caging late; and RP-RP, Rat Park both early and late. At age 80 days the rats began a sequence of choice tests, starting with a sucrose and a quinine–sucrose pretest, proceeding through the usual sequence of morphine–sucrose solutions, and ending with a sucrose posttest.

Figure 4–6 depicts results of this experiment for male rats (data on female rats indicate the same effects, although not with the same degree of statistical significance; see Alexander et al. 1981). No significant pretest or posttest difference appeared. Significant results were found for late housing, with rats housed in cages consuming much more morphine than did rats

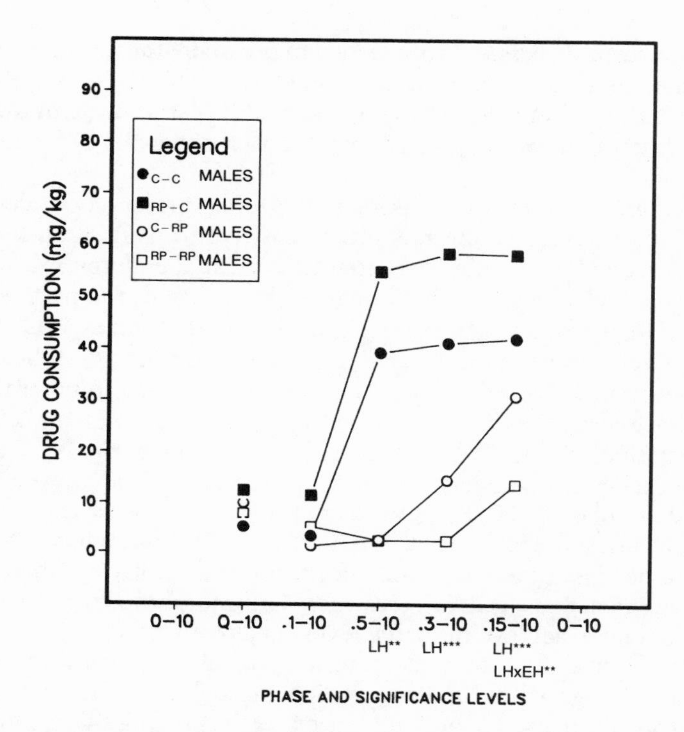

Morphine consumption as mg morphine/kg body weight/day. Additional abbreviations for housing conditions are C for caged and RP for Rat Park and for analysis of variance significance levels are EH for early housing and LH for late housing.

Figure 4–6. Morphine Consumption for Rats Housed Early/Late in Cages and Rat Park

living in Rat Park. Early experience had no consistent effect on the rats in this experiment, although there was a slight tendency for the C-RP rats to consume more morphine than RP-RP rats over all the measures reported in Alexander et al. (1981). These data showed clearly that the Rat Park housing effect is more the result of the environment of the animal at the time it is tested than of its early postweaning experiences and is less attributable to constitutional differences than to situational factors.

Interference with normal activity. The importance of contemporaneous environment for morphine consumption supports the results of the study of penned and caged rats. Both indicate that it is the inhibition of current opportunities for activity that favors the animals' consumption of morphine. The comparison of caged and penned rats alone and together showed that neither space nor companionship taken separately suppressed rats'

morphine consumption as much as both together did. Perhaps this is because rats housed in a spacious environment with others of their species perform many complex social activities that are inherently rewarding and with which the drug's effects interfere. Rat sexual behavior, for example, occurs on the run with the female starting and stopping over several square meters while the male keeps up as best he can. Perhaps the caged duos consumed more morphine than caged singles because putting two rats in a cage restricted their individual activities while not providing enough space for interactive ones. For rats—a colonial species and not a pair-bonding one (Lore and Flannelly 1977)—larger, more populated housing conditions would most closely resemble their natural habitats and might be most effective for inhibiting drug use.

There are other indications that rats learn to avoid morphine because it interferes with complex rodent activity. Even small doses of narcotics significantly reduce sexual behavior (Mumford and Kumar 1979; McIntosh et al. 1980) and social cohesion among rats (Panksepp et al. 1979). Alexander et al. (1978) noted a marked reduction in activity of all sorts among animals forced to drink morphine solution. The case that species-typical behavior is in and of itself reinforcing has been forcefully argued by Glickman and Schiff (1967). Garcia et al. (1974) have meanwhile shown that rats learn to avoid foods or solutions that produce sickness even hours after consumption. Taken together, this information suggests that rats could learn to avoid narcosis when it prevents them from experiencing the rewards brought on by normal activity.

What comes through most strongly in the Rat Park and related studies is how much experimental pressure is required—including heavy sweetening of morphine solutions and forced habituation in addition to deprivational housing—to cause rats regularly to self-administer a narcotic. The fact that rats reject morphine when offered a choice between unsweetened drug solution and water is usually attributed to the bitter taste of the opiate solution. This notion has not born up under testing, however. Huidobro (1964) reported that caged rats whose sense of taste was destroyed (through sectioning their lingual and glossopharyngeal nerves) rejected morphine solutions. Wikler and Pescor (1967) found that naive rats rejected the opiate drug etonitazine even though it was essentially tasteless in the concentration used.

The alternate possibility—that the effects of narcotics themselves are what prevent animals from drinking a morphine solution—was tested in two studies at the Drug Addiction Research Laboratory. In the first of these experiments, rats in cages and in Rat Park were given twenty-four-hour-a-day access to two bittersweet solutions. The bitter taste in one solution came from quinine sulphate and in the other from morphine hydrochloride. The two tasted almost identical to human taste. In this arrangement, rats

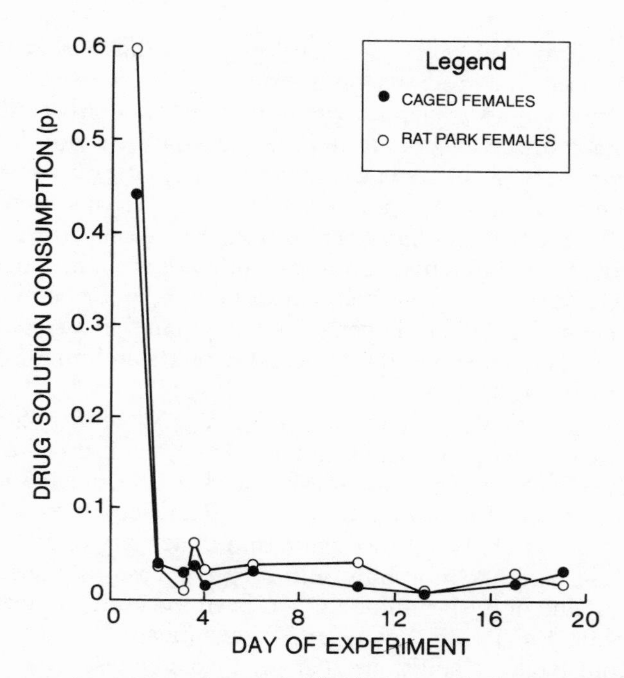

Morphine consumption as proportion of total fluid consumed. Choice was between morphine–sucrose (.5–5) solution and quinine–sulfate solution (.1–5) that were equally bitter to taste. The decline in morphine consumption after the first eight-hour test period was significant at $p < .001$, while differences between housing groups were not significant.

Figure 4–7. Morphine Consumption by Females in Rat Park and in Cages Given Choice of Quinine and Morphine Solutions

did not have to sacrifice palatability in order to obtain a drug effect. The results in figure 4–7 for female rats confirm that the solutions were equally tasty to the animals, with both caged and Rat Park animals drinking about half their total fluid intake as morphine for the first eight hours of the experiment. Then both sets of rats drank very little morphine for the remaining nineteen days (Coambs 1977). Caged males did drink significantly more morphine than Rat Park males for the last ten days of the experiment. In the absence of such a difference between Rat Park and caged females, however, the best overall summary of these results is that rats under both housing conditions will not ingest appreciable amounts of morphine when there is an equally palatable and inert alternative.

In a follow-up experiment, Coambs (1980) gave a choice between sweetened quinine and morphine solutions to caged rats. The quinine con-

centration was increased with the intention of forcing the animal to drink morphine. The initial effect of what appeared to be an unpleasant choice for the animals was that they did not drink at all for the first few days. In a result that did not occur with any other experimental procedure, the rats eventually split into two distinct groups: Roughly half the rats drank mostly the morphine solution, while the other half drank mostly the quinine. On day 15, naltrexone was introduced into both solutions with the effect of neutralizing the action of the morphine solution. Figure 4–8 shows that there was a dramatic jump in morphine consumption at this point. While the rats that had initially preferred the morphine continued to do so, the rats that had preferred the more bitter quinine solution quickly shifted to the morphine *once its psychoactivity had been removed.* The results of this study unambiguously indicated that even caged rats find the psychotropic effects of morphine to be aversive.

The evidence from both these studies seemingly contradicts a body of research that shows laboratory animals will inject themselves with opiates

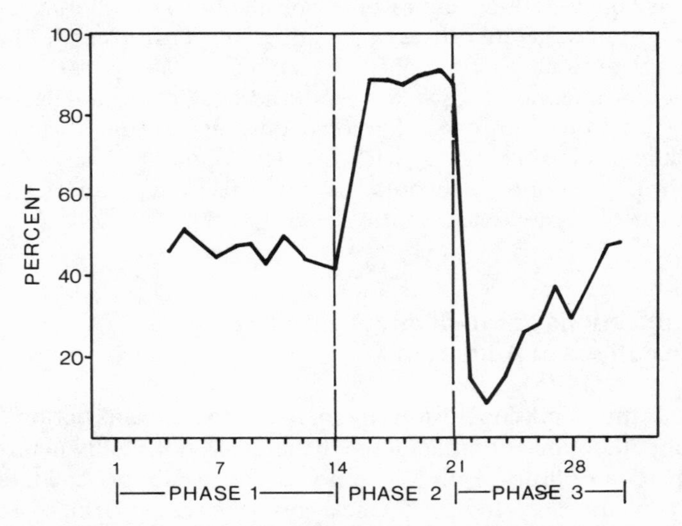

Morphine consumption as proportion of total fluid consumed. In Phase 1, rats chose between .5 mg morphine hydrochloride/ml water + 8 percent sucrose and .2 mg quinine sulfate/ml water + 8 percent sucrose (first three days omitted because very low intake made calculation of proportions unreliable). In Phase 2, 0.1 naltrexone hydrochloride added to both solutions. In Phase 3, the choice was the above morphine and naltrexone solution and a solution of 0.1 mg naltrexone/ml water + 8 percent sucrose.

Figure 4–8. Morphine Consumption by Caged Rats Given Choice of Quinine and Sweetened Morphine Solutions and Quinine and Morphine–Naltrexone Solutions

continuously without added inducements. The differential performance of animals in the morphine solution and the self-injection experiments may highlight the abnormality of the latter setting (Peele 1977; Yanagita 1970). For caged animals implanted with catheters, normal gratifications are curtailed at the same time that animals are able to produce—almost effortlessly—an immediate, reliable infusion of a drug. Yet research has shown that modifying these forces even slightly, as by increasing the amount of bar pressing required to produce an injection of drug, will reduce the doses that animals self-administer (Kumar and Stolerman 1977).

Self-injection research has been built on optimum situations for inducing an organism to ingest narcotics. Rats in experiments employing narcotic solutions, on the other hand, must drink an appreciable volume of fluid to gain a somewhat delayed effect in an environment that permits them a wider range of alternative activities. Under these conditions, which better correspond to those naturally obtaining for the animals, most animals seem to react with the same distaste for narcotics that most humans express in ordinary circumstances (see chapter 3). The same holds for alcohol, which laboratory animals regularly reject in preference to water. Falk (1981) was able to induce rats to consume alcohol and other drugs (such as barbiturates) in large quantities by creating an intermittent feeding schedule that the animals found highly disturbing. As Falk (1983) summarized over a decade's research: "Schedule-induced drug overindulgence remains strictly a function of current induction conditions. Even with a long history of schedule-induced drinking, with the development of physical dependence, termination of the scheduled aspect of feeding produces an immediate fall in alcohol intake to a control level" (p. 389).

The Implications of Infant and Animal Research for Conceptions of Addiction

The most important conclusion to emerge from an examination of animal and infant addiction is that addictive behavior is not rigidly determined by the properties of drugs. Falk (1983) noted the results of schedule-induced alcohol consumption studies: "Once again we have a picture of a reputedly enticing molecule failing to take over behavior in spite of chronic binging" (p. 389). Infants and animals continue to respond to such environmental factors as nurturance and a stimulating environment in the face of narcotic withdrawal pangs. The richness of the organism's repertoire of responses with regard to narcotics and other drugs may enhance our awareness of the complexity of the determinants of the behavior of all mammals and of human beings of all ages, including cognitive, emotional, and experiential complexity that has often gone unnoticed. In particular, the research on

animals and infants is reminiscent of findings about narcotics use by adults (such as the Vietnam War data)—namely, that full-fledged craving for narcotics and abhorrence of withdrawal appear mainly under abnormal conditions. Animals and infants apparently share with the adult human being an urge to experience life normally that outweighs the allure of narcosis.

At the same time, we must be careful to avoid the error of overgeneralization that has bedeviled animal self-injection research. Addiction as we know it is a purely human phenomenon (Peele 1977). This is because addiction entails behavior that gains its meaning only in human social and psychological context (see chapter 1). For example, we decide a person is addicted—as opposed to being a controlled user of a substance—when he or she disregards health, personal well-being, and social propriety in order to continue a behavior. There are no real parallels for this among animals and infants. Another distinction between adult human beings and other organisms is the greater cognitive and situational resources the adult human may counterpoise against addiction: Only an adult would quit an addiction like narcotics or cigarettes or overeating because it violates other values, such as a desire for self-control (see chapter 5). The animal or infant must face withdrawal without the benefit of any such salutary resolve.

On the other hand, adult human experience provides unusual opportunities for addiction to take hold. While Robins et al. (1974) found that most soldier narcotics users and addicts gave up their habits when returning home, a small percentage continued to be addicted. These veterans were more likely to have abused drugs before entering the service. What we see in these men is an enduring disposition—one that transcends situation—to seek narcosis or some other addiction. Peele and Brodsky (1975: 63) attempted to analyze this phenomenon in terms of animal and infant research:

> When we think of the conditions under which animals and infants become addicted, we can better appreciate the situation of the addict. Aside from their relatively simple motivations, monkeys kept in a small cage with an injection apparatus strapped to their backs are deprived of the variety of stimulation their natural environment provides. All they can do is push the lever. Obviously, an infant is also not capable of sampling life's full complexity. Yet these physically or biologically limiting factors are not unlike the psychological constraints the addict lives with.

While a concept of addictive personality that disregards the individual's opportunities, life stage, and personal desires is a limited analytic tool, the *absence* of a conception of personal disposition is also limiting in the analysis of addiction. Animal research can illuminate such a personality construct only indirectly. Falk's (1983) insightful analysis of animal and human excess discerned that drug abuse "depends upon what behavior opportuni-

ties are available in life's situations, and *whether the individual is prepared to exploit these opportunities*" (p. 390, italics added). The reliance on addiction is, in other words, as much an indication of how people experience and react to their environment as it is a result of the particular addicting properties of a substance or of the environment's objective qualities, barring the most abject environmental impoverishment.

While situations predispose people to addiction, individuals also show greater or lesser susceptibility to it. At one extreme, people who cannot generate productive or rewarding experiences are at a disadvantage in avoiding addiction. Lower achievement values (or greater fear of failure), fewer interests, an inability to structure one's time, less concern for health or other moderating values, and an unfamiliarity with functional coping techniques are elements in the addictive equation. Animal research reminds us that the sources of addiction lie in the ways human beings are denied—or deny themselves—the opportunities for rewarding experiences that characterize life for our species. As Peele and Brodsky (1975) evoked this idea, "The difference between not being addicted and being addicted is the difference between seeing the world as your arena and seeing the world as your prison" (p. 64)—or is it cage? It is striking that animal research in laboratories, even that conducted with a reductionist bent of mind, affirms this complex truth about addiction.

5
Addiction to an Experience

People become addicted to experiences. The addictive experience is the totality of effect produced by an involvement; it stems from pharmacological and physiological sources but takes its ultimate form from cultural and individual constructions of experience. The most recognizable form of addiction is an extreme, dysfunctional attachment to an experience that is acutely harmful to a person, but that is an essential part of the person's ecology and that the person cannot relinquish. This state is the result of a dynamic social-learning process in which the person finds an experience rewarding because it ameliorates urgently felt needs, while in the long run it damages the person's capacity to cope and ability to generate stable sources of environmental gratification.

Because addiction is finally a human phenomenon, it engages every aspect of a person's functioning, starting with the rewards (as interpreted by the individual) that an involvement provides and the individual's need for these rewards. The motivation to pursue the involvement, as compared with other alternatives, is a function of an additional layer of social, situational, and personality variables. All of these elements are in flux as the individual grows up, changes environments, develops more mature coping mechanisms, loses and gains new opportunities for satisfaction, and is supported or undermined in forming new outlooks and self-conceptions. There are indeterminate elements—for example, those activated by the person's value commitments—affecting whether the person will continue to return to an experience that is progressively more damaging to the rest of the person's life. Even after the person has developed an addictive attachment, he or she can suddenly (as well as gradually) rearrange the values that maintain the addiction. This process is the remarkable one of maturing out, or natural remission in addiction.

Elements of the Addictive Experience

Addictive experiences are not random; people become addicted to experiences that have clear-cut and specifiable elements. First and foremost, ad-

dictive experiences are potent modifiers of mood and sensation, in part because of their direct pharmacological action or physical impact and in part because of their learned and symbolic significance. In the United States, for example, both heroin and one-to-one love relationships have extreme cultural weight placed upon what are inherently affecting experiences (Peele and Brodsky 1975). The centrality of experiential effects in addiction makes clear why and how nondrug involvements become addictive; experiential definitions of addiction encompass all those powerful involvements noted as addictive. Falk et al. (1983) described the commonalities among the objects of excessive involvement: "Drugs, foods, gambling, and aggressive episodes all have *prompt effects on the person or upon their immediate environment.* The preferred drugs of abuse are typically those with a rapid onset of effect. Gamblers prefer fast 'action,' that is, a high rate of play with an immediacy of consequence for each wager" (p. 92; italics in original).

In addition to explaining the prevalence of nondrug addictions, the notion that addiction takes place with regard to an experience does away once and for all with such thoroughly debunked misconceptions as that addiction is maintained by the desire for pleasure or the avoidance of withdrawal (see chapter 3). Rather, an addictive experience is rewarding because it provides gratifications that the addict acknowledges are inferior to genuinely pleasurable and satisfying involvements; withdrawal is, in this context, better described as the absence of either such primary gratification or the ameliorative, substitute gratification sought from the addictive involvement. Consider Robbins and Joseph's (1982, cited in Sachs and Pargman 1984: 235) description of the kind of withdrawal observed in runners:

> Among runners for whom the activity serves to modify dysphoric mood states of psychophysiological distress, return of distress once the effects of the run have decreased may be misunderstood as symptoms of physiological withdrawal. In this instance, withdrawal may not be the pain associated with the body adjusting to the physiological changes of nonrunning, but a reexperience of the pain felt *before* the physiological changes of running.

If theorists could resist reducing self-destructive running or other, similar behavior to neurological terms or contrasting it with mythical visions of drug addiction, such compulsive involvements would shed essential light on the nature of addiction. Both the analysis of such involvements and what they highlight in the effects of drug involvements focus attention on the crucial matter of addiction: namely, what about drug and other potent experiences is attractive to people predisposed by personality and situation to addiction, and what additional elements besides their power characterize addictive experiences?

The Diminution of Pain, Tension, and Awareness

Although addiction has parallels to everyday, ordinary experiences, a model of addiction must explain the clinical extremities of the behavior of those who devote their lives—and sometimes destroy themselves—in the pursuit of an addiction. These people experience the addiction as being necessary for their continued existence. The most powerful descriptions of this outlook come from interviews with narcotics addicts. Zinberg et al. (1978) revealed that their subjects underwent a change in consciousness that was "characterized by increased emotional distance from external stimuli and internal response, but it is a long way from euphoria." The desire for this consciousness change "had little to do with warding off withdrawal sickness" and did not "stem from a wish to feel normal." For these addicts, "the ordinary, rational, self-aware state was an uncomfortable one" (p. 19). In Peele and Brodsky's (1975) formulation, "opiates are desired because they bring welcome relief from other sensations and feelings which the addict finds unpleasant," including a "distasteful consciousness of . . . life" (pp. 51, 61).

The erasure of sensation and of awareness that mark the heroin experience are a result of that drug's depressant action on the central nervous system—a characteristic of all drugs used for analgesic, or pain-relief, purposes. This recalls a peculiar anomaly in twentieth-century pharmacologia: the search for a nonaddictive analgesic (Eddy and May 1973; Peele 1977, 1978, 1979). Beginning with the introduction of heroin in 1898, new pharmacological discoveries have regularly been promoted as offering potent pain relief that will not create addiction. A substance with these combined qualities has yet to be identified, however. The history of sedatives is also typified by initial optimism about a new drug's usefulness, followed by increasing reports of abuse and eventual classification of the drug as being addictive or incurring physical dependence (Kales et al. 1974; Solomon et al. 1979). Having pain, anxiety, or other negative emotional states relieved through a loss of consciousness or a heightened threshold of sensation is a primary component of addictive experience; for this reason, all effective pain relievers will inevitably be addicting for some people.

That pain and tension reduction are essential functions of addictive chemical experiences is challenged by the appearance of addiction to stimulant drugs such as cocaine, amphetamines, nicotine, and caffeine. Research with smoking has been instructive in this regard. Nesbitt (1972), Gilbert (1979), and others have noted a paradoxical tranquilizing component to tobacco use. That is, while nicotine is a stimulant, habitual smokers report that the drug relaxes them and relieves tension. Apparently, the increased activity in the nervous and circulatory systems of smokers lessens their sensitivity to outside stimuli. In this way habitual drug stimulation inures them to events that they otherwise find anxiety-producing; as a

result, smokers smoke more when tense (Leventhal and Cleary 1980). The same kind of paradoxical tension relief is apparent in the excitatory atmosphere surrounding gambling (Boyd 1976).

Findings about the relief of tension through drinking alcohol have been complex. Alcohol is a depressant drug; all levels of drinkers cite alcohol's relaxing quality as a motivation for drinking. McClelland et al. (1972) found only heavy alcohol consumption actually reduced tension. Selzen and his colleagues (1977) found alcoholics—compared with both drunken drivers and ordinary populations—were the most likely to drink for tension relief. Several major experimental studies, on the other hand, have failed to detect any tension reduction from heavy drinking (Cappell and Herman 1972; Marlatt 1976). What research has consistently shown is that alcoholics drink in the *expectation* of reducing tensions, even though—as their drinking proceeds—they do not experience this effect and instead become even more tense (Mello and Mendelson 1978; Stockwell et al. 1982). This paradoxical component to addictive drinking—that it intensifies negative sensations that drinking is sought to relieve—is a crucial component in addiction (see the section of *The Addiction Cycle* below).

Bruch (1973) proposed that eating was a tranquilizer for the obese, who had learned to rely on food as a form of emotional reassurance due to childhood feeding patterns. The systematic research spawned by the internal–external model of obesity originally rejected the idea that overeating was a response to negative emotions (Schachter 1968). However, Schachter and Rodin (1974) discovered the obese were hyperresponsive to emotional stimuli and ate more when afraid or uncomfortable. Herman and Polivy (1975) found overweight people ate more when depressed or anxious because, these researchers felt, the obese are usually trying to diet and emotional distress overcomes their eating restraint. Slochower (1983) has found this to be an incomplete explanation of overeating by the obese. She showed in several laboratory studies that obese subjects ate in response to anxiety (although only when they could not affect the source of their anxiety directly) and that eating *did* reduce their anxiety, at least temporarily.

Social-learning models propose that addicts learn from past experience and social conditioning to anticipate that alcohol and other drugs solve specific dilemmas about which they are concerned. In other words, highly charged emotional states or settings evoke the addictive behavior in response. In Tokar et al. (1973), alcoholics reported that they went to bars or drank when they were depressed, anxious, or angry but that they pursued other activities when feeling comfortable. Leventhal and Cleary (1980) suggested that smokers learn to rely on nicotine's pharmacological effects as a way of coping with negative feelings. Zinberg (1984) noted that addicts were distinguished from controlled users of heroin in that addicts used the

drug to escape depression and intolerable conditions, while controlled users took the drug for diversion and entertainment. Similarly, Russell and Bond (1980) found that alcoholic subjects more often believed drinking would compensate for unpleasant feelings, while most normal college students believed that alcohol magnified existing feelings. Beckman (1978) reported that alcoholics of both sexes drank more when tense or depressed or when feeling powerless, inadequate, or out of control.

An Enhanced Sense of Control, Power, and Self-Esteem

An overall rubric for the variety of functions drug experiences serve in addiction is that they offer addicts control over areas of behavior or emotions that they otherwise feel unable to cope with. Power and control are frequent images offered by cocaine users to describe the effects of the drug (Stone et al. 1984). Power and aggressiveness have been strongly implicated in the nexus of emotions, expectations, and pharmacological effects surrounding drinking by men. Lang et al. (1975) found that the belief by men that they had drunk alcohol—whether or not they had—led to increased aggressiveness. McClelland and his co-workers (1972) explored the inner experiences connected with drinking among college students and blue-collar drinkers. For the college students, McClelland et al. found that men with a high need for power but little opportunity to exercise power developed extravagant fantasies of personal domination when intoxicated. Heavy drinkers among the blue-collar sample expressed similar images when drinking, which the researchers termed fantasies of personalized power. Brown et al. (1980) discovered that the heavier drinkers in their study expected greater enhancement of their aggressiveness and their sexual responsiveness than did lighter drinkers.

There was a gender distinction in Brown et al.'s (1980) findings for those at all levels of drinking: Women were motivated by expectations of generally positive social experiences from drinking, while men's drinking expectations centered around sexual arousal and potential aggressive behavior. Differences have consistently been uncovered between male and female drinking. Unlike the McClelland et al. model of male drinking, Wilsnak (1976) found that women drank to allay their anxieties about their femininity rather than to induce feelings of power. While males who believe they have drunk alcohol become more sexually aroused regardless of having actually consumed alcohol (particularly if they are guilty about and repress sexual feelings, Lang et al. 1980), women's sexual responses are diminished by actual alcohol consumption. Yet women also associate sexual arousal with the effects of alcohol (Wilson and Lawson 1978). It seems that men

and women act out reciprocal sex roles when drinking, where men become more desirous and sexually aggressive while women, although less sexually motivated, become more accommodating sexually (Wilson 1981). Burnett (1979) maintained, based on clinical experience, that alcoholic women use the drug to assist them in fulfilling a hyperfeminine role just as males rely on alcohol to produce stereotypical feelings of machismo.

A theme that unifies the drinking experiences of men and women is that alcohol enables both sexes to feel more adequate to their sex roles. That is, while gender-typical behavior varies between men and women, both sexes rely on alcohol to enhance self-esteem by making them feel closer to an ideal sex type. McGuire et al. (1966: 25) summarized the effects male alcoholics expected from drinking and how these related to subjects' self-esteem:

> The chronic alcoholic subjects expected transformations in their relationships and feelings when they became intoxicated. They believed they would become "masculine," "admired by women," more sociable, and better able to carry out tasks, and that they would have a better estimate of themselves, feel less "anxious," and become more "integrated" as individuals. No similar expectations or beliefs were noted in the nonalcoholic subjects.

Cocaine addicts frequently report sexual mastery to be a primary motivation for drug use (Stone et al. 1984), and heroin addicts have been noted to use the drug to remedy feelings of personal inadequacy (Krystal and Raskin 1970; Wurmser 1978) and specific sexual dysfunctions, such as premature ejaculation (Khantzian et al. 1974).

When asked to describe their normal, ideal, and drugged selves on an adjective checklist, heroin addicts rated their drugged selves closer to their ideal than they rated their normal selves, particularly on a dominance dimension (Teasdale 1972). Chemicals may be particularly suited for fulfilling an ego-boosting function through their success in supressing the negative self-attributions with which addicts are ordinarily weighed down. Hull and Young (1983) have proposed such a model for the effects of alcohol. These researchers found that alcohol reduced self-awareness for all drinkers and that alcoholics and those predisposed to alcoholism were particularly sensitive to this result of drinking. Alcoholics were more likely to return to drinking following treatment if they encountered situations that damaged their self-esteem. In a very different area, Robbins and Joseph (1982) found that running addicts—unlike other frequent runners—believed the activity was a sign of their mastery and used running as a "regular experience that acts to reinforce one's perception of competence and self-worth" (cited in Sachs and Pargman, 1984: 235). Slochower (1983) found overeating by the obese to be related to periods of self-doubt and low self-esteem.

Simplification, Predictability, and Immediacy of Experience

That alcoholics anticipate they will be better at handling life when drinking (McGuire et al. 1966) suggests the alcohol experience is valued for making the world appear to be a more manageable place. Zismer and Holloway (1984) validated a measure of alcohol reinforcement that identified five factors distinguishing between treated alcohol abusers and a general population of drinkers. Along with the familiar dimensions of self-confidence, social adequacy, and sociability, the instrument labeled factors of cognitive control (sample item: "alcohol makes thoughts flow better") and reduction of complexity ("life is easier to figure out after a few drinks" and "people are honest only when they drink"). This cognitive focusing and simplification is independent of any other psychological goals addicts seek to achieve and stands as a separate dimension of addictive experience.

The importance of ritual in addiction—for example, heroin addicts' rejection of noninjectable substitutes for heroin or other departures from their addictive routines (Solomon 1977) and their acceptance of nonnarcotic injections in place of heroin (Light and Torrance 1929)—also reflects the value addicts place on the simplification of experience. The repetition of a highly focused activity is rewarding for addicts in itself. Beyond the specific effects powerful psychoactive substances and other mood-altering involvements offer, they attract people because of their immediacy and predictability, or what Falk et al. (1983) termed their "ritualized saliency" (p. 92). They enable addicts to bypass the ordinary efforts required to bring about a desired state, thus eliminating the anxiety such taxing and uncertain real-world activities cause addicts.

The Range of Addictive Objects and Its Consequences

That addiction takes place with a range of objects, including quite common activities, drives home that no involvement or object is inherently addictive. Rather, people become addicted to a given involvement due to a combination of social and cultural, situational, personality, and developmental factors; these factors identify the topics of the following sections. Addiction can be understood only as a multifactorial phenomenon: It takes place along a continuum, in degrees, and is not limited to a single object. Unless we measure the range of addictive possibilities in a person's life, we cannot evaluate the degree to which the person is addicted (Peele 1983c). Switching from heroin to alcohol or methadone or from alcohol to compulsive eating or running or from any of these things to compulsive group involvements may mark an improvement in a person's life (or it may not). However, focusing on any one such involvement will not tell us to what extent the person is addicted.

The criteria that establish if an individual is addicted must be independent of type of involvement and must instead focus on the involvement's harmfulness to the individual, its limiting of other sources of gratification, the perception by the individual that the involvement is essential to his or her functioning, and the upset to the person's overall social, psychological, and physical system from deprivation of the involvement (see Peele 1981a; Peele and Brodsky 1975). The combination of these criteria eliminates from consideration both trivial activities, such as hair brushing, and activities that are functionally necessary to existence but that do not normally interfere with life, such as breathing and drinking water. Rejecting the idea that we can look to one activity, object, or set of involvements to discover addictions raises two questions: What causes a given individual to become addicted, and to which involvement or object will the person become addicted? The following sections address these fundamental issues in addiction.

Susceptibility to Addiction and the Choice of Addictive Object: Social and Cultural Factors

Social Class

Social class has little relationship to *initiation* of drug or alcohol use (Jessor and Jessor 1977; Kandel et al. 1978). However, social class is strongly related to problem drinking (Cahalan and Room 1974), to overweight (Garn, Bailey, and Higgins 1980), and to health behaviors in general (Becker 1974). Some of the social-class differences that have been uncovered are massive; in Stunkard et al. (1972) lower-class girls were obese nine times as often as girls from upper-class homes. What complicates relationships between socioeconomic status (SES) and drug behavior is that lower-SES groups are more likely both to be abstinent (in the case of alcohol) and to show high levels of treated alcoholism (Armor et al. 1978). While lower-SES groups may insist on avoiding drugs and alcohol altogether, they inspire less commitment to health as a general positive value (Becker 1974). For example, the value placed on weight control is primarily an upper-middle-class one, and immigrant groups show reduced weight levels as they adopt middle-class value orientations (Goldblatt et al. 1965). Alcohol intoxication also conflicts with the more stringent middle-class emphasis on sobriety.

It has become fashionable to deny that lower-SES groups differ from higher-SES groups in anything but money and what it can buy. Investigators who focus on social and political forces maintain that greater incidences of self-destructive or unhealthy behavior are simply the results of poverty, enforced repression, and perhaps resulting self-hate (cf. Lewontin et al. 1984;

Pelton 1981). From the other direction, disease and biological determinists like Vaillant (1983) deny that alcoholism can be socially caused, despite Vaillant's finding that his lower-class subjects were more than three times as likely to be alcoholic as those in his middle-class college sample. Social-class differences in addiction nonetheless appear to be persistent and substantial and to be based in differences in attitudes as well as behavior. Whether these differences mean that some groups are less susceptible to addiction overall remains cloudy, however. The broadening of an awareness of the forms of addiction may indicate that higher-SES addictions simply occur in different guises. For example, Yates et al. (1983) found anorexics (who were all women in this study) and compulsive runners (who were usually men) came from uniformly middle-class backgrounds. Subjects were preoccupied with their appearance and health, which in these extreme cases led to behavior that contributed to the physical deterioration subjects dreaded.

Peer and Parental Influence

Cahalan and Room (1974) found that social drinking context was more important than demographic factors in predicting drinking problems. That is, who one drinks with determines drinking problems more than one's social background. The study of adolescent drug and alcohol use has identified important strands of both peer and parental influence on the initiation of marijuana, alcohol, and other illicit drug use (Jessor and Jessor 1977; Kandel et al. 1978), as well as smoking (Williams 1971). Different constellations were apparent for each type of drug use: Peer influence was most important for initiation of marijuana use, somewhat less important for drinking, and least important for other illicit drug use, where parent–child closeness was the major determining factor (Kandel et al. 1978). Parents' influence was felt both through their modeling of alcohol (and cigarette) use and other values they conveyed. The connection between peer group influence and drug taking combined equally the shaping of attitudes and behaviors by the peer group with the seeking out by adolescents of peers who shared already existing attitudes (Kandel 1978).

Cahalan and Room's findings indicated that more than the initiation of drinking, actual *patterns* of drinking were determined by the social context. Such social drinking influences have been studied over a range of contexts (Harford and Gaines 1982). Peer social influence has an even larger role to play in the case of illicit substances, where parents and other social figures do not ordinarily provide models of behavior. Becker's (1953) work is a landmark in the description of social learning and drug effects. In his study of marijuana use, Becker found novices were instructed by experienced users not only how to notice and interpret the drug's effects, but why

these effects were positive ones. Jacobson and Zinberg (1975) found that groups that fostered controlled use of narcotics were typified by values encouraging moderate use; the maintenance of outside professional, scholastic, and social interests and connections; and rules limiting drug use to certain occasions and specific settings.

Culture and Ethnicity

Cultural outlooks on the appropriate use and the corrupting influence of a substance affect its addictive potential. In cultures where use of a substance is comfortable, familiar, and socially regulated both as to style of use and appropriate time and place for such use, addiction is less likely and may be practically unknown. Addiction is prevalent, however, when a substance is seen culturewide as both an effective mood modifier and as dangerous and difficult to control. These societal variables act on the inner experience produced by a substance and the individual's sense of his ability to control this experience. Chapter 2 described the historical evolution of views of alcohol in this country and the implications these have had for approaches to and conceptions of alcoholism, as opposed to the ideas about narcotic addiction that have grown up in this country and the Western world generally (see chapter 1). Historically, within the United States, narcotics and alcohol have exchanged places more than once as embodiments of chemical enslavement.

Within these larger cultural patterns dwell substantial group differences, particularly in attitudes toward alcohol. Ethnic patterns of drinking are robust, even for groups that have been otherwise assimilated into mainstream American values (Greeley et al. 1980). This suggests that the stylistic aspects of socialization into drinking practices—such as the introduction of children to mild spirits in ritual and family contexts (as discussed in chapter 2)—may not be as important as more basic views that are communicated to the child about what alcohol does to the individual. The kinds of mood-modifying and spiritual efficacy that are a part of addictive alcohol experiences can underlie cultural and parental socialization of drinking practices (Christiansen and Goldman 1983; Zucker 1976). Moderate versus excessive drinking practices may then be more the result than the cause of attitudes toward alcohol. Attitudes about alcohol can also be part of a larger perspective toward experience. For example, some have connected Irish intemperance to an Irish ethos that is at once mystical and tragic (cf. Bales 1946), while Jewish sobriety is seen to stem from Jews' traditional dedication to rationality and self-control (Glazer 1952; Keller 1970). The opposite poles of Eskimo and Indian drinking, on the one hand, and Chinese and Japanese drinking, on the other, exist within larger value contexts. The

Chinese and Japanese in the United States have embraced achievement—a value with which alcohol intoxication is incompatible—while Eskimos and Indians do not measure high in achievement. Observers have noted instead that Eskimos simply place a different value on the sobriety and moderation that limit alcohol intoxication for other groups (cf. Klausner et al. 1980).

MacAndrew and Edgerton (1969) painstakingly analyzed historical data to show that American Indians were *not* intrinsically debauched drinkers but that white traders encouraged the development of rampant alcoholism among Indian groups. Mangin (1957) found universal drinking but few signs of drinking pathology among the Andean Indians, who had strong ceremonial drinking customs. Mohatt's (1972) fascinating analysis of the role of alcohol in the Teton Sioux culture traced alcoholism in this tribe to the destruction by whites of the traditional means Indians had used to achieve adulthood and a sense of masculine competence. Before the advent of whites, the brave became an adult through displays of courage and underwent a mystical transformation brought on by fasting and prayer in an isolated setting. As the opportunities for exercising personal competence and undergoing psychic journeys were reduced and denigrated by the intrusion of whites, alcohol—which produced similar kinds of experiences—became a debilitating replacement source of fantasy and male sense of self. McClelland et al. (1972) analyzed this as a typical instance of cultural sources of heavy drinking. They found in societies that valued the demonstration of male power, but that made the achievement of such power difficult, drinking was heavier and was associated with antisocial aggression.

Bales (1946) provided a general analysis of the relation between problem drinking and cultural dilemmas such as the one McClelland et al. described in the case of male power. Bales saw three general cultural factors leading to alcoholism: (1) "the degree to which the culture operates to bring about acute needs for adjustment, or inner tensions, in its members"—whether connected to sex, guilt, aggression, and so on; (2) whether cultural attitudes toward alcohol suggest drinking "as a means of relieving . . . inner tensions"; and (3) "the degree to which the culture provides suitable substitute means of satisfaction" (p. 482). MacAndrew and Edgerton (1969), in their classic work *Drunken Comportment,* have provided the most detailed survey of the behaviors and feelings that result from imbibing alcohol. Cultures vary tremendously in the extent to which alcohol leads to aggressive and other socially disruptive behavior. MacAndrew and Edgerton further noted that the cultures in which such drinking appears see drinking as a time out from ordinary societal standards and as offering an excuse for antisocial behavior that otherwise is not tolerated. This is in sharp distinction to the moderate drinking of Jews, Italians, Chinese, et al., who disapprove strongly of drinking that leads to antisocial behavior.

These moderate-drinking cultures do not seem to have a category for loss of control of drinking. Paradoxically, those cultures and groups most fearful that substance use will become uncontrolled are those that display the highest incidence of abuse of the substance. It was among Irish subjects—those who expressed the most pronounced views of alcohol's good and evil qualities—that Vaillant (1983) discovered by far the largest amount of alcohol dependence. Compared with other ethnic groups, it was also Irish subjects in the study who were most likely to respond to drinking problems by abstaining entirely, while other ethnics were more likely simply to cut back their drinking. This perspective on alcohol's effects is similar to cultural views of other potent drugs of abuse, like the opiates. All such substances have been "deemed capable of tempting, possessing, corrupting, and destroying persons without regard to the prior conduct or condition of those persons" (Blum 1969: 327).

Such views are not inherent to a drug or fixed in a given culture, as Blum made clear in tracing the development of opium as anathema in China in the eighteenth century, despite the drug's long historical presence as an indigenous substance in Asia. Berridge and Edwards (1981) described a similar evolution of views of opiates in nineteenth-century Britain, one that led to the modern definition of addiction as an uncontrollable physical urge for a drug. Levine's (1978) analysis carefully detailed how, in a relatively short time, large parts of American society came to conceive of alcoholism as an uncontrollable disease commonly induced by regular drinking. Nineteenth-century temperance adherents were unable to discover (despite assiduous efforts) historical first-person accounts of loss of control of drinking by colonial Americans. By the 1830s, however, loss of control had become a stereotyped feature of the public confessions of drunkards who took up the temperance pledge.

These cultural perceptions of drugs and their effects are fundamental to the entire debate in the United States about the nature, incidence, and cure of addiction (see chapters 1 and 2). The notions of uncontrollable alcoholism and narcotic addiction are the results of complex social processes in this country. These processes include population shifts, urbanization, and the breakdown of stable community structures (Clausen 1961; Rothman 1971; Zinberg and Fraser 1979); nativistic sentiments, the assertion of Puritanical values, and social stereotyping of drug or alcohol use with foreign or outcast elements in the society (Clausen 1961; Goode 1972; Gusfield 1963); the medicalization of psychic maladies and deviant behavior and the assertiveness of key organizations such as the Federal Bureau of Narcotics, the American Medical Association, and the National Council on Alcoholism (Foucault 1973; King 1972; Wiener 1981). In pivotal eras, as groups of people lost both real and perceived control of their lives and as excess characterized major areas of social behavior, concepts of addiction

were presented that embodied and explained prevalent feelings (cf. Peele and Brodsky 1975).

Although these social developments cannot be reduced to psychological terms, their impact on individual psychology is monumental. Paradoxically, those people most ready to acknowledge their addictions are those most susceptible to cultural stereotypes about these addictions, despite their own often contrary experiences. Consider that Robins et al. (1980) discovered that heroin users among Vietnam veterans were no more likely to become regular users than were amphetamine and barbiturate users; nor did regular heroin users suffer more adverse consequences in their lives than did regular users of the other drugs. Yet heroin users in the study *claimed* that heroin was more dependence-producing and more dangerous. Confessed alcoholics typically trumpet the uncontrollable nature of their disease, while their own behavior bespeaks a range of motivations and variations in drinking; those mired in heroin addiction most vividly describe the withdrawal and craving that they themselves have often overcome. Thus the cultural stereotype of a drug infiltrates the kinds of relationships people believe they have with a substance. Addiction becomes a label and an explanation those who behave addictively apply to themselves.

The cultural analysis suggesting that drug addiction occurs to the extent that a drug experience serves crucial emotional functions and is viewed as having power over the individual applies to other experiences as well. This view helps to answer the question of whether cultures or groups with high rates of alcoholism or drug addiction suffer more psychopathology than other cultural groups. While this idea may hold for certain severely stressed groups like Indians, Eskimos, and blacks, it makes less sense as a description of comparably assimilated and well-off ethnic groups. For example, it does not seem possible that Irish Americans in Vaillant's inner-city group are seven times more often the victims of psychopathology than inner-city Italians and Jews, as their alcoholism rates alone would indicate.

What rather seems to be the case is that groups with lower drug or alcohol addiction rates express their distress and potential for addiction in other ways. Glassner and Berg (1980) noted that Jews referred to overeating as the Jewish version of alcoholism. "What this quasi-joking reference meant is that Jews who have emotional and coping problems that lead to substance use that is harmful and degrading would be more likely to eat than to drink excessively" (Peele 1983c: 964). Indeed, Jewish and some other ethnic groups with low rates of alcoholism do show greater overweight and obesity problems (Patai 1977: 447–53; Stunkard 1967), perhaps because it is more common for such groups to invest eating and food with emotional significance as signs of love and caring (cf. Bruch 1973). In our contemporary youth culture, the preoccupation is with thinness as a signal

of a person's worth and ability to inspire love, an ethos of which compulsive exercise and bulimia are symptomatic (Boskind-White and White 1983; Polivy and Herman 1983). Accompanying this development is the tendency for runners to describe themselves as addicts and to refer, however vaguely, to endorphins as the source of their addiction. Peele and Brodsky (1975) meanwhile found interpersonal addictions to be more prevalent for the middle class. Peele (1977) described the social setting in which relationships are more often addictive as being one "where social values hold out the possibility of falling in love as a life solution, where love is seen as a transcendent experience and as a rite of passage into adulthood, and where social life is organized almost entirely around being with the one you love" (p. 121).

Susceptibility to and Choice of Addiction: Situational Factors

The Vietnam War experience offered something as close to an experimental study of the effect of environment on human susceptibility to narcotic addiction as we are ever likely to have. That is, drug abusers (or others rated high in susceptibility to drug abuse) and those not previously involved with drugs (or likely to become so) were exposed to a setting where narcotics were readily available and drug use was accepted. Follow-up investigations assessed how many of these men became addicted in Vietnam and evaluated how many of those addicted remained addicted in the States and how many achieved permanent remission here. Within the broad outcomes of using narcotics or not after returning to the United States, it was possible to compare those who became readdicted with those who did not. Although data were collected on groups of men comparable to those who served in Vietnam but who did not enter military service, these data were analyzed mainly for initiation to drug use and not addiction to drugs (Robins 1978), so that comparisons with nonsoldier addicts are implicit rather than direct.

The analysis of these data under the direction of Lee Robins, a sociologist, has overwhelmingly pointed to situational determination of drug addiction. Around 50 percent of the men in Vietnam used a narcotic, and about 20 percent became addicted there, figures far greater than occur for even highly susceptible populations in the United States (Robins 1978; Robins et al. 1975). What is more, addiction largely disappeared on returning to the United States, even for those who used narcotics at home (Robins et al. 1975; Robins et al. 1980). The most obvious feature of the Vietnam environment from the standpoint of narcotic addiction was the ready availability of drugs. However, this does not clearly or entirely explain the addic-

tion of Vietnam soldiers and veterans. Soldiers in other parts of Asia who had easy access to drugs showed nothing like Vietnam addiction levels (Zinberg 1974). Among those veterans who used narcotics at home, 84 percent quickly found a supplier in the United States, yet most still did not become addicted (Robins et al. 1975). Thus, the elements in the Vietnam or U.S. environment that caused people to respond addictively to narcotics or other drugs went beyond simple availability.

The variables Robins and her co-workers found to predict drug use in Vietnam and post-Vietnam addiction were prior abuse of drugs and other deviant behavior (Robins et al. 1980). Those who came from settings where drug use was likely, such as inner-city ghettos, were most likely to use drugs in Vietnam even if they had not previously used drugs (Robins 1978). Robins et al.'s data do not point to personality traits but rather to aspects of the soldiers' pre-Vietnam environment as factors predisposing to addiction. The complex interaction between home and neighborhood environment and the personal disposition to be addicted is perhaps best described in Chein et al.'s (1964) classic work, *The Road to H.* These investigators also found it hard to separate personality from situation. The kind of bleak inner-city existences that typified most of their addict subjects were reflected in a personal outlook that welcomed narcosis just as much as the outlook engendered by serving in an Asian war zone.

Stress and Control of Stress

Stress is often proposed as a likely candidate for causing and maintaining addiction. Smokers smoke more when stressed and find it easier to cut back or quit when not stressed (Caplan et al. 1975; Leventhal and Cleary 1980). Relapse in all types of addiction, including smoking, drinking, gambling, overeating, and narcotics, is most frequently prompted by situational stressors and negative emotional reactions to them (Marlatt 1982). However, it was not stress alone that caused overeating by obese subjects in Slochower (1983), but rather the presence of stress that subjects could not affect directly. Lazarus (1966), Leventhal and Nerenz (1983), and Sarason and Sarason (1981) have proposed inclusive models of stress reactions that combine people's subjective interpretation of stressful events, their resources—both psychological and situational—for dealing with stress, and their belief in their ability to cope with it along with the beliefs and support of those around them. Both the Vietnam and ghetto settings were ones where sources of stressful feelings were not readily addressed and where deeply engrained pessimism about the possibility of ameliorating the situation reigned.

Uncontrollable stress at a microsituational level seems to parallel the larger societal conditions that encourage addiction. That is, groups whose

values and social structure are disturbed (e.g., by foreign invasion or economic underclass status) and who then show pathological extremes in behavior, including addiction, can be thought of as undergoing stress they cannot realistically hope to modify. Do cultures in general show historical shifts in addiction that correspond to the greater stressfulness of life? A more complex, interactive model suggests that it is the socially available means to handle what might be stressful situations that is at issue. In Bales's (1946) and McClelland et al.'s (1972) analyses, the question is how readily culture members can find concrete ways to deal with central, tension-producing demands made on them by the society rather than accept society's offer of magical, chemical, or other nonrealistic means for responding to these demands.

Social Support and Intimacy

Allen (1984) proposed a model for health behavior change and maintenance that focuses on the strength of the social group's support for such change. On the other hand, the Vietnam and inner-city ghetto situations are ones where social supports have often encouraged narcotic addiction. These addictive support groups are composed of young male peers, the same kind of peer groups Cahalan and Room (1974) connected with the highest rates of problem drinking. What was lacking for the soldiers in Vietnam was the presence of people to whom they could turn for emotional support that did not involve taking drugs. This deficiency was part of the general absence of opportunity for the kinds of intimacy provided by family, older people, and women. Chein et al. (1964) noted that ghetto adolescent addicts did not view family, friends, and sexual relationships as offering intimacy so much as holding out contacts and money for obtaining drugs. Schur's (1962) description of British addicts who were maintained on heroin also emphasized their lack of intimate social networks, even though the British addicts as a group were more often from the middle class and came from less socially disturbed environments than U.S. addicts.

Opportunity for Enterprise and Positive Rewards

Along with the absence of a range of emotional supports, the soldier in Vietnam was deprived of rewarding, productive activity. While many people find the work of war—combined with its lethargy and boredom—difficult to tolerate under any circumstances, the Vietnam soldier had in addition to withstand intense moral questioning of his purpose and effort. The street heroin addict Chein and his co-workers studied was likewise deprived of the opportunity for positive enterprise. "Unlike others, . . . he could not find a vocation, a career, a meaningful, sustained activity around

which he could . . . wrap his life." Instead, he relied on the addiction to provide "a vocation around which . . . [he could] build a reasonably full life" and establish an identity, albeit a negative one (Chein 1969: 23–24). More fundamentally, the ghetto addict saw the entire world as a dreary and dangerous place, one it was just as well to avoid. As chapter 4 demonstrated, it is not possible to separate the appeal of a drug from the environment in which it is administered and especially the richness of the environment, or at least the drug user's perception of its richness.

The ghetto addict interviewed by Chein and his colleagues (1964) demonstrated that "the likelihood . . . [a person] will become an addictive user of opiate drugs is most significantly affected by his experiences with drug use in the context of his current situation *as this has been structured by his entire experience*" (in Shaffer and Burglass 1981: 95, italics added). Chein et al.'s exploration of the heroin addict's world revealed this experience to be similar to that brought on for many young men by the Vietnam War, only the domestic addict's outlook was not so easily remedied by a change in external circumstances. For Chein et al., the New York City addict's very craving during addiction was "an expression of the preferred modes of gratification adopted by the individual and, as such, is dependent on the individual's attitudes toward objects and sources of satisfaction independently of and preceding experience with opiate drugs" (in Shaffer and Burglass 1981: 106). In other words, this addict showed a residual—or personality—effect from his deprived surroundings, one that is not likely to be exclusively a property of ghetto inhabitants.

Susceptibility to and Choice of Addiction: Individual Factors

Only a small minority of users of the most powerful psychoactive agents become addicted, even in the most barren of urban environments (Lukoff and Brook 1974). At the same time, there are notable individuals who consistently create addictions out of all their involvements (Peele 1982b). That either the resistance most people show to addiction or the panaddictive tendencies displayed by others is due to physiological make-up cannot be maintained; nor is it possible that people become addicted solely as a result of the cumulative, excessive use of a substance (see chapter 3). On the other hand, since the 1970s, the tide has run strongly against the belief in personality determinants of addiction. A survey of assessments of alcoholics by Miller (1976) found that they did not have significantly abnormal personality traits. Vaillant (1983) likewise found no reliable indication of personality-based sources for alcoholism. Research with narcotics addicts has yielded similar results (Platt and Labate 1976; Robins et al. 1980), and Lang

(1983), examining studies of both alcohol and drug abuse, found few indications of universal personality patterns.

The complex relationships between personality and behavior extend beyond addiction. Because personality traits do not reliably predict people's actions in all situations, interactive, personality-situation models now dominate psychological thinking (Magnuson 1981; Mischel 1984). The template-matching procedure is a variety of this approach in which a situation is specified and the different types of behavior possible within it are delineated (Bem and Funder 1978). An ideal type of person is then described who would be most likely to behave one way or the other. Actual individuals are evaluated in terms of how close to an ideal type they are, and their likelihood of performing the various behaviors is thereby gauged. For example, Bem and Lord (1979) hypothesized that an intensely competitive and undermining person would be most likely to undercut a potential partner in a mixed-motive game. Subjects who fit this description most closely (measured by their roommates' descriptions of them) did most often choose the competitive strategy.

A completed model of addiction requires that a template be constructed of the person most likely to be addicted. The analysis of addictive experiences and of the situational and social pressures most likely to encourage addiction creates a complementary mold of a person to whom addictive experiences are appealing and who is susceptible to addictive pressures. The mold is a composite construction and includes individual value orientations along with personality traits that have been discovered to be relevant to addiction. What guide this analysis of the addicted person are the linkages among behavior, setting, and individual characteristics and the need for a model to make sense out of these complex relationships.

Interpreting the Meaning of the Individual's Choice of Addictive Object

Some people will become addicted to one object and show no interest, even after frequent exposure, in another. Addicts—even after having demonstrated panaddictive tendencies—will express a preference for one object of addiction. There is some evidence relating personality type to choice of addictive drug. Spotts and Shontz (1982) related the life histories and psychological profiles of abusers of different classes of drugs to psychoanalytic, developmental crises; the investigators later (Spotts and Shontz 1983) found some basis for these differences in MMPI and other quantitative personality measures. Kern (1984) found that preference for stimulant versus depressant drugs was a function of the user's need for augmentation versus suppression of incoming stimuli. Milkman and Sunderwirth (1983) sug-

gested that drug users and others were responsive to three classes of stimulation: arousal, depression, and fantasy experiences.

While indicating an appropriate emphasis on the addict's relationship to an experience, these perspectives on personality leave out central elements in the addictive formula and, at their worst, mirror useless reductionist assumptions about addiction. Preference for a type of stimulus is not equivalent to addiction and, indeed, does not address the essential question of when, how, and why a person becomes addicted to any class or source of stimulation. Moreover, addicts do not seem to be responding exclusively, or even largely, to a physiological dimension of the drug experience. For example, the hospital patients who almost never report a desire to continue drug use (generally of narcotics) after leaving the hospital may be addicted to cigarettes or other drugs or involvements. In particular, some will be alcohol abusers. Yet their abhorrence of the narcotic addict role prevents them from experiencing narcotic drug effects as an appealing, everyday involvement.

In an almost total reversal of this kind of rejection of the pursuit of illicit drug experiences are the outsiders Becker (1963) identified who preferred these experiences. Such differences in attitudes toward licit and illicit drugs are sometimes mirrored by particular ethnic groups. In his autobiography, *Mine Enemy Grows Older,* Alexander King (1958) claimed never to have known a Jewish alcoholic, although many of the heroin addicts he encountered in treatment were Jewish (among whom he himself was numbered). The Jews as a group epitomize the way ethnic attitudes influence the desire for drug experiences. Eddie Fisher (1981), in his autobiography *Eddie: My Life, My Loves,* described himself as a lifelong—if irreligious—Jew. He began getting amphetamine injections early in his career and depended on the drug to perform. Later, Fisher injected the drugs himself, became addicted both to amphetamines and cocaine, and also became strongly dependent on sedatives (Fisher reported experiencing withdrawal from all these substances).

Yet despite being part of a heavy-drinking world and periodically becoming intoxicated, Fisher never developed an urge to drink. Similarly, when forced to inhale cigarettes for over a year for a television sponsor (and being married to at least one smoker), he detested the experience and never took up smoking on his own. Fisher is an example of how ethnic, social, and parental socialization colors experience so as to permit addiction to take place to some varieties of drugs in a given pharmacological class but not others. The legality of a substance is one salient dimension of the preference for drug experiences: It explains why narcotics addicts will often readily turn to alcohol (O'Donnell 1969), but why the reverse shift rarely occurs. There are other attitudinal dimensions to the preference for a given drug or addictive involvement. For example, a person can inherit attitudes

that make cigarette smoking an acceptable habit but that rule out overweight at any cost.

Lack of Values Toward Moderation, Self-Restraint, and Health

While addicts may find special or idiosyncratic rewards in the addictive experience, it is also possible they seek the same rewards as nonaddicts do from these involvements, only they seek them without restraint. For example, findings on social assertiveness and drinking indicate that normal drinkers (as opposed to alcoholics) use alcohol to facilitate social interactions (Beckman 1978) *and* that men use alcohol to feel dominant and sexually aggressive (Brown et al. 1980). The difference in alcohol-related social experiences here may not be so much one of type as degree. Similarly, Robbins and Joseph (1982) distinguished nonaddicted runners from addicted runners on the grounds that the former used running as an escape, while the latter used it as an essential means of coping with stress. Both may find that running relaxes tensions, but the addict seems to crave this effect in an extravagant way.

That the same people abuse all kinds of substances has been a regular and notable finding in the addiction field (cf. Kandel 1984; Robins et al. 1980). In his formulation of "Drug Abuse as Excessive Behavior," Gilbert (1981) analyzed drug abuse as a tendency some people have toward excess in general. For example, Gilbert noted in reviewing a study by Marlatt et al. (1973)—which demonstrated that alcoholics drank more when they thought a drink contained alcohol whether it actually did or not—that alcoholics drank more than nonalcoholics in *all* experimental conditions. "One might conclude from these data that alcoholics drink a lot of alcohol because they drink a lot of all fluids" (p. 233). Recently, Istvan and Matarazzo (1984) summarized a large number of studies that have examined the correlations among consumption of alcohol, tobacco, and caffeine. Relationships were generally positive and in many cases quite strong—particularly at the highest levels of consumption. For example, most studies have found that over 90 percent of alcoholics smoke. Dielman (1979) found heavy gamblers drank heavily.

People who behave excessively are characterized by their failure to delay gratification. Mischel (1979) has analyzed the "development of self-control competencies" among children and their awareness of "effective delay rules" (p. 750). Combined with this ability to moderate consumption is the *value* people place on avoiding excess or postponing gratification. No matter how much some people enjoy eating banana splits, they restrain themselves in line with other values they have. One such value is a generalized desire to be healthy; valuing health may be an important component in the

attitudes that are communicated from parent to child (Peele 1983b) and within social groups (Becker 1974) that influence the likelihood of drug, alcohol, and other harmful excess. Those who use substances dangerously have regularly been found to take risks with their health generally (Istvan and Matarazzo 1984); for example, Kalant and Kalant (1976) showed that users of psychoactive substances—both licit and illicit—engaged in a variety of behaviors that led to illness, injury, and death. In addition, people may value sobriety sufficiently so that even if they find drinking or sedatives to bring welcome tension relief, they refuse regularly to resort to emotional palliatives that would cloud their awareness.

Antisocial Attitudes and Aggression, Alienation, and Lack of Achievement

After a time when the emphasis has been exclusively on addiction as a behavioral, physical, or psychological—and not a moral—problem, Jessor and Jessor (1977), Kandel (1984), Peele (1981a), and others have reemphasized the relationship between values and drug and alcohol use. Drug and alcohol abuse among the young is connected to antisocial acting out (Jessor et al. 1980; Wingard et al. 1979) and to independence, nonconformity, and autonomy (Jessor and Jessor 1977). Unfortunately, this literature generally does not distinguish degree of harmfulness of drug use, so that relationships between measures of drug use and of independence and autonomy confuse destructive alienation and the desire for exploration and new experience (cf. Jessor and Jessor 1977; Kandel et al. 1978). Several studies of marijuana users have found them to be more spontaneous, open, and inquisitive than their nondrug-using peers (Goldstein and Sappington 1977; Kay et al. 1978; Segal 1977), although heavier users show poorer psychological adjustment (Kilpatrick et al. 1976). Prison inmates who used only marijuana were significantly less likely to become alcoholic than those who used *no* illicit drugs (Lewis et al. 1983).

Problem drinking, narcotics use and addiction, and smoking have been repeatedly related to deviance-proneness, rebelliousness, disturbed family backgrounds, and antisocial behavior generally (Cahalan and Room 1974; Newman 1970; Robins et al. 1980). Robins et al. (1980) found that social deviance was related to all kinds of illicit drug use, but more so to heroin use. "That we find higher levels of social disability among heroin users . . . is probably attributable to the kinds of people who use heroin. Men disposed to social problems are likely to use drugs, and those with the very greatest predisposition . . . are the ones likely to use heroin" (p. 229). An important component in the constellation of heavy drug and alcohol use for men is aggressive and violent behavior. MacAndrew (1965) noted that personality inventory items indicating pathological aggression distin-

guished alcoholics from nonalcoholic psychiatric outpatients; the same test items also identified drug abusers and addicts in later studies (Burke and Marcus 1977; MacAndrew 1981). A similar MMPI profile characterized compulsive gamblers (Roston 1961). McClelland et al. (1972) focused on an individual's desire for dominance or personalized power as being at the core of heavy drinking. Lewis et al. (1983) found in a prison population that alcoholism and drug abuse were more common for men with antisocial personalities.

Vaillant (1983) strenuously argued that rather than drinking in line with their antisocial and aggressive tendencies, alcoholics have these tendencies instigated by their drinking regardless of their values and personalities. He cited the case of the subject "James O'Neill," who was a model of socialized behavior when sober but who became totally irresponsible and a reckless philanderer when drunk. In Vaillant's (1977) previous work with the same subject population, he identified alcoholism as a form of psychological adaptation. There he discussed the case of "Robert Hood" (pp. 177–80)—who was a juvenile delinquent who became an early smoker and heavy drinker (and an eventual alcoholic) and who was sexually promiscuous and beat his child—in the context of the "less adaptive aspects of acting out." Promiscuity and child abuse cannot be explained exclusively as the result of drinking too much; for example, Hood never saw his child after he stopped drinking. Vaillant's change of heart on this issue from his 1977 perspective to the one he adopted in 1983 was due to his conversion to the view that alcoholism is a so-called primary disease and not the result of psychological dysfunction.

Vaillant's two views of alcoholics do serve to illustrate, however, the difficulties in determining the nature of addictive behavior as a cause or as a consequence of the characteristics of addicts. Robins et al. (1980) found that regular or addicted users of heroin, amphetamines, and barbiturates showed more social disturbance than did nonusers or casual users. This was due *both* to their predispositions before initiating drug use and to the consequences of their involvement with drugs. Jessor (1979) has established prospectively that a lack of achievement and of other positive social values causes drug use. This lack of positive values in turn makes achievement and constructive involvements less likely (Jones and Berglas 1978). Kandel (1984) found that greater use of marijuana (combined with other drug use) was associated with increasing disaffection and alienation from social institutions.

Fear of Failure, Intolerance of Uncertainty, and the Belief in Magical Solutions

The lack of positive motivation that Jessor (1979) uncovered in young drug users was part of a larger negative outlook in which these users doubt the

possibility of gaining satisfaction from the world. Jessor's portrait is very close to that of the adolescent addicts Chein et al. (1964) depicted, who pursue a life centered around drugs as part of an alternative value system that offers them "a sense of a personal identity, a place in society, a commitment, personal associations based on a seemingly common purpose, a feeling of belonging to an in-group, a vocation and an avocation, and a means of filling the void in an otherwise empty life" (in Shaffer and Burglass 1981: 106). Chein and his co-workers found that addiction served as a life- and consciousness-organizing principle for those who were overwhelmed by fear and pessimism at the same time that the addiction confirmed these addicts' world view.

Achievement-oriented behavior is positively motivated by one stable personality disposition—the need to achieve—and negatively motivated by another—the desire to avoid failure. Fear of failure is the disposition to regard challenging situations solely for their potential to bring about failure and embarrassment. Atkinson and Feather (1966: 369) provided the classic description of the person whose behavior is dominated by the fear of failure. Such a person

> resists activities in which his competence might be evaluated against a standard or the competence of others. Were he not surrounded by social constraints . . . he would never voluntarily undertake an activity requiring skill when there is any uncertainty about the outcome. . . . [Thus] constrained, . . . he will defend himself by undertaking activities in which success is virtually assured or activities which offer so little real chance of success that the appearance of trying to do a very difficult thing . . . more than compensates for repeated and minimally embarrassing failures. Given an opportunity to quit an activity that entails evaluation of his performance for some other kind of activity, he is quick to take it . . . [while displaying] dogged determination in the pursuit of the highly improbable goal. . . . [His] general resistance to achievement-oriented activity opposes any and all sources of positive motivation to undertake the customary competitive activities of life . . . [and] his long history of relative failure means he will view his chances in new ventures more pessimistically.

What is most telling in the description of the person high in fear of failure is how he tolerates the assured failure from self-defeating activity better than he does the middling probability of success in ordinary involvements. There are many harkenings here to the behavior of addicts and drug abusers: a lack of feeling for positive opportunity, ritualized behavior as a replacement for fear-inspiring challenge, and the self-handicapping strategy by which the person's previous failures (brought on by involvement in ill-fated activities highly unlikely to bear fruit) are used as excuses for continued failure (Jones and Berglas 1978). Indeed, Birney et al. (1969) have analyzed the rise in drug abuse through the 1960s as the result of the increase

in learned fear of failure. The addict too prefers highly ritualized behaviors in place of engaging in uncertain and challenging enterprise where he will be evaluated by dominant cultural standards. More generally, addicts show great "difficulty in tolerating ambiguity and ambivalence" (Zinberg et al. 1978: 19). Focusing attention on a drug and its effects eliminates the anxiety created by unstructured activities and their uncertain results.

Chein et al. (1964, in Shaffer and Burglass 1981: 111–112) noted this characteristic in addicts' search for "kicks":

> Normally, the search for new experience leads to the broadening of one's intellectual and sensory horizons and to the pleasures of working at challenging and difficult situations and tasks which, despite anxiety and strain, are capped with some degree of mastery or even with nondisgraceful failure. . . . In other instances, the outcome is not so fortunate. At one extreme, there is the total blunting of this complex drive; these are people who lead a life of stultifying routine. . . . The search for kicks is, on the surface, at the other pole. . . . [However, it actually represents a comparable experience to stultifying routine] as though the experience of novelty per se were substituted for the confrontation and mastery of ever-new and challenging situations. . . . The kicks they seek are inseparably linked with trouble from the onset. Their kicks are usually highly mannered, group-oriented, and stereotyped. . . . [and] are limited to new ways of being intoxicated and . . . mannerisms of dress, hair style, speech and gesture.

Because of a lack of persistence in goal-oriented activity, the person high in fear of failure prefers easy and quick solutions over ferreting out the roots of a problem. Drugs provide a means of modifying troubling feelings and sensations without influencing their actual causes. Those who rely on drug-induced moods want simply to modify their feelings, since they don't genuinely believe they can influence the situations that cause these feelings through real activity. Peele (1982a) labeled this method of coping as one involving "magical solutions." Such solutions include drug addiction and involvements like binge shopping, compulsive gambling, destructive love relationships, and even murder said to be the result of insanity. In all these cases, people are drawn to a conclusive resolution for their existential problems that has no chance for actual success and that paradoxically provides its own excuse for failure: that is, perpetrators are claimed to be addicted, insane, in love, or otherwise under the control of inexorable urges.

Low Self-Esteem, Lack of Self-Efficacy, and External Locus of Control

The connections between the measures in this section and addiction are marked by the intuitive sense they make, the important theories and some

findings that favor them, and the lack of definitive support for them. Addicts have repeatedly been described as having low self-esteem, based primarily on clinical impressions. There have been findings of low self-esteem in surveys of drug abusers (cf. Lang 1983; Lindblad 1977). As Benson and Wilsnack (1983: 66) found, for example, "the composite picture . . . on female alcoholics is that of a woman who is uncertain or conflicted about her womanliness, who has little self-esteem, [and] who has no clear sense of identity." Yet consistent differences in self-esteem have not been uncovered between alcoholics, addicts, or drug users and other groups, perhaps because many people who have low self-esteem still do not end up taking drugs or becoming addicts (Lang 1983; Miller 1976). Discussions of addicts' self-concepts include that of Peele and Brodsky (1975), who saw addicts of all kinds—including those involved in addictive interpersonal relationships—as lacking a sense of self in the absence of which the addiction becomes the core of their identity. Chein (1969) described how addicts acquire "a socially validated human identity, [albeit] a despised identity" through their addiction to heroin (p. 23). That is, the very self-esteem function that the addiction is required to serve itself contributes to the maintenance of addicts' negative self-images.

For Chein (1969), the addict's need for self-esteem is a result of his life history: "From his earliest days, the addict has been systematically educated and trained into incompetence" (p. 23). This incompetence refers both to an inability to arrive at a life vocation and also to a general inability to achieve desired results from life. Competence here suggests efficacy, or the ability to bring about desired aims for oneself. Bandura (1977a) has made the concept of self-efficacy a central one in psychology by asserting that therapeutic interventions achieve success by enhancing a person's sense of self-efficacy. At the same time, a general rubric for the problems that require therapy is the lack of self-efficacy. While competence describes objective coping abilities, self-efficacy connotes a person's subjective sense of his or her ability to control relevant aspects of the environment.

Since loss of control is a defining trait of alcoholism and other addictions, the belief in one's ability—and the actual ability—to harness drinking or other drug use has seemed to be a major factor in addiction. Laboratory investigations of alcoholics' drinking have made clear that no internal, biological mechanism leads to loss of control (see chapter 2). In lieu of such a mechanism, psychologists have investigated the internal–external locus of control of addicts—that is, their belief that they control the forces that regulate their lives (internal control) or else that their lives are controlled by forces outside themselves (external control). Different authors have provided divergent summaries of the results of such research in the case of alcoholism. Lang (1983) maintained that "In sum it appears that the popularity of I-E and related measures in personality and addictive behavior research is not supported by any decisive results they have produced" (p. 200).

Rohsenow (1983), on the other hand, claimed that "In summary, virtually all the studies that use adequate control groups have found that alcoholics and problem drinkers are more external in locus of control than nonproblem drinkers are" (p. 40).

Investigations have focused on alcoholics' beliefs about their ability to control their alcohol intake and their behavior while drinking and about the etiology of their drinking problems (cf. Stafford 1980: the Locus of Drinking Control Scale). For example, Heather et al. (1982) showed that alcoholics who believed that one drink inevitably led to relapse were more likely than other alcoholics to be drinking alcoholically six months after treatment and that alcoholics who viewed the nature of both their drinking problems and alcohol problems in general in uncontrollable, disease terms were more likely to drink destructively if they did drink (Heather et al. 1983). These studies are reminiscent of how heroin addicts' expectations about drugs affect their ability to withstand withdrawal and relapse pressures. Zinberg et al. (1978) remarked that addicts often "are well aware of their excessive fear of withdrawal" (p. 19). Peele and Brodsky (1975) reflected that the addict's sense of his impotence "has made him feel helpless not only against the rest of the world, but against the addictive object as well, so that he . . . believes he can neither live without it nor free himself from its grasp" (p. 62). Finally, Winick (1962) contrasted those addicts who matured out of addiction with those who remained lifelong addicts, "who decide that they are 'hooked,' make no effort to abandon addiction, and give in to what they regard as inevitable" (p. 6).

Susceptibility to and Choice of Addiction: Developmental Factors

> I am very grateful to old age because it has increased my desire for conversation and lessened my desire for food and drink.
>
> Cicero, *De Senectute*

The Incidence and Age of Remission in Addiction

Consistent findings indicate that alcohol, heroin, and other drug abuse are characteristic of young people, males in particular. Cahalan and Room (1974) described alcohol abuse as almost a rite of passage among certain groups of working-class males in their early twenties. Annual surveys of high school seniors throughout the 1970s and 1980s have shown that ritualized, weekend binge drinking has spread to a wider group, with approximately 50 percent of all high school senior males (and 30 percent of females) reporting having five or more drinks at one sitting in the previous two weeks (Johnston et al. 1981). In his pioneering study of maturing out of

narcotic addiction, Winick (1962) estimated from examining the rolls of known narcotic addicts that two-thirds outgrew their reliance on heroin. Community and national surveys have regularly found a lessening of heroin use among males through their twenties (Brunswick 1979; O'Donnell et al. 1976; Robins and Murphy 1967). Similarly, Johnston et al. (1978) found that—during the height of the American college drug culture—the percentage of regular users of marijuana and other popular illicit drugs declined after the ages 19 to 22.

Quitting cigarettes and alcohol do not typically occur at the same peak periods for cessation of illicit drug use. People begin smoking and drinking in the same late adolescent and early adulthood period when illicit drug use begins, and they do show some slight trends toward quitting these legal drugs in their late twenties (Fishburne et al. 1980). Men have far fewer drinking problems as they proceed through their twenties, but this is rarely accomplished through abstinence, and most continue to drink moderately (Cahalan 1970; Roizen et al. 1978). The continuation of cigarette use later in life does not bespeak the same kind of moderation that takes place with drinking: Most middle-age smokers are probably addicted. One type of drug use that begins and peaks later in life is that involving medically prescribed substances such as tranquilizers and sedatives (Kandel 1980).

Disease theorists argue that the kind of alcohol abuse that moderates with age cannot be genuine alcohol addiction (Keller 1975). While propounding this case, Vaillant (1983) reported more than half his sample of alcohol abusers—who had generally more severe and longer-lived drinking problems than those studied by Cahalan and his colleagues—achieved remission, most without any kind of therapy. Remission in this study and others occurs *throughout* the life span. Twenty percent of the former problem drinkers in Vaillant's study became moderate drinkers, while even among the rest (whom Vaillant termed abstainers) total abstinence was unusual. Along with Vaillant, Tuchfeld (1981)—in the case of alcoholism—and Waldorf and Biernacki (1981) and Maddux and Desmond (1981)—in the case of narcotics—have chronicled remission from addiction at later stages in life. Indeed, Cahalan et al. (1969) identified later age spans as representing the greatest drop-offs in heavy drinking: While 24 percent of men age 60 to 64 were heavy drinkers, only 7 percent of those over age 65 were thus classified; 10 percent of the women age 45 to 49 were heavy drinkers, after which ages the percentage of heavy drinkers never rose above 2 percent.

Because they do not disturb normal life patterns in the same way that illicit drug use does, licit addictions such as smoking and overeating are more readily maintained into adulthood and beyond. While such eating disorders as anorexia and bulimia reach their greatest proportions in young age groups (Boskind-White and White 1983; Bruch 1973), the long-term excessive consumption that often leads to obesity is more of a middle-age phe-

nomenon. The very range of ages over which overweight appears might be thought to argue against its essential addictive nature, at the same time that popular theories of overweight—particularly the set-point model (Bennett and Gurin 1982; Nisbett 1972; Polivy and Herman 1983)—present a physiologically deterministic basis for obesity. In fact, the gradualness, variety, and discontinuity of the behaviors leading to overweight are a sound paradigm for addictions of every type. Substantial remission in cigarette addiction and obesity may provide the best illustration of the essential—if inexact—self-regulating nature of much of human behavior including addiction.

Schachter (1982) countermanded his own and his co-workers' theories of obesity and smoking by discovering remission rates in the 50 to 60 percent range for both addictions (see chapter 3). Longitudinal and retrospective community surveys provide general support for his findings. Garn, Bailey, and Cole (1980) found in a longitudinal study that two-thirds of men (though only about 20 percent of women) lost their overweight within a ten-year period. Twenty-nine million Americans quit smoking between 1965 and 1975 (*Adult Use of Tobacco* 1975). A survey by the Public Health Service (1979) found three-quarters of those who had ever smoked had tried to quit and over half of this group had succeeded. In other words, even for addictive behaviors that are not illegal and that do not call into play the same level of social sanction as heroin addiction (or alcoholism), people are generally capable of eliminating self-destructive involvements to which they have become wedded.

The Meaning and the Means of Remission in Addiction

Schachter (1982) noted that the remission rates he uncovered were far superior to the typical 10 to 25 percent cure rates reported by therapy programs for smoking and obesity. These differences are not due to the severity of treated patients' smoking or obesity problems: Schachter found no differences in remission rates between heavy and light smokers or severely and mildly obese subjects. Conclusions about the efficacy of self-cure versus therapeutic cure are hard to draw from Schachter's and similar studies, however, because untreated and treated subjects are self-selected and because community studies like Schachter's examine outcomes over people's lifetimes, while therapy programs often report the success of a single therapeutic effort. On the other hand, Vaillant (1983) did not find differences in outcomes for his alcoholic hospital patients and comparable groups of untreated alcoholics at standardized two- and eight-year follow-up periods, while programs for alcoholics and narcotics addicts rarely show as much as 10 percent remission rates for follow-up periods from one to several years (Califano 1983; Emrick and Hansen 1983; Gordis et al. 1981).

Studies that uncover mild but distinct treatment effects for alcoholism have emphasized that what improvement does occur is traceable to developments in patients' lives outside the therapeutic milieu (Baekeland et al. 1975; Costello 1975; Orford and Edwards 1977), leading some theorists to maintain that a model linking cure solely to treatment inputs is inadequate and inaccurate (Moos and Finney 1982). That is, even when remission occurs following treatment, it is the result of improvements in a person's external involvements. Waldorf (1983) identified the same processes as accompanying cures both for heroin addicts who achieved remission on their own and for those who succeeded via treatment. The factors identified with cure in all these studies represent the basic building blocks in human functioning: improvement in intimate relationships (like marriage), changes in social networks, increased work opportunities and other professional considerations, health concerns, and more global factors such as maturation and a sense of who the addict is or wishes to be. These factors alternately stand for gratifications that will replace those from the addiction or that will be lost to people if they persist in the addictive behavior.

Divergent approaches to assessing natural remission in addiction disclose two different views of the phenomenon. Interviews with ex-addicts—particularly those who put themselves forward as having quit an addiction—emphasize subjective epiphanies or moments when people recognized their problems clearly and once and for all cast their addictions off (cf. Peele 1983d; Tuchfeld 1981; Waldorf and Biernacki 1981). Studies that on the other hand trace populations of people over their lifespans point toward natural progressions in habits dictated by age and other demographic factors (cf. Cahalan et al. 1969; Cahalan and Room 1974; Winick 1962). The former perspective depicts a sudden realignment of people's values and self-image that propels them to change; the latter describes a gradual process whereby people develop the emotional strength and environmental supports to find a new lifestyle.

Peele (1983d) found that the sudden insights that led to remission for all addictions involve people's juxtaposing an irrefutable image of their behavior against their self-image; they find they can no longer justify their behavior in terms of basic values they hold about themselves as parents, people in control of themselves, or people who would not consciously harm themselves. Greaves (1980) likewise saw the quitting of addiction to represent an existential realization and resolve, one that withstood nearly all pressures toward relapse. The opposite perspective—that of a gradual ripening into remission—is provided by the maturing out process. Winick (1962) and others have described adolescent addiction as an evasion of the responsibilities of adulthood. As addicts develop the emotional and practical resources to meet these demands, they find adulthood less frightening and its rewards more desirable and attainable. Consider the enigmatic love

relationships that teenagers and young adults often pursue compulsively while finding only fleeting (or nonexistent) satisfaction from these connections (Peele and Brodsky 1975). As most young people become more confident with age, they make commitments to relationships that entail more realistic personal and practical satisfactions.

Shifting life pressures and subjective rewards continue to characterize remission through the life span. Caplan et al. (1975) detected that middle-age blue-collar workers who quit smoking had become more comfortable with the requirements of their jobs. Gomberg (1980) speculated that a principal cause of the drop in heavy drinking among retired men was relief from the pressures of the daily work grind, in combination with a loss of income for buying liquor and physiological changes that made heavy drinking more unpleasant. Nowhere is addicts' awareness of the continuing costs of an addiction more pronounced than among seasoned heroin users who decide to get free of their drug habits. Repeatedly such people indicate they were no longer willing to incur the damage to their lives from every aspect of the addiction (cf. McAuliffe and Gordon 1980; Waldorf and Biernacki 1981). Explanations by former overeaters and smokers who changed compulsive habits also often reflected a sound evaluation of health and other practical considerations (cf. Gerin 1982).

In a larger sense, there may be no contradiction between the perspective that people change their behavior as a result of sudden insight and the view that they become able to change over time as they mature. Vaillant (1966, 1983) reported that both recovered heroin addicts and former alcoholics usually identified a specific moment when they decided to quit drinking or drugs. Yet Vaillant doubted the decisiveness of these individual events, preferring to see instead the ripening of forces that had been incubating for months or years. It is true, for example, that former addicts both to cigarettes and heroin have often experienced previous revelations or made similar resolves to quit that did not produce lasting results (Marlatt and Gordon 1980; Jorquez 1983). Whatever means addicts do use to eliminate their addictions, they very often restructure their lives to facilitate a nonaddicted lifestyle. In the one view, they intentionally make such changes in line with their resolve to go straight; in the other view, the changes already had to be in progress in order for them to eschew their addictions (cf. Wille 1983).

In leaving behind one addiction, the person may simply adopt another one, or may retain a simultaneous addiction. Robins et al. (1975) reported that although addicted narcotic use fell off for the large majority of returned Vietnam veterans, a sizeable minority replaced narcotic addiction with unhealthy drinking or dependency on non-narcotic drugs. Eighty-three percent of Zinberg's (1984) sample of controlled narcotics users—many of whom had been addicted to narcotics previously—still smoked cigarettes

daily. The correlations Istvan and Matarazzo (1984) noted among different forms of substance use remained, even for those who had been (but no longer were) addicted to one of the substances. For example, former smokers drank more coffee than those who had never smoked. Vaillant (1983) found that many abstinent alcohol abusers (although not those who had moderated their drinking) created substitute dependencies. The range of these correlations between both former and current substance abuse and other compulsive attachments affirms that a general tendency toward addiction is an often persistent part of a person's style of dealing with the world.

For Vaillant (1983), addicts' substitute dependencies included religious commitments and AA membership and often constituted a positive step for the addict. Other studies of reformed addicts have highlighted the changes addicts make in their social networks, such as joining religious groups or other organizations that, while not explicitly therapeutic, do rule out drug use (cf. Tuchfeld et al. 1983; Waldorf 1983; Wille 1983). At the same time, some addicts retain old lifestyles and acquaintances while changing addicted behavior, seemingly performing nothing more than an intrapsychic reappraisal of who they want to be (Jorquez 1983; Peele 1983d; Waldorf and Biernacki 1981). This latter approach is typical of reformed smokers and overeaters, who are unlikely to reject spouses, friends, and jobs when they shift behavior. Most subjects in Schachter's (1982) study of remission in smoking and obesity reported employing conscious policies for modifying their habits while making few external changes in their lives (cf. Gerin 1982). Again, the dichotomy may be more apparent than real. Group support is an indisputably central factor in people's ability to select and maintain a course of action (cf. Allen 1984), yet subjective factors such as identity, personal values, and the degree of satisfaction obtained from an activity play key roles in addiction.

Lastly, personality dispositions are part and parcel of the escape from addiction as well as its formation. These dispositions influence both the success of efforts at cure and the methods attempted for such cures. Condiotte and Lichtenstein (1981) found that smokers' feelings of self-efficacy predicted the success of outcomes of a smoking cessation program. On the other hand, high self-efficacy may be the best description of those who refuse therapeutic help and attempt self-cures (Peele 1983d). Tuchfeld's (1981) presentation of self-reports by those who quit or cut back drinking revealed an almost willful independence and a rejection of outside support: One man reported he would rather die than seek help from a therapist. Whereas disease theorists see such attitudes as proof of a defensive inability to change, these dispositions may actually hold out the most positive prognosis. Schachter (1982) found remission rates to be higher for those who never sought treatment than for those who had, no matter how severe the

person's overweight or reliance on nicotine. Wille (1983) noted that heroin addicts who found it most difficult to kick the habit were those who believed they needed institutional support the most and who had the greatest trouble making social changes and developing a new identity on their own.

The Nature of Addiction: The Addiction Cycle

Substantial life-span variations in addiction—along with the findings that addictive behavior is situationally, socially, and culturally determined—vitiates disease views of addiction. Responding to these findings, sociologists, clinical psychologists, and social psychiatrists often lose sight of the reality of addiction as a recognizable syndrome, and of people's personal dispositions to be addicted. Paradoxically, when confronted with the extremities of addictive behavior or with the degree of substitution of addictions, these social scientists suspect the operation of the same inbred and/or biological mechanisms that disease theorists posit for addiction. The interpretation of addiction among opposing theorists simply becomes a matter of degree, whereby all concede that the most severe instances of addiction or addictiveness represent the same biological imperatives. The authorities agree that if addiction is real and persistent, it *must* be biological. The same limitations in imagination cause scientists—as well as addicts themselves—to reify into concrete entities what are, in fact, relativistic personal impulses. Loss of control is real to the person; the effort of conceiving that it is also a culturally and subjectively induced sensation is insurmountable. Human thought is not well-equipped for understanding that intense motivations are not inevitably biological at their source and do not necessarily hold true for all humans, at all times, in all places.

That the addiction syndrome can appear with any type of involvement has led to the same conceptual difficulties, in the form of the denial or trivialization of nondrug addictions or of the claim that they are biological syndromes like those that alcoholism and opiate addiction supposedly represent. Compulsive gambling, running, overeating, etc., actually offer clear insights into the nature of addiction as an experience. Runners such as those interviewed by Robbins and Joseph (1982), who experienced cessation of running as traumatic because it removed what had become a shield against previously overwhelming pressures, reveal the fundamental nature of aversive withdrawal. Recognizing such truths means we no longer have to separate addiction from other human experiences and that we can bring to bear on the syndrome all the knowledge we have about human social and psychological functioning.

The addiction-experience model incorporates cultural processes with individual and situational vectors and includes all the experiences people

find to be addictive (Peele 1980). A society—and all the subsocieties to which people belong—creates a need for an addictive experience by setting forth key values that are not realizable. The society simultaneously presents alternative experiences as having the power and quality to fulfill these needs in other than realistic ways. As summarized in this chapter, people are susceptible to these addictive experiences to the extent that they occupy unsatisfying and stressful postions in the society, to the extent that they feel concrete consensual social rewards are unobtainable or not worthwhile, and to the extent that they relate to the world through dependencies and believe in the efficacy of external forces. (See figure 5–1.)

Becoming involved in substitute experiences offered by the social milieu as a resolution for crucial but unsatisfied needs limits people's abilities to fulfill these needs naturalistically, through functional effort and acknowledged accomplishment. People experience a consequent drop in their self-efficacy and social worth, and the ritualized addictive involvement becomes more firmly ensconced as an admittedly inferior—but nonetheless essential—source of gratification. Addicts seek an addictive experience to achieve a desired feeling—a state of being—that is not otherwise available to them. The experience is powerful and gratifying and ultimately becomes both necessary and distressing. Through habit and inclination, those who are addicted participate immoderately in these involvements, while perceiving this excess to signal a lack of control that defines addiction for themselves and others.

This is an exacerbating cycle of experience where the results of exposure to the involvement ensure continued involvement, and the life of the involvement perpetuates its own existence. Not an abnormal dimension of human experience, the process achieves the extremes of addiction when people—in turning to the experience to modify feelings—abandon all functional coping efforts. At this point, the addictive experience becomes the sole means for asserting control over addicts' emotional lives and becomes the core of their self-concepts (Peele and Brodsky 1975). No additional constructs are necessary to account for the fervor of pursuit of an addictive object (craving) and the anguish resulting from its abandonment (withdrawal). Shorn of the reassurance of the addictive involvement, addicts reemerge into worlds from which they have "grown increasingly alienated" (p. 62) and face physical readjustments that they understand as a sickness and feel inadequate to cope with.

With drugs, the reliance on pharmacological effects to create a desired state of being makes the achievement of this state through other means more difficult. McClelland et al. (1972) noted the inherent futility in alcohol intoxication as a fulfillment of power needs, since drunkenness *detracts* from the recognition and influence that the drinker is seeking. Such paradoxical temporary or illusory gratifications are a regular part of addic-

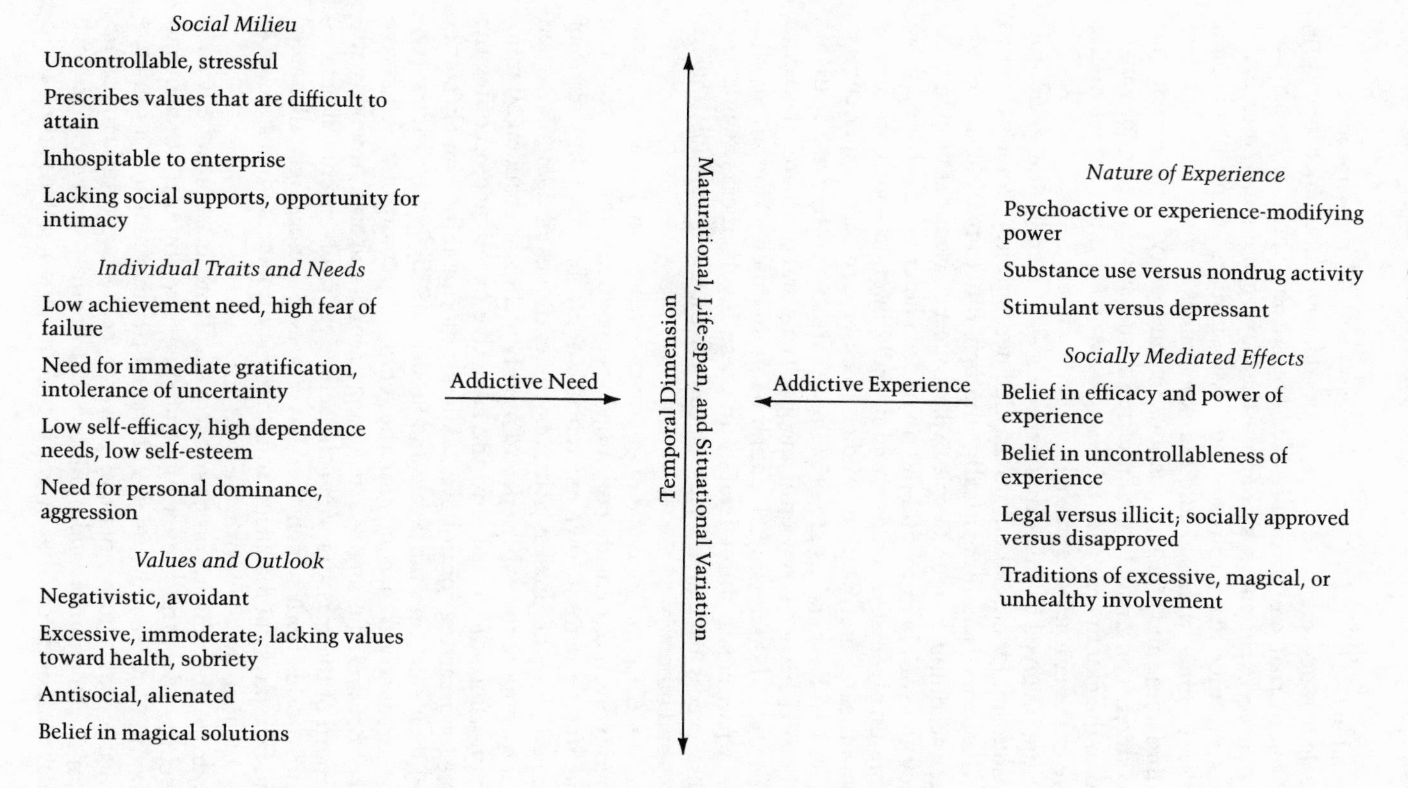

Figure 5–1. The Addiction Formula

tion. Nathan and his colleagues (1970) found short-term reduction of anxiety from drinking for alcoholics but long-term augmentation of anxiety. This is very similar to the paradoxical effects noted from smoking for nicotine addicts (Gilbert 1979; Nesbitt 1972). Aneshensel and Huba (1983) detected the same sequencing of improved mood followed by greater depression with drinking. Overall, while alcoholics *anticipate* positive affects from drinking, they in fact become more dysphoric, agitated, and depressed during drunken episodes (Mello and Mendelson 1978).

The failure of addicts either to find sufficient satisfaction in an act to resort to it only when appropriate, or else to quit because of continuing dissatisfaction, is the core paradox of addiction. Gray (1978) analyzed the use of tranquilizers to allay anxiety as having an inherently dysfunctional character. If anxiety is a signal of some inadequacy in coping, then blocking this signal makes appropriate responses less likely—because drug users become less aware of the sources of their anxiety—and the need for the drug greater. Illicit drug use and other activities carry with them feelings of shame or guilt that then add to the motivation to return to the drug or other experience. Thus drinkers who seek a sense of power from alcohol are aware that this is not a socially approved means of asserting oneself. They feel more debased by this guilty realization and experience simultaneously an increased need for intoxication as an illusory way of fulfilling power needs.

Addictive eating offers a commonsensical illustration of this central addictive process. The binge eater undergoes a similar cycle of emotions to those experienced by drug addicts and alcoholics, whereby the guilt and bad feelings that result from immoderation prompt greater excess (cf. Bruch 1973). Bulimics in one study were asked to report in to investigators whenever they were beeped on an electrical device they carried. Subjects revealed that they ate to escape anxiety, loneliness, and self-doubt: the very feelings that were exacerbated by their eating (Johnson and Larson 1982). In the reaction-formation characteristic of addiction, bulimic subjects then induced vomiting to regain a sense of control and self-worth. Television viewers studied by the same research group (Csikszentmihalyi and Kubey 1981) also indicated that they felt depressed while watching TV and, although they chose to continue doing so, the longer they watched the more depressed they became! A frequent element in this addictive cycle is that a single violation by binge eaters (or other addicts) of their intermittent resolutions to curtail their behavior often leads to a binge episode (Herman and Polivy 1980; Marlatt 1978; Peele and Brodsky 1975; Rollnick and Heather 1982). The addicts see any such slips as proof of their lack of control and as an indication that relapse is inevitable.

Over time, the mix of addictive and functional coping can shift. When stress lessens and situations improve or when successful experiences buoy

addicts' sense of efficacy, the addictive involvement becomes less necessary and appealing. Addicts finally break out of the small world of addiction through combinations of changes in their external situations (such as removal from war zones or ghettos), changes in self-efficacy that enable them to achieve personal goals, and shifts in the reward value addicts attach to the addictive experience relative to their other values. The escape from the addiction becomes permanent as they invest themselves more heavily in the involvements that drug use interferes with or detracts from—involvements that provide rewards that are stronger and more valued than those from the addiction. The final stage of remission is one in which these rewards are so firmly established that some people no longer imagine the possibility of returning to the addictive involvement or that it ever held any appeal. Former addicts may, at this final stage, revise entirely their self-estimates so as no longer to conceive of themselves as addicts or potential addicts; indeed, this is customary for youthful addicts when they mature into their adult lives. Strangely, it is the primary aim of our current policies toward drug and alcohol addiction to deny that this possibility exists and thereby to eliminate it.

6
The Impaired Society

A model of addiction must be judged on its ability to ameliorate a society's addictive problems. The dominant disease and exposure models of addiction have been widely marketed with the promise of reducing drug and alcohol abuse. The models propose that the behavior we are concerned to rectify cannot be stopped without external therapeutic intervention and that controlled use of some substances is never possible (at least for certain people who are congenital addicts). They attribute virtually all the motivation in addictive behavior to factors over which the individual has no control once initial contact is made with a substance. These views of addiction, as I have shown, do not fit the facts. The model of addiction I put forward in this book calls into question all the treatment programs and public policies that rely on such models of addiction for their support.

The dangers in misperceiving the nature of the problem are more than that a futile effort will be mounted that will then die of its own inconsistency, vagueness, and failure. Disease notions of addiction undermine actual successes, as when they deny that alcoholics can incur fewer drinking problems without abstaining entirely or that people can quit addictions themselves (one television advertisement likened a person trying to cure his own alcoholism to someone trying to operate on himself). More strikingly, disease notions of addiction have an uncanny ability to redefine their own failures as successes. A close look at the correlations between drug (most notably heroin) and alcohol abuse and the monies and effort spent on them reveal a relationship that is not random, as would occur if contemporary approaches were simply harmless. Indeed, the relationship is a positive one: The more effort and money spent on drug and alcohol problems, the greater their magnitude.

There are two possible explanations for this phenomenon. One is that current approaches represent futile attempts to catch up with addiction: We are always chasing, but never get a grip on, its causes. The other possibility is more insidious—that our very efforts contribute to and worsen ad-

diction. This has been a characteristic of the attention the United States has focused on heroin since the beginning of the century and now extends to its exporting concerns and policies about drugs to the rest of the world. In large part, what have been exported are U.S. drug-policing efforts, efforts that originated early in this century and that have grown exponentially in the last two decades. Early opponents of the law enforcement approach to narcotic addiction problems frequently endorsed a medical, or treatment, model as a superior alternative. In the United States today, enforcement and treatment approaches have been combined; their convergence is based on *essential commonalities in assumptions about the nature of addiction.* Both assume that addiction is primarily a function of exposure to substances and that prohibiting drug use or drinking by specified individuals and groups can eliminate addiction. Doctors, legislators, and the police increasingly agree that Americans need to be protected against themselves and their own desires.

Medical conceptions of alcoholism and addiction grew in the United States during the nineteenth and twentieth centuries as part of the idea that mental and emotional disorder was an illness. Yet the number of people that could be affected by conceptions of mental illness was limited. Not so the case with alcohol abuse and drug use, since they describe a range of behaviors and apply to a large portion of the population at one point or another in their lives. The application of disease notions to alcohol- and drug-related problems has accelerated in recent decades, at the same time that health professionals have found the disease model to describe eating disorders, destructive sexual relationships, compulsive gambling, child and wife abuse, and even such disparate maladies as phobias, anxiety, and depression. Disease conceptions of substance abuse may be a paradigm for self and cultural conceptions in our era.

None of these approaches has had much success in treating or preventing the disorders that are being addressed. The focus on physiological mechanisms in substance abuse has been completely wrongheaded, with any benefits that appear from it stemming from artifacts connected with natural remission or simply paying some attention to the addicted individual; yet research on inherited sources of addiction is now the primary focus of the funding for explorations of substance abuse. Nor has labeling compulsive gamblers or self-destructive lovers as diseased produced any additional benefits for such people beyond those resulting from religious conversions, growing up, or the act of getting hold of oneself. The dominant approaches to these and other psychic and social disorders are nonetheless hailed as successful because they conform to cultural stereotypes of individual treatment and cure, medical infallibility, and a kind of scientific mysticism that has grown up around the neurosciences in the 1970s and 1980s.

People do improve, from addiction and other maladies, and there are ways in which individual therapy can help this process. Treatment must be mediated, however, by the crucial awareness that a functioning individual's relationships to other people, to work, and to the environment are essential to keeping any healthy behaviors in place and any behavioral dysfunctions at bay. The failure to acknowledge these connections has hindered behavioral psychologists as much as it has medical therapists and disease counselors. An even more difficult connection for those concerned about drug abuse to make has been that between the social order and addiction. In order to deal with addiction on a scale that will make a difference in the United States, we need to understand what about our society encourages addiction, often in forms besides the abuse of the particular substances that attract our attention in any given era.

The Narcotic Connection—Supply and Demand

Interdicting narcotics and other imported drug supply lines has been a major preoccupation in U.S. addiction policy since the beginning of the century. This approach is notable for its failure. It has not limited addiction. It has had little impact on the availability of the drugs concerned, and where it has demonstrated momentary success in curtailing a drug's availability it has still had negative consequences. The entire legal apparatus for arresting drug dealers and users has produced a major enforcement industry that is self-perpetuating without ameliorating drug problems; in fact, even when failure is widely acknowledged (as in the 1982 "War on Cocaine"), the response has been to redouble the efforts that have led to the consequent failure.

The story of the legal proscription, demonization, and rise of narcotic addiction in the United States has by now been thoroughly, even conclusively told (Brecher 1972; Clausen 1961; King 1972; Musto 1973; Peele and Brodsky 1975; Trebach 1982). Abundantly present in nineteenth-century America, narcotics use had decreased considerably by the turn of the century and at the same time shifted in nature from use of opium and morphine to heroin and from the middle to the lower class. After the passage of the Harrison Act of 1914, the extent and the damaging nature of addiction were dramatically portrayed by medical organizations and Harry Anslinger's Federal Bureau of Narcotics, leading to the eventual elimination of legal heroin prescription in the United States. At the time of the Harrison Act and the vigorous propaganda campaign that followed it, there were perhaps 100,000 American heroin addicts (or, more likely, users of any sort), yet the public believed the number to be in the millions. When narcotic clinics were set up in major U.S. cities to replace maintenance of opiate

addicts by private physicians, no more than 15,000 addicts showed up for treatment (Trebach 1982).

Thus began an extended period when a hard core of heroin users and addicts maintained their habits illegally in numbers that probably increased gradually (until numbering 500,000 daily users by the 1970s) and that were certainly higher than for any other advanced country and probably any nation in the world but were minuscule compared with the number of active alcoholics. The 1960s saw the development of methadone maintenance programs, in which addicts were given the substitute narcotic while (ideally) being treated for their drug dependence. The 1960s, when drug use of various kinds became highly visible, marked a period of increased awareness of and alarm about narcotics use. It is still not clear to what extent this concern was justified by an actual rise in the supply and use of narcotics and to what extent it was caused by moral and political issues that determined social reactions to what usage existed (Lidz and Walker 1980).

The concern about heroin peaked in the late 1960s and early 1970s under the Nixon administration and was accompanied by an unprecedented international police and public relations effort directed against heroin suppliers and heroin use. In his exhaustive study of this period, Epstein (1977) has made clear exactly how this campaign was orchestrated exclusively according to political considerations. Throughout the 1970s—during and following this campaign—heroin use and addiction *increased* dramatically worldwide (Ball et al. 1977), including a tenfold increase in Western Europe (Trebach 1982). The U.S. information program about the dangers of narcotics actually fueled heroin problems. For example, Epstein described how U.S.-inspired television commercials about the drug propelled heroin addiction from a nonexistent concern in France to a position as the country's number one health problem. Despite these developments, President Richard Nixon announced in 1973 that the corner had been turned in dealing with heroin around the world.

Nixon made his announcement after enlisting the active support of the Turkish government in eradicating its poppy fields—then the major source for American markets. By 1974, Mexico had assumed this position, auguring a new epidemic and eventual headlines that "Mexico Making Progress in War on . . . Opium Poppies" (1980). The articles about the Mexican war on poppy growers revealed that new sources for heroin were appearing in Asia's Golden Triangle region, leading to subsequent announcements—one year later—of "Heroin Trade Rising Despite U.S. Efforts" (1981) and of "Heroin in West a 'Widening Crisis'" (1981). This led President Reagan to announce his own War on Drugs in 1982, although this time the focus was on a new drug scourge: cocaine. Two years later, in 1984, the suppliers of street cocaine had increased, prices had actually fallen, and estimates of

both the number of users and compulsive users had jumped ("U.S. Is Seen as Losing War on Cocaine Smuggling . . ." 1984). The response: an intensification of efforts to intercept drug supplies and drug dealers and to frighten Americans and supplier nations about the dangers of cocaine.

The New York region is a bellwether for drug use trends. It was in 1973 that Governor Nelson Rockefeller authored the most draconian drug measure ever, providing for mandatory life sentences for people convicted of selling or *possessing* heroin or cocaine. By 1979, Governor Hugh Carey—noting the ineffectuality of this legislation—oversaw major revisions in the law. In 1980, Carey announced a new "state of emergency because of the heroin epidemic" and pledged a war "against terrorists of the drug trade, both here and abroad" (cited in Peele 1982c). This concern for the epidemic proportions of drug abuse in New York carried over to Governor Mario Cuomo's regime. Coordinated city, state, and federal task forces raided drug dealers on New York City streets in 1984. This too proved largely ineffectual—except for moving the drug markets around the city—and New York Mayor Edward Koch was moved to up the ante from the Rockefeller laws by suggesting that pushers convicted repeatedly be executed.

Public policy toward illicit drug use has assumed a pattern—alarm and rising concern about the extent of the problem, strict laws and increased police activity, visible arrests and incidental drops in drug supplies, reemergence of the problem (often at a higher level)—that appears as ineluctable as it is doomed. What drives this approach to preventing addiction, given its futility? From a political standpoint, there is no cost and considerable benefit to embracing tougher laws and enforcement, even if several years later the same politician is forced to report a new wave of drug abuse (and in fact it is often not the same political figure who confronts the fruits of previous policies). Apparently there is something inherently rewarding to politician and public alike about tough drug policies. Adherents of the get-tough approach are not challenged if abuse levels set new records: They instead point to these data as signaling how appropriate and necessary their efforts were in the first place (cf. Peele 1982c).

These policies do not work because they focus on supply and not demand. Given the number of potential producers of heroin and other drugs among third-world nations, there will always be another region ready to take on the role of supplying the United States and other consumer nations. Within the United States, the profits to be made from the drug trade likewise guarantee a steady stream of drug dealers. This very fecundity of drug-trade labor makes the laws against individuals futile. As it is, the dealers rounded up by police in New York City are nearly all released immediately because they are too numerous to be retained by the justice system ("For Drug Prosecutor, A Sense of Frustration" 1984). The punitiveness of the Rockefeller legislation (and Koch's suggested amplification of this ap-

proach) cannot work because it is patently unjust—as well as useless—to penalize so severely the small minority of those apprehended from among the overwhelming numbers of people engaged in similar activities.

What would be the result if somehow, magically, it were possible to shut off the supply of drugs from outside the country? All indications are that committed drug users—the group toward which these efforts are targeted—would simply switch to available alternatives (which they often do of their own choice already). In the case of heroin, these substitutes include barbiturates and other sedatives, alcohol, and synthetic narcotics such as Demerol, Talwin, and methadone itself. Yet nearly everyone is persuaded by prima facie logic that the simple abundance of a drug like cocaine affects the extent of its abuse. For this and other reasons, even commentators like Zinberg (1984) will not endorse legalizing such illicit substances as heroin and cocaine. Berridge and Edwards (1981), while noting that the gradual and arbitrary entrenchment of increasingly negative public attitudes and laws toward narcotics has not improved—and often seems to have exacerbated—narcotic abuse, maintain that legalizing heroin would not reverse the social trends that cause addiction and thus legalization would result only in more drug abuse.

There is surprisingly little evidence to indicate that shorter supplies of drugs like heroin, cocaine, and marijuana translate into fewer drug abusers or addicts. What evidence there is for such a supply-side view comes mainly from epidemiological studies of alcoholism suggesting that individual drinkers consume a relatively fixed proportion of the total supply of alcohol, so that those who drink the most are pushed toward excessive consumption when more alcohol is consumed society-wide (Beauchamp 1980; Room 1984). Yet projected public policies making use of this finding involve such relatively minor steps (compared with prohibition) as raising taxes on alcoholic beverages. That is, the drug will still be readily available but somewhat more costly to procure. Considering that more or less the same can be said of marijuana (Johnston et al. 1981, reported 85 percent of high school seniors could obtain marijuana) or cocaine (at least among certain groups of affluent professionals), controlled legalization would hardly change the availability picture for these drugs.

Discussing drug policy rationally is, unfortunately, an anomalous activity. The proscription of cocaine, heroin, and marijuana is no more nor less than an expression of cultural prejudice. Although banning substances is a prerogative of any society—and one in which all societies indulge—we deny this arbitrariness by justifying prohibition on scientific grounds. The ordinary explanation offered is the harmfulness of these substances. Yet smoking tobacco is inherently harmful—but legal—while heavy drinking is more toxic than the heavy administration (if antiseptic) of a narcotic. Defenders of the public good point out that many of the known users of

illicit substances use them compulsively, as though this were the natural order of things. This impression is created by studiously ignoring all indications of controlled use of these substances. Zinberg (1979) argued that our policy seems best geared to making sure that as high a percentage as possible of those who use illicit drugs will not find out how to do so moderately. (The editors of the volume in which Zinberg's article appeared felt it necessary—while acknowledging the value of his research—to disown his treatment policy recommendations.)

The very discrepant perspectives that evolve from realistic versus moralistic stances is evident in an article in the *New York Times* about high school cocaine use ("Prep Schools in a Struggle to Curb Spread of Cocaine" 1984). One student claimed, "It used to be such a big thing to have it, . . . now everyone's so blasé," and another said, "I never met anybody who was really messed up by cocaine." The students' statements were contradicted by the former NIDA director Robert Dupont, who asserted that "Cocaine is the most powerfully reinforcing [i.e., addictive] of all drugs. . . . These kids don't have a clue of what they're fooling around with."

Why should we disregard the beliefs of these users in favor of the experiences of cocaine addicts who seek treatment? In addition, a systematic research program found regular cocaine users could not distinguish the drug's effects from standard pharmaceutical applications of amphetamines (Van Dyke and Byck 1982). These researchers questioned "whether the potential for the abuse of cocaine justifies the intensity" of current international policing efforts. They noted that "in Andean Indian societies blood-plasma levels comparable to those encountered among intranasal cocaine users are common, yet there is little evidence of physical harm" and Indian ceremonial "use of cocaine cannot be termed drug abuse." Nonetheless, they correctly concluded, "cocaine policy and regulations take little account of these conclusions" and "the final decisions about cocaine will be political and economic, not scientific" (p. 141).

Oddly, the traditional battlelines have been realigned on this issue. Heroin iconoclast Norman Zinberg has publicly agreed that cocaine use is unusually likely to become compulsive and that we should focus on limiting the drug's availability ("U.S. Social Tolerance of Drugs Found on Rise" 1983), apparently as a result of his active involvement in a cocaine hotline network that has turned up large numbers of cocaine addicts. Thus Zinberg contributes to the hysteria surrounding the glamor drug of the 1980s (cf. Peele 1984b), despite having fought irrationality about heroin in previous decades. Meanwhile, disease theory proponent David Smith, director of the Haight-Ashbury Free Medical Clinic, has correctly noted that equivalent percentages of cocaine, Valium, and alcohol users—involving often the same individuals—become addicted (while incorrectly deducing from this the existence of some genetic malady). As a result, Smith has come under

attack from the conservative groups one thinks of as forming the constituency for disease views, which claim Smith is endorsing drug use for those who don't have a tendency to be addicted ("The Collision of Prevention and Treatment" 1984).

The Negative Effects of the Belief in Chemical Dependence

In the period extending from the outlawing of the private prescription of heroin and the brief lifespan of public clinics for heroin users to the emergence of methadone maintenance as the preferred mode of treatment for heroin addicts, nearly all acknowledged narcotics users were sent to federal hospitals for treatment, most notably the Public Health Service Hospital in Lexington, Kentucky. Although research conducted at Lexington has provided important glimpses of the lives and habits of addicts, it appears no one actually was cured there. That is, when the heroin-user net apprehended successful physicians due to their suspicious prescription records, the hospital was provided with patients who naturally could return to work after treatment without difficulty (Winick 1961). Street addicts, however, presented a different picture (Brecher 1972: 71):

> At any given time after being "cured" at Lexington, from 10 to 25 percent of graduates may appear to be abstinent, nonalcoholic, employed and law abiding. But only a handful at most can maintain this level of functioning throughout the ten-year period after "cure." Almost all become readdicted and reimprisoned early in the decade, and for most the process is repeated over and over again.

Brecher estimated that relapse to addiction among such patients was closer to 100 percent than to 90 percent.

Prior to his 1973 life imprisonment law, Rockefeller had directed passage of the 1966 Narcotics Addiction Control Act providing for the civil commitment and treatment of heroin addicts in New York state. By 1972, $224 million had been spent on this program. According to one source, "Of 5,172 individuals treated and released under the . . . compulsory treatment program, only 141 managed to stay drug-free at the end of a year and a half, which meant each cure [this is assuming that those drug-free at a year and a half remained so for the rest of the decade] had cost New Yorkers about $1.6 million" (Collier and Horowitz 1976: 473). At the end of this period, Rockefeller announced the existence of the heroin "epidemic" that prompted his life imprisonment plan.

By the mid-1970s, the developers of methadone maintenance, Drs. Dole and Nyswander (1976), were forced to concede that the benefits of the

program had been "small at best" (p. 2118). This admission does not tell the full story, however. Epstein (1977) revealed that addicts often used other drugs in conjunction with their methadone and that there was an active black market in the drug. In the midst of Governor Carey's war on drugs, a consultant's report he commissioned claimed that no more than 10 percent of those in treatment in the state got off heroin permanently, while those taking methadone were *at least* as likely to be using other illicit drugs as were street heroin addicts (Califano 1983; Peele 1982c).

From its inception, some have questioned the rationale behind methadone maintenance (Lennard et al. 1972; Peele and Brodsky 1975). On what basis was the replacement of one narcotic drug with another considered to contribute to the cure of addiction? For psychopharmacologists like Dole (1980), Goldstein (1976b), and Snyder (1977), addiction is a metabolic process from which the addict is to be weaned. This can be accomplished through gradually replacing the effects of heroin with another drug (for Dole, 1980, this means permanent maintenance with methadone) or through blocking heroin's effects with antagonistic drugs such as naltrexone (Goldstein 1976a). There are exactly comparable procedures for nicotine weaning, by replacing cigarette-induced nicotine levels with gradually reduced levels of chemically pure nicotine. Based on nicotine dependence models that conceive of addicted smokers as striving to maintain habitual nicotine levels (cf. Krasnegor 1979), conferences on nicotine addiction are now sponsored by drug companies promising eventual drug remedies for the problem ("Tobacco Use as an Addiction" 1982). In fact, chemically supported nicotine withdrawal has shown no better results than has medical supervision of heroin withdrawal. There may be marginally greater success at cigarette withdrawal when nicotine is administered, although research has indicated little effect over that produced by administering a placebo (Best and Bloch 1979). Nonetheless, withdrawal is incidental to the actual problem of living a nonaddicted life, and the large majority of withdrawn cigarette addicts—like narcotics addicts—ultimately relapse. Yet metabolic theorists assert the primary nature of chemical reactions in the addiction syndrome, along with the centrality of managing the withdrawal syndrome for escaping addiction.

As a result, popular therapeutic programs for cigarette and illicit drug addiction advertise their ability to alleviate withdrawal distress. One noteworthy example of this approach was the highly publicized treatment of former rock star John Phillips under the supervision of Dr. Mark Gold at the Fair Oaks Hospital in Summit, New Jersey. Phillips—who had been taking enormous amounts of heroin, cocaine, and other drugs—was carefully guided through withdrawal through the use of clonidine to suppress withdrawal symptoms and then naltrexone to eliminate craving. In media interviews and magazine articles about the case, Phillips reported having gone through detoxification many times. Why should this last drug-aided

withdrawal have led to any greater success than his prior efforts to quit drugs after detoxification? What Phillips's experience actually indicates is the secondary importance of withdrawal to the outcome of treatment, suggesting that the entire focus on withdrawal is wrongheaded.

Withdrawal from alcohol—as represented by delirium tremens—became a major topic for medical research in the United States in the 1950s. One puzzling aspect of this emphasis has been that Canadian physicians regularly report finding the phenomenon to be less severe. A study at Toronto's Addiction Research Foundation, for example, indicated that skid-row alcoholics could have their symptoms suppressed in a supportive environment populated by other alcoholics who likewise did not experience withdrawal (Oki 1974). In a debate entitled "Is Inpatient Rehabilitation of the Alcoholic Cost Effective? (1984), Joseph Pursch, a clinician and medical director of the American CompCare Corporation, found the severely alcoholic patients he saw could rarely function outside the hospital. Helen Annis of the Canadian Addiction Research Foundation reported, on the other hand, that all the data indicated "outpatient treatment methods to have equal or even better chances of success" than inpatient care. She noted that well over 90 percent of Canadian patients weathered detoxification without need for hospitalization and in fact benefited from detoxifying in a social, rather than a medical setting ("Inpatient vs. Outpatient Treatment" 1984). Even given Dr. Pursch's pessimistic appraisal of the American alcohol detoxification experience, other researchers—such as Tarter et al. (1983)—have found that only a minority of alcoholics undergo severe withdrawal (the alcoholics in this study had exhibited numerous impairments on intellectual and neuropsychological tests and had histories of heavy drinking averaging over fifteen years).

Can We Treat Away the Drug Problem?

As detailed in chapter 5, the role of withdrawal in the maintenance of addictive behavior is secondary at most. Indeed, any cured addict will have withstood both withdrawal and periodic urges to return to addicted use even—as with the returned Vietnam Veteran—if they continue to use the drug periodically. When alcoholics, narcotics addicts, and smokers do relapse, it is seldom because they have experienced unusual physical symptoms or craving for a substance (Marlatt and Gordon 1980). Furthermore, indications are that people can fortify themselves quite well to resist relapse, often appearing to do so better without the aid of treatment. Wille (1983) found that heroin addicts who were the least confident in their ability to overcome their physical need for the drug and who required the most

institutional support to do so were those who had the most difficulty creating a nonaddicted lifestyle following treatment.

Addicts who are convinced they cannot escape their addictions are those particularly unlikely to believe they can manage their own physical discomfort, at the same time that they display a heightened respect for medical manipulations. Consider that the subject in the Light and Torrance (1929) study who expressed the greatest physical need for heroin was the one whose symptoms were relieved by an injection of saline solution. The addict least prepared for remission is the one who dreads getting off the drug and requires the greatest medical and chemical support for doing so. As a drug counselor exasperatedly told me, after one of his clients requested she be put in a hospital with doctors standing by to give her Demerol should her withdrawal from methadone prove too painful, "It's only called withdrawal if people *stop* taking drugs." From a commonsense standpoint, would one expect greater success at quitting smoking for the person who purchases a set of filters to step down the amount of nicotine he inhales or for the one who declares, "I'm going to quit smoking even if it kills me"?

By convincing addicts that remission from drug abuse is a severe metabolic strain, that their addiction is either inbred or deeply a part of their constitution, and that periodic desires to return to the drug represent powerful (albeit conditioned) physiological cravings, medical, pharmacological, and psychological treatment attack the very feelings of self-efficacy addicts need to achieve remission. Rather then warning addicts about how difficult quitting drugs is—and how much assistance they will need—the very opposite approach seems to be called for. That is, patients would benefit from being told that however tough the experience of withdrawal will be, they are capable of handling it. In any case, there is no alternative for such addicts to the recognition that the only way out of addiction is for them to be able to control their own craving and their desire for relief of discomfort or pain.

Bandura (1977a) signaled a major direction for modern therapies with his analysis that whatever improvement occurred in therapy was inevitably the result of patients' increased feeling of self-efficacy. Improved health outcomes of many types have been connected with enhanced self-efficacy, such as preventing the negative consequences of aging and even postponing death (Rodin and Langer 1977). On the other hand, people's belief that their own efforts are inadequate to affect their outcomes creates depression (Seligman 1975) and what Langer (1978) and Langer and Benevento (1978) labeled "self-induced dependence." The addicts who found quitting heroin easiest in therapy in Wille's (1983) study were those who began the process with the greatest expectation of success. Condiotte and Lichtenstein (1981) made a similar discovery about those with the best outcomes in a smoking cessation program. When smokers attribute their immediate cessation of

smoking in such programs to their own efforts rather than to the skill of the therapist or the efficacy of the therapy, they are more likely to maintain abstinence (Colletti and Kopel 1979; Fisher et al. 1982).

If those who quit addiction already have such feelings of self-efficacy, or must acquire them, does therapy help? Hodgson and Miller's (1982) text outlining a record-keeping and behavior modification procedure for treating addictions and compulsions described a single case of a man who quit smoking on his own after having a religious vision one night (cf. Marlatt 1981). What are we to make of the fact that about 20 million Americans quit smoking on their own in the decade from 1965 to 1975 ("Adult Use of Tobacco" 1975)? Surely most did so without employing elaborate behavioral techniques or undergoing religious experiences (Peele 1983a). The self-curers in Schachter's (1982) study of natural remission among smokers and overeaters appeared to take the most straightforward approaches: simply resolving to quit cigarettes or to eat less, cut out desserts, eat less fattening foods, and so forth (Gerin 1982). Schachter actually found those who had never been in therapy to have higher remission rates than those who had. Is it possible that the very act of turning oneself over to a treatment program is antagonistic to the feeling of self-efficacy necessary to succeed at cure? While the Schachter comparison of those who relied on treatment or not involved very small numbers, the 1982 Surgeon General's Report on Smoking, based on a survey of the research and a large data base, intriguingly summarized that "outcomes are sometimes better with less rather than more therapeutic contact" (p. 284).

Therapy works best when it requires clients to change attitudes, practice skills, and make life changes and when it attributes these changes to the client. Therapy that instead convinces clients they have inbred weaknesses that require the permanent intervention of the therapy attack the beliefs necessary for cure and effective self-management. All therapy is a mixed bag conveying, often simultaneously, elements of both messages. Yet disease views have at their core a vision of the intractability of the client's malady and of the essentialness of therapy's role. The strange story of Synanon epitomizes these attitudes. The best-known therapeutic community for drug addicts in the United States, Synanon (under its founder Charles Dederich) became obsessed with the idea that clients leaving the organization obviated their own cures and undercut the organization. Dederich employed a security force to coerce clients to stay in the treatment community, and he was eventually convicted of placing a rattlesnake in the mailbox of a lawyer representing dissident clients trying to leave the organization ("Synanon Founder . . . Convicted in Attack With a Snake" 1980).

Former Dederich supporters (like Jane Fonda and other luminaries of the entertainment industry) may regard Dederich's actions to be aberrations from Synanon's original philosophy. In fact, his response was the nat-

ural consequence of the Synanon credo that membership in the community is a lifetime proposition, a credo it shares with the most popular brand of alcoholism therapy: Alcoholics Anonymous. Popular stump speakers like Father Joseph Martin have been widely successful in promoting AA's own claims of near-infallibility into tenets of faith. In contrast, the only controlled comparison of AA with other treatments reported the highest dropout and relapse rate for those randomly assigned to AA (Brandsma et al. 1980; see Miller and Hester 1980). For therapies that involve alcoholics in nonreligious AA-type groups, the only two studies again favored the untreated comparisons (Pattison et al. 1967; Zimberg 1974). A survey of group therapies with nonalcoholic or drug-abusing college students found that the Synanon version of group therapy, called "the game," produced the most frequent cases of extremely negative outcomes (Lieberman et al. 1973).

Groups like Synanon and Alcoholics Anonymous have offered effective group support for abstinence for some people. At the same time, their demands for a consuming, full-time commitment have their own negative sequelae; for example, encouraging a totalitarian outlook that denies the possibility of self-cure or of pursuing other goals (such as cutting back drinking) or other therapies. Despite their considerable drawbacks, and no signs that they can work for other than self-selected populations, AA and related organizations completely dominate the U.S. treatment field, and their principles and policies are widely regarded to be the main hope for reducing drug and alcohol abuse in this country. Moreover, the religious absolutism of AA has been carefully melded with medical dogma. This modern synthesis is embodied in Harvard psychiatrist George Vaillant's acclaimed book, *The Natural History of Alcoholism*. In this remarkable work, Vaillant argued with his subjects against their claims that they could drink again nonaddictively or go it alone without AA (a majority of his subjects did both) and demanded that alcohol abusers be funneled through the health care system (while finding medical treatment did not improve the prognosis for severe alcoholism and was positively unnecessary for less severe alcohol abuse). Vaillant's research has been widely hailed as a defense of conventional treatments of alcoholism.

The Alcoholism and Chemical Dependence Industry

At the time the first edition of the Alcoholics Anonymous "Big Book" appeared in 1939, AA claimed no more than 100 active members. There was little public concern or awareness about the extent and the danger of alcoholism in the United States. The National Committee for Education on Alcoholism (the progenitor of the National Council on Alcoholism, created

in 1944 by AA members with the aid of the faculty of the Yale University Center of Alcohol Studies) identified its mandate to be alerting the public to these dangers as well as helping alcoholics to understand the nature of their problem. Between 1942 and 1976, Room (1980) estimated, the number of people receiving treatment for alcoholism increased twentyfold. Yet an even more rapid growth in the delivery of alcoholism services has occurred since the mid-1970s, when funding for alcoholism treatment shifted from large public institutions to service contracts and third-party payments provided to private alcoholism organizations. A 1982 Gallup Poll revealed that fully one-third of U.S. families believed one of their members had a drinking problem, a figure that had doubled over the previous six years.

Industry spokespeople now indicate more than 15 million Americans require treatment for alcoholism (Hackler 1983). This is to be compared with estimates by NCA founder Marty Mann (1970) that there were 3 million alcoholics in the United States in 1943, 5 million in 1956, and 6.5 million in 1965. By reckoning that the relatives of alcoholics need treatment as urgently as alcoholics themselves, the treatment industry now considers perhaps one in three or four Americans a potential beneficiary of therapy for alcoholism. In the 1980s, for-profit alcoholism clinics have become a $400 million-a-year industry with stocks traded on the exchanges and with fees ranging from $2,500 to $13,000 a month (Hackler 1983). This is in addition to the nearly $900 million earmarked by the Reagan administration in its 1985 budget for programs in Alcohol, Drug Abuse, and Mental Health. The public inebriates and skid-row denizens who once typified the alcoholic for the average American have been replaced by prominent public figures who announce their alcoholism and enroll in elite private clinics.

The economic strength and public allure of this growth industry has been matched by its political clout. In the fall of 1983, Medicare proposed that reimbursement for hospital stays for alcoholism treatment be calculated on an average length of 8.1 days. Immediately, the NIAAA, NCA, and organizations of treatment centers and counselors inundated DHHS with protests. The standards were suspended. Particularly effective was said to have been Betty Ford's personal appeal to Health and Human Services secretary Margaret Heckler ("Anatomy of a Victory: The DRG Exemption" 1984). Lost in the ballyhoo were the recently released findings of the U.S. Congressional Office of Technology Assessment: "controlled studies have typically found no differences in outcomes according to intensity and duration of treatment . . . with respect to treatment setting, there is little evidence for the superiority of either inpatient or outpatient care alone . . ." (Saxe et al. 1983: 4–5).

With the shift in funding mechanisms for alcoholism has come the aggressive marketing of disease concepts and alcoholism treatment services and identification of new client groups (Weisner and Room 1984). In addi-

tion to middle-class drinkers and children of alcoholics, these groups include teenage problem drinkers, women, minorities, functioning workers, and so on. An important change has also taken place in the traditional AA attitude that only those who indicated a readiness could be helped in combatting their alcoholism. Instead, the emphasis is now on active intervention and confrontational strategies, so-called outreach approaches (Weisner and Room 1984). From this perspective denial has become the defining trait of alcoholism, with alcoholics being identifiable by their inability or unwillingness to acknowledge the nature of their problems. This view is opposed by evidence that alcoholics have a good notion of what their drinking problems are and that contradicting these self-conceptions *impedes* treatment (Miller 1983c).

Because alcoholics are considered incapable of deciding what is best for themselves, most patients are now mandated into treatment through either industrial employee assistance programs or the court system. The largest group of treatment clients are those who are offered therapy as an alternative to a jail sentence for drunk driving or for such other crimes as wife battery, child abuse, writing bad checks, and even robbery (Weisner 1983). The programs are nearly all AA-based and demand that participants acknowledge that they are alcoholics. This is despite the repeated finding that drunk drivers and others convicted of alcohol-related offenses do not conform to the typical alcoholic profile (Vingilis 1983). Such individuals are now likely to be instructed that they are alcoholics, but will this label help them? Salzberg and Klingberg (1983) actually found that subjects who received ordinary judicial sanctions for drunk driving had significantly fewer subsequent alcohol-related traffic violations than those who were remanded to treatment. An earlier study discovered that simply putting people on probation was superior to compelling them to attend either clinical treatment or AA meetings (Ditman and Crawford 1966; Ditman et al. 1967).

The awareness that treatment produces very small and inexact benefits for alcoholics points to the prevention of alcohol problems as the most effective means of dealing with alcoholism. What does prevention look like from a disease framework? The bulk of the research money spent by the Alcohol, Drug Abuse, and Mental Health Administration (ADAMHA) is for biological investigation; the major focus of this research is on identifying inherited biological traits that cause alcoholism and drug dependence. According to acting ADAMHA director Robert Trachtenberg, "This research will have great impact upon the prevention of alcoholism as well as the understanding of the biological mechanisms that determine the onset of this disease" ("Biomed Research Gets Top Priority" 1984). In his presidential message in the *Bulletin of the Society of Psychologists in Addictive Behaviors,* Marlatt (1984) sounded the cry that psychosocial and epidemiological research is in danger of being submerged entirely by "the emergent

political strength of the biomedical researchers" (p. 2, quoting Robin Room). Ironically, the bulk of articles by the *psychologists* in this issue of the *Bulletin* concerned animal and human biological research.

The leading proponent of biological predispositions in alcoholism, Schuckit (1984), enthusiastically looked forward to the development of tests for a variety of potential biological markers for the malady, with the aim of being better able to indicate which young people should be told never to drink ("Alcoholism Not Inherited: Predisposition Does Exist" 1984). He added, "If we ever get to that point, where these kinds of tests are used to screen people [for example, for job applications], we're going to have to fight to make sure they don't get misused" (p. 15). Another proponent of this futuristic vision is the National Foundation for Prevention of Chemical Dependency Disease (1984), whose mission is:

> To sponsor scientific research and development of a simple biochemical test that can be administered to our young children to determine any predisposition for chemical dependency disease; to promote greater awareness, understanding and acceptance of the disease by the general public so prevention or treatment can be commenced at the age youngsters are most vulnerable.

What are the dangers of this method of prevention? The research and point of view behind this book indicate that (1) alcoholism and addiction do not exist at the level of biological determinants, so that no individual genetic predisposition indicates if addiction will or will not appear; (2) there is strong situational and lifespan variation in the appearance of addiction, so that those addicted at one time and place—and *particularly the young*—will often outgrow severe addiction; (3) the *belief* in one's susceptibility to addiction is itself a strong predisposing factor in addiction and that labeling oneself as an addict is the strongest guarantee of perpetuating an addiction; and (4) a cultural milieu in which the imminence, innateness, and inevitability of addiction are emphasized is associated with the highest addiction rates. In other words, the approach now favored by the official institutional leadership in the field is one whose only efficacy had been in the direction of creating addiction.

While the research program to uncover biological markers in alcoholism searches for ways to identify future alcoholics, active interventions with young people are already very much a part of the current treatment scene. Concern over epic rates of alcohol and drug abuse has prompted a huge public awareness campaign that emphasizes not only the dangers in drug use but the identification of children who use drugs as being chemically dependent (as exemplified by the two public television programs "Chemical People" shown nationally in November 1983). Like alcoholism,

chemical dependence is seen to be a permanent condition requiring lifetime prophylactic measures. One program for diagnosing children as dependent involves gathering family members and others close to the child to confront the child about drug use and other aberrant behaviors. The aim of the intervention is to have the child acknowledge his or her illness and to enter treatment.

Residential treatments in which children are stripped of their possessions and other signs of their status in the outside world in order to eradicate their prior identities as drug users have received mixed ratings from the media. Many observers have been shocked by depictions of verbal and emotional abuse of the children in such get-tough or tough-love programs. The techniques the programs utilize borrow from the Synanon group therapy or "game" and resemble the process by which the individual is forced to admit previous ideological errors and to adopt a new, approved group identity that Schein (1961) described in his analysis of brainwashing techniques. Underlying all these methods is an AA—and a religious—concept termed *surrender,* or the sacrifice of the individual's critical self-awareness for a subservience to God or the treatment authorities. It is only at the point of total self-abnegation, this belief has it, that meaningful therapy can take place. The Addiction Recovery Corporation—a treatment center in Concord, Massachusetts—advertises itself to parents with the chilling claim: "We Hang On Until They Let Go."

Interventions with the young are not reserved for those who have actually used drugs or alcohol. One thrust of the idea that children of alcoholics are at a high risk to have drinking problems is the identification of such children for special attention even before they are teens. They may as children be educated about the nature of alcoholism, taught to abstain themselves, and made aware of the kinds of roles that family members are said to assume around the figure of a drunken parent. It is such roles that are the object of treatment for nonalcoholic relatives of alcoholics. The treatment of family members of alcoholics has exploded since the late 1970s. The National Association for Children of Alcoholics was established in 1983 with aims described by one of its founders, Dr. Timmen Cermak ("The Founding, Future and Vision of NACoA" 1983: 19):

> Children of alcoholics require and deserve treatment in and of themselves, not as mere adjuncts of alcoholics. . . . [T]hat entails . . . accepting the concept of co-alcoholism . . . [as being as legitimate] as the diagnosis of alcoholism.

These children include the adult children of alcoholics, themselves not presently living with alcoholics, who are still thought to bear the brunt of

childhood identities fashioned by having grown up with a parent with a drinking problem (cf. Black 1982; Woititz 1983).

In his play *Our Town* (published the year before Alcoholics Anonymous was officially established), Thornton Wilder (1938: 931) recorded the following exchange:

> WOMAN IN THE BALCONY: Is there much drinking in Grover's Corners?
> MR. WEBB: Well, ma'am, I wouldn't know what you'd call *much.* Sattidy nights the farmhands meet down in Ellery Greenough's stable and holler some. Fourth of July I've been known to taste a drop myself—and Decoration Day, of course. We've got one or two town drunks [Grover's Corners' population is approximately 3,000], but they're always having remorses every time an evangelist comes to town.

From this off-hand, humorous image of alcoholism—in the person of the occasional town drunk who sobers up whenever an itinerant preacher arrives in town—the United States has developed a notion of alcoholism as an overwhelming specter that potentially clouds the lives of nearly every citizen. It might be said that the disease of alcoholism and related maladies have become a primary component of Americans' self-conception, one requiring constant vigilance, the segregation and re-education of many of our young—including some who have never had a drink—and the coerced treatment of many young and adult alike.

Spreading Diseases

The concept that adults who may never have been drunk warrant the same disease diagnosis and treatment as the alcoholic represents a monumental advance in the spread of alcoholism and disease in general. The concept has infinite ramifications: for example, if people need to be confronted about their unacknowledged drinking problems, then must others be confronted and treated for their unacknowledged relationship to an alcoholic or to a person who has failed to acknowledge his alcoholism? Although many more people will come under the purview of alcoholism treatment in this way, other trends signify that still larger numbers of people will be labeled as having a disease and as requiring medical attention.

The broadest view yet of the disease of alcoholism was offered by alcoholism researcher and psychiatrist Donald Goodwin (1984) when he argued that "One reason to believe alcoholism is a real disease—as real as a houseboat or a rose bush or double pneumonia—is that it has a natural history" (p. 1). For Goodwin, a disease is anything that can be identified and traced

over time—even should it disappear! Apparently, for Goodwin, if something exists at all, then it is a disease. The possibility that disease theorizing would move in this direction was anticipated by Jules Masserman (1976), another alcohol researcher and psychiatrist, when he wrote that "Addiction to drink . . . is a 'disease' only in the sense that excessive eating, sleeping, smoking, gambling, wandering, or lechery may also be so classified. All are attempts to deny conscious or unconscious insecurities and apprehensions, to challenge the milieu, and to escape onerous responsibility" (p. 4).

Masserman could as well have added stealing, overwork, worrying, sadness, fear, incompetence, forgetfulness, stage fright, procrastination, anger, child abuse, murder, premenstrual tension, sloppiness, and the host of other problems people seek treatment for. What he quite correctly meant to indicate was that regarding alcoholism as a disease denuded that word of all its commonsensical meaning. Masserman's work—along with Szasz's (1974) and my own book, *Love and Addiction*—was part of a movement that indicated compulsive chemical use was no less subject to individual self-control and cognitive and social influence than was any other strongly felt urge. This whole line of reasoning has now been turned on its ear, so that all involvements that are broadly similar to alcoholism and drug addiction can be reclassified as diseases, as if in having thus labeled such activities and states of being clinicians had made a scientific contribution akin to discovering a new planet or life form. In this way, as Masserman (1976) noted, what has historically been referred to as lechery can now be called "sexual addiction" (Carnes 1983), requiring that sufferers join groups constructed along AA lines for its cure.

That more and more behaviors are being called diseases does not rule out a moralistic characterization of the same actions. In fact, as Marlatt (1983) observed, the modern disease model "is little more than the old 'moral model' (drinking as sinful behavior) dressed up in sheep's clothing (or at least a white coat)" (p. 1107), in which abstinence signifies repentance. When professional football player Art Schlichter, who had been suspended for gambling, was readmitted to the National Football League, NFL commissioner Pete Rozelle declared: "We . . . reviewed medical views of physicians qualified in the care of compulsive gambling . . . [and] the doctors believe Art's condition is under control" ("Schlichter Suspension Lifted by Rozelle" 1984: 31). Here is how Schlichter himself described his remission on his reinstatement: "There are choices in everybody's lives. There is a bad side of the road and a good side of the road. The bad side is easier to take, but it will lead you into trouble. Do it the difficult, the good way" ("People" 1984: B9).

There is nothing the matter, of course, with people resolving to change the "side of the road" they travel on. The difficulty enters with considering

this street crossing to be a medical matter. Those societies in which alcohol (or anything else) is seen to provide an explanation for uncontrolled behavior—be the explanation magical or medical—are those with the highest incidence of alcohol-related antisocial behavior. Telling drunk drivers they cannot control their drinking or be responsible for their actions once they have drunk is tantamount to allowing them to disregard the law and social regulation when they are drinking. Accepting drug and alcohol intoxication or withdrawal, premenstrual tension, love sickness, eating junk food, and so on as extenuating circumstances in the commission of a crime is to guarantee that more crimes will be committed under these circumstances (Peele 1982a). Consider, in this light, Schachter's (1980: 156–157) explanation for social disintegration as a result of nicotine withdrawal:

> When a large portion of an addicted population is attempting to quit smoking or switches to low nicotine brands, a very large number of people in that population will be in withdrawal. Given what we know of withdrawal, this means large numbers of people simultaneously in a state of irritability, irascibility, short temper, and so on. One could with reason anticipate high rates of divorce, assault, and general mayhem in such a population.

Diseases have made tremendous inroads not only in explaining crime but in defining the innermost feelings people, sometimes quite ordinary people, have. Depression has for some years been promoted as a disease (cf. Kline 1981). Now irrational love attractions (Liebowitz 1983) and phobias (Sheehan 1984)—the latter of which constitute the second-most common mental health problem (after alcoholism) in America—are called diseases. Unlike garden-variety sadness, attachment to a lover, and anxiety or fear, disease-based versions of these maladies are termed endogenous and conceived as biochemical or neurological anomalies requiring drug treatments. Oddly enough, given the quite different behavioral manifestations and settings of these diseases, all seem to respond best to the administration of antidepressant drugs. Just as with alcoholism and the metabolic disease of narcotic addiction, these latter-day maladies are seen to be lifetime characteristics of people that require them always to be aware of their illness and to be on guard against it. Since prescribed medications only arrest the problem without curing it, as in the case of methadone treatment for heroin addiction, such drugs are considered a necessary and permanent adjunct to the person's functioning.

The same course of discovery and the same scientific problems appear with the modern diseases of depression, love sickness, and phobias as with alcoholism and narcotic addiction. That is, clinicians remark on the severity and resistance to treatment of some cases of irrational behavior. In frus-

tration, some physicians try different drugs until they find one that provides symptom relief. They then infer the existence of an endogenous biochemical source for the observed behaviors and feelings. The discoveries are in this way invariably made by exclusion, with neurological sources for a malady being deduced from the flagrance and persistence of its symptoms and its intractability to conventional psychotherapy. Never is the diagnosis of an individual case suggested by a biochemical analysis instead of by self-report, nor are hypotheses about the nature of the disease ever originally generated by neurochemical research.

The same baffling definitional problems remain for these contemporary diseases as have been noted for addiction. For example, they are all heavily linked to gender; more apparent among women than men are depression (by a 3:1 ratio, Weissman and Klerman 1977), severe phobias (4:1, Sheehan 1984) and love sickness or "hysteroid dysphoria" (10+:1, Liebowitz and Klein 1979), while alcoholism remains the prototypical male disease (found ten or more times as often with men as women; Öjesjö 1984). In accounting for the greater frequency of a purportedly biological form of anxiety among women, Sheehan (1984) adopts a rather old saw by suggesting female hormones may be the culprit. In fact, no reasonable biological relationship has been shown to underlie all the sex-linked emotional diseases (cf., in the case of alcohol, Cloninger et al. 1978). Moreover, similar sex ratios are apparent in the milder versions of these same diseases, such as problem drinking and less severe anxiety and depression. It defies scientific rationality and parsimony to imagine that social causes create a set of problems, while an entirely different collection of factors comes into play for the same groups of people at the point at which their problems become diseases.

As with addictive diseases, notions about these new diseases rest on the feelings and self-conceptions of a relatively small group of individuals who seek therapeutic help. Missing in the analysis of the problem are surveys of broader populations, accounts by those who choose to treat their own symptoms, natural histories of young people and others whose difficulties fall away as their lives evolve, and the complicated feelings of all the other groups that consistently confound disease views of addiction. In the past, people who felt they were in the throes of an inescapable sickness were free to choose help on their own. Today, public health campaigns actively promote the existence of these emotional diseases and encourage doctors, teachers, and child-care providers to search for victims among the young. In schools and elsewhere, young people are identified as hyperkinetic, learning-disabled, maladjusted, abuse victims, offspring of alcoholics, and so forth, with the *purpose* of convincing them they are truly ill. The most ready means for dealing with all those who are different or who have problems is to label their diseases and submit them for treatment.

George Orwell's *1984* found nearly everyone voluntarily cooperating with a military dictatorship because they accepted its rendition of history and willingly policed themselves. In the historic 1984, we see a revised version of mind control. People eagerly seek out, or have forced upon them, self-designations that are even more comprehensive than the social and political roles in Orwell's futuristic society. These roles tell us not only how we feel and who we are, but how we *should* feel and how we *will* behave into the unlimited future. The nineteenth-century revolution in thinking about mental illness, analyzed by some as a social-control mechanism for the deviant and those who cannot be assimilated into society, has been supplanted by a far more thorough psychological categorization. Affecting practically everyone in one fashion or another, it is a vision of normal life as being rife with emotional disease.

The Cure for Addiction

> The nineteenth-century discovery [in Britain] that the [narcotic] addict is a suitable case for treatment is today an entrenched and unquestioned premise, with society unaware of the arbitrariness of this come-lately assumption. . . . Any suggestion that the current model is fundamentally mistaken in its assumption, that the treatment enterprise should be closed down and people with bad habits left to their own devices, would be dismissed only as outrageous and bizarre.
>
> (Berridge and Edwards 1981: 251)

Even with government and other reports showing minimal and sometimes double-edged benefits from therapy for addiction, there is no slowing down the rush to have all addicts treated. In imagining how the results of this gigantic enterprise can be maximized, it is good to recall an evaluation of treatment outcomes for an alcoholism program by Gerard et al. (1962) in which the authors noted that improvement was a consequence of "a change in the alcoholic's attitude toward the use of alcohol based on a person's own experiences, which in the vast majority of cases took place outside any clinical interactions" (p. 94). The insight these researchers had more than two decades ago has not been improved on by all the research on treatment cited in this book.

Whether in therapy or not, addicts improve when their relationships to work, family, and other aspects of their environment improve. Addicts have come to count on the regular rewards they get from their addictive involvement. They can give up these rewards when they believe they will find superior gratifications from other activities in the regular fiber of their lives. Therapy helps this process by focusing on external rewards and by

assisting addicts in conceptualizing these rewards and obtaining them. Any rewards therapy itself produces must be regarded as intermediate and time-limited, as a passage to the stable, environmental rewards that are necessary to create a nonaddictive equilibrium in people's lives. Only when such everyday but potent reinforcements are firmly in place is an addiction cured. (See figure 6–1.)

Therapy—whether behavioral, group, or psychodynamic—errs when it designates its rewards and addicts' functioning in the therapeutic environment to be its goals. Similarly, by focusing solely on the addictive involvement as the object of change and not on addicts' life context, such therapy becomes too inward-focused to have real meaning or impact. For example, if conducted in splendid isolation within the laboratory, aversion training (or antabuse drug therapy or hypnotic suggestions) that attaches negative feelings to the addiction will be overwhelmed by outside pressures in addicts' lives. The idea that people can cease addictions by replacing them with so-called positive addictions like running or meditation is likewise a simplistic reduction of the role of addiction in people's lives. Like all-encompassing group involvements, activity substitution mainly holds out the opportunity for alternate addictions that may not be any less self-destructive than the original one (Peele 1981a).

Establishing systematic, ingrained rewards in people's lives is an imperfect, difficult process. The avoidance of this complexity marks addicts' pursuit and acceptance of addictive rewards in the first place. Preparation

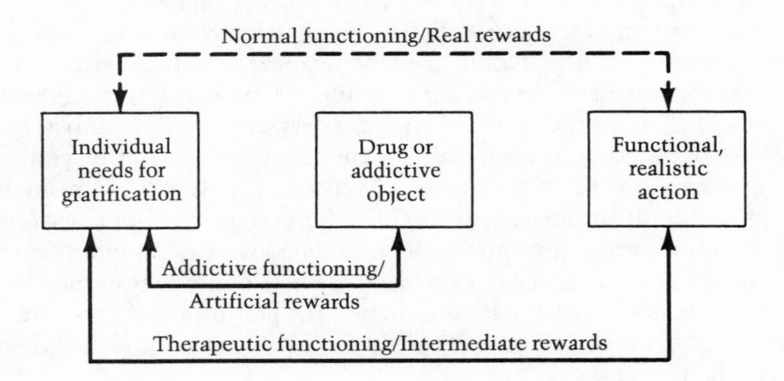

Addiction short-circuits a person's achievement of real-world rewards through normal functioning. Therapy must remove the barrier presented by an addiction so that a person can experience these real rewards. One way for therapy to do this is to provide intermediate rewards that lead to realistic action.

Source: Peele 1981a.

Figure 6–1. Breaking the Addiction Cycle

for a nonaddicted lifestyle includes an awareness that this imperfection exists, that negative feelings will return, that slips will occur, and that insoluble problems and a sense of inadequate rewards will never disappear entirely. The discovery that prior motivation is the most important element in predicting successful outcomes for addiction treatment is a restatement of the evident truth that only those who are willing to tolerate the uncertainty of a life without the addiction and who believe they can tolerate it will succeed at doing so. Therapy fails by causing addicts to imagine there is some way to short-circuit this fundamental self-reliance. It succeeds when it increases people's sense of their strength to withstand the uncertainty and discomfort as well as to generate positive rewards for themselves.

The summary of the steps out of an addiction that this book has highlighted—that people recover to the extent that they (1) believe an addiction is hurting them and wish to overcome it, (2) feel enough efficacy to manage their withdrawal and life without the addiction, and (3) find sufficient alternative rewards to make life without the addiction worthwhile—cannot make us optimistic about dramatic techniques for curing addiction. As an approach to our major problems of addiction, individual, therapeutic remedies obviously do not have the necessary breadth and depth of impact. Therapy is no more likely to eliminate addiction overall than is spontaneous recovery. While some seem to be aided to recovery through treatment, we can never get enough people to accept therapy, cure enough people through therapy, and keep enough people from relapsing after therapy to change fundamentally our society-wide levels of addiction.

More than anything, our failure at combatting addiction is due to our inability to prevent new addicts from being created. While use of major illicit drugs has receded somewhat for younger Americans in the 1980s, it is still greater than for the youth of any other Western nation (Johnston et al. 1981). Alcohol intoxication remains extremely common in this group, and both excessive alcohol and drug use by adolescents signal a dangerous future of addiction in our country. While the extremity of our response to these trends indicates how justifiably frightened we are, the efforts we have made over two decades have been futile. Indeed, extreme reactions to drug use and other addictive problems—such as the promotion of alternate compulsive activities as remedies—constitute major social and health problems in themselves.

Future generations of addicts—the enemy within—are the focus of a continual barrage of information about drugs and alcohol. My analysis in this book agrees with the assumption behind antidrug campaigns that there is something fundamentally wrong with the need many young people show—and some express consistently—for the modification of experience brought on by drugs and alcohol. However, I analyze the regular pursuit by

many of an eradication of awareness to be an expression of mainstream cultural trends. There is no reason to assume that at any given time and place people are being prepared psychologically and practically by social institutions for what they must deal with. If addiction is a retreat from the attempt to attain a balanced set of gratifications in life, then its increase means that more people are finding their resources for coping to be insufficient relative to the benefits they believe an active involvement in this world will yield. This chronic deficiency can be traced to a lack of practice at self-reliance, of feelings of competence, of an ability to tolerate discomfort, and of self-confidence combined with the absence of positive values toward achievement, toward experience, toward society and community (and, in the most extreme cases of addictiveness, toward health and toward the self; cf. Peele 1983b). What we are missing in our culture today is a sense of our capacities, a moderation of our fear of the world, and positive expectations about what can be gained from life.

As I wrote with Archie Brodsky in 1975 (p. 145):

> The best antidotes to addiction are joy and competence—joy as the capacity to take pleasure in the people, activities, and things that are available to us; competence as the ability to master relevant parts of the environment and the confidence that our actions make a difference for ourselves and others.

Preparing people better to achieve joy and competence offers us our only substantial chance at affecting the incidence of addiction. It is certainly not a modest goal: Some might call it utopian or quixotic. Yet to the extent that our addiction theories avoid this realization—whether these theories come from pharmacologists, from clinicians and self-help groups who see themselves as combatting a disease, from sociologists, from psychologists—we will only obfuscate and exacerbate the addictive tendencies of our society.

Our current approaches to tackling addiction are defeated before they begin and stand no hope of success, since they misappraise the nature and the solution of the problem. What we need, in Henry Murray's (1981: 533–534) words, is "the conception of a better world composed of better societies composed of better persons" and a drive "to actualize it by self-transformations and social reconstructions." Yet often scientists dealing with behavior "prevent all development in this direction by shattering man's faith in the existence of the necessary potentialities within himself and reducing him to cynicism and despair" as though these scientists were "intending out of malice to reduce the concept of human nature to its lowest common denominators, and were gloating" about having done so. Nowhere is the description more apt than in our theories of addiction.

References

Addicted mothers and babies. 1984. *Journal,* Addiction Research Foundation (April): 12.

Adler, M.W.; Bendotti, C.; Ghezzi, D.; Samanin, R.; and Valzelli, L. 1975. Dependence to morphine in differentially housed rats. *Psychopharmacologia* 41:15–18.

Adult use of tobacco. 1975. Washington, DC: Center for Disease Control and National Cancer Institute.

Alcoholics Anonymous. 1939. *Alcoholics Anonymous.* New York: Works Publishing.

Alcoholism not inherited: Predisposition does exist. 1984. *U.S. Journal of Drug and Alcohol Dependence* (January): 1; 15.

Alexander, B.K.; Beyerstein, B.L.; Hadaway, P.F.; and Coambs, R.B. 1981. Effects of early and later colony housing on oral ingestion of morphine in rats. *Pharmacology Biochemistry and Behavior* 15:571–576.

Alexander, B.K.; Coambs, R.B.; and Hadaway, P.F. 1978. The effect of housing and gender on morphine self-administration in rats. *Psychopharmacology* 58:175–179.

Alexander, B.K., and Hadaway, P.F. 1982. Opiate addiction: The case for an adaptive orientation. *Psychological Bulletin* 92:367–381.

Allen, J. 1984. Correlates of success in health change efforts. Paper presented at Annual Conference of the American Psychological Association, Toronto, August.

American Psychiatric Association. 1980. *Diagnostic and statistical manual of mental disorders.* 3rd ed. Washington DC: American Psychiatric Association.

Anatomy of a victory: The DRG exemption. 1984. *U.S. Journal of Drug and Alcohol Dependence* (January): 3.

Aneshensel, C.S., and Huba, G.J. 1983. Depression, alcohol use, and smoking over one year. *Journal of Abnormal Psychology* 92:134–150.

Appenzeller, O.; Standefer, J.; Appenzeller, J.; and Atkinson, R. 1980. Neurology of endurance training V: Endorphins. *Neurology* 30:418–419.

Apsler, R. 1978. Untangling the conceptual jungle of "drug abuse." *Contemporary Drug Problems* 7:55–80.

Armor, D.J.; Polich, J.M.; and Stambul, H.B. 1978. *Alcoholism and treatment.* New York: Wiley.

Atkinson, J.W., and Feather, N.T., eds. 1966. *A theory of achievement motivation.* New York: Wiley.

Ausubel, D.P. 1961. Causes and types of narcotic addiction: A psychosocial view. *Psychiatric Quarterly* 35:523–531.

Baekeland, F.; Lundwall, L.; and Kissin B. 1975. Methods for the treatment of chronic alcoholism: A critical appraisal. In *Research advances in alcohol and drug problems,* eds. R.J. Gibbons, Y. Israel, H. Kalant, R.E. Popham, W. Schmidt, and R.G. Smart. vol. 2. New York: Wiley.

Bales, R.F. 1946. Cultural differences in rates of alcoholism. *Quarterly Journal of Studies on Alcohol* 6:480–499.

Ball, J.C.; Smith, J.P.; and Graff, H., eds. 1977. International survey. *Addictive Diseases* 3 (1):entire issue.

Bandura, A. 1977a. Self-efficacy: Toward a unifying theory of behavioral change. *Pychological Review* 84:191–215.

———. 1977b. *Social learning theory.* Englewood Cliffs, NJ: Prentice-Hall.

Barnett, M.L. 1955. Alcoholism in the Cantonese of New York City: An anthropological study. In *Etiology of chronic alcoholism,* ed. O. Diethelm. Springfield, IL: Charles C Thomas.

Beauchamp, D.E. 1980. *Beyond alcoholism: Alcoholism and public health policy.* Philadelphia, PA: Temple University Press.

Beauchamp, D.E., et al. 1980. Comments on "Patterns of Alcoholism over Four Years"; and a response. *Journal of Studies on Alcohol* 41:760–796.

Becker, H.S. 1953. Becoming a marijuana user. *American Journal of Sociology* 59:235–242.

———. 1963. *Outsiders.* London: Free Press of Glencoe.

Becker, M., ed. 1974. *The health belief model and personal health behavior.* Thorofare, NJ: Charles B. Slack.

Beckman, L.J. 1978. The psychosocial characteristics of alcoholic women. *Drug abuse and alcoholism review* (September/December): 1–12.

Beecher, H.K. 1959. *Measurement of subjective responses: Quantitative effects of drugs.* New York: Oxford University Press.

The behaviorists. 1984. *Journal,* Addiction Research Foundation (February): 9–10.

Bejerot, N. 1980. Addiction to pleasure: A biological and social-psychological theory of addiction. In *Theories on drug abuse,* eds. D.J. Lettieri, M. Sayers, and H.W. Pearson. Research Monograph 30. Rockville, MD: National Institute on Drug Abuse.

Bem, D.J., and Funder, D.C. 1978. Predicting more of the people more of the time: Assessing the personality of situations. *Psychological Review* 85:485–501.

Bem, D.J., and Lord, C.G. 1979. The template-matching technique. *Journal of Personality and Social Psychology* 37:833–846.

Bennett, R.; Batenhorst, R.L.; Graves, D.; Foster, T.S.; Bauman, T.; Griffen, W.O.; and Wright, B.D. 1982. Morphine titration in positive laparotomy patients using patient-controlled analgesia. *Current Therapeutic Research* 32:45–51.

Bennett, W., and Gurin, J. 1982. *The dieter's dilemma.* New York: Basic Books.

Benson, C.S., and Wilsnack, S.C. 1983. Gender differences in alcoholic personality characteristics and life experiences. In *Identifying and measuring alcoholic personality characteristics,* ed. W. M. Cox. San Francisco: Jossey-Bass.

Berridge, V., and Edwards, G. 1981. *Opium and the people: Opiate use in nineteenth-century England.* New York: St. Martin's.

Best, J.A., and Bloch, M. 1979. Compliance in the control of cigarette smoking. In *Compliance in health care,* eds. R.E. Haynes, D.W. Taylor, and D.L. Sackett. Baltimore: Johns Hopkins University Press.

Best, J.A., and Hakstian, A.R. 1978. A situation-specific model for smoking behavior. *Addictive Behaviors* 3:79–92.

Biomed research gets top priority. 1984. *U.S. Journal of Drug and Alcohol Dependence* (May): 1; 21.

Birney, R.C.; Burdick, H.; and Teevan, R.C. 1969. *Fear of failure.* New York: Van Nostrand.

Black, C. 1982. *It will never happen to me.* Denver: M.A.C.

Blum, R.H. 1969. On the presence of demons. In *Drugs I: Drugs and society,* eds. R.H. Blum et al. San Francisco: Jossey-Bass.

Blum, R.H., and associates. 1969. *Drugs I: Society and drugs.* San Francisco: Jossey-Bass.

Blum, R.H., and Blum, E.M. 1969. A cultural case study. In *Drugs I: Drugs and society,* eds. R.H. Blum et al. San Francisco: Jossey-Bass.

Boland, F.J. 1983. Open letter concerning failure to replicate with new colony Wistar rats. Queen's University, Kingston, Canada, June 30.

Boskind-White, M., and White, W.C. 1983. *Bulimarexia: The binge/purge cycle.* New York: Norton.

Boyd, W. 1976. Excitement: The gambler's drug. In *Gambling and society*, ed. W.R. Eadington. Springfield, IL: Charles C Thomas.

Brandsma, J.M.; Maultsby, M.C.; and Welsh, R.J. 1980. *The outpatient treatment of alcoholism: A review and comparative study.* Baltimore: University Park Press.

Brecher, E.M. 1972. *Licit and illicit drugs.* Mount Vernon, NY: Consumers Union.

Brown, S.A.; Goldman, M.S.; Inn, A.; and Anderson, L.R. 1980. Expectations of reinforcement from alcohol: Their domain and relation to drinking patterns. *Journal of Consulting and Clinical Psychology* 48:419–426.

Bruch, H. 1973. *Eating Disorders.* New York: Basic Books.

Brunke, M.L.; Bowman, M.; Alexander, B.K.; and Coambs, R.B. 1980. Failure to find an effect of catheterization on oral morphine consumption in rats. *Psychological Reports* 47:444–446.

Brunswick, A.F. 1979. Black youth and drug use behavior. In *Youth drug abuse: Problems, issues and treatment,* eds. G. Beschner and A. Friedman. Lexington, MA: Lexington.

Burke, H., and Marcus, R. 1977. MacAndrew MMPI alcoholism scale: Alcoholism and drug addictiveness. *Journal of Psychology* 96:141–148.

Burnett, M. 1979. Understanding and overcoming addictions. In *Helping clients with special concerns,* eds. S. Eisenberg and L.E. Patterson. Chicago: Rand McNally.

Cahalan, D. 1970. *Problem drinkers: A national survey.* San Francisco: Jossey-Bass.

Cahalan, D.; Cisin, I.H.; and Crossley, H.M. 1969. *American drinking practices.* Monograph 6. New Brunswick, NJ: Rutgers Center of Alcohol Studies.

Cahalan, D., and Room, R. 1974. *Problem drinking among American men.* Mono-

graph 7. New Brunswick, NJ: Rutgers Center of Alcohol Studies.

Califano, J.E. 1983. *The 1982 report on drug abuse and alcoholism.* New York: Warner.

Cameron, D.C. 1971a. Abuse of alcohol and drugs: Concepts and planning. *World Health Organization Chronicle* 25:8–16.

———. 1971b. Facts about drugs. *World Health* (April): 4–11.

Caplan, R.D.; Cobb, S.; and French, J.R.P., Jr. 1975. Relationships of cessation of smoking with job stress, personality, and social support. *Journal of Applied Psychology* 60:211–219.

Cappell, H., and Herman, C.P. 1972. Alcohol and tension reduction—a review. *Quarterly Journal of Studies on Alcohol* 33:33–64.

Carnes, P. 1983. *The sexual addiction.* Minneapolis: CompCare.

Caudill, B.D., and Marlatt, G.A. 1975. Modeling influences in social drinking: An experimental analogue. *Journal of Consulting and Clinical Psychology* 43:405–415.

Chaney, E.F.; O'Leary, M.R.; and Marlatt, G.A. 1978. Skill training with alcoholics. *Journal of Consulting and Clinical Psychology* 46:1092–1096.

Chein, I. 1969. Psychological functions of drug use. In *Scientific basis of drug dependence,* ed. H. Steinberg. London: Churchill.

Chein, I.; Gerard, D.L.; Lee, R.S.; and Rosenfeld, E. 1964. *The road to H.* New York: Basic Books.

Chernick, V.; Childiaeva, R.; and Ioffe, S. 1983. Effects of maternal alcohol intake and smoking on neonatal electroencephalogram and anthropometric measurements. *American Journal of Obstetrics and Gynecology* 146:41–47.

Chipkin, R.E. 1976. Aversiveness of oral methadone in rats. Doctoral dissertation, Medical College of Virginia, Richmond, VA.

Christiansen, B.A., and Goldman, M.S. 1983. Alcohol-related expectancies versus demographic/background variables in the prediction of adolescent drinking. *Journal of Consulting and Clinical Psychology* 51:249–257.

Clark, W.B. 1976. Loss of control, heavy drinking and drinking problems in a longitudinal study. *Journal of Studies on Alcohol* 37:1256–1290.

———. 1982. Public drinking contexts: Bars and taverns. In *Social drinking contexts,* eds. T.C. Harford and L.S. Gaines. Research Monograph 7. Rockville, MD: National Institute on Alcohol Abuse and Alcoholism.

Clark, W.B., and Cahalan, D. 1976. Changes in problem drinking over a four-year span. *Addictive Behaviors* 1:251–260.

Clausen, J.A. 1961. Drug addiction. In *Contemporary social problems,* eds. R.K. Merton and R.A. Nisbet. New York: Harcourt.

Cloninger, C.R.; Christiansen, K.O.; Reich, T.; and Gottesman, I.I. 1978. Implications of sex differences in the prevalences of antisocial personality, alcoholism, and criminality for family transmission. *Archives of General Psychiatry* 35:941–951.

Coambs, R.B. 1977. The effect of environment on morphine consumption in opiate naive rats. Honors essay, Simon Fraser University, Burnaby, BC.

———. 1980. Aversiveness of orally administered morphine in rats. Masters thesis, Simon Fraser University, Burnaby, BC.

Coambs, R.B.; Alexander, B.K.; Davis, C.M.; Hadaway, P.F.; and Tressel, W.K. 1980.

A drug dispenser to measure individual drinking in rat colonies. *Pharmacology Biochemistry and Behavior* 13:593–595.

Cocaine: middle class high. 1981. *Time* (July 6):56–63.

Cohen, S. 1983. Current attitudes about the benzodiazepines: Trial by media. *Journal of Psychoactive Drugs* 15:109–113.

Colletti, G., and Kopel, S.A. 1979. Maintaining behavior change: An investigation of three maintenance strategies and the relationship of self-attribution to the long-term reduction of cigarette smoking. *Journal of Consulting and Clinical Psychology* 47:614–617.

Collier, P., and Horowitz, D. 1976. *The Rockefellers: An American dynasty.* New York: New American Library.

The collision of prevention and treatment. 1984. *Journal,* Addiction Research Foundation (February):16.

Colt, E.W.D.; Wardlaw, S.L.; and Frantz, A.G. 1981. The effect of running on plasma β-endorphin. *Life Sciences* 28:1637–1640.

Condiotte, M.M., and Lichtenstein, E. 1981. Self-efficacy and relapse in smoking cessation programs. *Journal of Consulting and Clinical Psychology* 49:648–658.

Coppolillo, H.P. 1975. Drug impediments to mothering behavior. *Addictive Diseases* 2:201–208.

Costello, R.M. 1975. Alcoholism treatment and evaluation II: Collation of two year follow-up studies. *International Journal of Addictions* 10:857–867.

Courtwright, D.T. 1982. *Dark paradise: Opiate addiction in America before 1940.* Cambridge, MA: Harvard University Press.

Csikszentmihalyi, M., and Kubey, R. 1981. Television and the rest of life. *Public Opinion Quarterly* 45:317–328.

Cummings, N.A. 1979. Turning bread into stones: Our modern antimiracle. *American Psychologist* 34:1119–1124.

Cushner, I.M. 1981. Maternal behavior and perinatal risks: Alcohol, smoking, and drugs. *Annual Review of Public Health* 2:201–218.

Davies, D.L. 1962. Normal drinking in recovered alcohol addicts. *Quarterly Journal of Studies on Alcohol* 23:94–104.

Davis, M., and Shanks, B. 1975. Neurological aspects of perinatal narcotic addiction and methadone treatment. *Addictive Diseases* 2:213–226.

Debate rages on 1973 Sobell study. 1982. *Monitor,* American Psychological Association (November):8–9.

DeFeudis, F.V.; DeFeudis, P.A.; and Samoza, E. 1976. Altered analgesic responses to morphine in differentially housed mice. *Psychopharmacology* 49:117–118.

Desmond, M.M., and Wilson, G.S. 1975. Neonátal abstinence syndrome: Recognition and diagnosis. *Addictive Diseases* 2:113–121.

Dickens, B.M.; Doob, A.N.; Warwick, O.H.; and Winegard, W.C. 1982. *Report of the Committee of Enquiry into Allegations Concerning Drs. Linda and Mark Sobell.* Toronto: Addiction Research Foundation.

Dielman, T.E. 1979. Gambling: A social problem? *Journal of Social Issues* 35:36–42.

Ditman, K.S., and Crawford, G.G. 1966. The use of court probation in the management of the alcohol addict. *American Journal of Psychiatry* 122:757–762.

Ditman, K.S.; Crawford, G.G.; Forgy, E.W.; Moskowitz, H.; and MacAndrew, C. 1967. A controlled experiment on the use of court probation for drunk arrests. *American Journal of Psychiatry* 124:160–163.

Dole, V.P. 1972. Narcotic addiction, physical dependence and relapse. *New England Journal of Medicine* 286:988–992.

———. 1980. Addictive behavior. *Scientific American* (June): 138–154.

Dole, V.P., and Nyswander, M.E. 1967. Heroin addiction: A metabolic disease. *Archives of Internal Medicine* 120:19–24.

———. 1976. Methadone maintenance treatment: A ten-year perspective. *Journal of the American Medical Association* 235:2117–2119.

Donegan, N.H.; Rodin, J.; O'Brien, C.P.; and Solomon, R.L. 1983. A learning theory approach to commonalities. In *Commonalities in substance abuse and habitual behavior,* eds. P.K. Levison, D.R. Gerstein, and D.R. Maloff. Lexington, MA: Lexington.

Drink/smoke combo significant risk to fetus. 1983. *Journal,* Addiction Research Foundation (May):3.

Drinking problem dispute. 1980. *New York Times* (January 30):20.

Dunwiddie, T. 1983. Neurobiology of cocaine and opiate abuse. *U.S. Journal of Drug and Alcohol Dependence* (December):17.

Eddy, N.B.; Halbach, H.; Isbell, H.; and Seevers, M.H. 1965. Drug dependence: Its significance and characteristics. *Bulletin of the World Health Organization* 32:721–733.

Eddy, N.B., and May, E.L. 1973. The search for a better analgesic. *Science* 181:407–414.

Edwards, G., and Gross, M.M. 1976. Alcohol dependence: Provisional description of a clinical syndrome. *British Medical Journal* 1:1058–1061.

Efron, V.; Keller, M.; and Gurioli, C. 1974. *Statistics on consumption of alcohol and on alcoholism.* New Brunswick, NJ: Rutgers Center of Alcohol Studies.

Emrick, C.D. 1975. A review of psychologically oriented treatment of alcoholism II: The relative effectiveness of different treatment approaches and the effectiveness of treatment versus no treatment. *Journal of Studies on Alcohol* 36:88–109.

Emrick, C.D., and Hansen, J. 1983. Assertions regarding effectiveness of treatment for alcoholism: Fact or fantasy? *American Psychologist* 38:1078–1088.

Engle, K.B., and Williams, T.K. 1972. Effect of an ounce of vodka on alcoholics' desire for alcohol. *Quarterly Journal of Studies on Alcohol* 33:1099–1105.

Epstein, E.J. 1977. *Agency of fear: Opiates and political power in America.* New York: Putnam.

Falk, J.L. 1981. The environmental generation of excessive behavior. In *Behavior in excess,* ed. S.J. Mulé. New York: Free Press.

———. 1983. Drug dependence: Myth or motive? *Pharmacology Biochemistry and Behavior* 19:385–391.

Falk, J.L.; Dews, P.B.; and Schuster, C.R. 1983. Commonalities in the environmental control of behavior. In *Commonalities in substance abuse and habitual behavior,* eds. P.K. Levison, D.R. Gerstein, and D.R. Maloff. Lexington, MA: Lexington.

Ferguson, G.A. 1981. *Statistical analysis in psychology and education.* 5th ed. New

York: McGraw-Hill.

Fillmore, K.M. 1975. Relationships between specific drinking problems in early adulthood and middle age: An exploratory 20 year follow-up study. *Journal of Studies on Alcohol* 36:882–907.

Fishburne, P.M.; Abelson, H.I.; and Cisin, I. 1980. *National survey on drug abuse, main findings: 1979.* Rockville, MD: National Institute on Drug Abuse.

Fisher, E. 1981. *Eddie: My life, my loves.* New York: Harper & Row.

Fisher, E.B., Jr.; Levenkron, J.C.; Lowe, M.R.; Loro, A.D., Jr.; and Green, L. 1982. Self-initiated self-control in risk reduction. In *Adherence, compliance and generalization in behavioral medicine,* ed. R.B. Stuart. New York: Brunner/Mazel.

Fisher, J.C.; Mason, R.L.; and Fisher, J.V. 1976. A diagnostic formula for alcoholism. *Journal of Studies on Alcohol* 37:1247–1255.

For drug prosecutor, a sense of frustration. 1984. *New York Times* (May 22): B4.

Foucault, M. 1973. *Madness and civilization: A history of insanity in the age of reason.* New York: Random House.

The founding, future and vision of NACoA. 1983. *U.S. Journal of Drug and Alcohol Dependence* (December): 19.

Fuentes, V.O.; Hunt, W.B.; and Crossland, J. 1978. The production of morphine tolerance and physical dependence by the oral route in the rat. *Psychopharmacology* 59:65–69.

Garcia, J.; Hankins, W.G.; and Rusniak, K.W. 1974. Behavioral regulation of the milieu interne in man and rat. *Science* 185:824–831.

Garn, S.M.; Bailey, S.M.; and Cole, P.E. 1980. Continuities and changes in fatness and obesity. In *Nutrition, physiology and obesity,* ed. R. Schemmel. Palm Beach, FL: CRC Press.

Garn, S.M.; Bailey, S.M.; and Higgins, T.T. 1980. Effects of socioeconomic status, family line, and living together on fatness and obesity. In *Childhood prevention of atherosclerosis and hypertension,* eds. R.M. Lauer and R.B. Shekelle. New York: Raven.

Garn, S.M.; Cole, P.E.; and Bailey, S.M. 1979. Living together as a factor in family-line resemblances. *Human Biology* 51:565–587.

Garn, S.M.; LaVelle, M.; and Pilkington, J.J. 1984. Obesity and living together. *Marriage and Family Review* 7:33–47.

Garn, S.M.; Pilkington, J.J.; and LaVelle, M. 1984. Relationship between initial fatness level and long-term fatness change. *Ecology of Food and Nutrition* 14:85–92.

Gay, G.R.; Senay, E.C.; and Newmeyer, J.A. 1973. The pseudo-junkie: Evolution of the heroin lifestyle in the nonaddicted individual. *Drug Forum* 2:279–290.

Gerard, D.L., and Saenger, G. 1966. *Out-patient treatment of alcoholism: A study of outcome and its determinants.* Toronto: University of Toronto Press.

Gerard, D.L.; Saenger, G.; and Wile, R. 1962. The abstinent alcoholic. *Archives of General Psychiatry* 6:83–95.

Gerin, W. 1982. (No) accounting for results. *Psychology Today* (August): 32.

Gilbert, D.G. 1979. Paradoxical tranquilizing and emotion-reducing effects of nicotine. *Psychological Bulletin* 86:643–661.

Gilbert, R.M. 1981. Drug abuse as excessive behavior. In *Classic contributions in the addictions,* eds. H. Shaffer and M.E. Burglass. New York: Brunner/Mazel.

Glaser, F.B. 1974. Psychologic vs. pharmacologic heroin dependence. *New England Journal of Medicine* 290:231.

Glassner, B. and Berg, B. 1980. How Jews avoid alcohol problems. *American Sociological Review* 45:647–664.

Glazer, N. 1952. Why Jews stay sober. *Commentary* 13:181–186.

Glickman, S.E., and Schiff, B.B. 1967. A biological theory of reinforcement. *Psychological Review* 74:81–109.

Goldblatt, P.B.; Moore, M.E.; and Stunkard, A.J. 1965. Social factors in obesity. *Journal of the American Medical Association* 192:1039–1044.

Goldstein, A. 1972. Heroin addiction and the role of methadone in its treatment. *Archives of General Psychiatry* 26:291–297.

———. 1976a. Heroin addiction: Sequential treatment employing pharmacological supports. *Archives of General Psychiatry* 33:353–358.

———. 1976b. Opioid peptides (endorphins) in pituitary and brain. *Science* 193:1081–1086.

Goldstein, A.; Kaizer, S.; and Whitby, O. 1969. Psychotropic effects of caffeine in man IV: Quantitative and qualitative differences associated with habituation to coffee. *Clinical Pharmacology and Therapeutics* 10:489–497.

Goldstein, J.W., and Sappington, J.T. 1977. Personality characteristics of students who become heavy drug users: An MMPI study of an avant-garde. *American Journal of Drug and Alcohol Abuse* 4:401–412.

Gomberg, E.L. 1980. Drinking and problem drinking among the elderly. *Alcohol, drugs and aging: Usage and problems series.* I. Institute of Gerontology, University of Michigan, Ann Arbor.

Goode, E. 1972. *Drugs in American society*. New York: Knopf.

Goodwin, D.W. 1976. *Is alcoholism hereditary?* New York: Oxford University Press.

———. 1979. Alcoholism and heredity. *Archives of General Psychiatry* 36:57–61.

———. 1980. The bad-habit theory of drug abuse. In *Theories on drug abuse,* eds. D.J. Lettieri, M. Sayers, and H.W. Pearson. Research Monograph 30. Rockville, MD: National Institute on Drug Abuse.

———. 1984. A paean to the follow-up. In *Longitudinal research in alcoholism,* eds. D.W. Goodwin, K.T. van Dusen, and S.A. Mednick. Boston: Kluwer-Nijhoff.

Goodwin, D.W.; Crane, J.B.; and Guze, S.B. 1971. Felons who drink: An 8-year follow-up. *Quarterly Journal of Studies on Alcohol* 32:136–147.

Goodwin, D.W.; Schulsinger, F.; Hermansen, L.; Guze, S.B.; and Winokur, G. 1973. Alcohol problems in adoptees raised apart from biological parents. *Archives of General Psychiatry* 28:238–243.

Gordis, E.; Dorph, D.; Sepe, V.; and Smith, H. 1981. Outcome of alcoholism treatment among 5578 patients in an urban comprehensive hospital-based program: Application of a computerized data system. *Alcoholism: Clinical and Experimental Research* 5:509–522.

Gordon, B. 1979. *I'm dancing as fast as I can.* New York: Harper & Row.

Grant, E.C. 1963. An analysis of the social behavior of the male laboratory rat. *Behavior* 21:260–281.

Gray, J.A. 1978. Anxiety. *Human Nature* (July): 38–45.

Greaves, G. 1974. Toward an existential theory of drug dependence. *Journal of*

Nervous and Mental Disease 159:263–274.

———. 1980. An existential theory of drug dependence. In *Theories on drug abuse,* eds. D.J. Lettieri, M. Sayers, H.W. Pearson. Research Monograph 30. Rockville, MD: National Institute on Drug Abuse.

Greeley, A.M.; McCready, W.C.; and Theisen, G. 1980. *Ethnic drinking subcultures.* New York: Praeger.

Greenough, W.T. 1975. Experimental modification of the developing brain. *American Scientist* 63:37–46.

Griffiths, R.R.; Brady, J.V.; and Bradford, L.D. 1979. Predicting the abuse liability of drugs with animal drug self-administration procedures: Psychomotor stimulants and hallucinogens. In *Advances in behavioral pharmacology,* eds. T.T. Thompson and P.B. Dews. vol. 2. New York: Academic.

Gross, M.M. 1977. Psychobiological contributions to the Alcohol Dependence Syndrome: A selective review of recent literature. In *Alcohol related disabilities,* eds. G. Edwards et al. WHO Offset Publication 32. Geneva: World Health Organization.

Gusfield, J.R. 1963. *Symbolic crusade: Status politics and the American temperance movement.* Urbana: University of Illinois Press.

———. 1981. *The culture of public problems: Drinking-driving and the symbolic order.* Chicago: University of Chicago Press.

Hackler, T. 1983. The road to recovery. *United Airlines Magazine* (September): 39–42.

Hadaway, P.F.; Alexander, B.K.; Coambs, R.B.; and Beyerstein, B. 1979. The effect of housing and gender on preference for morphine-sucrose solutions in rats. *Psychopharmacology* 66:87–91.

Hansen, J., and Emrick, C.D. 1983. Whom are we calling "alcoholic"? *Bulletin of the Society of Psychologists in Addictive Behaviors* 2:164–178.

Hanson, J.W.; Jones, K.L.; and Smith, D.W. 1976. Fetal alcohol syndrome: Experience with 41 patients. *Journal of the American Medical Association* 235:1458–1460.

Harding, W.M.; Zinberg, N.E.; Stelmack, S.M.; and Barry, M. 1980. Formerly-addicted-now-controlled opiate users. *International Journal of the Addictions* 15:47–60.

Harford, T.C. 1979. Ecological factors in drinking. In *Youth, alcohol and social policy,* eds. H.T. Blane and M.E. Chafetz. New York: Plenum.

Harford, T.C., and Gaines, L.S., eds. 1982. *Social drinking contexts.* Research Monograph 7. Rockville, MD: National Institute on Alcohol Abuse and Alcoholism.

Hatterer, L. 1980. *The pleasure addicts.* New York: A.S. Barnes.

Hawley, L.M., and Butterfield, G.E. 1981. Exercise and the endogenous opioids. *New England Journal of Medicine* 305:1591.

Heather, N., and Robertson, I. 1981. *Controlled drinking.* London: Methuen.

———. 1983. Why is abstinence necessary for the recovery of some problem drinkers? *British Journal of Addiction* 78:139–144.

Heather, N.; Rollnick, S.; and Winton, M. 1983. A comparison of objective and subjective measures of alcohol dependence as predictors of relapse following treatment. *British Journal of Clinical Psychology* 22:11–17.

Heather, N.; Winton, M.; and Rollnick, S. 1982. An empirical test of "a cultural

delusion of alcoholics." *Psychological Reports* 50:379–382.

Herman, C.P., and Polivy, J. 1975. Anxiety, restraint and eating behavior. *Journal of Abnormal Psychology* 84:666–672.

———. 1980. Restrained eating. In *Obesity,* ed. A.J. Stunkard, Philadelphia: Saunders.

Heroin in West a 'widening crisis': INCB. 1981. *Journal,* Addiction Research Foundation (March): 1.

Heroin trade rising despite U.S. efforts. 1981. *New York Times* (February 15): 1; 32.

Hingson, R; Alpert, J.J.; Day, N., et al. 1982. Effects of maternal drinking and marijuana use on fetal growth and development. *Pediatrics* 70:539–546.

Hodgson, R., and Miller, P. 1982. *Self-watching: Addictions, habits, compulsions; what to do about them.* London: Century.

Hodgson, R.; Rankin, H.; and Stockwell, T. 1979. Alcohol dependence and the priming effect. *Behavior Research and Therapy* 17:379–387.

Hodgson, R.; Stockwell, T.; Rankin, H.; and Edwards, G. 1978. Alcohol dependence: The concept, its utility and measurement. *British Journal of Addiction* 73:339–342.

Hooper, H.E., and Santo, Y. 1980. Use of propoxyohene (Darvon) by adolescents admitted to drug abuse programs. *Contemporary Drug Problems* 9:357–368.

Horn, G.; Rose, S.P.R.; and Bateson, P.P.G. 1979. Experience and plasticity in the central nervous system. *Science* 203:75–78.

Huidobro, F. 1964. Studies on morphine VI: Ingestion of morphine solutions in normal mice and rats and in animals with chronic morphinism. *Archives Internationales de Pharmacodynamie et de Therapie* 151:299–312.

Hull, J.G., and Young, R.D. 1983. The self-awareness reducing effects of alcohol: Evidence and implications. In *Psychological perspectives on the self,* eds. J. Suls and A.G. Greenwald. vol. 2. Hillsdale, NJ: Erlbaum.

Inpatient vs. outpatient treatment. 1984. *U.S. Journal of Drug and Alcohol Dependence* (May): 3.

Is inpatient rehabilitation of the alcoholic cost effective? 1984. Session at Conference on Controversies in Alcoholism and Substance Abuse, National Association on Drug Abuse Problems, New York, March.

Isbell, H. 1958. Clinical research on addiction in the United States. In *Narcotic drug addiction problems,* ed. R.B. Livingston. Bethesda, MD: Public Health Service.

Istvan, J., and Matarazzo J.D. 1984. Tobacco, alcohol, and caffeine use: A review of their interrelationships. *Psychological Bulletin* 95:301–326.

Jacobson, R.C., and Zinberg, N.E. 1975. *The social basis of drug abuse prevention.* Publication SS-5. Washington, DC: Drug Abuse Council.

Jaffe, J.H. 1980. Drug addiction and drug abuse. In *Goodman and Gilman's The pharmacological basis of therapeutics,* eds. A.G. Gilman, L.S. Goodman, and B.A. Gilman. 6th ed. New York: Macmillan.

Jaffe, J.H., and Harris, T.G. 1973. As far as heroin is concerned, the worst is over. *Psychology Today* (August): 68–79, 85.

Jaffe, J.H., and Martin, W.R. 1980. Opioid analgesics and antagonists. In *Goodman and Gilman's The pharmacological basis of therapeutics,* eds. A.G. Gilman, L.S. Goodman, and B.A. Gilman. 6th ed. New York: Macmillan.

Jarvik, M.E. 1973. Further observations on nicotine as the reinforcing agent in smoking. In *Smoking behavior: Motives and incentives,* ed. W.L. Dunn, Jr. Washington, DC: Winston.

Jarvik, M.E.; Glick, S.D.; and Nakamura, R.K. 1970. Inhibition of cigarette smoking by orally administered nicotine. *Clinical Pharmacology and Therapeutics* 11:574–576.

Jellinek, E.M. 1946. Phases in the drinking history of alcoholics: Analysis of a survey conducted by the official organ of Alcoholics Anonymous. *Quarterly Journal of Studies on Alcohol* 7:1–88.

———. 1952. Phases of alcohol addiction. *Quarterly Journal of Studies on Alcohol* 13:637–684.

———. 1960. *The disease concept of alcoholism.* New Haven: Hillhouse Press.

Jessor, R. 1979. Marijuana: A review of recent psychosocial research. In *Handbook on drug abuse,* eds. R.L. Dupont, A. Goldstein, and J. O'Donnell. Rockville, MD: National Institute on Drug Abuse.

Jessor, R.; Chase, J.; and Donovan, J. 1980. Psychosocial correlates of marijuana use and problem drinking in a national sample of adolescents. *American Journal of Public Health* 70:604–613.

Jessor, R., and Jessor, S.L. 1975. Adolescent development and the onset of drinking. *Journal of Studies on Alcohol* 36:27–51.

———. 1977. *Problem behavior and psychosocial development: A longitudinal study of youth.* New York: Academic.

Johanson, C.E., and Uhlenhuth, E.H. 1981. Drug preference and mood in humans: Repeated assessment of d-amphetamine. *Pharmacology Biochemistry and Behavior* 14:159–163.

Johnson, C., and Larson, R. 1982. Bulimia: An analysis of moods and behavior. *Psychosomatic Medicine* 44:341–351.

Johnston, L.D.; Bachman, J.G.; and O'Malley, P.M. 1981. *Highlights from "Student Drug Use in America 1975–1981."* Rockville, MD: National Institute on Drug Abuse.

Johnston, L.; O'Malley, P.; and Eveland, L. 1978. Drugs and delinquency: A search for causal connections. In *Longitudinal research on drug issues,* ed. D.B. Kandel. Washington, DC: Hemisphere.

Jones, H.B., and Jones, H.C. 1977. *Sensual drugs.* Cambridge, England: Cambridge University Press.

Jones, E., and Berglas, S. 1978. Control of attributions about the self through self-handicapping strategies: The appeal of alcohol and the role of underachievement. *Personality and Social Psychology Bulletin* 4:200–206.

Jones, K.L., and Smith, D.W. 1973. Recognition of the fetal alcohol syndrome in early infancy. *Lancet* 2:999–1001.

Jorquez, J.S. 1983. The retirement phase of heroin using careers. *Journal of Drug Issues* 13:343–365.

Kalant, H. 1982. Drug research is muddied by sundry dependence concepts. Paper presented at the Annual Meeting of the Canadian Psychological Association, Montreal, June (cited in *Journal,* Addiction Research Foundation [September 1982]: 12).

Kalant, O.J., and Kalant, H. 1976. Death in amphetamine users: Causes and estimates of mortality. In *Research advances in alcohol and drug problems,* eds. R.J. Gibbins, Y. Israel, H. Kalant, R.E. Popham, W. Schmidt, and R.G. Smart. vol. 3. New York: Wiley.

Kales, A.; Bixler, E.O.; Tjiauw-Ling, T.; Scharf, M.B.; and Kales, J.D. 1974. Chronic hypnotic-drug use: Ineffectiveness, drug-withdrawal insomnia, and dependence. *Journal of the American Medical Association* 227:513–517.

Kandel, D.B. 1978. Homophily, selection, and socialization in adolescent friendships. *American Journal of Sociology* 84:427–436.

———. 1980. Drug and drinking behavior among youth. In *Annual review of sociology,* eds. J. Coleman, A. Inkeles, and M. Smelser. vol. 6. Palo Alto, CA: Annual Reviews.

———. 1984. Marijuana users in young adulthood. *Archives of General Psychiatry* 41:200–209.

Kandel, D.B.; Kessler, R.C.; and Margulies, R.Z. 1978. Antecedents of adolescent initiation into stages of drug use: A developmental analysis. In *Longitudinal research on drug use,* ed. D.B. Kandel. Washington, DC: Hemisphere.

Kaplan, E.H., and Wieder, H. 1974. *Drugs don't take people, people take drugs.* Secaucus, NJ: Lyle Stuart.

Katz, D.M., and Steinberg, H. 1970. Long term isolation in rats reduces morphine response. *Nature* 228:469–471.

Kay, E.; Lyons, A.; Newman, W.; Mankin, D.; and Loeb, R. 1978. A longitudinal study of the personality correlates of marijuana use. *Journal of Counsulting and Clinical Psychology* 46:470–477.

Keller, M. 1969. Some views on the nature of addiction. First E.M. Jellinek Memorial Lecture presented at 15th International Institute on the Prevention and Treatment of Alcoholism, Budapest, Hungry, June (available from Publications Division, Rutgers Center of Alcohol Studies, New Brunswick, NJ).

———. 1970. The great Jewish drink mystery. *British Journal of Addiction* 64:287–295.

———. 1975. Problems of epidemiology in alcohol problems. *Journal of Studies on Alcohol* 36:1442–1451.

———. 1981. Perspective on medicine and alcoholism. Paper delivered at National Council on Alcoholism–American Medical Society on Alcoholism Medical-Scientific Luncheon, New Orleans, April 13.

Kendell, R.E. 1979. Alcoholism: A medical or a political problem? *British Medical Journal* 1:367–371.

Kern, M. 1984. Arousal modification in preferential drug use. Paper presented at meeting of Western Psychological Association, Los Angeles, April.

Khantzian, E.J. 1975. Self selection and progression in drug dependence. *Psychiatry Digest* 36:19–22.

Khantzian, E.J.; Mack, J.E.; and Schatzberg, A.F. 1974. Heroin use as an attempt to cope: Clinical observations. *American Journal of Psychiatry* 131:160–164.

Khavari, K.A.; Peters, T.C.; and Baity, P.L. 1975. Voluntary morphine ingestion, morphine dependence, and recovery from withdrawal signs. *Pharmacology Biochemistry and Behavior* 3:1093–1096.

Kilpatrick, D.G.; Sutker, P.B.; and Smith, A.D. 1976. Deviant drug and alcohol use:

The role of anxiety, sensation seeking, and other personality variables. In *Emotions and anxiety,* eds. M. Zuckerman and C.D. Speilberger. Hillsdale, NJ: Erlbaum.

King, A. 1958. *Mine enemy grows older.* New York: Simon and Schuster.

King, R. 1972. *The drug hang-up.* New York: Norton.

Kissin, B.; Lowinson, J.H.; and Millman, R.B. 1978. *Recent developments in chemotherapy of narcotic addiction.* New York: New York Academy of Sciences.

Klaus, M.H., and Kennell, J.H. 1981. *Parent-infant bonding.* 2d ed. St. Louis: C.V. Mosby.

Klausner, S.Z.; Foulks, E.F.; and Moore, M.H. 1980. The Inupiat, economics and alcohol on the Alaskan North Slope. Center for Research on the Acts of Man, University of Pennsylvania, Philadelphia, PA.

Kline, N.S. 1981. *From sad to glad.* New York: Ballantine.

Knop, J.; Goodwin, D.W.; Teasdale, T.W.; Mikkelsen, U.; and Schulsinger, F. 1984. A Danish prospective study of young males at high risk for alcoholism. In *Longitudinal research in alcoholism,* eds. D.W. Goodwin, K.T. van Dusen, and S.A. Mednick. Boston: Kluwer-Nijhoff.

Knupfer, G. 1972. Ex-problem drinkers. In *Life history research in psychopathology,* eds. M.A. Roff, L.N. Robins, and M. Pollack. vol. 2. Minneapolis: University of Minnesota Press.

Kolata, G.B. 1981. Fetal alcohol advisory debated. *Science* 214:642–645.

Kolb, L. 1958. Factors that have influenced the management and treatment of drug addicts. In *Narcotic drug addiction problems,* ed. R.B. Livingston. Bethesda, MD: Public Health Service.

———. 1962. *Drug addiction: A medical problem.* Springfield, IL: Charles C Thomas.

Kosterlitz, H.W. 1979. Endogenous opioid peptides and the control of pain. *Psychological Medicine* 9:1–4.

Kostowski, W.; Czlonkowski, A.; Rewerski, W.; and Piechocki, T. 1977. Morphine action in grouped and isolated rats and mice. *Psychopharmacology* 53:191–193.

Kraft, D.P. 1982. Public drinking practices of college youths: Implications for prevention programs. In *Social drinking contexts,* eds. T.C. Harford and L.S. Gaines. Research Monograph 7. Rockville, MD: National Institute on Alcohol Abuse and Alcoholism.

Krasnegor, N.A., ed. 1979. *Cigarette smoking as a dependence process.* Research Monograph 23. Rockville, MD: National Institute on Drug Abuse.

Kron, R.E.; Kaplan, S.L.; Finnegan, L.P.; Litt, M.; and Phoenix, M.D. 1975. The assessment of behavior change in infants undergoing narcotic withdrawal. *Addictive Diseases* 2:257–275.

Krystal, H., and Raskin, H.A. 1970. *Drug dependence: Aspects of ego function.* Detroit: Wayne State University.

Kumar, R., and Stolerman, I.P. 1977. Experimental and clinical aspects of drug dependence. In *Handbook of psychopharmacology,* eds. L.L. Iverson, S.D. Iverson, and S.H. Snyder. vol. 7. New York: Plenum.

Lang, A.R. 1983. Addictive personality: A viable construct? In *Commonalities in substance abuse and habitual behavior,* eds. P.K. Levison, D.R. Gerstein, and

D.R. Maloff. Lexington, MA: Lexington.

Lang, A.R.; Goeckner, D.J.; Adesso, V.J.; and Marlatt, G.A. 1975. Effects of alcohol on aggression in male social drinkers. *Journal of Abnormal Psychology* 84:508–518.

Lang, A.R.; Searles, J.; Lauerman, R.; and Adesso, V. 1980. Expectancy, alcohol, and sex guilt as determinants of interest in and reaction to sexual stimuli. *Journal of Abnormal Psychology* 89: 644–653.

Langer, E.J. 1978. The illusion of incompetence. In *Choice and perceived control,* eds. L. Perlmuter and R. Monty. Hillsdale, NJ: Erlbaum.

Langer, E.J., and Benevento, A. 1978. Self-induced dependence. *Journal of Personality and Social Psychology* 36:886–893.

Lasagna, L. 1981. Heroin: A medical "me too." *New England Journal of Medicine* 304:1539–1540.

Lasagna, L.; Mosteller, F.; von Felsinger, J.M.; and Beecher, H.K. 1954. A study of the placebo response. *American Journal of Medicine* 16:770–779.

Lasagna, L.; von Felsinger, J.M.; and Beecher, H.K. 1955. Drug-induced mood changes in man. *Journal of the American Medical Association* 157:1006–1020. 1020.

Lazarus, R. 1966. *Psychological stress and the coping process.* New York: McGraw-Hill.

Lear, M.W. 1974. All the warnings, gone up in smoke. *New York Times Magazine* (March 10): 18–19, 86–91.

LeFlore, R., and Hawkins, J. 1978. Stealing was my speciality. *Sports Illustrated* (February 6): 62–74.

Lender, M.E., and Martin, J.K. 1982. *Drinking in America: A history.* New York: Free Press.

Lennard, H.L.; Epstein, L.J.; Bernstein, A.; and Ransom, D. 1971. *Mystification and drug misuse.* San Francisco: Jossey-Bass.

Lennard, H.L.; Epstein, L.J.; and Rosenthal, M.S. 1972. The methadone illusion. *Science* 176:881–884.

Leventhal, H. 1980. Toward a comprehensive theory of emotion. In *Advances in experimental social psychology,* ed. L. Berkowitz. vol. 13. New York: Academic.

Leventhal, H., and Cleary, P.D. 1980. The smoking problem: A review of the research and theory in behavioral risk modification. *Psychological Bulletin* 88:370–405.

Leventhal, H., and Nerenz, D. 1983. A model for stress research and some implications for the control of stress disorders. In *Stress prevention and management,* eds. D. Meichenbaum and M. Jaremko. New York: Plenum.

Levine, H.G. 1978. The discovery of addiction: Changing conceptions of habitual drunkenness in America. *Journal of Studies on Alcohol* 39:143–174.

Lewis, A. 1969. Introduction: Definitions and perspectives. In *Scientific basis of drug dependence,* ed. H. Steinberg. London: Churchill.

Lewis, C.E.; Cloninger, C.R.; and Pais, J. 1983. Alcoholism, antisocial personality, and drug use in a criminal population. *Alcohol and Alcoholism* 18:53–60.

Lewontin, R.C.; Rose, S.; and Kamin, L.J. 1984. *Not in our genes.* New York: Pantheon.

Lidz, C.W., and Walker, A.L. 1980. *Heroin, deviance and morality.* Beverley Hills,

CA: Sage.
Lieberman, M.; Yalom, I.; and Miles, M. 1973. *Encounter groups: First facts.* New York: Basic Books.
Liebowitz, M.R. 1983. *The chemistry of love.* Boston: Little-Brown.
Liebowitz, M.R., and Klein, D.F. 1979. Hysteroid dysphoria. *Psychiatric Clinics of North America* 2:555–575.
Light, A.B., and Torrance, E.G. 1929. Opiate addiction VI: The effects of abrupt withdrawal followed by readministration of morphine in human addicts, with special reference to the composition of the blood, the circulation and the metabolism. *Archives of Internal Medicine* 44:1–16.
Lindblad, R.A. 1977. Self-concept of white, middle socioeconomic status addicts: A controlled study. *International Journal of the Addictions* 12:137–151.
Lindesmith, A.R. 1968. *Addiction and opiates.* Chicago: Aldine.
Lipscomb, T.R., and Nathan, P.E. 1980. Blood alcohol level discrimination: The effects of family history of alcoholism, drinking pattern, and tolerance. *Archives of General Psychiatry* 37:571–576.
Lolli, G.; Serianni, E.; Golder, G.M.; and Luzzatto-Fegiz, P. 1958. *Alcohol in Italian culture.* Glencoe, IL: Free Press.
Lore, R., and Flannelly, K. 1977. Rat societies. *Scientific American* (May): 106–116.
Lovibund, S.H., and Caddy, G. 1970. Discriminative aversive control in the moderation of alcoholics' drinking behavior. *Behavior Therapy* 1:437–444.
Lukoff, I.F., and Brook, J.S. 1974. A sociocultural exploration of reported heroin use. In *Sociological aspects of drug dependence,* ed. C. Winick. Cleveland: CRC Press.
MacAndrew, C. 1965. The differentiation of male alcoholic outpatients from nonalcoholic psychiatric outpatients. *Quarterly Journal of Studies on Alcohol* 26:238–246.
———. 1981. What the MAC scale tells us about alcoholic men: An interpretative review. *Journal of Studies on Alcohol* 42:604–625.
MacAndrew, C., and Edgerton, R.B. 1969. *Drunken comportment: A social explanation.* Chicago: Aldine.
Maddux, J.F., and Desmond, D.P. 1981. *Careers of opioid users.* New York: Praeger.
Magnusson, D., ed. 1981. *Toward a psychology of situations.* Hillsdale, NJ: Erlbaum.
Mangin, W. 1957. Drinking among the Andean Indians. *Quarterly Journal of Studies on Alcohol.* 18:55–66.
Mann, M. 1970. *Marty Mann answers your questions about drinking and alcoholism.* New York: Holt, Rinehart & Winston.
Many addicts have family alcoholism history. 1983. *Journal,* Addiction Research Foundation (November):3.
Markoff, R.; Ryan, P.; and Young, T. 1982. Endorphins and mood changes in long distance running. *Medicine and Science in Sports and Exercise* 14:11–15.
Marlatt, G.A. 1976. Alcohol, stress, and cognitive control. In *Stress and anxiety,* eds. I.G. Sarason and C.D. Speilberger. vol. 3. Washington, DC: Hemisphere.
———. 1978. Craving for alcohol, loss of control, and relapse: A cognitive-behavioral analysis. In *Alcoholism: New directions in behavioral research and treatment,* eds. P.E. Nathan, G.A. Marlatt, and T. Loberg. New York: Plenum.
———. 1981. Perception of "control" and its relation to behavior change. *Behav-*

ioral Psychotherapy 9:190–193.

———. 1982. Relapse prevention: A self-control program for the treatment of addictive behaviors. In *Adherence, compliance and generalization in behavioral medicine,* ed. R.B. Stuart. New York: Brunner/Mazel.

———. 1983. The controlled-drinking controversy: A commentary. *American Psychologist* 38:1097–1110.

———. 1984. President's message. *Bulletin of the Society of Psychologists in Addictive Behaviors* 3:2.

Marlatt, G.A.; Demming, B.; and Reid, J.B. 1973. Loss of control drinking in alcoholics: An experimental analogue. *Journal of Abnormal Psychology* 81:223–241.

Marlatt, G.A., and Gordon, J.R. 1980. Determinants of relapse: Implications for the maintenance of behavior change. In *Behavioral medicine: Changing health lifestyles,* eds. P.O. Davidson and S.M. Davidson. New York: Brunner/Mazel.

Marlatt, G.A., and Rohsenow, D.J. 1980. Cognitive processes in alcohol use: Expectancy and the balanced placebo design. In *Advances in substance abuse,* ed. N.K. Mello. vol. 1. Greenwich, CT: JAI Press.

Masserman, J.H. 1976. Alcoholism: Disease or dis-ease? *International Journal of Mental Health* 5:3–15.

Mayer, W. 1983. Alcohol abuse and alcoholism: The psychologist's role in prevention, research, and treatment. *American Psychologist* 38:1116–1121.

McAuliffe, W.E., and Gordon, R.A. 1974. A test of Lindesmith's theory of addiction: The frequency of euphoria among long-term addicts. *American Journal of Sociology* 79:795–840.

———. 1980. Reinforcement and the combination of effects: Summary of a theory of opiate addiction. In *Theories on drug abuse,* eds. D.J. Lettieri, M. Sayers, and H.W. Pearson. Research Monograph 30. Rockville, MD: National Institute on Drug Abuse.

McClelland, D.C.; Davis, W.N.; Kalin, R.; and Wanner, E. 1972. *The drinking man.* New York: Free Press.

McGuire, M.T.; Stein, S.; and Mendelson, J.H. 1966. Comparative psychosocial studies of alcoholic and nonalcoholic subjects undergoing experimentally induced ethanol intoxication. *Psychosomatic Medicine* 28:13–25.

McIntosh, T.K.; Vallano, M.L.; and Barfield, R.J. 1980. Effects of morphine, β-endorphin and naloxone on catecholamine levels and sexual behavior in the male rat. *Pharmacology Biochemistry and Behavior* 13:435–441.

McMurray, R.G.; Sheps, D.S.; and Guinan, D.M. 1984. Effects of naloxone on maximal stress testing in females. *Journal of Applied Physiology* 56:436–440.

Mello, N.K., and Mendelson, J.H. 1971. A quantitative analysis of drinking patterns in alcoholics. *Archives of General Psychiatry* 25:527–539.

———. 1972. Drinking patterns during work-contingent and non-contingent alcohol acquisition. *Psychosomatic Medicine* 34:1116–1121.

———. 1977. Clinical aspects of alcohol dependence. In *Handbook of psychopharmacology.* vol. 45/I. Berlin: Springer-Verlag.

———. 1978. Alcohol and human behavior. In *Handbook of psychopharmacology,* eds. L.L. Iverson, S.D. Iverson, and S.H. Snyder. vol. 12. New York: Plenum.

Mendelson, J.H., and Mello, N.K. 1979a. Biological concomitants of alcoholism. *New England Journal of Medicine* 301:912–921.

———. 1979b. One unanswered question about alcoholism. *British Journal of Ad-*

diction 74:11–14.

Merry, J. 1966. The "loss of control" myth. *Lancet* 4:1257–1258.

Mexico making progress in war on cultivation of opium poppies. 1980. *New York Times* (February 24): 12.

Milkman, H., and Sunderwirth, S. 1983. The chemistry of craving. *Psychology Today* (October): 36–44.

Miller, W.R. 1976. Alcoholism scales and objective assessment methods: A review. *Psychological Bulletin* 83:649–674.

———. 1983a. Controlled drinking: A history and critical review. *Journal of Studies on Alcohol* 44:68–83.

———. 1983b. Haunted by the Zeitgeists: Reflections on contrasting treatment goals and concepts of alcoholism in Europe and America. Paper presented at Conference on Alcohol and Culture, Farmington, CT, May.

———. 1983c. Motivational interviewing with problem drinkers. *Behavioral Psychotherapy* 11:147–172.

Miller, W.R., and Hester, R.K. 1980. Treating the problem drinker: Modern approaches. In *The addictive behaviors: Treatment of alcoholism, drug abuse, smoking, and obesity,* ed. W.R. Miller. Oxford: Pergamon.

Miller, W.R., and Muñoz, R.F. 1976. *How to control your drinking.* Englewood Cliffs, NJ: Prentice-Hall.

———. 1982. *How to control your drinking.* rev. ed. Albuquerque, NM: University of New Mexico Press.

Miller, W.R., and Saucedo, C.F. 1983. Neuropsychological impairment and brain damage in problem drinkers: A critical review. In *Behavioral effects of neurological disorders,* eds. C.J. Golden et al. New York: Grune & Stratton.

Mischel, W. 1974. Process in delay of gratification. In *Advances in experimental social psychology,* ed. L. Berkowitz. vol. 7. New York: Academic.

———. 1979. On the interface of cognition and personality: Beyond the person-situation debate. *American Psychologist* 34:740–754.

———. 1984. Convergences and challenges in the search for consistency. *American Psychologist* 39:351–364.

Mohatt, G. 1972. The sacred water: The quest for personal power through drinking among the Teton Sioux. In *The drinking man,* eds. D. McClelland, W.N. Davis, R. Kalin, and E. Wanner. New York: Free Press.

Moos, R.H., and Finney, J.W. 1982. New directions in program evaluation: Implications for expanding the role of alcoholism researchers. Paper presented at Conference on New Directions in Alcohol Abuse Treatment Research, Newport, Rhode Island, October.

Morgan, W.P. 1979. Negative addiction in runners. *Physician and Sportsmedicine* 7(2):55–70.

Mumford, L., and Kumar, R. 1979. Sexual behavior of morphine-dependent and abstinent male rats. *Psychopharmacology* 65:179–185.

Murray, H.A. 1981. *Endeavors in psychology,* ed. E.S. Shneidman. New York: Harper & Row.

Musto, D.F. 1973. *The American disease: Origins of narcotic control.* New Haven: Yale University Press.

Nathan, P.E. 1980. Ideal mental health services for alcoholics and problem drinkers: An exercise in pragmatics. In *Behavioral medicine: Changing health lifestyles,* eds. P.O. Davidson and S.M. Davidson. New York: Brunner/Mazel.

Nathan, P.E., and O'Brien, J.S. 1971. An experimental analysis of the behavior of alcoholics and nonalcoholics during prolonged experimental drinking: A necessary precursor of behavior therapy? *Behavior Therapy* 2:455–476.

Nathan, P.E.; Titler, N.A.; Lowenstein, L.M.; Solomon, P.; and Rossi, A.M. 1970. Behavioral analysis of chronic alcoholism. *Archives of General Psychiatry* 22:419–430.

National Foundation for Prevention of Chemical Dependency Disease. 1984. Mission statement, March 1, Omaha.

Nesbitt, P.D. 1972. Chronic smoking and emotionality. *Journal of Applied Social Psychology* 2:187–196.

New insights into alcoholism. 1983. *Time* (April 25):64, 69.

Newman, J.M. 1970. Peer pressure hypothesis for adolescent cigarette smoking. *School Health Review* 1:15–18.

Nichols, J.R.; Headlee, C.P.; Coppock, H.W. 1956. Drug addiction I: Addiction by escape training. *Journal of the American Pharmacological Association* 45:788–791.

Nisbett, R.E. 1968. Taste, deprivation, and weight determinants of eating behavior. *Journal of Personality and Social Psychology* 10:107–116.

———. 1972. Hunger, obesity, and the ventromedial hypothalamus. *Psychological Review* 79:433–453.

Nurco, D.N.; Cisin, I.H.; and Balter, M.B. 1981. Addict careers III: Trends across time. *International Journal of the Addictions* 16:1353–1372.

Oates, W. 1971. *Confessions of a workaholic.* New York: World.

O'Brien, C.P. 1975. Experimental analysis of conditioning factors in human narcotic addiction. *Pharmacological Review* 27:533–543.

O'Brien, C.P.; Nace, E.P.; Mintz, J.; Meyers, A.L.; and Ream, N. 1980. Follow-up of Vietnam veterans I: Relapse to drug use after Vietnam service. *Drug and Alcohol Dependence* 5:333–340.

O'Brien, C.P.; Testa, T.; O'Brien, T.J.; Brady, J.P.; and Wells, B. 1977. Conditioned narcotic withdrawal in humans. *Science* 195:1000–1002.

O'Donnell, J.A. 1969. *Narcotic addicts in Kentucky.* Chevy Chase, MD: National Institute of Mental Health.

O'Donnell, J.A.; Voss, H.; Clayton R.; Slatin, G.; and Room, R. 1976. *Young men and drugs: A nationwide survey.* Research Monograph 5. Rockville, MD: National Institute on Drug Abuse.

Öjesjö, L. 1984. Risks for alcoholism by age and class among males. In *Longitudinal research in alcoholism,* eds. D.W. Goodwin, K.T. van Dusen, and S.A. Mednick. Boston: Kluwer-Nijhoff.

Oki, G. 1974. Alcohol use by Skid Row alcoholics I: Drinking at Bon Accord. Substudy 612. Toronto: Addiction Research Foundation.

Orford, J., and Edwards, G. 1977. *Alcoholism.* New York: Oxford University Press.

Ostrea, E.M.; Chavez, C.J.; and Strauss, M.E. 1975. A study of factors that influence the severity of neonatal narcotic withdrawal. *Addictive Diseases* 2:187–199.

Ouellette, E.M.; Rosett, H.L.; Rosman, N.P.; and Weiner, L. 1977. Adverse effects on offspring of maternal alcohol abuse during pregnancy. *New England Journal of Medicine* 297:528–530.

Panksepp, J. 1980. Brief isolation, pain responsivity, and morphine analgesia in young rats. *Psychopharmacology* 72:111–112.

Panksepp, J.; Najam, N.; and Soares, F. 1979. Morphine reduces social cohesion in rats. *Pharmacology Biochemistry and Behavior* 11:131–134.

Paredes, A.; Hood, W.R.; Seymour, H.; and Gollob, M. 1973. Loss of control in alcoholism. *Quarterly Journal of Studies on Alcoholism* 34:1141–1161.

Pargman, D., and Baker, M.C. 1980. Running high: Enkephalin indicated. *Journal of Drug Issues* 10:341–349.

Patai, R. 1977. *The Jewish mind.* New York: Scribners.

Pattison, E.M.; Brissenden, A.; and Wohl, T. 1967. Assessing specific effects of inpatient group psychotherapy. *International Journal of Group Psychotherapy* 17:283–297.

Pattison, E.M.; Sobell, M.B.; and Sobell, L.C. 1977. *Emerging concepts of alcohol dependence.* New York: Springer.

Peele, S. 1977. Redefining addiction I: Making addiction a scientifically and socially useful concept. *International Journal of Health Services* 7:103–124.

———. 1978. Addiction: The analgesic experience. *Human Nature* (September): 61–67.

———. 1979. Redefining addiction II: The meaning of addiction in our lives. *Journal of Psychedelic Drugs* 11:289–297.

———. 1980. Addiction to an experience: A social-psychological-pharmacological theory of addiction. In *Theories on drug abuse,* eds. D.J. Lettieri, M. Sayers, and H.W. Pearson. Research Monograph 30. Rockville, MD: National Institute on Drug Abuse.

———. 1981a. *How much is too much: Healthy habits or destructive addictions.* Englewood Cliffs, NJ: Prentice-Hall.

———. 1981b. Reductionism in the psychology of the eighties: Can biochemistry eliminate addiction, mental illness, and pain? *American Psychologist* 36:807–818.

———. 1982a. Love, sex, drugs and other magical solutions to life. *Journal of Psychoactive Drugs* 14:125–131.

———. 1982b. What caused John Belushi's death? *U.S. Journal of Drug and Alcohol Dependence* (April): 7.

———. 1982c. When governments get tough on drugs. *U.S. Journal of Drug and Alcohol Dependence* (July): 7.

———. 1983a. Behavior therapy, the hardest way: Natural remission in alcoholism and controlled drinking. Discussant's remarks on the Panel of Controlled Drinking, 4th World Congress on Behavior Therapy, Washington, DC, December.

———. 1983b. *Don't panic: A parent's guide to understanding and preventing alcohol and drug abuse.* Minneapolis: CompCare.

———. 1983c. Is alcoholism different from other substance abuse? *American Psychologist* 38:963–964.

———. 1983d. Out of the habit trap. *American Health* (September/October): 42–47.

———. 1983e. *The science of experience: A direction for psychology.* Lexington, MA: Lexington.

———. 1983f. Through a glass darkly: Can some alcoholics learn to drink in moderation? *Psychology Today* (April): 38–42.

———. 1984a. The internal–external model and beyond: Reductionist approaches

to smoking and obesity in the context of social psychological theory. Unpublished manuscript, Morristown, NJ.

———. 1984b. The media and the latest glamor drug. In *The human side of addiction: Unpopular ideas on the drug and alcohol scene,* S. Peele. Morristown, NJ: Author.

———. 1984c. *Sixty Minutes'* report on the Sobell–Pendery controlled drinking dispute. In *The human side of addiction: Unpopular ideas on the drug and alcohol scene,* S. Peele. Morristown, NJ: Author.

Peele, S., with Brodsky, A. 1975. *Love and addiction.* New York: Taplinger, 1975.

Pelton, L.H., ed. 1981. *The social context of child abuse and neglect.* New York: Human Sciences Press.

Pendery, M.L.; Maltzman, I.M.; and West, L.J. 1982. Controlled drinking by alcoholics? New findings and a reevaluation of a major affirmative study. *Science* 217:169–174.

People. 1984. *New York Times* (June 28): B9.

Platt, J., and Labate, C. 1976. *Heroin addiction: Theory, research, and treatment.* New York: Wiley.

Polich, J.M.; Armor, D.J.; and Braiker, H.B. 1981. *The course of alcoholism: Four years after treatment.* New York: Wiley.

Polivy, J., and Herman, C.P. 1983. *Breaking the diet habit: The natural weight alternative.* New York: Basic Books.

Pollock, V.E.; Volavka, J.; Mednick, S.A.; Goodwin, D.W.; Knop, J.; and Schulsinger, F. 1984. A prospective study of alcoholism: Electroencephalographic findings. In *Longitudinal research in alcoholism,* eds. D.W. Goodwin, K.T. van Dusen, and S.A. Mednick. Boston: Kluwer-Nijhoff.

Porjesz, B., and Begleiter, H. 1982. Evoked brain potential deficits in alcoholism and aging. *Alcoholism: Clinical and Experimental Research* 6:53–63.

Prep schools in a struggle to curb spread of cocaine. 1984. *New York Times* (May 27): 1; 50.

Prescott, J.W. 1980. Somatosensory affectional deprivation (SAD) theory of drug and alcohol use. In *Theories on drug abuse,* eds. D.J. Lettieri, M. Sayers, and H.W. Pearson. Research Monograph 30. Rockville, MD: National Institute on Drug Abuse.

Prial, F.J. 1984. Criticism of the alcohol industry has grown lately. *New York Times* (February 22): C13.

Primm, B.J. 1977. Pseudoheroinism. In *Drug abuse: Clinical and basic aspects,* eds. S. N. Pradhan and S.N. Dutta. St. Louis, MO: C.V. Mosby.

Public Health Service. 1979. Change in cigarette smoking and current smoking practices among adults: United States, 1978. *Advance Data* 52:1–16.

Rado, S. 1933. The psychoanalysis of pharmacothymia (drug addiction). *Psychoanalytic Quarterly* 2:1–23.

Restak, R. 1979. *The brain.* Garden City, NY: Doubleday.

Riggs, C.E. 1981. Endorphins, neurotransmitters, and/or neuromodulators and exercise. In *Psychology of running,* ed. M.H. Sacks and M.L. Sachs. Champaign, IL: Human Kinetics.

Robbins, J.M., and Joseph. P. 1982. Behavioral components of exercise addiction. Unpublished manuscript, Jewish General Hospital, Montreal.

Robertson, I.H., and Heather, N. 1982. A survey of controlled drinking treatment in Britain. *British Journal on Alcohol and Alcoholism* 17:102–105.

Robins, L.N. 1978. The interaction of setting and predisposition in explaining novel behavior: Drug initiations before, in, and after Vietnam. In *Longitudinal research on drug use,* ed. D.B. Kandel. Washington, DC: Hemisphere.

———. 1980. The natural history of drug abuse. In *Theories on drug abuse: Selected contemporary perspectives,* eds. D.J. Lettieri, M. Sayers, and H.W. Pearson. Research Monograph 30. Rockville, MD: National Institute on Drug Abuse.

Robins, L.N.; Davis, D.H.; and Goodwin, D.W. 1974. Drug use by U.S. army enlisted men in Vietnam: A follow-up on their return home. *American Journal of Epidemiology* 99:235–249.

Robins, L.N.; Davis, D.H.; and Wish, E. 1977. Detecting predictors of rare events: Demographic, family, and personal deviance as predictors of stages in the progression toward narcotic addiction. In *The origins and course of psychopathology,* eds. J.S. Straug, B. Haroutun, and M. Roff. New York: Plenum.

Robins, L.N.; Helzer, J.E.; and Davis, D.H. 1975. Narcotic use in Southeast Asia and afterward. *Archives of General Psychiatry* 32:955–961.

Robins, L.N.; Helzer, J.E.; Hesselbrock, M.; and Wish, E. 1980. Vietnam veterans three years after Vietnam: How our study changed our view of heroin. In *The yearbook of substance use and abuse,* eds. L. Brill and C. Winick. vol. 2. New York: Human Sciences Press.

Robins, L.N., and Murphy, G.E. 1967. Drug use in a normal population of young Negro men. *American Journal of Public Health* 57:1580–1596.

Rodin, J. 1981. Current status of the internal-external hypothesis for obesity: What went wrong? *American Psychologist* 36:361–372.

Rodin, J., and Langer, E.J. 1977. Long-term effects of a control-relevant intervention with the institutionalized aged. *Journal of Personality and Social Psychology* 35:897–902.

Rohsenow, D.J. 1983. Alcoholics' perceptions of control. In *Identifying and measuring alcoholic personality characteristics,* ed. W.M. Cox. San Francisco: Jossey-Bass.

Roizen, R. 1978. Comment on the Rand Report. In *Alcoholism and treatment,* eds. D.J. Armor, J.M. Polich, and H.B. Stambul. New York: Wiley.

Roizen, R.; Cahalan, D.; and Shanks, P. 1978. "Spontaneous remission" among untreated problem drinkers. In *Longitudinal research on drug use,* ed. D.B. Kandel, Washington, DC: Hemisphere.

Rollnick, S., and Heather, N. 1982. The application of Bandura's self-efficacy theory to abstinence-oriented alcoholism treatment. *Addictive Behaviors* 7:243–250.

Room, R. 1976. Ambivalence as a sociological explanation: The case of cultural explanations of alcohol problems. *American Sociological Review* 41:1047–1065.

———. 1977. Measurement and distribution of drinking patterns and problems in general populations. In *Alcohol related disabilities,* eds. G. Edwards et al. WHO Offset Publication 32. Geneva: World Health Organization.

———. 1980. Treatment seeking populations and larger realities. In *Alcoholism treatment in transition,* eds. G. Edwards and M. Grant. London: Croom Helm.

———. 1983. Sociological aspects of the disease concept of alcoholism. In *Research*

advances in alcohol and drug problems, eds. R.G. Smart, F.B. Glaser, Y. Israel, H. Kalant, R.E. Popham, and W. Schmidt. vol. 7. New York: Plenum.

———. 1984. Alcohol control and public health. *Annual Review of Public Health* 5:293–317.

Rosensweig, M.R. 1971. Effects of environment on development of brain and of behavior. In *The biopsychology of development,* eds. E. Tobach, L. Aronson, and E. Shaw. New York: Academic.

Roston, R.A. 1961. Some personality characteristics of compulsive gamblers. Unpublished doctoral dissertation, University of California, Los Angeles.

Rothman, D.J. 1971. *The discovery of the asylum.* Boston: Little, Brown.

Rubington, E. 1967. Drug addiction as a deviant career. *International Journal of the Addictions* 2:3–20.

Russell, J.A., and Bond, C.R. 1980. Individual differences in beliefs concerning emotions conducive to alcohol use. *Journal of Studies on Alcohol* 41:753–759.

Sachs, M.L., and Pargman, D. 1984. Running addiction. In *Running as therapy,* eds. M.L. Sachs and G.W. Buffone. Lincoln: University of Nebraska Press.

Salzberg, P.M., and Klingberg, C.L. 1983. The effectiveness of deferred prosecution for driving while intoxicated. *Journal of Studies on Alcohol* 44:299–306.

Sanchez-Craig, M. 1980. Random assignment to abstinence or controlled drinking in a cognitive-behavioral program: Short term effects on drinking behavior. *Addictive Behaviors* 5:35–39.

———. 1983. The role of the drinker in determining how much is too much: In search of nonobjective indices. Paper presented at International Alcohol Research Seminar, National Institute on Alcohol Abuse and Alcoholism, Washington, DC, October.

Sanchez-Craig, M.; Annis, H.M.; Bornet, A.R.; and MacDonald, K.R. 1984. Random assignment to abstinence and controlled drinking: Evaluation of a cognitive-behavioral program for problem drinkers. *Journal of Consulting and Clinical Psychology* 52:390–403.

Sarason, I.G., and Sarason, B.R. 1981. The importance of cognition and moderator variables in stress. In *Toward a psychology of situations,* ed. D. Magnusson. Hillsdale, NJ: Erlbaum.

Saxe, L.; Dougherty, D.; and Esty, J. 1983. *The effectiveness and costs of alcoholism treatment.* Washington, DC: Congressional Office of Technology Assessment.

Schachter, S. 1968. Obesity and eating. *Science* 161:751–756.

———. 1971. Some extraordinary facts about obese humans and rats. *American Psychologist* 26:129–144.

———. 1977. Nicotine regulation in heavy and light smokers. *Journal of Experimental Psychology: General* 106:13–19.

———. 1978. Pharmacological and psychological determinants of smoking. *Annals of Internal Medicine* 88:104–114.

———. 1980. Non-psychological explanations of behavior. In *Retrospections on social psychology,* ed. L. Festinger. New York: Oxford University Press.

———. 1982. Recidivism and self-cure of smoking and obesity. *American Psychologist* 37:436–444.

Schachter, S., and Rodin, J. 1974. *Obese humans and rats.* Washington, DC: Erlbaum.

Schachter, S., and Singer, J.E. 1962. Cognitive, social, and physiological determinants of emotional state. *Psychological Review* 69:379–399.

Schaefer, H.H. 1971. A cultural delusion of alcoholics. *Psychological Reports* 29:587–589.

———. 1972. Twelve-month follow-up of behaviorally trained ex–alcoholic social drinkers. *Behavior Therapy* 3:286–289.

Schein, E.H. 1961. *Coercive persuasion.* New York: Norton.

Schlichter suspension lifted by Rozelle. 1984. *New York Times* (June 23): 31.

Schuckit, M.A. 1984. Prospective markers for alcoholism. In *Longitudinal research in alcoholism,* eds. D.W. Goodwin, K.T. van Dusen, and S.A. Mednick. Boston: Kluwer-Nijhoff.

Schur, E.M. 1962. *Narcotic addiction in Britain and America.* Bloomington: Indiana University Press.

Seevers, M.H. 1936. Opiate addiction in the monkey I: Methods of study. *Journal of Pharmacology and Experimental Therapeutics* 56:147–156.

———. 1963. Laboratory approach to the problem of addiction. In *Narcotic drug addiction problems,* ed. R.B. Livingston. Public Health Service Publication 1050. Bethesda, MD: National Institute of Mental Health.

Segal, B. 1977. Reasons for marijuana use and personality: A canonical analysis. *Journal of Alcohol and Drug Education* 22:64–67.

Seligman, M.E.P. 1975. *Helplessness.* San Francisco: Freeman.

Selzer, M.L.; Vinokur, A.; and Wilson, T.D. 1977. A psychosocial comparison of drunken drivers and alcoholics. *Journal of Studies on Alcohol* 38:1294–1312.

Shaffer, H., and Burglass, M.E., eds. 1981. *Classic contributions in the addictions.* New York: Brunner/Mazel.

Shaw, S. 1979. A critique of the concept of the alcohol dependence syndrome. *British Journal of Addiction* 74:339–348.

Sheehan, D.V. 1984. *The anxiety disease and how to overcome it.* New York: Scribner.

Siegel, R.K. 1979. Natural animal addictions: An ethological perspective. In *Psychopathology in animals,* ed. J.D. Keehn. New York: Academic.

Siegel, R.K., and Jarvik, M.E. 1980. DMT self-administration by monkeys in isolation. *Bulletin of the Psychonomic Society* 16:117–120.

Siegel, S. 1975. Evidence from rats that morphine tolerance is a learned response. *Journal of Comparative and Physiological Psychology* 89:498–506.

———. 1979. The role of conditioning in drug tolerance and addiction. In *Psychopathology in animals: Research and treatment implications,* ed. J.D. Keehn. New York: Academic.

———. 1983. Classical conditioning, drug tolerance, and drug dependence. In *Research advances in alcohol and drug problems,* eds. R.G. Smart, F.B. Glasser, Y. Israel, H. Kalant, R.E. Popham, and W. Schmidt. vol. 7. New York: Plenum.

Skinner, H.A.; Glaser, F.B.; and Annis, H.M. 1982. Crossing the threshold: Factors in self-identification as an alcoholic. *British Journal of Addiction* 77:51–64.

Skinner, H.A.; Holt, S.; Allen, B.A.; and Haakonson, N.H. 1980. Correlation between medical and behavioral data in the assessment of alcoholism. *Alcoholism: Clinical and Experimental Research* 4:371–377.

Slater, P. 1980. *Wealth addiction.* New York: Dutton.

Slochower, J.A. 1983. *Excessive eating: The role of emotions and environment.* New York: Human Sciences Press.

Smith, D. 1981. The benzodiazepines and alcohol. Paper presented at Third World Congress of Biological Psychiatry, Stockholm, July.

Smith, D.E., ed. 1983. The benzodiazepines: Two decades of research and clinical experience. *Journal of Psychoactive Drugs* 15(1–2):entire issue.

Smith, D.E., and Wesson, D.R. 1983. Benzodiazepine dependency syndromes. *Journal of Psychoactive Drugs* 15:85–95.

Smith, G.M., and Beecher, H.K. 1962. Subjective effects of heroin and morphine in normal subjects. *Journal of Pharmacology and Experimental Therapeutics* 136:47–52.

Snyder, S.H. 1977. Opiate receptors and internal opiates. *Scientific American* (March): 44–56.

Sobell, M.B., and Sobell, L.C. 1973. Alcoholics treated by individualized behavior therapy: One year treatment outcomes. *Behavior Research and Therapy* 11:599–618.

———. 1976. Second year treatment outcome of alcoholics treated by individualized behavior therapy: Results. *Behavior Research and Therapy* 14:195–215.

———. 1982. Controlled drinking: A concept coming of age. In *Self-control and self-modification of emotional behavior,* eds. K.R. Blanstein and J. Polivy. New York: Plenum.

———. 1984. The aftermath of heresy: A response to Pendery et al.'s (1982) critique of "Individualized Behavior Therapy for Alcoholics." *Behavior Research and Therapy* 22:413–447.

Solomon, F.; White, C.C.; Parron, D.L.; and Mendelson, W.B. 1979. Sleeping pills, insomnia and medical practice. *New England Journal of Medicine* 300:803–808.

Solomon, R. 1977. The evolution of non-medical opiate use in Canada II: 1930–1970. *Drug Forum* 6:1–25.

Solomon, R.L. 1980. The opponent-process theory of acquired motivation: The costs of pleasure and the benefits of pain. *American Psychologist* 35:691–712.

Solomon, R.L., and Corbit, J.D. 1973. An opponent-process theory of motivation II: Cigarette addiction. *Journal of Abnormal Psychology* 81:158–171.

———. 1974. An opponent-process theory of motivation I: Temporal dynamics of affect. *Psychological Review* 81:119–145.

Sonnedecker, G. 1958. Emergence and concept of the addiction problem. In *Narcotic drug addiction problems,* ed. R.B. Livingston. Bethesda, MD: Public Health Service.

Spotts, J.V., and Shontz, F.C. 1982. Ego development, dragon fights, and chronic drug abusers. *International Journal of the Addictions* 17:945–976.

———. 1983. Psychopathology and chronic drug use: A methodological paradigm. *International Journal of the Addictions* 18:633–680.

Stafford, R.A. 1980. Alcoholics' perception of the internal–external locus of their drinking problem. *Journal of Studies on Alcohol* 41:300–309.

Steiner, C. 1971. *Games alcoholics play.* New York: Grove.

Stewart, O. 1964. Questions regarding American Indian criminality. *Human Organization* 23:61–66.

Stockwell, T.; Hodgson, R.; and Rankin, H. 1982. Tension reduction and the effects of prolonged alcohol consumption. *British Journal of Addiction* 77:65–73.

Stone, N.; Fromme, M.; and Kagan, D. 1984. *Cocaine: Seduction and solution.* New York: Potter.

Stunkard, A.J. 1958. The results of treatment for obesity. *New York State Journal of Medicine* 58:79–87.

———. 1967. Obesity. In *Comprehensive textbook of psychiatry,* eds. A.M. Freedman and W.I. Kaplan. Baltimore: Williams & Wilkins.

Stunkard, A.J., ed. 1980. *Obesity.* Philadelphia: Saunders.

Stunkard, A.J.; d'Aquili, E.; Fox, S.; and Filion, R.D.L. 1972. Influence of social class on obesity and thinness in children. *Journal of the American Medical Association* 221:579–584.

Surgeon General. 1982. *The health consequences of smoking: Cancer.* Rockville, MD: U.S. Department of Health and Human Services.

Synanon founder and two guards convicted in attack with a snake. 1980. *New York Times* (July 16): 1; 20.

Szasz, T.S. 1961. *The myth of mental illness.* New York: Hoeber–Harper.

———. 1974. *Ceremonial chemistry.* Garden City, NY: Anchor Press.

Tang, M.; Brown, C.; and Falk, J. 1982. Complete reversal of chronic ethanol polydipsia by schedule withdrawal. *Pharmacology Biochemistry and Behavior* 16:155–158.

Tarter, R.E.; Goldstein, G.; Alterman, A.; Petrarulo, E.W.; and Elmore, S. 1983. Alcoholic seizures: Intellectual and neuropsychological sequelae. *Journal of Nervous and Mental Disease* 171:123–125.

Teasdale, J.D. 1972. The perceived effect of heroin on the interpersonal behavior of heroin-dependent patients, and a comparison with stimulant dependent patients. *International Journal of the Addictions* 7:533–548.

———. 1973. Conditioned abstinence in narcotic addicts. *International Journal of the Addictions* 8:273–292.

Tennov, D. 1979. *Love and limerence.* New York: Stein and Day.

Tobacco use as an addiction. 1982. Special report on symposium sponsored by Merrell Dow Pharmaceuticals, New York City, March 12. *U.S. Journal of Drug and Alcohol Dependence.*

Tokar, J.T.; Brunse, A.J.; Stefflre, V.J.; and Napior, D.A. 1973. Emotional states and behavioral patterns in alcoholics and non-alcoholics. *Quarterly Journal of Studies on Alcohol* 34:133–143.

Trebach, A.S. 1982. *The heroin solution.* New Haven, CT: Yale University Press.

Trice, H.M., and Roman, P.M. 1970. Delabeling, relabeling, and Alcoholics Anonymous. *Social Problems* 17:538–546.

Tuchfeld, B.S. 1981. Spontaneous remission in alcoholics: Empirical observations and theoretical implications. *Journal of Studies on Alcohol* 42:626–641.

Tuchfeld, B.S.; Lipton, W.L.; and Lile, E.A. 1983. Social involvement and the resolution of alcoholism. *Journal of Drug Issues* 13–323–332.

U.S. is seen as losing war on cocaine smuggling as planes get through. 1984. *New York Times* (May 18): 12.

U.S. social tolerance of drugs found on rise. 1983. *New York Times.* (March 21): 1; B5.

Vaillant, G.E. 1966. A 12-year follow-up of New York addicts IV: Some characteristics and determinants of abstinence. *American Journal of Psychiatry* 123:573–584.

———. 1977. *Adaptation to life.* Boston: Little, Brown.

———. 1983. *The natural history of alcoholism.* Cambridge, MA: Harvard University Press.

Vaillant, G.E., and Milofsky, E.S. 1982. The etiology of alcoholism: A prospective viewpoint. *American Psychologist* 37:494–503.

Van Dyke, C., and Byck, R. 1982. Cocaine. *Scientific American* (March): 128–141.

Vingilis, E. 1983. Drinking drivers and alcoholics: Are they from the same population? In *Research advances in alcohol and drug problems,* eds. R.G. Smart, F.B. Glaser, Y. Israel, H. Kalant, R.E. Popham, and W. Schmidt. vol. 7. New York: Plenum.

Vogler, R.E., and Bartz, W.R. 1982. *The better way to drink.* New York: Simon & Schuster.

Vogler, R.E.; Compton, J.V.; and Weissbach, J.A. 1975. Integrated behavior change techniques for alcoholism. *Journal of Consulting and Clinical Psychology* 43:233–243.

Waldorf, D. 1973. *Careers in dope.* Englewood Cliffs, NJ: Prentice-Hall.

———. 1983. Natural recovery from opiate addiction: Some social-psychological processes of untreated recovery. *Journal of Drug Issues* 13:237–280.

Waldorf, D., and Biernacki, P. 1981. The natural recovery from opiate addiction: Some preliminary findings. *Journal of Drug Issues* 11:61–74.

Wallerstein, R.S.; Chotlos, J.W.; Friend, M.B.; Hammersley, D.W.; Perlswig, E.A.; and Winship, G.M. 1957. *Hospital treatment of alcoholism: A comparative experimental study.* New York: Basic Books.

Washton, A. 1983. Diagnostic and treatment strategies. Paper presented at Cocaine Update Conference, New York, December.

Weeks, J.R., and Collins, R.J. 1968. Patterns of intravenous self-injection by morphine-addicted rats. In *The addictive states,* ed. A.H. Wikler. Baltimore: Williams and Wilkins.

———. 1979. Dose and physical dependence as factors in the self administration of morphine by rats. *Psychopharmacology* 65:171–177.

Weisner, C. 1983. The alcohol treatment system and social control: A study in institutional change. *Journal of Drug Issues* 13:117–133.

Weisner, C., and Room, R. 1984. *Financing and ideology in human services: The alcohol treatment system as a case study.* Berkeley, CA: Alcohol Research Group.

Weissman, M.M., and Klerman, G.L. 1977. Sex differences and the epidemiology of depression. *Archives of General Psychiatry* 34:98–111.

Weisz, D.J., and Thompson, R.F. 1983. Endogenous opioids: Brain-behavior relations. In *Commonalities in substance abuse and habitual behavior,* eds. P.K. Levison, D.R. Gerstein, and D.R. Maloff. Lexington, MA: Lexington.

Wiener, C. 1981. *The politics of alcoholism: Building an arena around a social problem.* New Brunswick, NJ: Transaction Books.

Wikler, A. 1973. Dynamics of drug dependence. *Archives of General Psychiatry* 28:611–616.

———. 1980. *Opioid dependence.* New York: Plenum.

Wikler, A., and Pescor, F.T. 1967. Classical conditioning of a morphine abstinence phenomenon, reinforcement of opioid-drinking behavior and "relapse" in morphine-addicted rats. *Psychopharmacologia* 10:255–284.

Wilder, T. 1938. Our town. In *Best plays of 1937–38.*, ed. B. Mantle. New York: Dodd Mead.

Wilkinson, R.W. 1970. *The prevention of drinking problems: Alcohol control and cultural influences.* New York: Oxford University Press.

Wille, R. 1983. Processes of recovery from heroin dependence: Relationship to treatment, social changes and drug use. *Journal of Drug Issues* 13:333–342.

Williams, T. 1971. Summary and implications of review of literature related to adolescent smoking. National Clearinghouse for Smoking and Health, U.S. Department of Health, Education and Welfare, Bethesda, MD.

Wilsnack, S.C. 1976. The impact of sex roles and women's alcohol use and abuse. In *Alcoholism problems in women and children,* eds. M. Greenblatt and M.A. Schuckit. New York: Grune & Stratton.

Wilson, G.T. 1981. The effect of alcohol on human sexual behavior. In *Advances in substance abuse,* ed. N.K. Mello. vol. 2. Greenwich, CT.

Wilson, G.T., and Lawson, D.M. 1978. Expectancies, alcohol, and sexual arousal in women. *Journal of Abnormal Psychology* 85:489–497.

Wingard, J.A.; Huba, J.V.; and Bentler, P.M. 1979. The relationship of personality structure to patterns of adolescent substance use. *Multivariate Behavioral Research* 14:131–143.

Winick, C. 1961. Physician narcotic addicts. *Social Problems* 9:174–186.

———. 1962. Maturing out of narcotic addiction. *Bulletin on Narcotics* 14:1–7.

Wishnie, H. 1977. *The impulsive personality.* New York: Plenum.

Woititz, J.G. 1983. *Adult children of alcoholics.* Hollywood, FL: Health Communications.

Woods, J.H. 1978. Behavioral pharmacology of drug self-administration. In *Psychopharmacology: A generation of progress,* eds. M.A. Lipton, A. DiMascio, and K.F. Killam. New York: Raven.

Woods, J.H., and Schuster, C.R. 1971. Opiates as reinforcing stimuli. *Stimulus properties of drugs,* eds. T. Thompson and R. Pickens. New York: Appleton-Century-Crofts.

World Health Organization Expert Committee on Mental Health. 1957. *Addiction producing drugs: 7th report of the WHO Expert Committee.* WHO Technical Report Series 116. Geneva: World Health Organization.

Wray, I., and Dickerson, M.G. 1981. Cessation of high frequency gambling and "withdrawal" symptoms. *British Journal of Addiction* 76:401–405.

Wright, J.T., et al. 1983. Alcohol consumption, pregnancy, and low birth-weight. *Lancet* 8326(1):663–665.

Wurmser, L. 1978. *The hidden dimension: Psychodynamics in compulsive drug use.* New York: Jason Aronson.

Yanagita, T. 1970. Self-administration studies on various dependence-producing agents in monkeys. *University of Michigan Medical Center Journal* 36(4, pt. 2):216–224.

Yates, A.; Leehey, K.; and Shisslak, C.M. 1983. Running: An analogue of anorexia? *New England Journal of Medicine* 308:251–255.

Zelson, C. 1975. Acute management of neonatal addiction. *Addictive Diseases* 2:159–168.

Zentner, J.L. 1979. Heroin: Devil drug or useful medicine? *Journal of Drug Issues* 9:333–340.

Zimberg, S. 1974. Evaluation of alcoholism treatment in Harlem. *Quarterly Journal of Studies on Alcohol* 35:550–557.

Zinberg, N.E. 1972. Heroin use in Vietnam and the United States. *Archives of General Psychiatry* 26:486–488.

———. 1974. The search for rational approaches to heroin use. In *Addiction,* ed. P.G. Bourne. New York: Academic Press.

———. 1979. Nonaddictive opiate use. In *Handbook on drug abuse,* eds. R.L. Dupont, A. Goldstein, J. O'Donnell. Rockville, MD: National Institute on Drug Abuse.

———. 1981. "High" states: A beginning study. In *Classic contributions in the addictions,* eds. H. Shaffer and M.E. Burglass. New York Brunner/Mazel.

———. 1984. *Drug, set, and setting: The basis for controlled intoxicant use.* New Haven, CT: Yale University Press.

Zinberg, N.E., and Fraser, K.M. 1979. The role of the social setting in the prevention and treatment of alcoholism. In *The diagnosis and treatment of alcoholism,* eds. J.H. Mendelson and N.K. Mello. New York: McGraw-Hill.

Zinberg, N.E., and Harding, W.M., eds. 1982. *Control over intoxicant use: Pharmacological, psychological, and social considerations.* New York: Human Sciences Press.

Zinberg, N.E.; Harding, W.M.; and Apsler, R. 1978. What is drug abuse? *Journal of Drug Issues* 8:9–35.

Zinberg, N.E.; Harding, W.M.; and Winkeller, M. 1977. A study of social regulatory mechanisms in controlled illicit drug users. *Journal of Drug Issues* 7:117–133.

Zinberg, N.E., and Jacobson, R.C. 1976. The natural history of chipping. *American Journal of Psychiatry* 133:37–40.

Zinberg, N.E:, and Lewis, D.C. 1964. Narcotic usage I: A spectrum of a difficult medical problem. *New England Journal of Medicine* 270:989–993.

Zinberg, N.E., and Robertson, J.A. 1972. *Drugs and the public.* New York: Simon & Schuster.

Zismer, D.K., and Holloway, R.L. 1984. The development and validation of an alcohol reinforcement value measure. Unpublished manuscript, Health Services Research Center, Minneapolis.

Zucker, R.A. 1976. Parental influence on the drinking patterns of their children. In *Alcoholism problems in women and children,* eds. M. Greenblatt and M.A. Schuckit. New York: Grune & Stratton.

Author Index

Adler, M.W., 89
Alcoholics Anonymous, 29, 31, 145
Alexander, B.K., 56, 68, 80, 81, 82, 88, 89–90, 91
Allen, J., 112, 127
American Psychiatric Association, 19
Aneshensel, C.S., 131
Annis, H.M., 43, 142
Appenzeller, O., 58
Apsler, R., 23–25, 64, 71, 99, 120, 122
Armor, D.J., 29, 33, 36–37, 39, 43, 62, 104
Atkinson, J.W., 119
Ausubel, D.P., 71

Baekeland, F., 44, 125
Baker, M.C., 57
Bales, R.F., 12, 106, 107, 112
Ball, J.C., 136
Bandura, A., 69, 121, 143
Barnett, M.L., 13, 133
Bartz, W.R., 39
Beauchamp, D.E., 11, 27, 31, 35, 36, 61, 138
Becker, H.S., 13, 71, 105, 115
Becker, M., 104, 117
Beckman, L.J., 101, 116
Beecher, H.K., 17, 64
Begleiter, H., 49
Bejerot, N., 63, 78
Bem, D.J., 114
Benevento, A., 143
Bennett, R., 57
Bennett, W., 53, 124
Benson, C.S., 121
Berg, B., 13, 33, 62, 109
Berglas, S., 118, 119
Berridge, V., 4, 5, 56, 75, 108, 138, 154
Best, J.A., 58, 141
Biernacki, P., 123, 125, 126, 127
Birney, R.C., 119
Black, C., 150
Bloch, M., 141
Blum, E.H., 13, 33
Blum, R.H., 4, 12, 13, 33, 108
Boland, F.J., 88
Bond, C.R., 101
Boskind-White, M., 110, 123
Boyd, W., 100
Brandsma, J.M., 145
Brecher, E.M., 4, 7, 64, 135, 140
Brodsky, A., 12, 40, 54–55, 66, 95, 96, 98, 99, 104, 109, 110, 121, 122, 126, 129, 131, 135, 141, 151, 157
Brook, J.S., 8, 28, 113
Brown, S.A., 101, 116
Bruch, H., 100, 109, 123, 131
Brunke, M.L., 89
Brunswick, A.F., 123
Burke, H., 118
Burnett, M., 102
Butterfield, G.E., 58
Byck, R., 19, 139

Caddy, G., 37
Cahalan, D., 13, 15, 16, 33–34, 39, 44, 62, 104, 105, 112, 117, 122, 123, 125
Califano, J.E., 10, 124, 141
Cameron, D.C., 20, 21–22
Caplan, R.D., 111, 126
Cappell, H., 100
Carnes, P., 151
Caudill, B.D., 34
Center for Disease Control, 124, 144

Cermak, T., 149
Chaney, E.F., 40
Chein, I., 16, 64, 65, 71, 111, 112–113, 119, 120, 121
Chernick, V., 76
Chipkin, R.E., 88
Christiansen, B.A., 106
Cisin, I.H., 8, 123, 125
Clark, W.B., 13, 34, 39
Clausen, J.A., 4, 10, 27, 108, 135
Cleary, P.D., 58–59, 70, 100, 111
Cloninger, C.R., 50, 117, 118, 158
Coambs, R.B., 68, 80, 81, 82, 88, 89–90, 91, 92–93
Cohen, S., 10
Colletti, G., 144
Collier, P., 140
Collins, R.J., 77
Colt, E.W.D., 58
Condiotte, M.M., 127, 143
Coppolillo, H.P., 75
Corbit, J.D., 65–66
Costello, R.M., 125
Courtwright, D.T., 4, 7, 27, 75
Crawford, G.G., 147
Csikszentmihalyi, M., 131
Cummings, N.A., 74
Cushner, I.M., 76

Davies, D.L., 35
Davis, M., 74
DeFeudis, F.V., 89
Desmond, D.P., 8, 123
Desmond, M.M., 74, 75
Dickens, B.M., 38
Dickerson, M.G., 25
Dielman, T.E., 116
Ditman, K.S., 147
Dole, V.P., 51, 56–57, 63, 78, 140, 141
Donegan, N.H., 62
Dunwiddie, T., 51

Eddy, N.B., 10, 11, 20, 99
Edgerton, B., 13, 33, 107
Edwards, G., 4, 5, 41, 44, 56, 59–60, 70, 75, 108, 125, 138, 154
Efron, V., 33
Emrick, C.D., 32, 39, 41, 43, 44, 124
Engle, K.B., 17
Epstein, E.J., 13, 136, 141

Falk, J.L., 13, 14, 60, 65, 94, 95, 98, 103
Feather, N.T., 119
Ferguson, G.A., 87
Fillmore, K.M., 44
Finney, J.W., 44, 125
Fishburne, P.M., 123
Fisher, E., 115
Fisher, E.B., Jr., 144
Fisher, J.C., 18
Flannelly, K., 80, 91
Foucault, M., 5, 32, 108
Fraser, K.M., 13, 30, 34, 108
Fuentes, V.O., 82
Funder, D.C., 114

Gaines, L.S., 105
Garcia, J., 91
Garn, S.M., 54, 104, 124
Gay, G.R., 18, 24, 71
Gerard, D.L., 33, 44, 154
Gerin, W., 126, 127, 144
Gilbert, D.G., 99, 131
Gilbert, R.M., 14, 16–17, 116
Glaser, F.B., 18, 24, 43
Glassner, B., 13, 33, 62, 109
Glazer, N., 106
Glickman, S.E., 91
Goldblatt, P.B., 104
Goldman, M.S., 101, 106, 116
Goldstein, A., 11, 19, 51, 57, 63, 78, 88, 89, 141
Goldstein, J.W., 117
Gomberg, E.L., 126
Goode, E., 108
Goodwin, D.W., 9, 11, 14, 48, 49, 66, 95, 150–151
Gordis, E., 44, 124
Gordon, B., 19
Gordon, J.R., 67, 126, 142
Gordon, R.A., 63, 64, 67, 78, 126
Grant, E.C., 80
Gray, J.A., 131
Greaves, G., 71, 125
Greeley, A.M., 33, 106
Greenough, W.T., 89
Griffiths, R.R., 79
Gross, M.M., 59, 61
Gurin, J., 53, 124
Gusfield, J.R., 31, 35, 108

Hackler, T., 146
Hadaway, P.F., 56, 68, 80, 81, 82, 88, 89–90, 91
Hakstian, A.R., 58
Hansen, J., 32, 39, 43, 44, 124
Hanson, J.W., 75
Harding, W.M., 8, 10, 23–25, 64, 71, 99, 122
Harford, T.C., 34, 105
Harris, T.G., 9, 19
Hatterer, L., 63
Hawkins, J., 9
Hawley, L.M., 158
Heather, N., 17, 18, 29, 35, 38, 39, 40, 43, 49, 122, 131
Herman, C.P., 53, 100, 110, 124, 131
Hester, R.K., 33, 43, 145
Hingson, R., 76
Hodgson, R., 43, 59–60, 67, 70, 100, 144
Holloway, R.L., 103
Hooper, H.E., 10
Horn, G., 89
Horowitz, D., 140
Huba, G.J., 117, 131
Huidobro, F., 91
Hull, J.G., 102

Isbell, H., 5, 11, 20
Istvan, J., 55, 116, 117, 127

Jacobson, R.C., 8, 24, 106
Jaffe, J.H., 9, 19, 20–21, 64, 78
Jarvik, M.E., 15, 79, 88
Jellinek, E.M., 29, 59
Jessor, R., 10, 13, 34, 104, 105, 117, 118
Jessor, S.L., 10, 13, 34, 104, 105, 117
Johanson, C.E., 14, 64–65
Johnson, C., 131
Johnston, L.D., 45, 122, 123, 138, 156
Jones, E., 118, 119
Jones, H.B., 19
Jones, H.C., 19
Jones, K.L., 75
Jorquez, J.S., 126, 127
Joseph, P., 98, 102, 116, 128

Kalant, H., 16, 23, 57, 60, 117
Kalant, O.J., 117
Kales, A., 19, 99
Kandel, D.B., 13, 104, 105, 116, 117, 118, 123
Kaplan, E.H., 71
Katz, D.M., 89
Kay, E., 117
Keller, M., 19, 33, 35, 79, 106, 123
Kendell, R.E., 11
Kennel, J.H., 75
Kern, M., 114
Khantzian, E.J., 71, 102
Khavari, K.A., 80
Kilpatrick, D.G., 117
King, A., 115
King, R., 4, 108, 135
Kissin, B., 9, 44, 125
Klaus, M.H., 75
Klausner, S.Z., 107
Klein, D.F., 153
Klerman, G.L., 153
Kline, N.S., 152
Klingberg, C.L., 147
Knop, J., 49, 50
Knupfer, G., 29
Kolata, G.B., 77
Kolb, L., 5, 7, 16, 64
Kopel, S.A., 144
Kosterlitz, H.W., 10
Kostowski, W., 89
Kraft, D.P., 34
Krasnegor, N.A., 11, 141
Kron, R.E., 74, 75
Krystal, H., 71, 102
Kubey, R., 131
Kumar, R., 78, 91, 94

Labate, C., 113
Lang, A.R., 16, 101, 113, 121
Langer, E.J., 143
Larson, R., 131
Lasagna, L., 17, 64, 80
Lawson, D.M., 101
Lazarus, R., 111
Lear, M.W., 19
LeFlore, R., 9
Lender, M.E., 13, 30
Lennard, H.L., 17, 141
Leventhal, H., 25, 58–59, 70, 100, 111
Levine, H.G., 6, 13, 27, 30, 32, 108
Lewis, A., 11, 19
Lewis, C.E., 117, 118

Lewis, D.C., 7, 28
Lewontin, R.C., 104
Lichtenstein, E., 127, 143
Lidz, C.W., 136
Lieberman, M., 145
Liebowitz, M.R., 12, 54, 55, 152–153
Light, A.B., 6, 15, 19, 103, 143
Lindblad, R.A., 121
Lindesmith, A.R., 17, 69
Lipscomb, T.R., 50
Lolli, G., 33
Lord, C.G., 114
Lore, R., 80, 91
Lovibund, S.H., 37
Lukoff, I.F., 8, 28, 113

MacAndrew, C., 13, 33, 107, 117, 118, 147
McAuliffe, W.E., 63, 64, 67, 78, 126
McClelland, D.C., 33, 70, 71, 100, 101, 107, 112, 118, 129
McGuire, M.T., 102, 103
McIntosh, T.K., 91
McMurray, R.G., 58
Maddux, J.F., 8, 123
Magnusson, D., 114
Mangin, W., 107
Mann, M., 29, 146
Marcus, R., 118
Markoff, R., 58
Marlatt, G.A., 17, 32, 34, 39, 40, 43, 67, 70, 100, 101, 111, 116, 126, 131, 142, 144, 147, 151
Martin, J.K., 13, 30
Martin, W.R., 64
Masserman, J.H., 151
Matarazzo, J.D., 55, 116, 117, 127
May, E.L., 10, 99
Mayer, W., 18
Mello, N.K., 29, 33, 34, 50, 60, 64, 70, 100, 131
Mendelson, J.H., 29, 33, 34, 50, 60, 64, 70, 100, 102, 103, 131
Merry, J., 33
Milkman, H., 56, 114
Miller, P., 67
Miller, W.R., 18, 29, 31, 33, 34, 35, 39, 41, 43, 113, 121, 144, 145, 147
Milofsky, E.S., 48
Mischel, W., 66, 114, 116
Mohatt, G., 107
Moos, R.H., 44, 125
Morgan, W.P., 12
Mumford, L., 91
Muñoz, R.F., 39
Murphy, G.E., 8, 123
Murray, H.A., 157
Musto, D.F., 4, 135

Nathan, P.E., 29, 44, 50, 131
National Association for Children of Alcoholics, 149
National Cancer Institute, 124, 144
National Foundation for Prevention of Chemical Dependency Disease, 148
Nerenz, D., 111
Nesbitt, P.D., 99, 131
Newman, J.M., 117
Nichols, J.R., 77, 82
Nisbett, R.E., 52–53, 124
Nurco, D.N., 8
Nyswander, M.E., 51, 56–57, 140

Oates, W., 12
O'Brien, C.P., 24, 62, 66–67
O'Brien, J.S., 29
O'Donnell, J.A., 15, 16, 62, 115, 123
Öjesjö, L., 153
Oki, G., 14, 19, 142
Orford, J., 41, 44, 125
Ostrea, E.M., 74
Ouellette, E.M., 76

Panksepp, J., 89, 91
Paredes, A., 33
Pargman, D., 57
Patai, R., 109
Pattison, E.M., 29, 145
Peele, S., 1, 3, 9, 10, 12, 16, 25, 38, 40, 43, 44, 48, 52, 54–55, 58, 59, 66, 72, 78, 94, 95, 96, 98, 99, 103, 104, 109, 110, 113, 117, 120, 121, 122, 125, 126, 127, 129, 131, 135, 137, 139, 141, 151, 152, 155, 157
Pelton, L., 104
Pendery, M.L., 37–39, 41, 43
Pescor, F.T., 67, 78, 91
Platt, J., 113
Polich, J.M., 29, 33, 36–37, 39, 43, 62, 104
Polivy, J., 53, 100, 110, 124, 131
Pollock, V.E., 49, 50

Porjesz, B., 49
Prescott, J.W., 89
Prial, F.J., 62
Primm, B.J., 18, 24
Public Health Service, 124

Rado, S., 71
Raskin, H.A., 71, 102
Restak, R., 78
Riggs, C.E., 57
Robbins, J.M., 98, 102, 116, 128
Robertson, I.H., 29, 35, 38, 39, 43, 49
Robertson, J.A., 14, 68
Robins, L.N., 8, 9, 14, 16, 18, 28, 66, 67, 95, 109, 110–111, 113, 116, 117, 118, 123, 126
Rodin, J., 15, 52, 53, 58, 62, 100, 143
Rohsenow, D.J., 17, 12
Roizen, R., 31, 36, 38, 44, 123
Rollnick, S., 17, 18, 40, 43, 122, 131
Roman, P.M., 31
Room, R., 13, 15, 16, 28, 29, 31, 32, 33–34, 35, 44, 45, 61, 62, 104, 105, 112, 117, 122, 123, 125, 138, 146–147, 148
Rosensweig, M.R., 89
Roston, R.A., 118
Rothman, D.J., 108
Rubington, E., 71
Russell, J.A., 101

Sachs, M.L., 57
Saenger, G., 33, 44, 154
Salzberg, P.M., 147
Sanchez-Craig, M., 18, 43, 44
Santo, Y., 10
Sappington, J.T., 117
Sarason, B.R., 111
Sarason, I.G., 111
Saucedo, C.F., 18, 34, 39
Saxe, L., 146
Schachter, S., 11, 13, 15, 17, 19, 52, 53, 58–59, 67, 100, 124, 127, 144, 152
Schaefer, H.H., 37, 40
Schein, E.H., 149
Schiff, B.B., 91
Schuckit, M.A., 11, 45, 49, 148
Schur, E.M., 112
Schuster, C.R., 14, 63, 77, 98, 103
Seevers, M.H., 11, 20, 56, 77, 78
Segal, B., 117
Seligman, M.E.P., 143
Selzer, M.L., 100
Shanks, B., 74
Shaw, S., 35, 60, 70
Sheehan, D.V., 152–153
Shontz, F.C., 16, 114
Siegel, R.K., 79, 88
Siegel, S., 63, 66–69
Singer, J.E., 13, 17
Skinner, H.A., 18, 43
Slater, P., 12
Slochower, J.A., 100, 102, 111
Smith, D.E., 10, 16, 19, 51, 139
Smith, D.W., 75
Smith, G.M., 64
Snyder, S.H., 51, 57, 141
Sobell, L.C., 29, 33, 37, 39, 41–42
Sobell, M.B., 29, 33, 37, 39, 41–42
Solomon, F., 10, 99
Solomon, R., 12, 14–15, 103
Solomon, R.L., 62, 63, 65–66
Sonnedecker, G., 4
Spotts, J.V., 16, 114
Stafford, R.A., 122
Steinberg, H., 89
Steiner, C., 39
Stewart, O., 33
Stockwell, T., 43, 59–60, 70, 100
Stolerman, I.P., 78, 94
Stone, N., 101, 102
Stunkard, A.J., 15, 53, 104, 109
Sunderwirth, S., 56, 114
Surgeon General, 144
Szasz, T.S., 5, 151

Tang, M., 14, 60
Tarter, R.E., 18, 142
Teasdale, J.D., 67, 102
Tennov, D., 12, 54, 55
Thompson, R.F., 12, 57
Tokar, J.D., 100
Torrance, E.G., 6, 15, 19, 103, 143
Trebach, A.S., 4, 28, 135–136
Trice, H.M., 31
Tuchfeld, B.S., 43, 123, 127

Uhlenhuth, E.H., 14, 65

Vaillant, G.E., 10, 13, 17, 29, 34, 36, 39, 40, 41, 44–45, 48, 49, 50, 62, 67, 105, 108, 118, 124, 126, 127, 145

Van Dyke, C., 19, 139
Vingilis, E., 147
Vogler, R.E., 37, 39

Waldorf, D., 8, 9, 15, 67, 123, 125, 126, 127
Walker, A.L., 136
Wallerstein, R.S., 35
Washton, A., 11, 19
Weeks, J.R., 77
Weisner, C., 32, 146–147
Weissman, M.M., 153
Weisz, D.J., 12, 57
Wesson, D.R., 10
White, W.C., 110, 123
Wieder, H., 71
Wiener, C., 31, 108
Wikler, A., 63, 66–67, 78, 91
Wilder, T., 150
Wilkinson, R.W., 33, 34
Wille, R., 126, 127, 128, 142, 143
Williams, T., 105
Williams, T.K., 17
Wilsnack, S.C., 101, 121
Wilson, G.S., 74, 75
Wilson, G.T., 17, 70, 101, 102
Wingard, J.A., 117
Winick, C., 7, 15, 71, 122, 123, 125, 140
Wishnie, H., 17
Woititz, J.G., 150
Woods, J.H., 63, 77
World Health Organization Expert Committee on Mental Health, 18
Wray, I., 25
Wright, J.T., 76
Wurmser, L., 71, 102

Yanagita, T., 79, 94
Yates, A., 105
Young, R.D., 102

Zelson, C., 74
Zentner, J.L., 80
Zimberg, S., 145
Zinberg, N.E., 7, 8, 10, 13, 14, 17, 19, 23–25, 28, 30, 34, 64, 68, 69, 71, 99, 100, 106, 108, 111, 120, 122, 126, 138, 139
Zismer, D.K., 103
Zucker, R.A., 106

Subject Index

Abstinence: cure for alcoholism, 30–31, 34, 38, 41, 42, 43, 49, 104, 123, 145, 149, 151; cure for smoking, 144; recommendation for pregnant women, 77; recovery without treatment and return to nonproblematic drinking, 29, 34, 35–45, 49, 122, 123. *See also* Controlled drinking; Moderation

Achievement, 17, 96, 107, 108, 119, 130, 157

Adaptation theories, 47, 69–72; adaptation to internal and external needs, 70; meekness of theorists inappropriate, 72; physiological mechanisms needed, 71

Addiction, causes: among animals, 88–94; any potent experience, 25, 55, 94–96, 97; avoidance of withdrawal (denied), 98; biological factors (inadequate), 12, 18, 54–62, 128, 147–148; cognitive factors, 17, 68–70, 95, 103, 106–110, 128, 138, 148; developmental factors, 15–16, 103, 122–128; exposure to narcotics (denied), 57, 94; personality factors, 1, 3, 9, 16–17, 43, 72, 95–98, 103, 111, 113–122, 127–128; pleasure (denied), 64, 98; ritualistic factors, 14–15, 33, 66, 103, 106, 107, 119, 122, 129; situational factors, 14, 19, 34, 47, 51, 63, 66, 71–73, 84, 90, 94, 96, 97, 103, 110–113, 128, 135, 148; social factors, 1, 2, 13–14, 19, 21, 23, 34, 52–54, 56, 79, 80, 85, 87, 95, 97, 103, 104–106, 127, 128, 130, 131, 135, 148, 151; susceptibility or disposition (psychosocial causes), 95, 96, 98, 104–128

Addiction, nature: adaptation to internal and external needs, 70; animal (no exact equivalent to human), 73, 77–96; behavioral pattern, 1, 2, 5, 10, 18–19, 20–21, 24, 26, 72, 75, 79, 94, 113–114, 127, 128, 133; compulsive, self-destructive activity, 12; concept, 1, 2, 3, 12, 17–26, 72; control issue, 5, 18, 108, 112, 121, 133, 139, 143–144, 151; cure (fundamental self-reliance), 154–157; cycle, 75, 128–132, 155; disease (disputed), 2, 3, 5–6, 47, 55, 57, 59, 72, 128, 133–134, 139, 152–154; drug dependence (denied), 2, 16–25, 39, 57, 60, 136; experience, 12, 25–26, 55, 94–95, 97–132; extreme on continuum of feeling and behavior, 2, 20, 25, 99, 103, 109; formula, 130; given to habit or vice, 3, 12; heroin model for medical definition, 2, 5, 6, 10, 26, 69; illustration, 130; infant (no exact equivalent to adult), 7, 73–77, 94–96; Jaffe's definition, 20–21; label for those who behave in socially unacceptable ways (perpetuating addiction), 21, 26, 56, 109, 134, 147–148, 151, 153; lack of control, 5, 18, 29, 31, 121, 129; overwhelming involvement, 20–21, 26, 47, 97, 98, 132; overworked term, 20; pathological, self-destructive, harmful nature, 1, 2, 26, 47, 95–97, 104, 129; Peele's

Addiction, nature *(continued)*
definition, 26, 72, 95–96, 97, 104, 128–132, 148, 150–157; personality disposition, 16, 95–96; physical dependence (disputed), 20, 23–25, 129; psychic dependence (qualified), 20–21; psychic and social disorder, 134; purely human phenomenon, 95, 97; reasons for broader concept, 2, 96, 132; recognizable syndrome, 23, 28, 128; remission, 6, 8, 15–16, 125–128, 132, 134, 156; requirements for successful model, 72; signs (tolerance, withdrawal, craving), 1, 2, 6, 8, 11, 12, 19, 26, 63, 67, 71, 95, 98, 142; simultaneous, 126–127, 141; style of coping, 2, 20, 47, 70, 127, 157; substitute, 8, 16, 98, 103, 127, 128, 129, 138, 141, 155; treatment (recommendations), 135, 142–145, 147–148, 154–157. *See also* Adaptation theories; Addictive behavior; Addictive experience; Addictive personality; Addicts; Alcohol; Alcoholism; Biological theories; Cognitive factors; Conditioning theories; Control of drug use; Controlled drinking; Craving; Cultural factors; Dependence; Developmental factors; Disease theories; Drug abuse; Drugs; Environment; Experience; Exposure theories; Genetic theories; Heroin; Heroin addiction; Lack of control; Metabolic theories; Moderation; Narcotics; Narcotic addiction; Nonaddictive narcotic use; Nonnarcotic addiction; Opiates; Personality factors; Pharmacology; Physiological factors; Pleasure theories; Policy; Remission; Ritualistic factors; Science; Self-efficacy; Situational factors; Social factors; Social-psychological theories; Society; Tolerance; Treatment; Values; Withdrawal
Addiction Recovery Corporation, 149
Addictive behavior, 1, 2, 5, 6, 10, 18–19, 20–21, 24, 26, 47, 49, 59, 72, 74, 75, 79, 94, 95, 108, 113–114, 118, 127, 128, 133; control impossible (prevailing notion), 10, 133; drugs not sufficient cause, 94; social and cultural determinants, 12–13. *See also* Behavior; Compulsive behavior; Craving
Addictive experience, 12, 25–26, 55, 94–95, 97–104, 104–128, 128–132; control and self-esteem, 101–102; developmental factors, 122–128; illustration, 130; individual factors, 113–122; power, 97–98, 101–102, 129, 131; range of involvements, 103–104; relief of pain, tension, awareness, 99–101, 131; simplification of experience, 103; situational factors, 110–113; social and cultural factors, 104–110. *See also* Cultural factors; Developmental factors; Experience; Personality factors; Situational factors; Social factors
Addictive personality, 16, 95–96, 98, 113, 118, 127–128. *See also* Personality factors; Physiological factors
Addicts: are regular users (not controlled users), 28; break out through changes in environment, self-efficacy, and values, 132; can become controlled users and quit, 8–10, 67–68, 133; educated into incompetence, 121; feel powerless, 6, 129; have addictive personality, 95–96; have degraded lifestyle, 74; have difficulty in tolerating ambiguity and ambivalence, 120; have low self-esteem, 16, 56, 121; have no habitual need for narcotics, 51; know when addicted and will tell, 10, 18–19, 24; mimic sociomedical model of behavior, 6, 143; see themselves as addicts, 17, 132; seek substitute experience, 129
Age factor, 15, 34, 40, 49, 97, 122, 123, 124, 125, 126, 128, 134, 143, 148. *See also* Personality factors; Social factors
Aggression, 13, 101, 116, 118
Alcohol, Drug Abuse, and Mental Health Administration

(ADAMHA), 147
Alcohol-dependence syndrome, 60–61. *See also* Fetal alcohol syndrome
Alcohol, nature: addictive drug (according to disease theory), 3, 10, 12, 15, 19, 24, 27, 64; American image, 27–28; compared to heroin (addictive), 27–28; confusion of study of abuse, 3, 27–28; demon rum, 30, 31; depressant (nonnarcotic), 10, 100; and infants (fetal alcohol syndrome disputed), 75–77; and other drugs, 2, 3, 8, 15, 16, 21, 22, 24, 47, 55, 74, 78, 106, 117, 126–127, 138; symbol of masculine independence, 30, 33, 101, 107, 129. *See also* Addictive experience; Heroin; Narcotics
Alcohol, use: American colonial use, 13; controlled drinking, 10, 29, 35–45, 68, 101–102, 116, 118, 122–123, 147; ethnic patterns of use, 13, 33–34, 44–45, 48–50, 62, 70, 115; Hopi use before Spanish conquest, 12; peer and parental influence, 33–34, 48, 105–106, 115, 122–123; use by animals, 78, 94; use with other drugs, 76, 116, 139
Alcoholism, causes: alcohol dependence (exposure theories), 59–61; biological factors (inadequate), 18, 148; cognitive factors, 17; cultural factors, 13; demographic factors, 34; excessive drinking (exposure theories), 59; expectation of positive benefits (power), 101–102, 118, 129, 131; exposure to drink (before Prohibition), 27; genetic susceptibility (after Prohibition), 11, 18, 27, 29, 45, 47–50, 58, 139, 148; habitual drinking (exposure and disease theories), 27, 30–31, 56, 108; relief of tensions (qualified), 100–101; social context (not alcohol dependence), 34; threshold level of consumption, 11, 61
Alcoholism, nature: abstinence as sole cure (disputed), 30–31, 34, 38, 41, 42, 49, 104, 123, 145, 149, 151; APA definition, 18–19; binges, 40, 45, 62, 110, 122; continuum of behavior, 29, 39; controlled drinking, 10, 29, 35–45, 68, 101–102, 116, 118, 122–123, 147; denial of drinking problem the defining trait (disease theory), 147; disease (disputed), 11, 18, 27–32, 35, 39, 42, 44–45, 59, 61, 108, 109, 118, 122–123, 134, 147–154; ethnic patterns, 13, 33–34, 44–45, 48–50, 62, 70, 115; femininity, 101, 102, 121; gamma alcoholics, 29, 31, 42, 59; gender distinction, 33, 50, 101, 121, 153; Jellinek's analysis, 29, 59; loss of control the defining trait (disease theory), 29, 31, 121; lower class prevalence, 34, 105; masculinity, 17, 30, 33, 101, 102, 107, 116, 153; moral deficiency, 28, 30, 41, 43, 117; number of alcoholics, 32, 33, 44–45, 136, 146; parental influence, 33–34, 48–49, 105–106; problem drinkers, 39, 42; prototypical male disease, 122, 153; relapse, 37, 38, 40–41, 122, 145; signs (blackout, tremors, lack of control), 18, 36, 39; social construction, 61, 97; social convention, 35; social science theory (not disease), 32–33; temperance movement, 27, 30–31, 108; treatment, 28–29, 32, 34, 35, 37–45, 122, 141–142, 145–150. *See also* Abstinence; Alcohol; Control; Controlled drinking; Dependence; Disease theories; Drinking; Ethnic patterns; Heroin addiction; Loss of control; Moderation; Relapse; Treatment
Alcoholics Anonymous (AA), 29, 31, 38, 41, 43, 44, 49, 127, 145, 147, 149, 151. *See also* Washingtonians
Alcohol supply model, 61, 138
Alienation, 118, 129, 130
American Medical Association (AMA), 5, 108
American Psychiatric Association (APA), 19
American Psychological Association (APA), 74
Amphetamines, 9, 11, 21, 24, 64–65, 77, 99, 109, 115, 118, 139

Analgesics, 10, 80, 89, 99
Anorexia, 123
Anxiety, 66, 99, 100, 120, 131, 134, 152, 153

Barbiturates, 9, 10, 16, 24, 94, 109, 118, 138
Behavior, 1, 24, 70, 105; appropriate (socially approved), 13, 21, 107, 131; healthy, 135; scientific concept including subjective perceptions, values, and personality differences, 3, 25; self-regulating, 124. *See also* Addictive behavior; Experience
Biological factors, 12, 18, 54–62, 128, 147–148; insufficient, 18, 148; necessary (disease theory), 128. *See also* Biological theories; Physiological factors
Biological theories, 1–2, 6, 12, 18, 20, 47, 49, 51, 54–62, 71, 73, 75, 78, 89, 105, 121, 128, 147–148, 152. *See also* Disease theories; Genetic theories; Metabolic theories; Neurological theories; Physiological factors
Blackout, 18, 36
Blood alcohol level (BAL), 49–50
Brainwashing, 149
Bulimia, 53, 110, 123, 131

Caffeine, 11, 55, 99, 116, 127
Children, 32, 33, 44–45, 48, 71, 105, 118, 134, 136, 146–150
Chinese attitude toward alcohol, 13, 33, 50, 106–107
Cigarettes, 11, 48, 58–59, 67, 68, 95, 105, 115, 116, 124, 141. *See also* Nicotine; Smoking
Clonidine, 141
Cocaine, 11, 16, 19, 21, 22, 55, 77, 99, 101, 102, 115, 135, 136–137, 138, 139; new drug scourge (1982), 136
Coffee, 4, 127. *See also* Caffeine
Cognitive conditioning model, 69
Cognitive factors, 2, 17, 68–69, 70, 95, 103, 143–144, 148, 151
Competence, 116, 121, 157
Compulsive behavior, 1, 2, 11, 16, 17, 18, 20, 21, 25, 26, 50, 63, 98, 103, 126, 137, 139. *See also* Addictive behavior; Craving
Conditioning theories, 1, 62–69; contribution to adequate theory of addiction, 70; "euphoric" state not inherently rewarding, 65; limited by inability to convey meaning individual attaches to addiction, 68; secondary reinforcement more important than unconditioned stimulus (drug use), 67
Controlled drinking, 35–45, 59, 122–123; applicable for problem drinkers rather than alcoholics, 39, 42; British practice, 38; contrasted with abstinence, 38–40; 123; determinant of success is client's motivation to control drinking, 43–44; extinct as treatment goal in U.S., 38, 42; failures 41–42; issue of relapse, 40; moderation, 39–40, 42–43, 49; successes, 41, 122, 125. *See also* Moderation; Abstinence
Control of drug use, 3, 7–10, 28, 29, 35–45, 49, 54, 68, 70, 71, 95–96, 101, 106, 111, 121, 123, 124, 125, 127, 129, 131, 133, 138, 143–145, 151, 153. *See also* Controlled drinking; Loss of control; Nonaddicted narcotics use; Remission; Self-efficacy
Coping: addictive 2, 20, 47, 70, 127, 129, 131; functional, 21, 96, 97, 101, 111, 116, 121, 125, 129, 131, 157
Craving: sign of addiction, 1, 2, 6, 8, 11, 12, 20, 21, 26, 63, 67, 71, 95, 109, 113, 129, 141, 142
Cultural factors, 1, 3, 12–13, 27, 28, 33, 44–45, 52–53, 70, 72, 98, 103, 106–110, 128, 138, 148; culture, 107–108; ethnicity, 106–107; social processes, 108–110. *See also* Social factors
Cure. *See* Abstinence; Control; Self-efficacy; Therapy; Treatment

Darvon, 10
Death, 41, 117, 143; penalty, 137
Demerol, 7, 10, 138, 143
Dependence, 2, 3, 16, 17, 20, 34, 39, 43, 51, 59–60, 109, 127, 129, 143, 148; concept distinguished from addiction, 20, 21, 23, 129; negative effects of belief in, 140–142;

physical, 20–25, 34, 94, 99; psychic, 20–22, 24
Depression, 1, 54, 64, 74, 100, 101, 115, 131, 134, 143, 152, 153
Detoxification, 41, 141, 142. *See also* Treatment
Developmental factors, 15–16, 103, 122–128
Disease theory of addiction, 2, 5, 6, 47, 55, 57, 59, 72, 128, 133–134, 139; implications for treatment, 53, 133–134, 142–145; paradigm for self and cultural conceptions in our era, 134; term criticized, 152–154. *See also* Biological theories; Conditioning theories; Metabolic theories; Policies; Society
Disease theory of alcoholism, 11, 18, 27–32, 35, 39, 42, 44–45, 47, 59, 61, 72, 108, 122–123, 134, 147–154; denial of drinking problem the defining trait, 147; origin in collapse of Prohibition, 30–31; primary component of America's self-conception, 150; regular drinking presumed cause, 31, 108; term extended beyond all meaning, 151. *See also* Alcoholism; Controlled drinking; Metabolic theories; Policies
DMT, 79
Drinking, 13, 18, 27–28, 30, 33–34, 35–45, 49–50, 54, 59–61, 70, 76–77, 100–102, 105–108, 115–118, 122, 123, 126, 129, 134, 146, 149–150; binges, 40, 45, 62, 110, 122; dominant and aggressive feelings, 116, 118; enhanced sense of power, 101–102, 118, 129, 131; facilitation of social interaction, 116; quitting, 127; relief of tensions, 100–101. *See also* Alcohol; Alcoholism; Controlled drinking
Drug abuse: alcohol, 12, 15, 16, 32, 35, 40, 44, 108, 115, 117, 123, 127, 133, 134, 148, 156; drug, 2, 6, 9, 12, 15, 20, 22, 27, 51, 55, 56, 62, 74, 95, 98, 110, 111, 116, 117, 118, 119, 120, 122, 133, 134, 135–140, 148, 156; meaning as excess, 116; overworked term, 20. *See also* Control of drug use; Illicit drugs; Moderation
Drugs: abuse, 2, 6, 9, 12, 15, 20, 22, 27, 148; addictive, 1–2, 3, 6, 16–26, 37, 56, 69, 71, 73, 94, 98, 99, 108, 129, 148; and alcohol, 2, 3, 8, 15, 16, 21, 22, 24, 47, 55, 74, 78, 106, 117, 126–127, 138; analgesics, 10, 80, 89, 99; conventional guide, 22; dangerous, 21, 106; dependence, 2, 16–25, 39, 57, 60, 136; depressants (alcohol, narcotics, sedatives, analgesics), 10, 99, 100, 130; hallucinogens, 21, 22, 63, 78, 79, 88; illicit, 3, 9, 10, 74, 75, 105, 115, 123, 131, 137, 139, 141, 150; narcotics (opium, morphine, heroin), 10–11, 57, 71, 112; New York bellwether for use, 137; not sufficient cause for addictive behavior, 94; peer pressure, 13, 56, 71, 105, 112, 122–123; personality and social factors in use, 9, 69, 95–98, 104–128; search for nonaddictive analgesics, 10, 94, 99; sedatives, 10, 19, 99, 115, 123, 138; stimulants (caffeine, nicotine, amphetamine, cocaine), 11, 23, 78, 99, 130; substances whose behavioral effects are physiologically determined, 1; trade, 135–140; tranquilizers, 21, 131; treatment for abuse, 5–6, 68, 140–145; use by animals, 77–79, 88–89, 93–94; use by mother of "addicted" infant, 73–77; used to infer existence of biochemical source for altered behavior, 153; use in moderation, 106, 116–117, 123, 124, 139, 157; wrongheaded ideas, 3, 134. *See also* Addictive experience; Alcohol; Drug abuse; Heroin; Narcotics; Opiates
Drug trade, 136–137

Emotional factors, 26, 28, 31, 70, 74, 94, 100, 101, 109, 125, 129, 131, 154. *See also* Euphoria; Personality factors; Psychological factors
Endorphins, 10, 51, 57–58, 78, 89, 110
Environment: need to take into account, 2, 14, 23, 26, 44, 47, 52, 60, 66, 68, 79, 80, 85, 88, 90, 94, 95, 96, 97, 110, 111, 113, 125, 135, 154. *See*

Environment *(continued)*
also Adaptation theories; Conditioning theories; Setting; Situational factors
Escape from reality, 16, 71, 99, 101, 103, 113, 119–120, 125, 129
Eskimo attitude toward alcohol, 13, 33, 50, 106, 109
Ethnic patterns of drug use, 13, 33–34, 44–45, 48–50, 62, 70, 115
Etonitazene, 88, 91
Euphoria, 63–65, 99; alcohol, 64; allure of narcosis, 95; heroin, 64; motivation for use of addictive drugs, 64; not produced by addictive drugs, 95
Experience: normal life, 26, 55, 70, 72, 94–96, 103, 106, 120, 132; potent, 25–26, 49, 55, 95, 96, 97, 110, 129. *See also* Addictive experience; Behavior; Situational factors
Exposure theories, 56–69, 133. *See also* Conditioning theories; Metabolic theories

Fear of failure, 118–120
Federal Bureau of Narcotics, 7, 108, 135
Feeling: and addiction, 1, 2, 66, 101, 109, 120, 129; state of being, 129. *See also* Emotional factors; Experience; Euphoria; Guilt
Fetal alcohol syndrome (FAS), 75–77
Fisher, Eddie, 115
Funding, 134, 146, 147

Gambling, 4, 21, 25, 63, 98, 100, 120, 134, 151
Genetic theories, 48–56, 133, 139, 148; biological mechanism not found, 49; endorphin deficiency exceptional, 51; ethnicity not controlled for, 48; genetic factor in alcoholism, 11, 18, 27, 29, 45, 47–50, 58, 139, 148; greater risk from certain biological abnormalities, 49–50; love not due to chemical imbalances, 54; obesity due to social factors, 52–54; one biological factor cannot explain myriad addictions, 55
Gratification, 2, 16, 66, 98, 113, 129, 130, 154, 155, 157
Guilt, 101, 131

Heroin, nature: analgesic, 10, 99; compared to alcohol (addictive), 27–28; depressant, 99; and euphoria, 63–66, 99; interchangeable with morphine, 80; legal suppression, 4–5, 135–140; medical prescription prohibited, 135, 140; most sinister drug of abuse (conventionally), 12, 27, 109, 117, 135; origin, 4, 10, 99; sources (Turkey, Mexico, Asia), 136; worse because "worse" people use it, 9, 74, 140. *See also* Opiates; Narcotics
Heroin, use: animals, 77–78; humans (addicting), 3, 10, 16, 27, 109, 122, 124; humans (controlled), 8–10, 16, 28, 67, 68, 100, 101, 109, 123, 139; pregnant women (effect on baby), 73–75
Heroin addiction, causes: association with deviant social groups, 13, 71, 74; diversion and entertainment, 101; escape from reality, 16, 71, 99, 101, 103, 113, 119–120, 125, 129; euphoria (disputed), 63–68, 99; feelings of personal inadequacy, 102, 121, 142–143; pleasure (debunked), 98; relief from unpleasant consciousness of life, 99; rite of self-injection, 14, 71, 103; withdrawal (debunked), 98
Heroin addiction, nature: 2, 3, 8, 9, 16, 78, 103, 118; "American disease," 12–13; among outsiders, 115; compared to dependent love relationships, 98; controlled use, 8–10, 16, 28, 67, 68, 100–101, 123; cure, 125, 140; degraded lifestyle, 74; "hooked" (dependent), 122; metabolic disease (disputed), 57; model for medical definition of all addictions, 2, 5–6, 9–10, 26, 69, 98, 100–101, 109, 117, 133–134; numbers of addicts (1920), 27, 135, 136; (1982), 28, 136, 137; quitting

the habit, 51, 67, 125–126, 128, 143; in Vietnam, 8–9, 14, 51, 110–111; youthful habit, 15, 122. *See also* Addicts; Alcoholism; Narcotic addiction; Nonnarcotic addiction
Hallucinogens, 21, 22, 63, 78, 79, 88
Harrison Act (1914), 4–5, 135
Health: moderating value, 96, 116, 130; positive value, 74, 104, 125, 157
History of drug use: alcohol, 12–13, 27, 30–32, 38, 145–146, 150; heroin, 4, 10, 14, 99, 134, 135; legal suppression, 135–140; opium, 3–5, 12, 27, 75, 108, 135
"Hooked," 122

Identity, 121, 127, 128
Illicit drugs, 3, 9, 74, 75, 105, 115, 123, 137, 139, 141, 150; degraded lifestyle, 74; feelings of guilt and shame, 131; nonconformity and independence predictors of use, 10, 117; peer and parental influence, 105; quitting, 123. *See also* Drug abuse; Drugs; Law
Indians, American: attitude toward alcohol, 13, 33, 50, 106–107, 109
Insanity, 120. *See also* Mental illness
Institute for the Study of Drug Dependence (ISDD), xi
Internal-external model of overeating, 52–54, 100, 121
Interpersonal addiction, 47, 54, 110, 121. *See also* Love
Irish attitude toward alcohol, 33, 34, 44–45, 48, 106, 109
Italian attitude toward alcohol, 13, 33, 45, 107, 109

Jaffe, J.K.: definition of addiction, 20–21
Japanese attitude toward alcohol, 13, 33, 50, 106–107
Jellinek, E.M.: disease theory of alcoholism, 29, 59
Jewish attitude toward alcohol, 13, 33, 62, 106, 109, 115
Joy, 157

Laudanum, 4, 7
Law: effort to suppress drug trade, 135–140; failure for focusing on supply, not demand, 137; invasion of everyday life to mandate treatment, 147; role in definition of addiction, 3, 4, 5, 7, 10, 27, 35, 115, 130, 134. *See also* Medicine; Police; Policies
Legalization, 138
"Limerant" people, 54
Liquor. *See* Alcohol
Loss of control, 1, 5, 6, 11, 13, 17, 21, 53, 62; sign of alcoholism, 18, 29, 30, 31, 32, 49, 53, 108, 109, 120, 121, 122, 128, 129, 149. *See also* Control; Compulsive behavior; Drug abuse
Love: and addiction, 12, 16, 47, 54, 65–66, 98, 109–110, 120, 126, 134; compared to heroin addiction, 98; and disease, 152, 153. *See also* Interpersonal addiction; Nonnarcotic addiction
Lower class factor, 4, 8, 16, 34, 101, 104, 122, 135, 140
LSD, 21

Magic, mystification, and myth, 1, 25, 98, 120, 130, 134, 152
Marijuana, 13–14, 21, 22, 63, 76, 105, 117, 118, 123, 138
Maturing out, 15, 97, 122, 125, 134. *See also* Age factor
Media: depiction of therapies that attack individuality, 149; role to discourage heroin use, 9. *See also* Television
Medicine, organized: role in changing definition of addiction, 4, 6, 7, 21–23, 28–30, 31, 32, 34, 38, 108, 123, 134, 145; treatment, 5–6, 32, 134, 140–157. *See also* Policy; Therapy; Treatment
Meditation, 155
Men, 4, 30, 50, 101, 102, 107, 112, 116, 117, 122, 123, 153. *See also* Women
Mental illness, 1, 120, 129, 134, 154. *See also* Disease theories; Medicine
Metabolic theories, 50, 51, 56–62, 141, 152; alcohol supply model does not

Metabolic theories *(continued)*
conform to facts of alcoholism rates, 61–62; cell metabolic mechanism still unknown, 56; lead to no cure, 141–143; naloxone does not stop addiction to running, 58; rats and people do not become "dependent" on alcohol, 60–61
Methadone and methadone maintenance, 78, 89, 103, 136, 138, 140–141
Middle class factor, 4, 8, 11, 34, 101, 104, 110, 112, 135. *See also* Lower class factor
Mind–body duality: source of obscurity about multifactorial nature of addiction, 25–26
Moderation: goal of treatment for alcoholism, 34, 39–40, 42–43, 49; value for controlled use of all drugs, 106, 116–117, 123, 124, 139, 157. *See also* Abstinence; Controlled drinking
Mood, 14, 25, 58, 65, 98, 103, 106, 131. *See also* Euphoria
Morning glory seeds, 22
Morphine: and addiction, 3, 4, 8, 10, 24, 27, 57, 80, 135; consumption by rats, 68, 77, 80–84, 86, 87, 90, 92, 93; interchangeable with heroin, 80; psychotropic effects aversive, 93
Motivation, 1, 14, 58, 64, 65, 88–89, 97, 101, 118, 128, 133, 156; as most important element of successful treatment, 43, 156. *See also* Self-efficacy

Naloxone, 58
Naltrexone, 93, 141
Narcosis, 88, 111: allure, 95. *See also* Euphoria
Narcotics, nature: compared to alcohol, 10–11, 47, 106; depressants, 10; euphoric (disputed), 63–64, 99; history, 2–4, 69, 135–137; not necessary for addiction, 57; psychotropic effects aversive to animals, 93; suppression by legal authorities, 135–140; trade, 135–140; universally addicting (by convention), 11, 47. *See also* Addictive experience; Alcohol; Drugs; Heroin; Opiates
Narcotics, use: animal, 77–94; human (addictive), 1, 3, 8, 10, 18–19, 65, 96; human (controlled), 6–10, 51, 57, 69, 71, 73–74, 106, 139; physicians, 7–8; recreation, 9
Narcotic addiction, causes: association with deviant social groups and lifestyles, 13–71, 74; constitutional differences in individuals (not found), 89–90; drug availability, 138; endorphin deficiency (disputed), 51; escape from realities of life, 16, 71, 99, 101, 103, 113, 119–120, 125, 129; exposure to narcotics (denied), 57, 73, 110–111; habitual use of drugs (exposure theories), 27, 56; not chemicals, but the socially available means to handle stress, 112; pleasure or euphoria (disputed), 63–65, 98; recreation, 9; reinforcement, 30, 47, 62, 63, 67, 69, 78, 84, 139, 155; relief of stress and pain 88–89, 99–101, 111–112; withdrawal (disputed), 58, 65, 98
Narcotic addiction, nature: 1, 2, 5, 7, 10, 12, 19, 27, 47, 63, 73, 106, 108, 110; avoided by hospital patients, 17, 24, 51, 57, 64, 69, 115; cases of nonaddiction, 7–10, 17, 24, 51, 57, 69; debased, immoral, debilitating practice and legal problem (conventional view), 5; inability to choose defining trait, 5, 18; infant withdrawal (disputed), 73–75; metabolic disease (disputed), 51, 57, 152; model for understanding other addictions, 2, 5. *See also* Addictive experience; Addicts; Alcoholism; Heroin addiction; Nonaddictive narcotics use; Nonnarcotic addiction
Narcotics Addiction Control Act (1966), 140
National Council on Alcoholism (NCA), 31, 36, 108, 145–146
National Foundation for Prevention of Chemical Dependency Disease, 148
National Institute on Alcohol Abuse

and Alcoholism (NIAAA), 18, 36, 146
Neurological model, 12, 16, 18, 52, 56–57, 65, 78, 98, 152
Nicotine, 11, 15, 19, 21, 47, 55, 58–59, 70, 78, 99, 100, 116, 131, 141, 152
Nixon, Richard, 136
Nonaddictive narcotics use: hospital patients, 17, 24, 51, 57, 64, 69, 115; physicians, addicts, and soldiers, 7–10, 12, 24, 51, 57, 69
Nonnarcotic addiction, 3–12, 47, 124; alcohol, 10–11, 21; analgesics, 10, 21; caffeine, 11, 19, 21; cocaine, 11, 19, 21; endorphins, 57, experience, 12, 25–26, 55, 94–95, 97–132; gambling, 63; nicotine, 11, 15, 19, 21, 58; other drugs, 16–17, 21; overeating, 63. *See also* Addictive behavior; Addictive experience; Addictive personality; Control; Moderation; Treatment

Obesity, 15, 48, 52–54, 123–124, 127; lower class prevalence, 104; search for genetic factors, 52–54. *See also* Overeating
Opiates: change in Western view, 4–5; consumption by animals, 84, 88–89, 93; nonaddictive, 7; substances producing dependence, 3; use, 3, 4, 6, 12, 24, 27, 56, 108, 113, 135. *See also* Heroin; Narcotics
Opponent-process model of motivation, 63, 65–67
Oriental flush, 50
Orwell, George, *1984*, 154
Overeating, 1, 12, 15, 17, 21, 47, 52–54, 63, 66, 95, 98, 100, 102, 103, 109, 111, 116, 123–124, 126, 127, 131, 134, 144. *See also* Bulimia; Obesity

Pain. *See* Stress
Paregoric, 4, 75
Pathology, 2, 19, 26, 47, 49, 74, 95–96, 109, 112, 117
Peer pressure: alcohol, 33–34, 48, 105–106, 122–123; drugs, 13, 56, 71, 105, 112, 122–123
Personality factors, 1, 3, 9, 16–17, 43, 72, 95, 97, 98, 103, 111, 113–122, 127–128; addictive personality, 95–96, 113, 118, 127–128; alienation, 118; antisocial attitudes and aggression, 117–118; fear of failure, 118–120; individual choice, 114–116, 127; internal or external control, 121–122; lack of achievement, 118–119; lack of moderation, 116–117; legality, 115; low self-esteem, 120–121; model personalities, 114; not determinative, 113–114. *See also* Cognitive factors; Social factors; Values
Peyote, 21
Pharmacology and pharmocological factors, 5, 10, 20–21, 23, 47, 55, 57, 63, 70, 72, 78, 98, 99, 100, 115, 129, 139, 143, 157. *See also* Physiological factors
Phobias, 134, 152
Physicians: own use of narcotics, 7–8, 24
Physiological factors: admitted, 15, 25, 26, 27, 47, 71, 97, 98, 102, 126; disputed, 2, 3, 17–25, 47, 49, 50, 52, 53–54, 56, 57, 59, 67, 73, 78, 109, 113, 115, 124, 134, 143, 148; no alteration in cell metabolism yet linked with addiction, 56, 78. *See also* Biological theories; Metabolic theories; Neurological Model; Social factors
Pleasure model, 63–66, 88–89, 98, 99. *See also* Rewards
Police, 134, 136
Policies toward drug addiction, 4–5, 132–133, 135–140, 145–150, 156–157; official biological approach creates addiction, 148, 156; policies fail because they focus on supply, not demand, 137; powerful treatment industry interest, 146. *See also* Law
Poverty, 104
Prayer, 17
Prohibition, 30–31, 138; effect of repeal on concept of alcoholism, 27, 31
Prostitutes, 74
Psilocybin, 21
Psychological factors, 2, 11, 18, 20, 23,

Psychological factors *(continued)* 24, 27, 68, 69, 71, 72, 73, 75, 77, 95, 103, 111, 117, 118, 128. *See also* Personality factors; Social factors

Quinine, 81, 85, 86, 87, 89, 91, 93
Quitting, 51, 125–128, 131, 132, 143, 144

Rand Reports, 36–38, 43
Rat park experiment, 80–88; first, 82; second, 83; Nichols cycle phase, 84
Reagan, Ronald, 136
Reinforcement: and addiction, 30, 47, 62, 63, 67, 69, 78, 84, 139, 155; models, 62–63, 66. *See also* Conditioning theories; Pleasure model
Relapse after treatment, 21; alcoholism, 37, 38, 40–41, 122, 145; drug, 6, 66–67, 78, 131, 140–142, 156. *See also* Remission; Withdrawal
Religious factors, 31, 127, 134, 144, 145, 149. *See also* Social factors; Cognitive factors
Remission, 15–16, 37, 39, 53, 67, 68, 97, 110, 123, 124–127, 132, 143; meaning (quitting or maturation), 125–126; means (resolves, aging, substitutions), 126–128, 132; spontaneous (natural), 6, 8, 134, 144, 156. *See also* Control; Relapse; Treatment; Withdrawal
Rewards, 55, 63, 64, 66, 67, 70, 77, 97, 98, 112–113, 116, 129, 132, 137, 154–156. *See also* Pleasure model
Ritualistic factors, 14–15, 33, 66, 103, 106, 107, 119, 122, 129
Rockefeller, Nelson, 137, 140
Running, 12, 47, 57–58, 98, 102, 103, 110, 116, 128, 155

Schizophrenia, 1
Science and research, 3, 6, 25–26, 56, 72, 96, 134, 138, 151. *See also* Funding
Self-efficacy, 6, 43, 121, 127, 129, 130, 132, 143–145
Set point, 52–54, 124
Setting: need to take into account, 6, 17, 19, 58, 68, 70, 75, 77, 85, 94, 110, 114, 152. *See also* Environment; Situational factors
Sex drive: and addiction, 4, 102; and alcoholism, 17, 101–102, 116; cognitive effect of liquor placebo, 17; destructive relationships, 134; of heavy drinkers, 101, 116; narcotics as antiaphrodisiacs, 64; of women drinkers, 101
Situational factors, 1, 14, 19, 34, 47, 51, 63, 66, 71, 72, 73, 84, 90, 94, 96, 97, 103, 110–113, 128, 135, 148; availability, 110–111; ghetto environment, 111–112; opportunity and rewards, 112–113; prior use, 111; social support and intimacy, 112; stress and control of stress, 111–112
Smoking, 4, 15, 48, 58, 59, 70, 76, 99, 100, 116, 117, 123, 124, 126, 127, 131, 143–144, 152. *See also* Nicotine
Social factors, 1, 2, 13–14, 19, 21, 23, 34, 52–54, 56, 79, 80, 85, 87, 95, 97, 103, 104–106, 127, 128, 130, 131, 135, 148, 151; class, 4, 8, 11, 16, 34, 101, 104–105; parental influence, 105–106; peer pressure, 105–106; socioeconomic status, 34, 104–105. *See also* Situational factors
Social learning theory, 15, 69–70, 97, 100, 105
Social-psychological theories, 32–33, 56, 71–72, 128. *See also* Adaptation theories; Social factors; Personality factors; Self-efficacy; Values
Society: impaired, 133–157; influence on addictive behavior, 2–3, 9, 129, 135, 148, 156–157. *See also* Social factors
Stress (and pain): cause for use of narcotics, 16, 19, 46, 79, 99, 101, 116, 121, 129, 130, 131; disputed, 88–89, 111–112
Surgeon General, 77
Surrender, 149
Synanon, 144–145, 149

Talwin, 138
Television: addiction to, 1, 21, 131;

role in public notion of addiction, 9, 133, 136, 148
Therapy, 35, 37–45, 135, 143–145, 147, 149, 154–157; lack of self-efficacy requires, 121; no short circuit of fundamental self-reliance, 156; recovery with understanding of addiction, self-efficacy, and alternative rewards, 156. *See also* Treatment
Tobacco. *See* Nicotine; Smoking
Tolerance: cross-tolerance, 57; sign of addiction, 1, 12, 16, 19, 26
Tranquilizers, 21, 131
Treatment, 5–6, 32, 37–45, 122, 133–135, 139, 140–157; alcoholism, 28, 29, 31, 32, 34, 35, 37–45, 122, 141–142, 145–150; authorities, 149; based on common assumptions about nature of addiction, 134; controlled drinking (extinct as goal in U.S.), 38, 42, 145; "disease" label, 153; improvement result of patient's self-efficacy, 143; industry, 32, 146; narcotic addiction, 5–6, 68, 140–141, 142–145; primary determinant of moderation as treatment outcome, 43; recommendations (individual responsibility and prevention), 135, 142–145, 147–148, 154–157; reform implied by new model, 133; rejection by willful individuals, 43, 127, 142, 153. *See also* Abstinence; Controlled drinking; Medicine; Moderation; Self-efficacy; Relapse; Remission; Therapy
Tremors: sign of alcoholism, 18, 36, 142

Valium, 10, 16, 55, 139
Values, 2, 3, 23, 34, 59, 69, 95, 96, 97, 106, 108, 110, 114, 116, 117, 118, 119, 125, 127, 129, 130, 132; addiction a moral problem, 59, 117, 151, 156–157; relationship between values and drug and alcohol use, 117, 132. *See also* Moderation; Social factors
Vietnam veterans, 8, 14, 51, 66, 67, 68, 95, 109, 110–111, 112–113, 126, 142

War on drugs, 137, 141
Washingtonians, 30–31
Withdrawal: contrasted with methadone maintenance, 141; meaning, 19; not primary factor in addiction, 98, 142; relapse, 20, 21; sign of addiction, 1, 2, 6, 8, 11, 12, 19, 26, 60, 63, 67, 68, 71, 73, 79, 84, 95, 98, 109, 115, 122, 128, 129, 141, 143. *See also* Relapse
Women, 4, 33, 54, 73–77, 101, 102, 121, 123; wife abuse, 32, 134, 147, 153. *See also* Men
World Health Organization (WHO): Expert Committee on Addiction-Producing Drugs, 20, 21; Expert Committee on Mental Health, 18

About the Author

Stanton Peele established himself as a leading theorist, clinician, and writer in the field of addiction with publication of his *Love and Addiction* twenty-five years ago. He is the author of six other books and over 120 professional and popular articles about addiction and alcoholism. Stanton has been awarded the prestigious Mark Keller Award by the Rutgers University Center of Alcohol Studies and the Lindesmith Award for lifetime achievement in scholarship and writing by the Drug Policy Foundation. Many of Stanton's "radical" concepts—including moderation training for problem drinkers, the application of the addiction concept to nondrug activities, and the frequent occurrence of natural remission among alcoholics and addicts—have become conventional wisdom in the field.